AS ONCE IN MAY

By ANTONIA WHITE

FICTION
Frost in May (D. Harmsworth, 1933; Virago, 1978)
The Lost Traveller (Eyre & Spottiswoode, 1950; Virago, 1979)
The Sugar House (Eyre & Spottiswoode, 1952; Virago, 1979)
Beyond the glass (Eyre & Spottiswoode, 1954; Virago, 1979)
Strangers (Harvill Press, 1954; Virago, 1981)

NON-FICTION
The Hound and the Falcon: The Story of a Reconversion to the Catholic Faith (Longmans, 1965; Virago, 1980)

CHILDREN'S BOOKS
Minka and Curdy (Harvill, 1957)
Living with Minka and Curdy (Harvill, 1970)

A PLAY
Three in a Room, a Comedy in 3 Acts (French's Acting Edition 1947)

AS ONCE IN MAY

— EDITED BY SUSAN CHITTY —

THE EARLY AUTOBIOGRAPHY OF
ANTONIA WHITE
— AND OTHER WRITINGS —

Virago

Published by VIRAGO PRESS Limited 1983
41 William IV Street, London WC2N 4DB

British Library Cataloguing in Publication Data
White, Antonia
   As once in May.
   I. Title   II. Chitty, Susan
   828'.91208   PR6045.H5634
   ISBN 0-86068-352-4

Typeset by Rowland Phototypesetting Limited
and printed by St Edmundsbury Press, both
of Bury St Edmunds, Suffolk

'I have a superb collection of beginnings'

The Hound and the Falcon

CONTENTS

ACKNOWLEDGEMENTS

I would like to acknowledge the advice of my half-sister Lyndall Passerini and Sir Thomas Hopkinson. Also the help of Phyllis Jones who did the typing.

For permission to reproduce the material listed below, grateful acknowledgement is made to the following: for 'What a Woman Does Alone', originally published in *Lilliput*, Syndication International Limited and IPC Magazines Limited; for *Harrods News*, April 1934, Harrods Limited; for the caricature of Cecil Botting, St Paul's School; for the map of Binesfield, the Royal Geographical Society.

The cover illustration is a portrait of Antonia White by Cedric Morris.

INTRODUCTION

Antonia White was born a year before the beginning of the twentieth century, of which she was so much a part. She was the only child of Cecil Botting and Christine White, and her real name was Eirene, spelled in the Greek manner. Her father came of a long line of Sussex yeomen but had risen to become head of the Classics Department at St Paul's School, London, and was co-author of the famous Hillard and Botting Latin and Greek text books. Antonia's early years were spent at 22 Perham Road, West Kensington, where she largely occupied herself by inventing adventures for her rocking horse, Sceptre and her toy poodle, Mr Dash. She was to relive those first four years with increasing affection and, even when she was in revolt against most of the things her father held dear, she never moved far from West Kensington.

The Sussex background, however, was very much part of her childhood and of her life. Her summer holidays were spent at Binesfield, the cottage standing back on Bines Common where Cecil Botting's maiden aunts, Clara and Agnes Jeffreys, lived. Bines Common is between the villages of Ashurst and Partridge Green, near Horsham and the South Downs. Old Stepney, the gardener, used to wheel a handcart four miles to Steyning, at the foot of the Downs, on market days. The chapters of her Autobiography, included here, describe these early years. The aunts in the country are also the subject of the piece 'The Most Unforgettable Characters I've Met'.

When Antonia was nine her father, who had become a convert to Catholicism, sent her as a boarder to the Convent of the Sacred Heart at Roehampton, a southern suburb of London, near Richmond Park and only a bus ride from West Kensington. The convent is the setting for 'A Child of the Five Wounds'. She worked hard there and won many prizes for work and morals, but disaster struck when she was fifteen. A book she was writing for her father was discovered in somebody else's desk. It was to have been a story of worldly sinners ultimately converted, but unfortunately Reverend Mother read it before the young author had had time to write the end and she was asked to leave the convent. The text of this, the first of Antonia's 'superb collection of beginnings' was never returned to her, but another piece, 'The Copper Beech', penned carefully in an exercise book and intended as a similar (but more satisfactory) present to her father, is illustrated in this collection.

Antonia was now sent to St Paul's Girls School. At St Paul's, the frivolous side of her nature came to the fore and, from wanting to please her father, she seemed only to wish to annoy him. She failed to work for the Cambridge Higher Local Examination and so to go on to Cambridge in his footsteps. Instead she experimented with clothes and make-up and, finding by chance that she had a knack for writing advertising copy, she earned £250 a year from Dearborn's Beauty Preparations advertising Mercolized wax.

Antonia left St Paul's at seventeen, as she had been offered a job which she held briefly as governess in a Catholic family. During the next three years she supported herself with odd teaching jobs and work in government offices. At this time she contributed some short stories to newspapers. Then she did something that must have deeply shocked her father: she took a year's course at what is now the Royal Academy of Dramatic Art (then known as ADA), and went on to tour the provinces as the ingénue in *The Private Secretary*. She never pretended to be a good actress but she had a fluffy blond charm which saw her through. Even in youth she was attractive rather than beautiful and her looks changed according to her mood. 'The First Time I Went on Tour' gives a vivid account of Antonia's only experience as a professional actress.

In 1921 Antonia made a disastrous and incomprehensible marriage. R.G.W. was a lovable if gangling young man whose passions were for driving cars and hanging about the theatre; he also drank too much. The only interest the young couple shared was playing toy soldiers in their toy house in Glebe Place in Chelsea.

After three years the marriage was annulled by the Catholic Church and Antonia returned to her parents. By now she had fallen in love with a handsome officer in the Scots Guards. He was called Robert, and he was lucky to have survived the trenches. The two appear to have quickly established telepathic powers of communication when apart. Soon afterwards Antonia was certified insane and spent a year in Bethlem Royal Hospital, often under restraint. *Clara IV*, an unfinished novel included in this volume, contains references to the asylum under its fictional name of Nazareth. In the fourth chapter is an account of a meeting with the two nurses who had attended her there. This description of a reunion on board a channel steamer is one of the few chapters of pure fiction Antonia ever wrote. The death of the little boy in *The Lost Traveller* is another.

The memory of her madness, and the fear that it might return, did not leave Antonia for the rest of her life. It may explain her second marriage which was not to Robert (who had married somebody else while Antonia was in Bethlem) but to E.E.S., a Cambridge educated civil servant whom she had venerated as little less than a seer since she was twenty-one. She went to live with him in his house at Paulton's Square, also in Chelsea. By now she had a well-paid job as head woman copywriter at Crawford's. Their antiseptic life together is described in *Julian Tye*, the other unfinished novel in this collection.

In 1928 a tall, handsome young man with a slightly melancholy charm, S.G., crashed into this airtight household. He was brought to the house by a friend because his motorbike had broken down outside. S.G. was (and is) my father. He was not the kind of person Antonia was likely to meet at the Chelsea parties she frequented. He was well read in French and English literature but, as a mining engineer, was often abroad. He was undoubtedly attracted by Antonia's literary powers as well as her charm. By now she had taken on a part-time job as assistant editor of *Life and Letters*, Desmond McCarthy's literary review. It was in this review that her first short story to be printed appeared. It was entitled 'The House of Clouds', and was based on her experiences in the asylum. She signed it with the pseudonym 'Antonia White'. White was her mother's maiden name and Tony was the name by which her friends knew her.

In 1929 I was born and Cecil Botting died. He was fifty-nine and had enjoyed only three years of his early retirement at Binesfield. To add to the complications of this period of her life, Antonia now fell in love with Tom Hopkinson, a junior copywriter at Crawford's. Tom was one of the four sons of a north country clergyman. He was recently down from Oxford and was considered a promising novelist. A fictional account of their first meeting occurs in the opening chapter of *Julian Tye*. Julian is simply Clara under a new name. Tom, under the guise of Mark Mayhew, is discovered occupying Julian's desk. Their interchange is spirited and, on her side, hostile, but, by the end, the young man's interest in Julian's writing is luring her from her sterile marriage to Clive Heron (E.E.S.).

After her divorce from E.E.S. Antonia had the greatest difficulty in deciding whether to marry S.G. or Tom. She kept both in suspense until S.G. took a mining post in Canada and went there to await her decision. In 1930 she married Tom and in 1931 my sister Lyndall was born. They moved into Cecil Court in Hollywood Road, Fulham, engaged a nurse for us children and, for a few years, established a somewhat more normal home than the one at Paulton's Square had been.

Antonia continued to work full time, now for Harrods rather than Crawford's. She always regarded her period in the advertising department there as 'Hell!' and claimed Harrods were her meanest employers. (A facsimile page from one of her Harrods catalogues is included here.) She and Tom spent two holidays in the south of France; one of these might well have been taken in the summer of 1931 just after Lyndall was born, and been used as the setting for 'The Painter's Wife', for the narrator in this short story is also a pregnant young wife.

Frost in May, Antonia's first novel, published in 1933, was written with Tom's encouragement. He insisted on having a new chapter read to him every weekend. The book was the first to be published by a new firm, Desmond Harmsworth – Harmsworth having set himself up with the money he'd won in a sweepstake – and its dust jacket was designed by Antonia's old friend the painter Joan Souter Robertson. Like her subsequent three novels it was largely autobiographical.

Antonia's new found celebrity did not have a good effect on her marriage. Although Tom was to have success with his short stories, and was later to achieve fame as the wartime editor of *Picture Post*, none of his novels received the attention of *Frost in May*. It was an even more cruel turn of fate for Antonia that, just at this moment of recognition, 'The Beast' returned. (The Beast was the name Antonia always gave to her madness.) This time it came in the form of neurosis rather than insanity and she underwent a Freudian analysis. In the meantime, she moved into a room in Oakley Street, Chelsea, and in 1937 she divorced Tom Hopkinson.

Then, quite unexpectedly, Antonia began a very successful career as a journalist. She became fashion editor of *The Sunday Pictorial* and was offered all the freelance work she could handle. She moved into a handsome two storey flat in Cornwall Gardens, South Kensington, with my sister and myself, and had several love affairs, including those with the brothers N.H. and I.H.

With the war the jobs folded, lovers vanished and the flat in Cornwall Gardens was bombed. Perhaps it was not surprising that Antonia should have chosen this moment to return to the

Catholic Church after a twenty year absence. She considered that the moment was chosen for her and now explored her religion intellectually with a thoroughness she had never employed in her youth. She wrote newspaper articles and lectures about it and contributed pieces, one on her beloved St Thomas Aquinas, to French and English religious periodicals. She also wrote a series of letters to Joseph Thorpe, a stranger who had once been a Jesuit and who was known to his friends as Peter. These were published much later under the title of *The Hound and the Falcon*.

During the war Antonia had been obliged to return to fulltime office work. She had a period in the BBC Overseas Department and then moved to the Political Intelligence Department of the Foreign Office. Once the war was over she determined to devote herself to writing novels.

It was not until 1950, sixteen years after *Frost in May*, that she produced the second novel in what is now known as the 'Frost in May' quartet, *The Lost Traveller*. It carried Nanda, now renamed Clara, through her late adolescence. In a period of rare fertility, Antonia produced two more novels in the next four years, *The Sugar House* (1952) and *Beyond the Glass* (1954). The first was based on Antonia's experiences in the theatre and her marriage to Archie Hughes-Follet (R.G.W.). The second was about her madness and her year in the asylum.

Now that Antonia no longer received a salary, much of her time had to be devoted to earning a living. She wrote novel reviews for Janet Adam Smith at the *New Statesman*, but relied for serious income on translations. With her first, Maupassant's *Une Vie*, she won the Denyse Clairouin prize in 1949. There were thirty-four to follow, many of them the novels of Colette, the last translation appearing in 1967.

Antonia never regarded translating as her profession. She was careful to allow gaps between translations during which she would go back to her own work. She had had no formal training in French after the age of eighteen and, although she had won prizes for French at school, she never lived in France, visiting Paris or the Midi only for short holidays. She did however read a great number of French writers and identified with the perfectionism of Flaubert. Julian Green, Jâcques Maritain and Alfred Perlès were all friends. Her spoken French was excellent and in *Clara IV*, one of the asylum nurses reminds her that she had often spoken in French when she was insane. Her mastery of the language presumably was a gift from the convent at Roehampton. After her return to the church she used to visit the Dominicans at the boulevard de la Tour Maubourg, and wrote two long articles in French for their periodical *La Vie Intellectuelle*.

At this time, Antonia also wrote some delightful and humorous pieces for such magazines as *Punch* and *Lilliput* (a pocket-size humorous magazine edited by Tom Hopkinson). Antonia's sense of humour unfortunately could no longer encompass her relations with Lyndall and myself. I had gone up to Oxford in 1947 and in 1948 Lyndall began a year's stage production course at the Old Vic Theatre School. Antonia's response to any success we had was ambivalent. When I came down from Oxford I married Thomas Hinde and did not communicate with her for five years. Lyndall moved to Italy permanently, but continued to write letters. Antonia was not an easy woman to be involved with emotionally. She needed constant reassurance and she had a bad temper. It was not only with her husbands and her daughters that she quarrelled. She had at least two intense (but presumably innocent) relationships with women during the post war period and both ended explosively.

My mother and I were reconciled after her return from a semester at the University of Notre Dame in Indiana, and she met her first two grandchildren. Lyndall also kept affectionately in touch, and I believed Antonia when she told me that the last twenty-five years of her life were the happiest. Alone in her fourth floor flat at 42 Courtfield Gardens, where her work room looked over the trees in the square, she spent most of the day working at her father's desk surrounded by her books. In the late afternoon, she liked to have a friend in for a glass of sherry (whisky for a priest). Her conversation was anecdotal and often very funny and she abandoned herself to it with obvious pleasure. She would end a particularly naughty story with a special laugh that I can still hear.

As her infirmities increased, the ninety-seven stairs up to the flat became a problem, but she would not move to the ground floor flat that Lyndall offered. Luckily, among her surviving friends, some were young. The greatest companion of her last years was Carmen Callil of Virago. Besides bringing Antonia's forgotten novels back into print, she did her shopping on the way to work, and Antonia earned enough money by then to spend her last years without the financial worries, many of them, admittedly, of her own making, that had dogged her all her life. Antonia was hopelessly extravagant and usually in debt to Harrods, Selfridges and Peter Jones. She inherited the characteristic from both her parents. As she explains in the *Autobiogra-phy*, both Cecil and Christine lived beyond their income.

Sadly, Antonia did not live to see the *Frost in May* series on BBC television in 1981. She died on April 10, 1980.

No account of Antonia White's life and work can ignore the condition known as 'writer's block' from which she suffered. The condition is illustrated in the three major pieces in this book, *Julian Tye*, *Clara IV* and the *Autobiography*. Antonia always blamed the block on the disgrace brought upon her by the story she wrote at the convent, the story which led to her rejection both by the nuns and by her father.

There may have been another reason for Antonia's inability to write her fifth novel: the nearer she came to the present the more likely she was to offend the living. Also, the closer events became, the less was she able to distance herself from them as was proved by an unreadable story written in the fifties about her daughters called 'Happy Release'.

The form that Antonia's block took was pathological inde-cision. She teased a sentence like a cat with a mouse, until the page was black with crossings out and rewritings. She claimed that translating had made her cease to know what was her own style, and she remembered with nostalgia the ease with which she had written *Frost in May*. Often one barely legible page was all she had to show for a morning's work. No wonder she was sometimes tempted to seek relief in *The Times* crossword.

A brief word must be said about the arrangement of the pieces in this book under their three headings, Fiction, Ephemera and *Autobiography*. The first and last sections are straightforward enough. In the middle stands Ephemera, the shortest of the three sections, consisting of three long autobiographical pieces. Antonia once remarked that during her working life she had pro-duced 150,000 words of ephemera a year, the equivalent of two novels. The list of material that has had to be excluded for lack of space would fill many pages. These include pre-war drama reviews for *The Spectator* and post-war novel reviews for the *New Statesman*, in which Antonia enthusiastically hailed, among others, the first novels of Barbara Pym, Doris Lessing and Elizabeth Jane Howard. Doris Lessing was to become a friend.

A solitary poem has also found its way into the ephemera section. Antonia did not write enough poems for them to merit a separate section yet the beautiful 'Ubi Sunt Gaudia' could not be excluded. Antonia did not regard herself as a poet, although she

had many friends who were, Dylan Thomas, David Gascoyne
and Kathleen Raine among them. A poem was something she
wrote under the pressure of emotion and was carefully worked,
often in the metaphysical style of the seventeenth century. A
second poem, 'Epitaph' ends the book.

Apart from her published works, and the writings collected
here, Antonia White's literary energies were devoted to the
journals she kept all her life – twenty-six volumes in all,
covering the years 1926 to 1980 – and to a considerable output of
letters. It is hoped that these will be published at a future date.

Susan Chitty, 1983

PART ONE
FICTION

CLARA IV
(*Unpublished: 1965*)

Antonia White spent the last thirty years of her life attempting to add a fifth novel to the 'Frost in May' quartet. She always claimed that she felt guilty about leaving Clara, aged twenty-four, on the steps of the asylum, waiting to get on with the rest of her life.

Clara IV and *Julian Tye* were alternative beginnings to this fifth novel. *Clara IV* (the title was, of course, only a working one) was the less successful. Three of its four chapters consisted of the story so far seen through the eyes of various members of Clara's family at Paget's Fold (Binesfield). Clara is now nearly thirty and is married to Clive Heron (E.E.S.).

The difficulty with which Antonia wrote these flashback chapters was painful to watch. She would spend a whole morning writing and rewriting one sentence. By the end of the day her desk would be strewn with sheets of closely written lines crossed out again and again. She had only to write a phrase to think of six other ways that phrase could have been written. As a result these early chapters are overweighted with unnecessary information.

In the fourth and last chapter is an episode as fresh as a sea breeze. We enter the present (1928) and Clara is returning from an unfortunate holiday in Austria. On the channel steamer she meets two of the nurses from the asylum and learns some things about herself she never knew. This is one of the few totally invented episodes in Antonia's *oeuvre*.

1.

On a blazing Sunday afternoon in the first week of August 1928, Claude Batchelor and his wife Isabel were sitting in deck-chairs under the huge walnut tree that cast its shadow over two-thirds of what, till this summer, had been the croquet lawn at Paget's Fold. Isabel was reading and Claude was smoking his after-lunch pipe and making it last as long as possible, for when it was finished he could not have another till after tea. Being cut down to four pipes a day was the only one of the doctor's restrictions that seriously irked him. When this one was finished, it would still be too glaringly hot on the new full-sized lawn to play croquet in any comfort. It lay beyond the boundary hedge of the old garden of Paget's Fold, on the half acre of field he had enclosed to make room for it and for Isabel's orchard when he had realised, last September, that he would have to retire from St Mark's this July, two years earlier than he intended.

That regulation-sized croquet lawn was only one of the new amenities that he had added to Paget's Fold now that it was to be his and Isabel's home as well as that of his two old aunts, Leah and Sophy, who had lived there all their lives. New rooms had been built on at the back of the small sixteenth-century Sussex farmhouse, hardly bigger than a cottage, and the ancient part completely remodelled inside. He and Isabel had arrived ten days ago to take up life in a transformed Paget's Fold with a bathroom, a hot water system and an electric light plant. Realising all these ambitions which for so long had seemed impossible dreams had given him intense pleasure, but even owning a car for the first time in his life did not afford him the peculiar private satisfaction of at last possessing a full-sized croquet lawn. It was something he had longed for, not merely for over twenty summer holidays at Paget's Fold, but ever since he was a small boy, playing solitary games with a warped mallet and small, chipped wooden balls of the old-fashioned kind with stripes on them, on the patch of grass behind his father's village shop in Storrington. Almost the moment they arrived, while the furniture was still being moved in, he had gone off to inspect the great level expanse of freshly laid turf. Only the fact that he had not unpacked his tennis shoes had prevented him from fetching a mallet and ball and trying a few shots on it. The next morning he had even foregone his after-breakfast pipe in order to get busy on hands and knees with a measuring tape and stake out the boundaries. Then he had spent hours directing the old gardener who had done odd jobs about the place for thirty years and was now to work full-time for him, and the new living-in handyman as they marked it with dazzling white lines and set up the brand-new hoops and sticks.

The first games he had played on it, more often by himself than with Isabel who, in the brilliant weather they had been having since they arrived, preferred lazing in a deck-chair or a hammock under the trees of the old garden to tramping long distances over its unshaded expanse, had been pure delight to him. But as the weather had daily grown hotter, the sun glared down so fiercely on the site where last year wheat had been ripening that he had had to abandon playing on it between noon and teatime. He had missed his after-breakfast game this morning because of going to Mass and, after tea, there would not be time for one before driving over to West Marling for Benediction. By the time he returned it would be nearly suppertime.

He could not help reflecting a little sadly as he puffed at his dwindling pipe that, had he been able to play real croquet in his own garden only a couple of years ago when his energy still equalled his enthusiasm, no heat, however scorching, would have deterred him from going up there, when he had finished his pipe, to practise difficult shots on that fine new lawn. What they had been playing for twenty summers on this inadequate, plantain-studded old one could hardly be called croquet; one could never have invited a serious player to a game on it. No amount of rolling would ever make it level this end where the ground swelled over the roots of the vast ancient tree which year by year littered the patchy, mossy grass with more and more twigs that deflected his most accurately aimed strokes. Nevertheless, on this broiling afternoon, he found himself regretting that it was no longer possible to play any kind of croquet on its shade-dappled sward. The modern reproduction of an antique stone sundial which had been set up at the far end in the centre of the patch the sun never reached effectively prevented its ever being used again for its old purpose. Grateful as he was to Upper Eighth Classical for their parting gift and obvious as it was that this was the ideal, indeed the only possible, site for the sundial, he gave an involuntary sigh.

Isabel, who had dropped her book and was lying back in her deckchair with closed eyelids, opened her great brown eyes, turned them towards him without shifting her head on the cushion and asked languidly:

'Why the sigh, dea'est?'

'Did I sigh? I wasn't aware of it.'

'You know what ears I have. I can hear a bat squeak.'

He checked himself from saying admiringly 'Still?' Isabel hated any suggestion that there was anything remarkable in the fact that her senses were as keen as ever. From long refusal to admit her age, even to herself, she had come to believe her own assertion that she had been married at seventeen to a man considerably older than she was. Once or twice lately he had heard her make it in his presence to new acquaintances. Appearances supported it more than ever now that he, though not yet fifty-eight, was white-haired and very bald. Looking at her, reclining in her deck-chair with her bronze shingled head tilted back in the shadow of the sunlit leaves at an angle that disguised the slight slackening of the flesh under her chin, he himself found it hard to believe that she was barely a year younger than he. Her sallow, chiselled beauty which even in her early twenties had never had the fresh bloom he normally admired in women (until he met Isabel he had been attracted only by pink-and-white blondes) seemed to have been arrested at the point where it had just begun to decay in her early forties.

Seeing him looking at her so intently, she asked:

'Why that critical stare?'

'Not critical, admiring,' he said, smiling at her.

He had an extraordinarily genial smile that made him look like a benevolent elderly cherub. His firmly fleshed face was almost as round as a full moon now that his broad, domed head was bald and the white hair on his temples emphasised the bright blue of his eyes and the patches of foxglove pink in his cheeks. People who did not know him well were deceived by that superficially cherubic appearance into supposing him a man who took life with easy good humour. The kindly creases round his eyes distracted attention from the vertical frown marks on his forehead and his moustache almost hid the compressed lips beneath it. No one who had not seen him stern or angry would have guessed how formidable his face could become, though a close observer would have noticed certain contradictions in his bold, rather handsome features, which in repose had a curious tension as if he had to make a continuous effort to keep them fixed in their habitual mould. The soft fold of flesh above the eyelids, the sensual nostrils and the dimple in the heavy chin implied a man self-indulgent by nature; the obstinate, under-hung jaw and the firmly compressed mouth were those of a disciplinarian who could impose his will on himself and others.

Now, as he smiled at Isabel, all the tensions relaxed in an expression of quizzical, half-rueful tenderness. 'The more I look at you, the more I feel like the ageing Tittonus contemplating his eternally young wife.'

'Who was Tittonus?'

'A mortal who married a goddess.'

'Which one – Diana? You wrote a poem to me when we were engaged comparing me to Diana.'

'No. Aurora, the goddess of dawn.'

'I'm sure I'm not a bit like the goddess of dawn. She ought to have pink cheeks and golden hair, like Clara. Anyway, if she was a goddess, why didn't she make him eternally young too?'

'She made him immortal but unfortunately not ageless. So when he became too decrepit she turned him into a grasshopper. At least I suppose it will be some comfort that your hyper-sensitive ears will be able to register my feeble stridulations.'

'Silly Claude! But I hate you to talk about being old and

decrepit, even in fun. It's such utter nonsense. You're not old by any standards. And when you've had even a few months of this heavenly, peaceful life, you'll feel a new man.' She added, a little anxiously, 'You didn't sigh just now because you were feeling ill?'

'Good Lord, no. Just a little nostalgic. I was thinking of our old games on this lawn and feeling rather sad to think we'd played the last of them. Even if they couldn't strictly speaking be called croquet, they had a peculiar charm, hadn't they?'

'*I* used to love them. At least I could sometimes beat you and Clara, the experts. It was so much a matter of luck who won. But you know how you always yearned for a proper croquet lawn. You were always cursing this one for not being level and ruining your shots.'

'Yes, I know. Naturally, from the point of view of the game there's no comparison. I can only curse myself, not the lawn, when I bungle a shot on the new one. Which I do all too frequently. I'm going to have to put in any amount of practice on it to get used to playing on a full-size lawn after footling about on this pint-size old one. All the same, on an afternoon like this, one forgets its drawbacks and remembers what a lot of pleasure we got out of it in spite of them.' He paused, and sucked at his almost dead pipe. 'Well, I suppose one's bound to lose something, even for the better.'

'*Le mieux est l'ennemi du bien*,' said Isabel, with a faintly mocking smile. 'You've so often used that as an excuse for never wanting to change anything. You disapproved dreadfully when I shingled my hair.'

'I admit I liked it as it was. But now I've got used to it, I think it suits you very well. It sets off your chiselled features. Most women's aren't good enough to stand it. Any more than their legs are good enough to stand these abbreviated skirts you all wear nowadays.'

'Hope mine are.'

'Yes, of course,' he said gallantly, privately thinking that, shapely as they still were, she was unwise to display so much of them now that a little patch of swollen veins was visible under her pale silk stockings. Averting his eyes from them, he fixed them once more on the sundial. Pointing his now completely dead pipe at it, he said:

'I daresay I shall take a bit of time to get used to *that* innovation. Obviously it was the only place to set it up. When the dear boys suggested giving me a sundial, I hadn't envisaged

such an imposing affair as this. I'd have been more than satisfied
with something quite small and unpretentious that we could
have put up on the little lawn behind the rose-bed . . . Once the
stone's weathered a bit – it looks a trifle glaring at the moment –
the effect should be very pleasing.'

'Oh, it'll soon lose that aggressively new look once it gathers
some moss – which it quickly will on this lawn. We must grow a
climbing rose up its pedestal.' Isabel screwed up her eyes and
some normally invisible wrinkles scribbled sharp little lines
round them, making her look almost her real age. 'Oh, I can see
this lawn in a year or two's time. It will be so charming and
picturesque – so right in this old-world garden. The pink roses
and the mossy stone against the clipped yew hedges – yes, I *know*
they're arbor vitae – but the effect's just the same. What could be
more in keeping with our lovely Elizabethan house . . . a lawn
with clipped hedges and a sundial?'

He smiled at her again. 'You make Paget's Fold sound like a
stately manor. In a moment you'll be adding peacock.'

'Oh, you're so aggravating! You're always accusing me of
turning geese into swans. It's just as ridiculous to go to the other
extreme as you do and persist in referring to Paget's Fold as a
"cottage" – which it never was, even before we built on to it.
That young architect said it was one of the most perfect specimens of an Elizabethan farmhouse he'd ever seen.'

'He also said it was one of the smallest.'

'There you go again. Always belittling everything, including
yourself. Why should you be so surprised that your old pupils
should have given you what you call such an imposing sundial?
Naturally they wanted to give you a handsome one to show how
much they appreciated you. It's so touching, the inscription on
it. Even I didn't need it translated. *Praeceptori dilectissimi.*'

'*No,* I implore you, *no!* Don't insult the Upper Eighth's
grammar.'

'Don't be so pedantic. *I* don't wince when you pronounce
French words wrong. Can't you remember you're not a schoolmaster any more?'

'Sorry, my dear, but once a schoolmaster, always a schoolmaster. I found myself gritting my teeth as usual at Mass when
Father Baines said *opera* instead of *opere* in the *Confiteor.* Then I

Cecil Botting when he was an undergraduate at Emmanuel College, Cambridge.

remembered that from now on I shall be hearing him say it on every Sunday of the year instead of just a few in the summer.'

'You'll have to endure it just as I shall have to endure his sermons. Well, at least we shall hear some we haven't heard.'

'I don't find *them* nearly so unendurable. But I'd better get used to it before the time comes for him to say my Requiem Mass. Otherwise I shall grit my teeth in my coffin when he says *opera*.'

'Don't be so morbid. What a thing to think of when we're just beginning our wonderful new life!'

'Oh, I shall last for a good while yet. After all, there's nothing seriously wrong with me, the old machinery's only slightly worn in places. If it weren't for these infernal restrictions on what I eat and drink and smoke, I could almost believe I was scrimshanking. Apart from not having just as much energy as I used to have, I feel very fit. In fact I feel slightly ashamed of myself chucking work two years earlier than I always intended to. Pleasant as it is to be a man of leisure, I don't feel I've properly earned it.'

'Oh, that outsize conscience of yours! As if any man ever earned it more. If you'd waited till 1930, there probably wouldn't have been a Claude to retire. I could have told you long ago what the doctor did – that you'd been overdriving yourself for years. But it was no good my talking to you . . . you know how obstinate you are. I believe you'd have dropped dead at your desk rather than drop one single pupil . . . even one of those wretched boys you took for nothing.'

He set his formidable jaw, and she took the hint.

'All right, I'll drop that subject. It's too heavenly an afternoon to argue and it's bad for you to get agitated.' She stretched luxuriously and her short sleeves fell back, revealing the thickened, flabbier flesh above her elbows. Her full tapering forearms were still firmly rounded and had a sheen on their skin that, as she clasped her hands above her head, made her powdered face look parched. 'The great thing is you're not going to have to work any more. I don't count that one lecture a week at that women's college in Hampstead in the autumn. That won't tire you too much and anyway it doesn't start till October. I know you'd hate giving up your beloved teaching entirely. Besides it will be fun for you to go up to town occasionally. I expect I shall come up with you and get my hair done. I don't suppose the hairdressers in Horsham have ever *seen* a shingle, let alone trimmed one. Perhaps I'll go dancing, sometimes. I enjoy it, apart from it's being so good for the figure. And I'm getting on so well. My partner says I have a natural gift for the tango . . . most Englishwomen are far too stiff and have no *temperament*. I do wish you'd let me teach you a few simple steps, Claude. I'm sure you could manage things like the slow foxtrot. Then we could drive over to Sherry's in Brighton and dance together.'

'My dear girl, I was never a dancing man, even in my youth. Now I'm fat and bald and white-haired I certainly don't propose to disgrace you in public by attempting these strange modern gyrations.'

'You're not fat any more. At least that's one compensation for having to diet for your horrid old diabetes. You're getting quite an elegant figure. That grey flannel suit fitted you last year – now it hangs quite loose on you. And *I* think your white hair makes you look very distinguished.'

'You won't flatter me into displaying either on a dance floor. But don't think I want to hinder your pleasure. If you can find some youthful expert in Brighton as you did in London . . . far be it from me.' Nevertheless he frowned slightly.

'You think I'm dreadfully frivolous, don't you, taking to going to these *thés dansants* at my age? But lots of terribly respectable married women do it, you know.'

'Oh, I realise it's the fashion. And you assure me these professional partners are quite decent young men. It still seems to me an odd way for a man to earn a living. However, I suppose no odder than many things in the way people behave nowadays that I find bewildering. I suppose it's part of your amazing youthfulness that you seem so much more at home in the modern world than I do.'

'But you were always ultra-conservative, weren't you?'

'Yes, I suppose so. And no doubt, as the arteries harden, I shall become more and more of an old die-hard.'

'Shan't let you. I think it's very good for you to have a frivolous wife.'

'So do I. I only hope you're not going to be too bored with the company of a heavy husband. Won't you miss all those feminine bridge parties and having other women to talk to about what-ever women *do* talk about?'

'The only reason I played so much bridge in London was because I got so little of your company. Pupils in the lunch hour, pupils waiting in the study when you got back from afternoon school, pupils up to eleven at night and after that you'd sit up writing your text-books. When did I ever see you except on

Saturday and Sunday nights and your poor little three weeks
down here. All the rest of the summer holiday you stayed up in
London working and only coming down at weekends.'

'How I used to look forward to that blessed three weeks.
They'd have been half over by now. I even caught myself
thinking in church this morning: "Our second Sunday already –
only one more before I have to go back to West Kensington and
the grindstone." It took me a moment or two to remember that
the old study in Valetta Road was no longer there to go back to. I
still find it hard to realise that house isn't ours any more, don't
you? After all, we lived in it ever since we were married.'

'I never could persuade you to move, could I? I used to pine to
get away from that dreary, shabby-genteel neighbourhood and
live in one of those charming, artistic little houses in Edwardes
Square or Chelsea like Clive and Clara's. But you never would
hear of it, so I had to put up with it all those years.'

'I'm sorry you were exposed to so many years of martyrdom.
I did what I could to make the house reasonably pleasant and
comfortable, even if it offended your aesthetic tastes.'

'Silly Claude, don't be so touchy. Anyway, now we've got
our heavenly Paget's Fold, I don't envy Clive and Clara their
exquisite little Chelsea house any more.'

'I'm glad to hear it. It's lucky your taste and mine seems to
have coincided for once in the matter of furnishing and so on.'

'You don't admire their home as much as I do, do you? I think
it is *so* charming – so utterly original. I don't wonder it was
photographed in *Vogue*.'

'Oh, I'm sure it's very pretty . . . very pretty indeed. It still
seems a trifle shocking to me that people should employ some
professional at a vast fee to "create" their own home. I should
think they were both perfectly capable of choosing their furniture and so on for three very moderate sized rooms. And I
confess I'm more than shocked at what they pay for them. One
hundred and thirty pounds a year, for barely a house, when I
think we paid sixty for Valetta Road, which had nine rooms, all
a decent size.'

'Yes, I know, dea'est, I know. But you can't compare Valetta
Road with an exquisite Regency square. After all, they can
afford it and they don't want lots of rooms, living the way they
do and having all their meals out. It's not as if they had children.'

'You don't need to remind me of that,' he said with some
bitterness.

'Claude, do give them time.'

'They've been married three years. After all she's twenty-nine.'

'Is she really as old as that?'

'She was twenty-nine this June.'

'What an alarming thought for me! Mercifully she doesn't look it. I hope this modern frankness of hers doesn't extend to proclaiming her age to all and sundry. Well, I'm in no hurry to be a grandmother . . . that *would* be a give-away. Don't look so shocked, dea'est. But, seriously I'm quite glad for Clara's sake there's no sign of a little Heron yet. It's so wonderful to see her well and happy after the appalling things that happened to her before she married Clive. I should have thought she'd had enough suffering to deserve a few years carefree happiness.'

'Heaven knows I'm glad to see her happy. All the same . . .'

'. . . And suppose she wasn't up to the strain yet? You don't realise what a woman goes through . . .' She broke off, staring straight ahead of her with a resentful, unfocused stare. 'Four times,' she said bitterly. 'And three times for nothing. If we'd become Catholics earlier, I suppose it would have been more. I should probably have been dead by now. It's the only thing I have against the Catholic Church, it's so cruelly unfair to women.'

He waited for a moment, to see if she was going to launch on one of three painful familiar themes: the agony of childbirth, the three stillborn daughters who had come after Clara and the inhumanity of the church's marriage laws, but to his relief her face resumed its normal expression and she said quite serenely:

'Well, I suppose it's really Clive and Clara's business, isn't it? And since Clive was never a Catholic . . .'

'And since Clara no longer regards herself as one,' he interrupted, his voice suddenly bitter as hers had been a moment ago. 'I presume they will continue to organise their life entirely for their own pleasure.'

Isabel waited for him in turn to launch on a painful, familiar theme. But though his face remained clouded, he said no more. After a brief pause, she risked asking:

'Don't you think you worry too much about Clara's having given up her religion?'

'Don't you worry too?'

'Well, of course I'm sorry. I often light candles for her. And it seems so surprising – she was always such an ultra-good Catholic – like you.'

'God knows, I'm not that.'

'Oh yes you are. But you were anything but religious when I first knew you, though you'd been brought up a pious Protestant. You stopped believing in anything when you were at Cambridge. And you went on being an agnostic for years. You only had Clara christened to please me and your parents. She was seven before you decided we were all to become Catholics.'

'One moment, Isabel . . . you know you were perfectly free to make your own choice.'

'Oh, I know. But naturally I wanted to be what you were. And, even if I hadn't the brains to go into all the intellectual arguments as you did, Roman Catholicism had always appealed to me – it's such a much more beautiful religion. But I don't suppose I'd have taken the step if you hadn't.'

'I took it because I believed it to be the truth. It wasn't an easy decision to make, as you know.'

'No, of course not. You had to choose between your career and your conscience. Becoming a Catholic meant you could never become a headmaster which you'd most certainly have done otherwise. Which meant I had to make sacrifices too. But at least you and I were able to choose for ourselves. Poor little Clara didn't have any choice – she was brought over willy-nilly. How could a child of seven realise what becoming a Catholic commits one to?'

'Seven is the age of reason. And Clara was exceptionally intelligent for her age. Father Crampton said he'd never instructed a child who showed more natural grasp of the fundamentals. And the nuns at Mount Hilary often told me they wished many cradle Catholics had as much understanding of their faith and devotion to it as Clara.'

'Oh, I know. And she stuck to it through such trying times . . . all that terrible, humiliating nullity suit – enough to make any sensitive girl rebel against the church.'

'Against ecclesiastical procedure perhaps, not the church itself.'

'Well, anyway she didn't. Though she had to wait nearly three years before she was free to marry again after that appalling marriage to that wretched, drunken Archie Hughes-Follett . . . Oh, I know you always had a soft spot for him. But when I think of the tragedy he brought on her, I find it hard to forgive him in spite of de mortuis and so on.'

'I don't think you can entirely blame poor Archie. I admit that, indirectly . . .'

'Then who and what do you blame?' she said heatedly.

There's never been anything of *that* kind in my family or, as far as we know, in yours. What else but the nervous strain of that disastrous marriage could so have affected her mind that she had to be . . . Oh, I can't bear even to think of it.' She closed her eyes and shuddered. 'That awful day when they thought she might never recover.'

Claude reached out his hand and took one of hers.

'Which, thank God, she did. So suddenly and completely that it was like a miracle. Sometimes I think all the suffering you and I went through all those months was worth it for the incredible joy of that day. Six years ago yesterday. August 4, 1922. The day we got that letter out of the blue in her own handwriting and I rushed up to London and, beyond our wildest hopes, they let me bring her back with me.'

'I'd forgotten the exact day. I knew it was during the summer holidays. Yes, that was wonderful, wasn't it? But it doesn't reconcile *me* to the agony of mind that went before it. *I* sometimes think you set a morbid premium on suffering, Claude. I remember your saying long ago that happiness wasn't the most important thing in life. Well, I should have thought if God was good, He *wanted* us to be happy.'

'I don't think I set a morbid premium on suffering. Heaven knows I enjoy the pleasures of the world only too well.'

'Yes, when that ferocious conscience of yours lets you. And if you keep worrying about other people's consciences too, you soon won't allow yourself to enjoy anything at all. After all, Clara's grown up. She has a right to her own opinions, even if you don't agree with them. You can't expect her to be influenced by you all her life, as she was when she was a child – and long, long after that. You should be thankful she's as fond of you as ever even if she doesn't tremble at your lightest word any more.'

'Was I such a tyrannical father?' he asked rather sadly.

'No, of course not. But she was terrified of your disapproval because she positively worshipped you. I used even to be a little jealous sometimes – you meant so much more to her than I did. But there *have* been times when I've understood her better than you have – after all, she *is* my daughter too. And, nowadays she and I seem to have more in common than we ever had before. Somehow, I feel nearer her generation.'

'As you have reason to,' he said, looking at her again and seeing something that vaguely troubled him in the fact that she had copied her hair-style from Clara's and wore a brief flowered dress that looked to him much the same as the one he had last seen Clara wearing. There was little physical resemblance between them, yet now and then a certain tone of voice, a certain gesture or facial expression made him sharply conscious that they were mother and daughter. At times it gave him pleasure, but at this moment it gave him a curious sense of isolation from both of them.

He rose rather abruptly from his deck-chair.

'I'm getting fidgety sitting still so long,' he said. 'I think I'd like to stretch my legs a little. The sun's not as hot as it was. I think I'll go up to the croquet lawn and try one or two shots before tea.'

2.

Isabel was rather surprised by Claude's sudden impulse to go off and practise croquet shots. If he wanted to stretch his legs before tea, a stroll round the garden would surely have been pleasanter in this heat, as well as better for his blood pressure. However she was too thankful for any sign that his energy was returning to try and dissuade him. In any case, she would not have succeeded. Since his illness he had become, if possible, more obstinate than ever.

As she watched his short, grey-flannelled figure march briskly away across the lawn, she thought, with a mixture of amusement and exasperated tenderness how forcibly his back view expressed his indomitable refusal to let himself 'slack' even if he had retired. If the hat he had just clapped on very straight had been a bowler and not a panama he might have been hurrying off to St Mark's, where in all his twenty-eight years, even this last one, he had never been a minute late for morning or afternoon school. Yet, though he was holding his head as stiffly erect as ever and keeping his shoulders braced back as he always did in his determination not to develop a stoop, it seemed to her that he did so with a hint of conscious effort. He had lost so much weight that his broad back seemed to have shrunk inside the jacket that hung so loose on it. It gave him a disconcertingly wasted, almost brittle look. The word 'brittle' was so absurd in connection with Claude that she had to smile. Of course it was only an optical illusion due to his wearing a suit she had not seen him in since last summer which had been made for him when he was at his stoutest. Nevertheless, she had an impulse to call after him, just to make him turn his head and let her see his reassuringly solid face. But before she could open her mouth, he had vanished behind the dark hedge.

She lay back in her deck-chair and gazed up at the patches of incandescent blue that showed through the rifts in the great dome of branches and golden-green foliage. The rifts were wider even than last year; the spread-finger leaves were smaller, as well as sparser, and spotted with rusty stains. In places there was only a fretwork of bare lichened twigs between her and the sky. When they had first begun coming down to Paget's Fold every year for their holiday, only the three main boughs that sprang from the huge triple trunk had been visible. All the rest had been hidden under such a dense canopy of leaves that when Claude lifted Clara up and perched her on the lowest branch, nothing could be seen of her but her little, dangling, black-stockinged legs. Even when Clara had grown into a schoolgirl, she had only to climb up a few feet to be invisible from the ground. Now, even in its full summer dress, all the articulations of its skeleton were visible. She could not bear to think there might come a day when the walnut would have to be cut down. Paget's Fold would not be Paget's Fold without it. She could no more imagine the house without its great, sheltering tree than she could imagine herself without Claude.

But she was not going to let herself think about gloomy things on such a glorious afternoon. Claude had spoilt it quite enough for her already by going off into one of his tiresome, moralising moods about Clara. How she wished the doctor would pre-scribe some drug for that over-active conscience of his! Why, oh why, couldn't he just relax and revel, as she did, in the prospect of the blissful, carefree life the two of them were going to lead down here in Sussex instead of fussing about how Clara and Clive led theirs in London.

Wasn't it enough for him to see Clara happy at last in a way that, some years ago, neither of them had dared to hope possible? When one thought of all those dreadful things that happened, one after another, to Clara in her early twenties, her disastrous first marriage and its even more disastrous conse-quences – the terrifying breakdown that had lasted the best par of a year and from which she had recovered only to find that, in the meantime, fate had dealt her an even crueller blow – it amazed her that Claude couldn't just be thankful she had survived them all so triumphantly. To look at her as she was nowadays, and as she had been ever since she had married that charming, civilised, brilliant Clive Heron who was as unlike that boorish, stupid, drunken Archie Hughes-Follett as it was possible to be, no one would believe she had ever experienced even normal unhappiness, let alone a series of tragedies of such an abnormal kind that any one of them would have been unusual in a lifetime.

She closed her eyes and tried to recapture that blissful sense of well-being, that delicious feeling of life beginning all over again and stretching ahead in a series of unclouded days in which there would be no more worries, no more of the tragedies of which, heaven knows, they had had more than their share, nothing to do but reign together over their delightful little kingdom – good King Claude and lovely Queen Isabel. But somehow she could not quite recover it.

After a minute or two, she opened her eyes again and decided to make a start on one of her long overdue letters. She had brought out the pretty little green leather writing-case that had been one of Claude's silver wedding presents to her, meaning to write one or two before tea. Perversely, the person to whom she felt most in the mood to write at the moment was Clara, though she certainly did not owe her a letter. But Clara was still in Austria, where she was spending her three weeks holiday from the advertising agency and had left no address. It was extraordinary how Clive made no objection to her taking her holiday without him – this was the third year she had gone off on her own. She smiled at the thought of Claude ever allowing *her* to do such a thing, but Clive was such a delightfully unconventional husband and obviously trusted his pretty wife among all those dangerously attractive foreigners. He did not even mind her going out alone with other men in London which Claude found almost as shocking as if she herself had done so. While she secretly envied Clara for being so wonderfully free, for having all the advantages of marriage and none of the disadvantages, she sometimes wondered how any husband, as obviously devoted as Clive, could be so – so *unpossessive*. But this charming son-in-law of hers was not like any other man she had ever known. Once she said to him chaffingly: 'I don't believe you have an ounce of the normal man in you.'

He had given her one of his most quizzical looks and asked:

'Precisely what do you mean by that?'

'Oh, I mean it as a compliment,' she had smilingly assured him. 'What a much happier world it would be for us women if all men were like you . . . Anyway, all husbands.'

For a moment he had stared at her very intently through his pince-nez. And such a pity he insisted on wearing pince-nez instead of the tortoise-shell-rimmed glasses that all smart young men wore nowadays and which even Claude had adopted for his new reading ones. They gave him a prim, old-fashioned look which entirely belied his nature, besides leaving an ugly red dint on either side of his delicate nose. Since he wore them all the time, it was only when he took them off to polish them that his pale, narrow face made any real impression on one. With his pince-nez on, it was so unobtrusive that one hardly thought of it as plain or handsome, merely as pleasant and highly intelligent. Without them, it had a kind of freakish, ethereal beauty, neither masculine nor feminine, not even quite human. She often told him that, as a boy, he must have looked just like Ariel and even now, with his white skin, red-gold hair and preternaturally long, slender limbs, there was something sprite-like about him as if, for all his convincing disguise as an earthly being, he really belonged to another world.

He had stared at her so questioningly that she wondered if he doubted the sincerity of her remark.

'No, I'm not joking, Clive,' she had said earnestly. 'I mean it quite literally. It must be wonderful to have a husband who adores you but doesn't want to possess you body and soul. Clara's lucky to have married a man who's so delightfully abnormal in that way.' Then she added, with her sweetest smile: 'Not to mention his being abnormally clever and charming into the bargain!'

He had blinked at her behind his pince-nez, then suddenly his intent expression dissolved into a mischievous grin. Slightly disconcerted, she had made a reproachful little *moue* at him.

'I think it's rather horrid of you to laugh at me when I'm saying such nice things to you. You ought to be very flattered to be told I think my darling daughter couldn't have found a more ideal husband. You don't deserve to have such an appreciative *belle-mère.*'

He had promptly suppressed the grin, taken one of her hands and raised it to his lips – he was the only Englishman she knew who could kiss a woman's hand gracefully – and, as he relinquished it, given it an unwonted, affectionate squeeze.

'Of course I don't.'

A little shyly, she had asked him:

'And what was it today?'

But he had only said, provocatively:

'I'll leave you to find that out,' and then maddeningly changed the subject and asked her how she was enjoying *Madame Bovary* which he had strongly recommended her to read. She had had to admit that, though it was very well written, she had found it dreadfully depressing and thought poor Emma should not have been so cruelly punished for wanting a little romance in her drab life.

At one time Clara's life had seemed to be going to be as tragic and frustrated as poor Emma's. She could have written a novel every bit as depressing as *Madame Bovary* about her own daughter if she had ended it at the point where the golden-haired heroine whom life had already treated so cruelly, involving her through no fault of her own in a child's tragic death and, as a result, in a hopeless marriage which had led to a mental breakdown – had emerged from the asylum to which ignorant doctors, believing her to be incurably insane, had cruelly consigned her, only to find that the handsome young soldier with whom she had fallen desperately in love at first sight – and he with her – like Romeo and Juliet – had been deluded into thinking she would never return to him and had, in his despair, married another. But this novel would have a happy ending. The broken heart had mended. The faithful, understanding friend who must have secretly loved her for so many years, since though he was so attractive and eligible he had remained a bachelor until she was once more free to marry, had banished even the memory of the dark shadows and filled her life with gaiety and sunshine.

As she took out a sheet of her lilac-coloured notepaper and shook the violet ink from her fountain pen, narrowly missing splashing the drops on Claude's copy of *The Georgics* that lay open on the grass beside his deck-chair, she had a sudden impulse to start writing a novel, instead of a letter. It would not be the first time she had secretly started one, but she never managed to get further than a few pages. Should she make Clara the heroine this time, instead of an imaginary woman who bore some resemblance to herself but lived in much more luxurious circumstances and was sometimes married to a rich professor, sometimes to an ambassador, who adored her, but neglected her for his work, and did not really understand her. However, she always finally resisted the advances of the other men who besieged her, though she was sometimes terribly tempted to yield to them, and returned to the strong, sheltering arms of her much older husband whom she loved too dearly to let him suspect how much romance she had renounced for his sake. On second thoughts, she decided not to start on a novel. She felt too lazy to go in and find some more suitable paper. The person she felt most guilty about not having written to for so many months

was her sister Blanche. Poor old Blanche, her life was so
dreadfully drab compared to her own. If she had been as plain as
Blanche, she too might have been still a governess, instead of
being married to Claude and just about to begin a delightful new
life in a delightful country home. After all, she had been very
kind to Clara in Vienna – so Clara's solitary postcard from
Salzburg had said. It had also said 'Do try and write to her if you
can bear to. She's longing to hear all about the Great Upheaval
and of course I couldn't give her any details till I see Paget's Fold
for myself.' She decided to be virtuous and write Blanche a
really long newsy letter. It would be fun to impress Blanche,
who still pretended she had never married because she would
rather remain a spinster teaching aristocrats, who recognised
another aristocrat, however poor, than marry any man, however clever and nice, who did not belong to her own class.
Paget's Fold was now almost the English equivalent of those
country *schlosse* where Blanch often spent holidays with *Gräfins*
and *Erzherzogins*. Not so big, of course, but infinitely more comfortable. She would tell her that, the next time she came to
England (the prospect was mercifully very remote) she must
come and stay with them in Sussex in Claude's dear old ancestral
home.

Station Crowfield   Paget's Fold,
Tel. Crowfield 12   Bellhurst,
                                       Nr Horsham,
                                       Sussex

Dearest Blanche,

You must not be cross with your naughty little sister. You are the
first person to be honoured with a letter on my new writing paper
(isn't it pretty?) from our lovely new – but of course in reality very *old*
– home. There was so much to do clearing up Valetta Road and
getting everything ready down here that I haven't had a moment to
myself for months. I had no idea what moving involved as we've
never moved since we were married.

But at least, for the first time I've had all the fun I never had as a
bride of being able to have a house done up and furnished as *I* wanted
it instead of having to put up with so much hideous furniture
belonging to Claude's parents or given us by people with no taste. We
have made a clean sweep of all the ugly cumbersome old things. I have
even persuaded Claude to part with his beloved 'Duke of Norfolk' –
that shabby old green plush chair that was in his study and that he's
had since he was at Cambridge – and now that his mother is dead and

can't be offended, I have at last been allowed to get rid of that *horrible* brass bedstead she gave us as a wedding present. We now have twin beds, like Clive and Clara. A reluctant concession to modernity on Claude's part, but so much more civilised.

Well, here we are, just settled in our adorable little place in Sussex which, as you know, has belonged to Claude's family for centuries. You never saw Paget's Fold in the old days when we used to refer to it merely as 'the cottage' – which of course it never was – but now that we have built on to it *most* artistically so that the new part blends perfectly with the original sixteenth century house and doubled the size of the already large (and heavenly) garden, not to mention installing *all* twentieth-century comforts, we have the most 'desirable residence' imaginable! Paget's Fold always looked deliciously quaint and charming, a typical old Sussex farmhouse with a porch smothered with honeysuckle and the walls thick with ivy and creepers and swallow's nests under the eaves. But now that the porch (Victorian addition) has gone and all the ivy etc. cleared away (I hope the swallows will come back next year) the facade is revealed in all its original beauty of mellow pink brick and ancient timbering. For in the course of the tremendous reconstructions, the architect discovered Paget's Fold to *be a gem of a small Elizabethan manor house*, with superb old oak floors and beams, all covered up by Claude's Victorian forebears who didn't appreciate their beauty. Now the house is restored to all its original dignity both within and without. In the old days you could hardly see it from the road – though it stands on a rise – for it was half hidden behind overgrown bushes and two ragged old box trees that grew right up to the bedroom windows. Now it stands clearly revealed, looking nearly twice as big, even from the front (the new additions are all at the back), framed on one side by the magnificent old walnut tree under which I am sitting and on the other by the row of tall elms reflected in the duck pond on the green that sweeps up to it. People stop their cars to look at it admiringly and more than one artist has already set up his easel, not to mention a photographer from Horsham who has asked permission to use a view of it for a picture postcard – permission we have graciously granted! I will send you one. If it turns out well, we might have it reproduced on our Christmas cards. Inside we have completely transformed it – or rather restored it to its true self. The walls that have been stripped of all the layers of wallpaper that hid the fine old timbering are now pure white, checkered with rough-hewn squares of age-darkened oak. And gone, except for the dear old grandfather clock and one or two really fine old chairs and tables which the dear little aunts either thought too shabby to be displayed or hid under antimacassars and bobbed cloths, is all that incredible medley of horsehair sofas, bamboo what-nots, Victorian armchairs upholstered in red rep or ginger plush, Berlin wool-work footstools, etc., etc. which seemed to them, poor darlings, the 'genteel' way to furnish *any* house.

Now we have furnished Paget's Fold as much as possible in the style of its proper period – simple dark oak to match the original beams, upholstery in Tudor designs and curtains to match. Claude was amazed (and relieved) at my not wanting to use 'contemporary' fabrics like the ones Clara and Clive have in *their* lovely home, but I have too much artistic sense of period. Delightful as they are – unlike Claude, I can appreciate modern art – 'impressionist' curtains would be as much of an anachronism at our Elizabethan casements as the dear old aunts' red blinds and lace 'drapes'. Such is my aesthetic sense of fitness that I have even found reproductions of carved Tudor stone chimney-pieces to put in the upstairs rooms in the old part which till now had no fireplaces, and copies of antique iron lanterns to hide the electric light bulbs. I'm afraid the aunts, particularly my darling Aunt Sophy, will take a little while to get used to seeing the home of their childhood restored to its ancient beauty. They do not altogether appreciate the artistic simplicity of bare oak and plaster walls. And they are quite shocked that I have adorned these with what they regard as 'kitchen utensils' to be hidden away – their own glorious old copper warming pans and preserving pans! But they do appreciate all the modern comforts we have installed – it is like magic to them to be able to switch on electric light, have hot water (they didn't even have cold water laid on before) a bathroom etc., etc. Yet I loved Paget's Fold, even in the old days, when we had to light ourselves up to bed with candles, and the *cabinet* was a wooden shed at the end of the garden, and we had to *buy* buckets of water when the well went dry in hot summers. There was a quaint charm even about the motley collection of furniture with which it was crammed and which always made me think of our old doll's house where nothing went with anything else and everything was out of scale – the jug and basin were bigger than the washstand and the kettle the same size as the coal scuttle. But everything was perfect to a child's vivid imagination, and to naive, uncritical little Belle it was a dream house.

And now she really does inhabit a dream house – perfect in every detail even to the grown-up Belle's fastidious eye! We have made Paget's Fold into the idyllic retreat we have always planned to make it when Claude was able at last to retire to his beloved native Sussex and lead the peaceful life of a country squire. I am so thankful I made him do so earlier than he intended. He is so much better already after even ten days of leisured life that I am not *in the least* worried about his health any more. Our dreams have come true earlier than we expected and they have been realised even beyond our hopes. Paget's Fold in its new glory is even more enchanting than we had visualised it. So rare in this world of disappointments where the best-planned schemes 'gang oft agley'!

The weather is divine and I am sitting on a yew-hedged lawn under the huge walnut tree planted nearly one hundred years ago by one of Claude's forebears. Last year it was the croquet lawn but now we have a magnificent full-sized one on which Claude is at the moment practising shots in this blazing heat. That shows there isn't much

wrong with him! At the end of it now stands a most handsome sundial with a beautiful Latin inscription presented to him by his adoring pupils. I attended his last Speech Day at St Mark's – so moving! My heart nearly burst with pride to hear all the tributes paid to him and the tremendous ovation the boys gave him. 'The most brilliant Classics Master St Mark's has ever had and as beloved as he was brilliant,' the Headmaster said. Also that the name Batchelor was respected throughout the scholastic world and known to thousands who had never had the privilege of meeting him. So Isabel Batchelor can now be proud of the surname (only for true love would she have married the bearer of such an ugly one!) in exchange for the much prettier – and far more distinguished one of Maule. How I wish Papa could have lived to see that day! He would have realised that his youngest daughter did not make such a *mésalliance* as he supposed. And quite apart from Claude's wonderful brain and his truly noble character, his people, the Batchelors, and Sayerses, have owned property in this part of Sussex for generations, even if they can't trace their ancestors back to the fourteenth century as we can. True, for some generations now they have come down to being not much more than yeomen, but we now know that Paget's Fold was originally a manor house and his ancestors settled here in Charles II's time. They must have been at one time squires and probably owned quite a big estate before it was whittled down to the forty acres Claude inherited at twenty-one. So sad he has had to sell in order to do all the rebuilding, etc. However, we are quite content with our modest but perfect estate of a single Sussex acre!'

You always said you could not picture me living permanently in the depths of the country. You do not really know the side of me that revels in the beauties of nature – birds, flowers, trees, the glorious Downs we can see from almost every window. I do not think I shall miss London at all. Besides, now that we have a car, the chauffeur can always run me up if I want to get new clothes or have my hair done, for your Belle has no intention of degenerating into the typical English county lady in ill-fitting tweeds, with hair like a bird's nest. Such a joy possessing a car at last though we did not really need one in London. Even Clive and Clara haven't got one. When Claude learns to drive it we shall not always use the chauffeur: there is plenty for him to do about the place running the electric-light plant, motor-mower, etc. He looks very well in his livery. As we drove to Mass this morning, it was *so* nice to be in one's own car, instead of having to hire the one local taxi whose driver does not bother even to wear a cap. The chauffeur's wife acts as cook; we also have a gardener and a weeding-boy – quite an 'establishment' for four people, but it takes a lot of work to keep the place up properly and we should need them all

Christine Botting (née White) photographed in 1898, a year after her wedding to Cecil, and exactly a year before the birth of Antonia.

even if Claude's two dear old aunts were not still with us. It was really a blessing in disguise that his mother died before we moved for we should have needed a nurse for her if she had recovered from her stroke. A merciful release for her too, poor thing, of course, for she would have been completely paralysed. It is no good pretending it wasn't a trial having had to have her living with us all those years at Valetta Road though I'm sure I did my best! Luckily I have always adored the old aunts Leah and Sophy – *so* unlike their elder sister! I was really sorry when Claude's father died in 1914. He was such a handsome old man with aristocratic features and hands and devoted to me. Poor Mrs Batchelor, she couldn't help being so plain, but she was so trying with her meek, martyred ways and so jealous of me and always making trouble between me and Claude. Still, *de mortuis*, etc. Anyhow now we can use the really lovely new room Claude built on specially for her (he was such a dutiful son though it was his father he worshipped) as a spare room and I *do* hope that one of these days, if you can tear yourself away from your beloved Vienna and all the *Grafins* who value their dear Miss Maule so highly, you will come for a nice long stay.

She paused, feeling a little guilty. She knew that she ought to add what Claude, with his usual sense of duty, had told her to tell Blanche – that if ever she wanted to give up her Austrian pupils and return to England he would gladly offer her a permanent home at Paget's Fold. The thought of having another relative, even one of her own, planted on her after having had to share her home for nearly twenty years with her mother-in-law, frankly horrified her. And Blanche was notoriously *difficile*, though in an entirely different way from old Mrs Batchelor. There was nothing of the meek, injured martyr about Blanche! She was fierce, domineering and had an explosive temper. She was fond of Blanche, of course – after all, she was her only surviving sister and, as the eldest, had taken the place of the mother who had died when she herself was a baby. But the only one of her three older sisters whom she had really loved had been Alicia, the one nearest her in age and the most like her in temperament. She still regretted Alicia, who had died so tragically young – only the age Clara was now. Sometimes Clara reminded her of her a little, especially her eyes which were neither blue like Claude's nor brown like her own, but a changeable greyish-green with hazel like Alicia's. Had darling Alicia been still alive, she would have welcomed the prospect of having her to live with them. But the idea of Blanche arriving some day, even in the distant future, to spend the rest of her life with them frankly appalled her. Besides it might not be so

distant! Horrid thought, poor old Blanche must be in her sixties
and, even more horrid thought, she was only six years older
than herself, though there had always seemed such an immense
gap between them. That was the worst of having an elder sister.
Even if one *looked* nothing like one's age, she had no scruples
about reminding one of it every birthday. After all, it wasn't
really Claude's responsibility to provide Blanche with a home
when she retired. It was their brother Henry's, who lived in
Omaha, Nebraska – such a nice long way off – and had done
very nicely for himself. She had better not make Paget's Fold
sound too attractive, she decided, as she resumed her letter.

However, I must not let my enthusiasm run away with me. Paget's
Fold, charming as *we* think it, would seem a very modest abode
compared to those splendid *schlosse* in Austria where you so often stay,
and which you have so vividly described to me. And obviously it is
not as luxurious as Henry and Mamie's American home. We could not
afford to make it so, even if we wanted to, for, alas, we are anything
but rich! I believe over there they have standards of comfort far
beyond anything *we* have in dear, backward old England! In any case,
I remember you were very critical of poor old England when you last
returned to it just before the hateful war. It seemed very *ungemutlich* to
you after your beloved Vienna. After all, you have lived there so long
that it is really your spiritual home and I doubt if you would find
anywhere else congenial for long. How I wish I could visit you in that
enchanting city – I know I should find it so *sympathique*. And how I
envy Clara for being lucky enough to do so! At least she will be able to
bring me back first-hand news of you – the next best thing to seeing
you in person, after all these years, though from your recent snapshots
you do not seem to have changed much. I think you are so wise to
stick to a particular dignified style of dressing that suits you, like
Queen Mary. I could never be so strong-minded! But then I have
always been a frivolous vain creature – as you used to tell me so often
in the old days.
Well, what do you think of the niece whom you haven't seen since
she was a child at her convent school? You must find a sensational
difference between that little girl in a prim blue uniform with her
golden hair scraped back in a plait (the nuns insisted on it!) and this
charming, chic grown-up Clara, so pretty and ultra-sophisticated! I
am sure you felt she was a credit to you, even if she doesn't take after
the Maules except that, thank goodness, she has the family hands. As
you so often say, 'If you want to judge race, look at hands before face.'

Isabel's lips twitched. Poor old Blanche, no wonder she was
so fond of this maxim. Her small white hands, with their
smooth, tapering fingers were her only beauty. But it was a

shame to laugh at her; she had had to fend for herself since she was eighteen, first as a governess, then as a private teacher of languages, and no man had ever shown the least inclination to love and cherish her. No wonder she had such exaggerated pride in her birth; it was the only thing she had to keep up her own self-esteem and make her employers and pupils treat her with the respect due to an English lady who, though forced to earn her own living, was as *wohlgeboren* as any Austrian *grafin* or *baronin*. Had she herself been dumpy and plain, like Blanche, she might have found herself in the same situation, for Grandfather Maule had speculated away the last of the family fortune and their father had had no scruples, when his young wife died, in purchasing an annuity for himself with her marriage portion and making no provision whatever for their children. He had decided very early that Blanche had no chance of finding a husband and despatched her abroad to earn her living, since he had no intention of having an unmarried daughter left on his hands to feed and clothe. Even she herself, his youngest and favourite child, of whom he had high matrimonial hopes as the beauty of the family, had been told she was an idle, undutiful hussy, not worth her keep, and packed off along with Alicia, who had dared to stand up for her, to be a governess in Hamburg when she had refused to marry a rich, gouty old baronet. She had not minded it too much for the son of the house had fallen in love with her and, though she hadn't returned his affection, she had enjoyed all the tributes of poems and flowers, and the young officers who came to the house paid far more attention to her than to her stolid, flaxen-haired *backfisch* pupils for whose benefit they were invited. Both she and Alicia had had so much fun with their German admirers and most of all in comparing their methods of approach to *die schone Englandein* when they met on their off days that they had on the whole preferred being governesses to living at home with their irascible father. Above all, there had been the wonderful excitement of earning their own money. Little as it was, at least they could afford to buy themselves a few clothes instead of having to cajole even the price of a rose to trim a hat out of Papa. *His* favourite maxim had been 'Beauty unadorned adorns the most'. Sometimes, after repeating it many times, he would reluctantly grant the request. More often he would fly into one of his rages and accuse them of wanting to bedizen themselves like the daughters of a horse-leech. But the excitement would soon have palled if they had had to go on being governesses all their lives. On their return to

England they had both met their true loves and become engaged to them. Alicia had married almost at once and gone to Canada with her husband and died without their seeing each other again, soon after Clara was born. For herself and Claude – he had only just come down from Cambridge when they met and, since he more than half supported his parents – it was four years before they could afford to marry. She had to go out and earn her living again, for Papa had made it very clear that if his daughter intended to demean herself by marrying this nobody of an usher she was not going to eat her head off at his expense during a long engagement. And since her scrappy education at the cheap French boarding school to which he had sent all his daughters for the sake of economy had not qualified her for being anything but a governess or a companion, there had been no other way of earning her keep and saving enough money to buy her trousseau. She could never have got through those four years of drudgery and boredom but for being passionately loved and in love and having marriage to look forward to at the end of them.

She had gone off into such a long reverie that she had lost the thread of her letter to Blanche. In any case her hand was tired with writing and it must be nearly tea-time. She would finish it after tea. It would be a good excuse for not accompanying Claude to Benediction.

She lay back in her deck-chair and closed her eyes, thinking how many things in those days for a woman had depended on whether or not she was good-looking and whether or not her family had money. Compared to Blanche, she herself had been lucky, but how much luckier Clara was in every way than the girls of her own generation. Even if she hadn't been, if not a beauty, at least decidedly pretty (for which she was thankful – she would have hated to have a plain daughter) with her brains and all the wonderful opportunities women had nowadays, she would have had a very pleasant life even if she had not married. As it was, she now had the best of both worlds. It was difficult not to envy her a little. Certainly she had had a bad time a few years ago – but after all, since they were both so devoted to her, it had been as bad, if not worse for her parents. But that was all over long ago, and here she was, still in her twenties, with everything she could possibly wish for, a perfectly charming husband who worshipped her, a delightful home and enough money to have everything, in reason, that she wanted, including the loveliest clothes. In *her* early married life she had had to dress on eighteen pounds a year because that was all Claude could afford, because of having to house and feed his parents as well as themselves. And later on, when he was earning more, she had still had to filch from the house-keeping money to be decently dressed (oh, the sordid rows there had been over bills!) because he had insisted on sending Clara to that expensive convent school which meant 'economising' – how she hated that word! What it meant, of course, was that he begrudged his wife even a small fraction of what he cheerfully spent on giving his daughter a Catholic education. She was the one who had had to be sacrificed on the altar of his conscience! And, after all that, Clara had given up her religion which proved that a convent education was no guarantee that a girl would remain a good Catholic all her life. Poor Claude, he took it so hardly!

She was sorry about it herself, of course, but there was no doubt that Clara was much more tolerant and easier to get on with than in the old days when she had been as strict as her father and decidedly critical of herself for not going to Mass except when one had to and being rather vague about dogma and so on. At least she was spared those endless discussions in which they ganged up together to prove that she was little better than a heretic on all sorts of matters of faith and morals. At one time Clara had been just like Claude, intolerant of any opinions but her own. No doubt Clive's influence had a great deal to do with that. That was one of the things she found most attractive in her son-in-law; he was always ready to listen to other people's point of view. In fact it was sometimes difficult to know what he really believed about anything. He had a way of producing such ingenious arguments on both sides of a question that you were never sure what his own convictions were or even if he had any fixed ones. He would put a case so clearly and logically that even *her* illogical mind could follow every step and then just as clearly and logically proceed to demolish it. Claude had once tried to make her read Plato and in her opinion Socrates was a pompous old bore who went about trying to confuse everybody to show off his own superiority and must have been an intolerable husband! No wonder his wife had been a shrew! But Clive never tried to make you feel a fool – on the contrary he took it for granted you were as clever as he was and listened to everything you said with the most flattering attention. She found it very refreshing to be treated by a man as if she were something more than a beautiful nitwit. Yet somehow she could not imagine wanting to be married to Clive, charming as she found him in every way. It was absurd to say that anyone could be *too* tolerant and sweet-tempered and yet there was no doubt that most women rather liked having domineering husbands, even ones with passionate tempers. She herself would have found marriage rather dull without scenes and squabbles and jealousies; besides it was rather fun to have to get one's own way by guile and exploiting one's femininity. A woman had weapons, if she knew how to use them, against a man arrayed against her in all his strength. There was always a chink in Goliath's armour if you knew where to aim that little pebble from your sling. However, perhaps Clive appealed so much to Clara precisely because he was utterly unlike Claude. Yet didn't they say that girls who adored their fathers usually married men of the same type? At any rate, it couldn't have been a more successful marriage. Yet, at the time, it had surprised her. For one thing Clara and Clive had been close friends long before she had married that wretched Archie Hughes-Follett and Clara had always assured her that he was such a confirmed bachelor that it was impossible to imagine him married to anyone. She had watched very carefully at Clara's twenty-first birthday party, which was the first occasion on which she herself had met this Clive of whom Clara had talked with almost awed admiration, for any sign of anything more than friendship but her sharp eye for such things had not been able to detect the least trace of it. Even when Clive had exerted himself so much to revive Clara's spirits after her nervous breakdown and the tragic end of her love-affair with Richard Crayshaw his whole attitude had been that of an affectionate brother to a favourite sister and not in any way suggesting that he wanted to be anything more to her. Stranger still, he had not only introduced her to his best friend but thrown the two of them so much together that it seemed obvious he was bent on matchmaking. The friend had indeed fallen in love with Clara and Clara had shown more and more signs of responding. Strangest of all, it was only when Nigel Bell had proposed to her and she had been on the verge of accepting him, that Clive, apparently to Clara's immense surprise, had proposed to her himself and she had said 'yes' without a moment's hesitation. Of course she was quite aware that Clara did not feel the same about either Clive or Nigel as she had felt about Richard – she would probably never feel the same about any other man – but what had puzzled her at the time and puzzled her still when she remembered it, was the suddenness with which she and Clive had discovered that if either of them was going to marry anyone it could be no one but each other.

And year by year it became more evident that they had been right. No two people could be more unlike – they seemed almost to belong to different species – so much so that she nicknamed them 'The Owl and the Pussy Cat' – but she could sense an extraordinary bond between them that was not of the same nature as that between Claude and herself but might be even more indissoluble. She had secrets she had never told Claude, he might even have secrets he had never told her. But now and then she had the oddest sense that Clive and Clara had no secrets from each other yet had a secret in common which it annoyed her to be unable to guess. She wasn't an inquisitive woman but it whetted her curiosity. It was all the more annoying because she was quite sure that if she knew the right question to ask and had the courage to ask it she would get a perfectly candid answer. She even had a strong suspicion that they were surprised she hadn't asked it long ago. Yet though plenty of questions had occurred to her, her feminine intuition assured her that none of them was the right one.

3.

As soon as Claude stepped into the full blaze of sunlight, he realised it would still be as scorching as ever up on the new lawn. However, since he had left Isabel so abruptly on the excuse of practising croquet shots, he felt bound at least to change into tennis shoes and collect a mallet and balls. Her feelings would be hurt if she suspected that all he wanted was to be alone for a while. Much as he loved her company, now that he had it all the time he was apt to feel suddenly oppressed by the weight of thoughts he could not share with her, most of all on the subject of Clara.

As he walked slowly towards the house, feeling more reluctant at every step to leave the shade-dappled garden for the glare of the croquet lawn, he saw Aunt Leah wandering alone down a path. The sight of her small, thin figure in the grey alpaca blouse and long black skirt that he had seen her wearing summer after summer on the Sundays of his holiday gave him a twinge of conscience. Since the move he had been so occupied in getting all the new arrangements working smoothly that he had not spent as much time as he should with the two old ladies. He felt particularly guilty in the case of Aunt Leah, the elder, for there had always been a special bond between them as there was between Isabel and Aunt Sophy. Moreover he knew she was too proud and sensitive to obtrude herself on him. If he did not seek her company of his own accord, nothing would have induced her to invent some excuse, as his mother had always done, to seek him. Seeing a chance to make up for his neglect, he went in pursuit of her.

'If you're going for a little stroll round the garden, Aunt, may I come with you?' he asked, as he caught her up and fell into step beside her.

'Why, Claude, there's nothing I should like more, if you've nothing else to do,' she said, smiling up at him from under the brim of a very ancient black straw hat with a faded mauve ribbon she always put on when she went into the garden whether the sun were shining or not, for she still considered it improper for any respectable woman to be seen out of doors with her head uncovered. By now she was inured to seeing Isabel and Clara bare-headed in the garden; she did not approve, though she refrained from criticism. But she severely reproved her younger sister Sophy for not putting on a hat, even if she had only gone out to pick a few flowers.

He smiled back, with a sudden rush of affection, at the thin, white face whose normally severe expression had melted into one of such pleasure that the delicate features lost all their primness. But the next moment they stiffened into an anxious look as she said:

'Oh dear, I wish I hadn't put on this shabby old hat. I'd no idea I was going to have the pleasure of your company. Of course I was going to put on my Sunday one when I appeared at tea-time. May I run in and change it?'

'No, I'm not going to let you escape now I've caught you,' he said firmly, tucking her arm under his – it felt like a frail, dry twig compared to the fleshy warmth of Isabel's – and drawing her along beside him down the grass path bordered with phlox and sunflowers and shaded by gnarled fruit trees. 'Anyway I like you in that hat. It reminds me of the old days. It gives me a sense of permanence which I find very comforting in this changing world.'

She looked up at him, surprised.

'Why, Claude, you're surely too young to feel like that? That's how we old people feel.'

'You forget I'm getting old myself. After all, in two years I shall be sixty.'

'I daresay you feel older than you should because of having to retire earlier than you meant to.'

'Well, certainly it makes one more conscious of being a has-been. After all, one's on the shelf. However pleasant the shelf, and heaven knows it couldn't be pleasanter, it takes one a little while to get over finding oneself on it sooner than one expected.

'I always knew it would be a wrench to give up your work; it meant so much to you. But you have so many good years ahead of you and I can't see you letting that splendid brain of yours lie idle.'

'Oh, I shall do a little lecturing in the autumn. And probably get down to doing another Cavell and Batchelor. But I've left it too late to do what I always dreamed of – make one original contribution however small to Homeric scholarship. When one's young one deludes oneself into thinking it's only a question of having enough leisure. One doesn't realise that by the time one has the leisure, one will no longer have the mental energy.'

'You only talk like that because you're not well and need a thorough rest. By this time next year you'll be talking very differently. Why, to hear you, anyone would think you were in your eighties, like me and your Aunt Sophy, instead of only in your fifties.

'Ah, but you two don't seem to have aged at all in the past twenty years. When Isabel and I first began coming down here regularly for our summer holidays, you both looked to me just the same as you do now. So does she . . . allowing for the changes in female fashions. I'm the only one of the four of us who has changed out of all recognition. Even to go back to not so very long before the war – do you remember that unusually hot summer of 1911?'

'Indeed I do. Farmers in Bellhurst still talk of that record hot summer.'

'Well, on the hottest day of that record hot summer, though I was considerably fatter than I am now, I walked twelve miles over the downs with Clara without turning a hair. Fat and forty as I was, at least I still had a reasonable amount of energy and a reasonable amount of hair to turn. Look at me now, a bald-headed crock, who finds it almost too much exertion to retrieve a croquet ball.'

She looked at him anxiously.

'Is that why you're feeling so tired? Don't tell me you've been playing croquet in this heat. It's enough to give you sunstroke – that new lawn is so exposed. Oh dear, I pictured you sitting peacefully under the walnut tree with Isabel, having a nice rest after lunch.'

He gave her a reassuring smile and patted the frail arm entwined with his.

'Don't worry. So I was, till I finished my pipe and got a little fidgety. Anyway, decrepit as I am, I have still enough energy to potter round the garden with my favourite aunt.'

'How dreadfully you do exaggerate, Claude. Still I don't deny you've aged faster than you should in the past few years. To my mind, you've never looked quite the same since all that grief and worry you had over Clara. I mean when she was struck down with that terrible brain disease and she had to spend so many months in hospital.' Though Aunt Leah knew as well as he did that what had struck Clara down was a violent attack of insanity and that the hospital where she had spent so many months was a public asylum known as Colney Hatch, she could not bring herself to use the word 'madness' even to him. 'Even though, mercifully, *she* got over it so completely, I think you yourself never quite recovered from what you went through in that anxious time. I think it left a permanent mark on you.'

He frowned and kicked a plum crawling with wasps off the grass into a lavender bush.

'Perhaps you're right,' he said thoughtfully. 'Thank God it has left no mark on her. Within a fortnight of her coming home, except that she was very thin, no one could ever have suspected there had been anything wrong with her. To look at her nowadays, I could almost feel, as Isabel does, that the whole thing was a bad dream. Nevertheless I can't forget that it happened. Though why to Clara, when there had never been anything to suggest such a possibility, and as far as I know, no history of insanity in either Isabel's family or ours.'

'Certainly not in ours,' said Aunt Leah indignantly. 'Our poor mother was sometimes a little confused in her head in her last years, but that often happens with old people. There was never any question of her having to be . . .' She broke off abruptly and gave a gentle tug at his sleeve. 'Excuse me, Claude, but would you mind if we turned round and went the other way?'

'Why, of course not,' he said, stopping at once. 'Are you finding the sun too hot, now we're out of the shade?' The path they were on led past the large sunny patch of ground where vegetables grew in orderly rows, in contrast to the unplanned confusion of fruit trees and bushes, herbs and cottage flowers of the plot they had just left.

'No, it isn't that,' she said, as they reversed their direction. 'But I just caught sight of a man over there picking peas. It can't be Kensett, because he doesn't come on Sundays. So it must be Mrs Smith's husband. I wouldn't like him to overhear our conversation. Sophy and I are always having to remind ourselves to be careful how we talk nowadays . . . one of them may be within earshot. We're not used to having servants always about the place, like you and Isabel.'

'We're not used to having a man and wife ourselves. We'd have brought the cook and housemaid from Valetta Road if it had been feasible. I was sorry to part with May and Gladys after all these years.'

'We were sorry you couldn't bring them with you. Such nice women, they were. We got used to them while we were staying with you in London during the alterations. But I quite see you had to have a man to drive the motorcar and run the electric light machine. That would be quite beyond Kensett.'

'Anyhow Kensett has more than enough to do in the garden, now he's working full time. At least we've got one familiar face about the place. However long has Kensett been doing jobs about the house and garden here, Aunt? I can remember him here when I was a boy and I used to come over with my parents from Hambleden. I daresay he wasn't much more than a boy himself but to me he seemed like a grown-up man.'

'Oh, I "dunnamany" years, as Kensett would say. He'd have been about fourteen when he first came to do a bit of digging now and then when the soil was too heavy for Aunt Sophy to turn. He must be well on into his sixties now, but he's wonderfully well and hearty and as good a worker as ever, though you can't hurry him. He's a real Sussex man and "won't be druv". We were so glad you kept him on as a full-time gardener. We thought you might want to get some younger man.'

'As if I'd dream of it. Kensett is as much part of Paget's Fold as the walnut tree.'

They were passing along the hawthorn hedge which marked the boundary of the old garden. Aunt Leah glanced over it at the rows of spindly little trees, looking almost too frail to bear the weight of their iron labels, which filled the smaller rectangle beside the new croquet lawn.

'What splendid fruit you'll be enjoying in years to come,' said Aunt Leah. 'All those wonderful new varieties specially chosen and planted for you by that expert. Poor Kensett, he thought that young "foreigner" from London was to be the new garden-

er and put his nose out of joint. But he still can't get over there
not being any strawberry pippins.'

'Neither can I. I'd have had a dozen put in if they were to be
had. To my mind, there isn't an apple to touch a strawberry
pippin. But they've disappeared, like so many good old-
fashioned things, worse luck. Isabel's fond of saying the good
gives way to the better. To my mind, nowadays, it more often
gives way to the worse.'

'Ah, you're not so fond of all the modern ways as Isabel is.'

'No, I haven't got her amazing adaptability . . . any more
than her amazing inability to age. I'm almost beginning to feel
she and I belong to different generations.'

'I admit she looks wonderfully young for her age. And they
say a woman is as young as she looks. But that doesn't alter the
fact that there's less than a year between you.'

'It's not so much a question of years as of our respective
mental outlook. She still instinctively looks forward and I look
back. I suppose that's the dividing line between young and old.'

'But at your age you've still so much to look forward to. It's
natural when you get to mine and Aunt Sophy's to dwell in the
past and find it difficult to adapt oneself to change. Even when
the change is for the better, like all the wonderful improvements
you've made down here.'

He smiled remorsefully: 'I realise all too well how you must
feel. I wish myself so many of the old, familiar things I've
known at Paget's Fold since my boyhood hadn't had to go in the
process. But it's far worse for you and Aunt Sophy who have
lived here all your lives.'

'Oh, we're getting used to them fast, even if we still make
stupid mistakes and keep looking for doors that aren't there any
more and forget the old stairs have been done away with. Nasty,
dangerous things they were, anyway. But it still feels a little
strange coming back after all these months . . . neither of us had
ever been away from here longer than a week . . . and finding
the old cottage transformed out of all recognition into quite a
grand place. Of course our shabby old furniture had to go – it
would have disgraced such fine new surroundings. Anyway, it
was old-fashioned stuff at the best and much of it only makeshift
we'd put together ourselves.'

'But you'd made it so beautifully and with such infinite care
and ingenuity. Isabel and I used to marvel every year at what you
two could conjure up out of nothing.'

'Well, necessity is the mother of invention. We found a use for most things. We used to hoard the oddest bits and pieces like two old jackdaws because they might come in handy.'

'What a brute I feel, disturbing your nest.'

'Oh you mustn't do that Claude. Look at the wonderful home you've given us. I'm sure we never dreamed of living in such luxury in our old age. Fancy, we shall even be able to have a fire in our bedroom in the cold weather: we've never had such a thing.'

'It horrified me to discover you hadn't even a fireplace up there. You must have frozen to death in the winter.'

'Oh, we could have moved into the big bedroom – the one that was our mother's and father's and is now yours and Isabel's – and lit a fire there. But we preferred to keep to the old room we've shared all our lives. Your poor mother, being the eldest, had a room to herself – the one Clara always used to sleep in. If it was very cold we'd have more candles than just the one to take the chill off. To think we have the electric light. It's like magic. Sophy keeps turning it on when it isn't dark enough to need it just to see it come on and I have to remind her not to waste it.'

'Well, I'm thankful there's something that makes you at least a little more comfortable.'

'Oh, please don't think we don't appreciate all you've done for us,' she said anxiously. 'We couldn't be more grateful. But I think what we appreciate most of all is you and Isabel letting us keep our bedroom otherwise as it was, with our own furniture and our queer old odds and ends. We've slept together in that same feather bed since we were children. And such a comfort, particularly to Sophy, to have all sorts of strange oddments she treasures still about her. Even a family of ancient dolls! And poor old Whiff. He's getting moth-eaten and I said we really ought to throw him away, but she couldn't bear to part with him.'

Seeing his puzzled look, she said:

'Ah, I daresay you don't remember Whiff, our old tabby cat. Clara does, though he died long ago when she was only a little girl. She pleased Sophy so much by mentioning Whiff when we went to see her and her husband in London and Sophy admired their black cat so much. What is its name, something rather unusual like that dog you had when you were at Cambridge – Socrates.'

'Augustus,' he said, involuntarily clenching his jaw. He was fond of animals, particularly of dogs, but he almost loathed Augustus. The sight of all the doting affection Clara and his son-in-law lavished on a wretched cat when they ought to have

A studio portrait taken at the age of fourteen.

been lavishing it on a child sickened him. He added hastily, with as much warmth as he could:

'Ah, of course I remember a cat here at one time, now you mention it. Shocking how bad my memory's getting.'

'It's not likely you'd remember Whiff. He was getting a very old gentleman when you and Isabel first started coming down here and he was always shy of strangers. Though he took wonderfully to Clara and never once scratched her. We were so frightened he might; he'd been ill-treated by children. Sophy rescued him as a tiny kitten from some cruel village boys throwing stones at him. Eighteen he lived to be, poor old Whiff, and Sophy was so fond of him that when he died she swore she'd never have another cat. She couldn't even bear to bury him herself, as she'd done all our others, and asked Kensett to. But do you know what Kensett did? He's very clever at stuffing birds and so on and out of the kindness of his heart, instead of burying

Whiff, he stuffed him. He'd taken so much pains and made such a beautiful job of it, Sophy couldn't hurt his feelings by refusing to take it. So we've had Whiff up in our bedroom ever since. You and Isabel wouldn't have seen him for of course neither of you have ever been in there.' She paused and added hesitantly: 'I hope you don't mind – we've asked Mrs Smith not to go in there, even to make the bed. We so much prefer to keep it tidy ourselves as we've always done. It's foolish of us, I know, but it makes it easier for us to get accustomed to all the new ways if we've got a little corner to retire to where everything is as we remember it and we can go on just as we used to.'

He said, gently, pressing the thin arm against his side:

'I won't ask to see that room. And of course I'll tell Mrs Smith that she's never to enter it without your express permission. But I like to know it's there – that one little bit of the house as I remember it still exists.'

'Now, now, Claude, don't sound so sad. You mustn't get sentimental, just because your queer old aunts cling to their queer old habits.'

'I have plenty of queer old habits myself,' he smiled at her. 'And I intend to develop a great many more in the course of the next few years. In spite of all Isabel's determination to prevent me from becoming even more hidebound than I am.'

By avoiding the vegetable patch and taking the opposite path they had now toured the whole of the smaller end of the garden and come in sight of the house again.

'It really does look nice,' she said. 'I liked the new part from the first, it harmonises so very well with the old.'

He could not help admiring it himself.

'That young man did a good job. After all, it's rather pleasant to know that he considered Paget's Fold an unusually good specimen of domestic Tudor. The original structure hasn't been altered since it was built, probably in the time of Queen Elizabeth.'

'I don't suppose it had. They built to last in those days. They say about here that some of those old oak beams came from the wreck of the Spanish Armada.'

'Perhaps they did. If so, I'm glad His Catholic Majesty lost his ships and provided us with some excellent timber.'

'Oh dear, I suppose, now you're a Roman Catholic yourself you wish the Spanish had won and all the English Protestants had been forced to become Roman Catholics or be burnt at the stake.'

'You'd have been burnt at the stake rather than do that, wouldn't you, Aunt?'

She said soberly:

'I don't think one should joke on such subjects, Claude. I am thankful I didn't live in those days when my faith might have been put to such a test.'

'Forgive me,' he said penitently. 'I only meant it in admiration. I know you would flinch from nothing rather than go against your religious conscience.'

'You cannot *know* such a thing,' she rebuked him. 'No one can foresee how anyone may act in moments of great temptation.'

'No, indeed,' he said with a sigh. For a moment he was silent, remembering one occasion on which he had compromised with his conscience. It was a painful memory and earlier that afternoon, when he and Isabel had been talking about Clara, it had begun suddenly after many years to rankle once more. The subject was one he had promised never to mention again to Isabel and one he could never, in any circumstances, mention to Aunt Leah.

The latter, obviously anxious to get on to a safer subject than religious liberty, observed, glancing at the new porch as they passed it: 'It's a great improvement having the entrance at the side now. It was so awkward having the front door opening straight into the living-room. And the house looks so much neater from the road without the old porch. It had got so overgrown with honeysuckle and so on, it looked shockingly untidy in winter.'

They turned the corner and stood for a moment on the strip of grass in front of the house, inside the white palings, beyond which there still stood a moss-covered boulder, the last mounting-block left in Bellhurst.

'And so much bigger,' she said, screwing up her eyes and surveying the now bare half-timbered facade. The small faded bricks were flushed to warm pink by the afternoon sun but the rough-hewn oak that framed them in irregular squares were no longer the silver grey produced by centuries of weathering. They had been coated with some chocolate-brown substance to preserve them from rotting, so that they made a staring criss-cross pattern of crooked dark lines against the mellow brick-work, instead of blending into it almost imperceptibly. To an unkind eye, Paget's Fold now looked a shade too much like the 'picturesque period residence' of estate agents' catalogues.

'One couldn't see its true proportions before,' said Claude, standing back to admire it. 'I'm amazed myself how much larger it looks from the front, now that the porch and all the ivy and stuff have gone.'

'And that old box tree that had grown so high, it was half-way up our bedroom window – it quite hid that end of the house,' said Aunt Leah, glancing up to a window on the upper floor, whose curtains were drawn. 'Poor Sophy, she thinks people can see in from the green now it's gone. She always pulls the curtains when she's up there. And she misses hearing the birds twittering – the box and the ivy were always full of nests. But now I'm getting used to the bare walls even indoors. I'm beginning quite to like them. It looks so much neater. And the ivy was really getting a nuisance. We used to get sprays growing right through the walls, thick as they are.'

'Yes, that really had to go. The architect said it was endangering the structure. Isabel wants to have roses climbing up the front but personally I think it's a pity to hide the half-timbering now that one can see it.'

'How you must be longing to show Clara all that you've done to the place. Will she and her husband soon be coming back from their holiday? Oh, I forgot, you said she'd gone to Austria alone. It seems such an extraordinary thing for a young wife to go off abroad by herself. I remember she did the same last year.'

'It seems extraordinary to me too. But no more extraordinary than the whole way she and Clive live. It's hardly my idea of married life – Clara working in an office and the two of them not having even what I consider a proper home, considering they never have a meal in it except breakfast. They don't even possess a dining-table, let alone a dining-room. Isabel thinks it all very smart and modern but I'm old-fashioned enough to think that if people are married, they should behave like normal married people. However, if I so much as hint that I think it's time they settled down and . . .' he broke off, suddenly remembering that Isabel was only a few yards away on the other side of the house and could catch every syllable.

He took Aunt Leah's arm again and turning back the way they came suggested they should go and sit on the lawn where he had originally planned to set up the sundial. It was sufficiently far from the walnut tree for any conversation to be out of range even of Isabel's ears.

'It *would* be nice to go somewhere more secluded,' Aunt Leah said gratefully. 'I was beginning to feel a little embarrassed standing out here in the front where anyone passing could see my shabby old hat. I wouldn't like to disgrace my smart nephew in front of the neighbours.'

A few minutes later they were seated on a slatted bench under two ancient apple trees, so bowed and twisted with age that their gnarled limbs were propped on crutches of forked stakes, on a grass plot bordered with flower beds and screened by a high laurel hedge. In one corner, all by itself, as if it had been thrust there so as not to embarrass the crippled old apple tree by flaunting its youth and vigour too near them, stood a stripling larch. It was a well-grown stripling; its slim, tapered trunk was already hardened and ran straight and firm as a masthead among the rigging of tasselled branches still lithe enough to dance when a blackbird perched on them. Nevertheless, beautiful as it was, Claude had as usual seated himself at an angle from which the larch was invisible.

'I always think this lawn is one of the pleasantest spots in the garden on a hot afternoon like this,' said Aunt Leah contentedly. 'Well, at least this is one thing Clara won't find changed since this time last year. No, now I come to think of it, it must be two years since she was last down here for a weekend.'

'Yes,' he said rather gloomily. 'I suppose that is partly my fault. I spoke my mind rather strongly that last Sunday she was down here when she calmly announced she was not coming to Mass as she no longer believed in Catholicism. So last year she said she wouldn't embarrass me by coming down for a weekend. By now I suppose I am more or less resigned, at least outwardly. But when she first told me, it came as such an appalling shock, that I said some rather harsh things to her. Isabel thinks it is no business of mine that Clara has given up her religion and I had no right even to make any comment. I don't agree. But I regret that I let my temper get the better of me. Since then, though of course Clara knows how I feel on the subject, I never mention it to her.'

'I know what a great grief it must be to you. I always thought the Catholic faith meant as much to her as it did to you.'

'So did I. She couldn't have been more loyal to it all through that difficult time when she might well have been tempted to waver. I mean all that time she had to wait for the Ecclesiastical Courts to annul her first marriage after the English courts had already done so.'

'I am afraid I never did quite understand about all that. I've always understood that Roman Catholics weren't allowed in any circumstances to divorce and remarry. I know you said this wasn't quite the same thing as a divorce – in fact I believe you told us the Pope decided in the end that Clara and Mr Hughes-Follett had never been properly married. But I confess that it seemed to me rather peculiar, considering they were both Roman Catholics and had been married in a Roman Catholic church by a Roman Catholic priest. However since you believe the Pope is infallible, of course you take his word for it that they weren't.'

Claude heaved a patient sigh, wondering whether to make one last despairing attempt to explain to Aunt Leah the difference between an annulment and a divorce. He had never succeeded in making it clear to her, mainly because he had never been able to find any way of conveying to Aunt Leah, without offending her modesty, what was meant by non-consummation of marriage. Luckily she rescued him from his dilemma by saying:

'Anyhow, it is none of our business. It was only a little awkward for us at the time, because people are so inquisitive in Bellhurst. But of course we had your word for it that there wasn't anything scandalous about it like an ordinary divorce so we held our heads high and refused to answer questions. Least said, soonest mended. I'm sure any spiteful gossip has long ago died down.'

'I sincerely hope so. I am very sorry indeed that you should have been subjected to it. But I can assure you that no stigma whatsoever attaches to either party when a marriage is declared null and void. Thank goodness, in this case, there is no family scandal to hush up or to live down. I'm as jealous of your good name here as you are.'

'I know you are. The Batchelors and Sayerses may not be grand people, but they've always been highly respected hereabouts. And I'm sure I'm very glad for your sake and Clara's that she was able to marry again with a good conscience. It would be sad, indeed, for her to have been tied for life to that young man whom Isabel said' – she lowered her voice almost to a whisper – '*drank*.'

'Unfortunately, yes. But I don't judge Archie Hughes-Follett as harshly as Isabel does. I was always fond of him, in spite of his obvious defects as a husband. I think the war was responsible for that particular weakness, as, alas, it was in so many cases.'

'You're so good-hearted, Claude. You always see the best in everyone. But you must rejoice to see Clara married so happily now and to such a very nice man. Sophy and I like Mr Heron so much, what little we've seen of him.'

'I like Clive immensely myself. I've always had a peculiar admiration for him, long before there was any question of their marrying. Something about him reminds me of the best friend I ever had – a man I knew at Cambridge – who died, alas all too early. Clive has something of the peculiar personal charm that poor Larry had, though of course a far better brain. He would certainly have got a first in Classics if he had stayed on at Oxford and taken his finals before joining up – for which, of course, I honour him. It proves he has some firm convictions, whatever he may say.'

'I know he isn't a Roman Catholic. But surely he has some religious convictions?'

'No. He is a complete agnostic, as I was at his age.'

'Oh dear – to all intents and purposes an unbeliever. Don't you think that may have affected Clara?'

He frowned and shook his head.

'No, I honestly think not. Not only because she assures me that Clive had nothing to do with it, but because I trust Clive himself to keep his promise not to interfere with her religion. He knew what was involved in marrying a Catholic. And far from having any prejudice against Catholicism, he says – forgive me, Aunt – that it is the only form of Christianity he could ever imagine adopting. He quite often went to Mass with Clara during that first year of their marriage when she was still a practising Catholic.'

'I suppose you had hopes she would convert him to your faith?'

'If I had, I naturally never expressed them. But at least I could have sworn that Clara would never apostatise from hers.' He sighed. 'After that, can I ever trust my judgment again in anything that concerns Clara?'

'I don't know how she could do anything she must have known would hurt you so much. She loves you so dearly and always has from a child. I've never known a father and daughter so devoted to each other. Apart from everything else, I don't see how she could bear to put such a division between you. Even if there were some things she objected to in Roman Catholicism – as I'm sorry to say I do – I should have thought the fact that it was *your* religion would have kept her in the Roman Church.'

He shook his head. 'No, Aunt, a sentimental reason like that wouldn't have justified her in remaining in it if she were no longer genuinely convinced it was the true one. If only she'd given me some hint beforehand that she had any doubts – was having any kind of struggle in her mind or even with her conscience, I'd have been only too glad to discuss the matter with her calmly. After all I'd spent years before I made up my mind that Catholicism was the only true religion.' Aunt Leah pursed her lips, but did not interrupt him. 'I would so gladly have listened to her objections – done my best to answer them. But she didn't give me a chance – that was what I resented so bitterly, her not even thinking it worth-while consulting me.'

'I'm sure you had every right to resent it. After all, you are very much older and wiser than she is. I think it showed a great lack of respect on her part.'

'It was the lack of confidence that hurt me most. But what really enraged me was the calm, almost casual way she announced it: "I hope you won't mind too much Daddy if I don't come to Mass with you. You see I'm no longer a Catholic." I don't remember exactly what she said afterwards: I was too stunned to take in much except something about intellectual honesty. But I do remember the expression on her face. I can see it now – an expression of hers that I have always found peculiarly irritating even at the best of times – a cool, superior little half smile. I've seen it too often on the faces of conceited boys, and, I may say, wiped it off pretty effectively, not to find it even more intolerable on Clara's. The first sight of it at that moment made me see red. I told her roundly that mental honesty is a cant phrase people use very glibly nowadays as an excuse for rejecting any form of religious discipline that interferes with their personal freedom. She simply shrugged her shoulders and said, "If you think that's so in my case, I'm afraid you will have to go on thinking so." But at least she stopped smiling.'

'Oh dear, it is all so sad,' sighed Aunt Leah. 'But I'm sure you only spoke sharply to her for her own good . . . to try and bring her into a better frame of mind. After all, it was your duty to show her that in your eyes – and in mine too – she was doing *very* wrong. It is a terrible thing for any Christian to give up their religion, no matter what excuse they give for it. But I know you can't be angry with Clara for long, even over such a serious matter as this. You are far too fond of her. When I saw you in London together, you looked at her and spoke to her as affectionately as ever.'

He sighed in turn.

'Yes, of course. Nothing could ever alter my affection for her.

As I say, I've never referred to the painful subject again. But it weighs on my mind, all the same.'

'I know it does, Claude,' she said gently. 'But you must try not to fret yourself too much. It's so bad for your health. Peace of mind is what you need more than anything else now after the way you've overtaxed yourself all your life. Oh dear, you've had so many anxieties and troubles over Clara in the past. I do so hope they were over for good. At least, praise be, the one great one is.'

'Praise be, indeed. I ought to go down on my knees every day and thank the Almighty for that. I was thinking so at Mass this morning. Yesterday was the sixth anniversary of the fourth of August, 1922. I believe that was the happiest day of my entire life.'

He turned his head away from Aunt Leah and gazed into the distance, deep in memory. For a moment, he could only see Clara's face as they clung together half-laughing, half-crying, in the bliss of reunion. Unwittingly he found himself gazing straight at the larch tree. He forced himself to go on looking at it, though it reminded him of the one thing that had marred the joy of the following day when he had brought Clara back to Paget's Fold. He had known the questions she would be bound to ask the moment she set eyes on the larch, then no bigger than a Christmas tree, that Richard Crayshaw had had planted for her during her absence. He dared not answer them truthfully for fear of giving her a shock that might unhinge her mind again. He told himself that he had no reason for feeling guilty when he looked at the larch tree. Clara had long ago forgiven him for having deceived her – for the only time in his life and for her own good. When she had discovered the truth for herself she had blamed him neither for deluding her with false hopes nor for having told Richard what he had been driven to believe himself, that there was little hope of her ever recovering. Indeed, she had taken the news of Crayshaw's marriage so stoically that he felt he had tortured himself for nothing. Now that she herself was happily married, he might have allowed himself to forget the whole episode, but for the larch tree. He could not cut it down, since it was Clara's. In any case, there was no excuse for cutting down such a fine young tree. Nevertheless, he could not help wishing it were not quite so aggressively thriving.

The sound of Aunt Leah's voice recalled his wandering thoughts. He jerked his head round sharply towards her; he had almost forgotten she was there.

'Yes, Aunt, you were saying?'

'Only that I think I can guess which day that was. The day you suddenly had that letter from Clara and went rushing up to London to find she was so much better – actually well enough to come home. Such a lovely surprise for you. I know it must have been August because you were down here for your summer holiday. But what a memory you have, fancy remembering the exact date! It shows how much it meant to you.'

'I think I'd remember it, even if it hadn't been one I'm always conscious of in any case. August the fourth . . . the first day of the war. Up to then it had always been a melancholy anniversary for me – so many of my boys and, alas so often the very best of them, were killed in the war. I used to think of all those parents who'd lost their sons – often only children like Clara. And to think how lucky I was that she hadn't been a boy – though before she was born, like most men, I had hoped for a son. And the very morning that letter came, I had been thinking that, after all, *my* only child was as good as dead. Because they had told me a few months earlier that if she ever recovered at all, it might not be till she was round about fifty.'

He was staring into the distance again, but, as his eyes caught the larch tree, he shifted his gaze away from it.

Aunt Leah exclaimed aghast: 'Oh, Claude, how dreadful. You never told us that at the time.'

'No, I didn't want to upset you. In any case, Isabel, mercifully, never believed it, no matter what the doctors might say. She had more faith than I had. But I still feel there was something miraculous about that sudden and, thank God, permanent recovery of Clara's.'

'I'm sure it must have seemed like a miracle to you. You must have felt almost as Jairus did when his daughter was raised from the dead and given back to him.'

He nodded.

'Yes, I don't think Jairus even could have rejoiced more than I did that day. It was against my wildest hopes that they would let me take her away with me then and there, even on probation. When we came out of that place together, I felt like Orpheus bringing Eurydice back from the underworld.' He smiled at the recollections of that perfect moment. Nothing could spoil that for him, though the days that followed had been clouded by the apprehension that, when the fortnight was over, she might have to return to the underworld. That was why he had to lie to her, torture her with false hopes, do anything rather than risk a relapse. It was during those days he had come more and more to hate the sight of the larch tree because, though he had told Richard Crayshaw only what he believed to be the truth, and for the boy's own good, there would have been no need to lie to Clara for hers.

'I shall never forget your radiant face when you came back the next day, with Clara on your arm,' Aunt Leah said tenderly. 'You yourself looked like someone who had been restored to life. You'd looked so sad and careworn all that holiday – it made my heart ache to see you. I knew you couldn't be expected to enjoy your holiday as usual, but I so hoped the change would do you good and take your mind off your trouble for a little.'

'For the only time in my life, I was longing for my holiday to be over and to get back to London. At least I could go over to the place every Sunday on the off-chance they would let me see her. Quite often they did though, except once, she was too ill to recognise me.'

'Isabel thought it was so bad for you – only making things worse. She said the time she went with you it upset her so much she couldn't bear to go again. Her nerves couldn't stand it. I know hers are particularly sensitive, but it must have been a dreadful strain, even on yours.'

'No, to me it was a kind of solace. Even if I wasn't allowed to see her, at least I could feel I was under the same roof. I didn't feel so utterly cut off from her. And there was that once, when she not only recognised me, she spoke to me in her normal voice. Quite early on, less than two months after it all started. She suddenly opened her eyes – she'd been asleep and I'd been sitting on her bed watching her – and smiled at me. And then she said, absolutely in her natural voice . . . "Hullo, Daddy, you're wearing a new scarf." And she was perfectly right. It was one she'd never seen before, a knitted silk muffler given me for Christmas. It was only for a flash, but it was a ray of hope. So you see, I couldn't bear to miss a visiting day in case it happened again.'

'I wonder if any daughter ever had so devoted a father.'

'Cicero would have done as much and more for his Tullia,' he smiled. 'I was luckier than Cicero. I haven't lost *my* Tullia.' But the smile was a bit rueful and he was tempted to add: 'At least not entirely.'

'Ah, you can smile now those sad days are over. But they've left such a deep impression on you. Even if you can never forget them, I don't think you should let yourself brood on them.'

'I don't brood on them. Sometimes I almost wish I could forget them. But at least, if I remember the suffering, I can remember the joy that came after. I think I could almost bear to relive all those months again for those few hours of pure bliss. That was something unlike anything I've experienced on this earth and don't expect to again. Mark you, I'm not saying I haven't had any amount of happiness in my life. I consider myself an extremely fortunate man in every way. But nothing can eclipse the ecstacy of that day.'

As he spoke he was already reliving it again – walking down to the gate to meet the postman, expecting at best a formal note from the asylum doctor to say that her condition, if no better, was at least no worse, and had hardly glanced at the cheap white envelope readdressed from Valetta Road in his mother's large, sprawling writing. And then suddenly he had seen his own name in Clara's handwriting – a trifle larger than its normal smallness, a little shaky, but unmistakably the neat, forward-sloping, legible handwriting he had helped to form himself; he had spent hours in her early childhood correcting her natural tendency to write back-hand, a form of script he abhorred. He had mentally taken out the letter, that was to mean more to him than even Isabel's most passionate love letter when Aunt Leah gently tugged at his sleeve.

'Oh Claude, I can't bear to interrupt our conversation. I was enjoying it so much, but I've just seen Mrs Smith through the gaps in the laurels, carrying the tea-tray. I must run in and change my hat. And I left Sophy asleep . . . she mightn't wake up if I don't call her.'

'Yes, of course, run along. Oh, and, by the way, Aunt, if either or both of you want to go to Evensong, I can drop you at Bellhurst on my way to Benediction.'

'Oh that would be kind, Claude, if it wouldn't be too much trouble, going out of your way.'

'Only five minutes in the car. What's the point of having a car if I can't give you a lift? The only thing is I'm afraid you'll get to church rather early. Benediction is at half-past five and your service isn't till half-past six.

'Oh, we should like that. We want to visit the family graves and put some flowers on them. It's worried us so that we haven't once put any on your mother's yet, though she's been gone all these months.'

'I'll come with you then,' he said, remembering with shame that he hadn't visited his mother's grave since she had died the previous winter. He was shocked that her memory had already become so dim. Loyally fond of her as he had been, he had never been able to return her passionate devotion to himself with the warmth it deserved. It was his father, his handsome, deaf, incompetent father, whom he had loved with a fierce protective love which he had cherished for no one else, not even Clara, for it had demanded nothing in return, only to be accepted. He still dreamt of his father and when he did, he awoke with a pang of

The Copper Beech.

The Copper Beech is a native of England, and grows extremely well there.

General Description. The trunk is smooth and not very thick; the leaves are a dark reddish colour, and the branches, slender, wavy, and graceful. The bark is often of a silvery hue. The branches, if allowed to grow, sweep the ground. It looks best, planted among other trees, whose leaves are green.

Parts in detail. The trunk, as has been said, is smooth, and the bark, a silvery grey. it does not peel off in patches like the Plane for instance. Sometimes the branches sweep the ground on one

[margin note:] It took me nearly a month & tons of nature books to get up all this, so do not smile.

A facsimile first page of 'The Copper Beech' written for her father before the age of nine. Her note in the margin reads, 'It took me nearly a month and tons of nature books to get up all this, so do not smile.'

utter bereavement which he had felt on the morning after his death, over fourteen years ago.

He was thinking of his father, as he watched Aunt Leah's small, stiff figure vanish behind the laurel hedge. It was strange that a father should mean so much more to a son, especially an only son, than a mother. Daughters, especially only daughters . . . But how much did he mean to Clara now?

That day, at least, he had meant everything to her. She had not so much as remembered the existence of anyone else when her reason began to come back to her. Not Richard Crayshaw. Not even her mother. There had not been so much as a mention of Isabel.

He knew the letter by heart. It would not be found among his papers, after his death, tied up with ribbon, like Isabel's love letters. He had burnt it long ago, for Clara's sake. Some stranger might have found it and discovered what he hoped no stranger would ever know, that she had once been in a public asylum. But it was printed on his brain like a photostat, every detail of it clear, down to the question mark in brackets, which for some reason had moved him more than anything . . . she had remembered, even with her mind still confused, how much she disliked inaccurate spelling.

Shutting his eyes, he re-read it again.

Dearest Daddy,

I do not know where I am but I think it is Nazareth Royal Hospital. That is what it says on the plates. Please try and find me. I want so much to see you again. Please try hard. Perhaps you thought I was dead. I am alive but in a very strange place. Doctor Bennett (?) has promised to post this.

Your loving daughter,
Clara

He opened his eyes again, and blinked hard. The grass lawn, the bed of hollyhocks and roses, swam a little in the dazzle of sunshine. Isabel's voice shrilly calling '*Clau*-aude, *tea*-time,' brought him sharply back to the present. He rose briskly to his feet, and stood for a moment surveying the far end of the lawn, where he had intended to put the sundial if it had been of a reasonable size. It would have looked well enough, against the hollyhocks. But now he saw that if he had set it up in the centre, the larch tree was already tall enough to cast a shadow on it. In any case, since he could never look at the larch tree without thinking of Clara nor at the sundial without thinking of that final speech day at St Mark's, he was glad the two were so widely separated. At least, when he looked at the sundial in its present position, there was less danger of his being reminded that Clara had not bothered to curtail her holiday in Austria by so much as one day to be present at his last speech day.

4·

Clara's relief, as she stepped on to the boat at Ostend, was so immense that she inwardly ejaculated 'Deo Gratias' before she remembered that she was an atheist. It was the final indication of the demoralised state to which the collapse of her civilised self had reduced her. During that sleepless night, sitting up in a crowded compartment reeking of sweat and garlic (she had mismanaged money as badly as everything else on this holiday and had had to travel back third-class) it had seemed to her that the journey would never end and that she would never find herself safely back in Caroline Square with Clive. After travelling for thirty-six hours with no sustenance but the sandwiches she had bought at the station buffet in Linz and those cups of coffee on the train that had cost her last few Austrian schillings and Belgian francs, she had reached Ostend in such a trance of weariness that only the fear that a porter might snatch her luggage before she could stop him had given her the energy to grab it herself and stumble out on to the platform. A porter was a luxury she could not afford for the only money left in the beautiful and expensive handbag she had bought in Vienna, and which, at this moment she would have gladly exchanged for a cup of tea and a couple of aspirin was five pfennigs and one English ten shilling note. Half-blinded by the headache which for the past few hours had made the wheels of the train seem to be throbbing inside her right temple and stopping every few yards to put down the heavy Veritton suitcase to rest her tired arms, she had somehow managed to reach the gangway and stagger up it, catching her Louis heels in the struts, until she was on deck. In a few more hours, in however battered a condition, she would be home again with Clive. And the first thing she was going to tell him was that never again was she going to go off on her own without him. These last two weeks in Austria had proved that, away from him, she could not be trusted to behave like a rational human being. There were things she had thought and done in these past two weeks she would be ashamed to tell even to Clive who understood and condoned everything.

The blast of the ship's siren exploded in her right ear and vibrated through her right temple like a dentist's drill on an exposed nerve. For a few moments she was dazzled with pain, but when the spasm had passed, her sense of relief returned more strongly than ever. As the boat began slowly to move, it increased to such a pitch that it dominated the drum-beat of her headache. She pulled off her hat and let the sea breeze blow on her closed eyes. For a few moments she was conscious of nothing but the wind on her face, the shuddering and creaking of the ship and the dull throbbing in her temple. Then, jostled out of her stupor, by people pushing past her, she decided to go below and try to get some sleep. Now that she was safely launched on an English boat, she could risk breaking into her ten shilling note to tip the stewardess to give her some aspirin.

In the crowded wash-room of the second-class ladies cabin, she caught sight of herself in a glass. Her kasha suit was grimy from the dirty compartment and creased from being sat in all the way from Linz to Ostend and her face looked as haggard as it felt. Her hair was dishevelled, her make-up, unrenewed since yesterday, had caked into a pitted mask, and her eyes were red-rimmed from lack of sleep. She was thankful she was not returning first-class; at least there was no risk of running into any client of the Meldrum Merchandising Service or, worse still, into one of its directors. 'Our Mrs Heron' was expected to look the part of their fashion and beauty expert, even off duty. At the moment she could hardly look it less or be a worse advertisement for the clothes and cosmetics of the two firms for which she wrote her most alluring copy and who supplied her with their wares at trade prices and sometimes even free because she was 'good publicity' for them. The present state of her complexion did no credit at all to Mary Bell Beauticare and that of her 'Chanel-inspired' three-piece was enough to deter any woman who might glimpse the label inside its cardigan jacket from buying a 'Paul and Paula Model'. And, if Monsieur Alex could see the hair which the great man condescended to cut and set with his own hands because 'it was so beautiful it did him justice', and had even had it photographed for *Vogue* as an example of his artistry, he would probably have withdrawn his account from Meldrum's.

However, even if her appearance was slatternly enough to lose her her job, as well as being an outrage to her vanity, she was too exhausted to do anything about it till she had done something about her headache. She procured some aspirin and, having asked the stewardess to call her well before they were due at Dover, she lay down on a bunk and closed her aching eyes. She did not sleep, but she fell into a drowsy stupor during which the throbbing in her temple gradually died down and gave way to a duller, more diffused pain which promised her some hope that this was, after all, what she called an 'honest' headache and not the beginning of one of those dreaded migraines which now and then prostrated her for three days on end. Though they had become more frequent this last year, there was still normally a long enough interval between them for Mavis Collins, the head of her department, not to be restive about her absences from work. Sickness, even vouched for by a doctor's certificate, was considered almost as a culpable offence at Meldrum's. Every day of the firm's time wasted in it was totted up at the end of the year and if there were too many of them, the offender had no hope of a rise on the grounds that he or she was not justifying their present salary. It would have been alarming if she had developed another migraine – even in her own time – so soon after the violent one she had had only the week before last in Salzburg. If they became habitual, she might lose her job. And, sick of it as she was beginning to be, she could not afford to do that. She and Clive had grown so used to living in what they called a civilized way, that they were always slightly in debt, even on their joint salaries.

After a while, she began to feel capable of getting up and attempting to make herself look a little more presentable. By the time she had washed, removed her stale make-up, re-done her face and combed her shingle, she was at least recognisable as Clive's 'other pussy-cat', however sadly out of condition. It was more difficult to recreate the image of 'our Mrs Heron'. All the clothes she could see, as she rummaged through the suitcases Clive had given her as a wedding present, looked as crushed and wilted as the suit she was wearing. She had packed in such a hurry when she left St Wolfgang the morning before yesterday, in her anxiety to start off on the journey home to Clive and Caroline Square as quickly as possible, even though a later train would have caught the same connection at Linz, that she had crammed everything in pell-mell instead of in methodical layers. The chaotic state of her suitcases reflected all too shamefully the way she had let herself go, physically, morally and mentally in the last half of her holiday. However she might have behaved on those two previous holidays abroad without him, at least she had retained some semblance of the tolerably civilised person she had become since their marriage, and whom they both fondly fancied to be permanent. He didn't expect her, of course, ever, to be wholly rational or even want her to be. She would not have sympathised so much with his particular brand of madness if she had not had her own to contend with, the exact opposite of Clive's, and, as he was fond of reminding her, a far more enviable type since it had once allowed her to escape for several months from the hideous necessity of *doing* anything. But there had been one or two days in the past fortnight when, for the first time since she had recovered from the outburst of certifiable insanity which Clive assured her was the best thing that had ever happened to her though he agreed that once was enough, she had wondered whether she were not going out of her mind again or had not even already done so. She had lost contact with her rational self to such an extent that she could not remember it well enough to reconstruct it.

One thing in her suitcase, however, she had packed carefully enough to be wearable, the off-white raincoat Clive had given her last June on her twenty-ninth birthday, bemoaning the fact that though she was older in cat-years than Augustus she was so much less prudent about keeping her fur dry that he had been unwillingly forced to *do* something about it for the sake of preserving at least one of her nine lives. She treasured it more than anything he had given her except his irreplaceable copy of the New York edition of *The Ambassadors* when he had 're-nounced her forever' for her own good a few months before their wedding. No one realised better than she what it must have cost him in mental agony to go into a women's shop, endure the torture of having to *commit* himself to a choice and the final humiliation of having to carry the garment home in a parcel. The sight of his anxious face as he added: 'I hope to God it's wearable,' would have made her say it was the most attractive raincoat she had ever seen, even if this had not been true, which it was.

When she had replaced her soiled and creased cardigan-jacket for the crisp, immaculate raincoat, which, buttoned up, completely hid the equally deplorable state of its matching hip-length jumper and brief pleated skirt, the improvement in her morale was even greater than the improvement in her appearance. Though she would not recover her looks until she had had a good night's sleep (mercifully tomorrow was Sunday and she could stay in bed as long as she liked) she had, at least partially, recovered her identity. She would not recover it wholly till she

was safe back with Clive; only his sure, delicate, almost impalp-
able touch could mould her back into the shape she almost feared
she had lost irretrievably. Yet she could already feel her numbed
brain beginning to revive and her muddled emotions to clarify.
It was as if the white raincoat were one of those magic garments
which restore their human form to people who have been turned
into animals. Indeed, at times lately, she really had felt as if she
were under an evil spell which degraded her to a condition less
than human. Her own personality seemed to have disintegrated
and been replaced by some alien one whose impulses, however
repellent and humiliating, she was compelled to obey. Now she
could feel Clive's beneficent influence counteracting the bad
spell. It was as if, merely by putting on his raincoat, she had
become once again the person both he and she recognised as
'Clara' and who bore only a surface resemblance to 'our Mrs
Heron' and inwardly hardly any resemblance to Clara Hughes-
Follet and Clara Batchelor.

The wash-room was no longer empty. Other women had
come in and were tidying themselves up preparatory to dis-
embarking. Clara glanced at her watch; in a little over half an
hour, the ship was due in dock. There was time to get herself the
cup of tea for which she was craving and which might finally
disperse her headache. Since she was also feeling very hungry,
she decided she could safely afford a ham sandwich out of her
remaining nine shillings. That would leave her enough for
porters at Dover and Victoria and if the taxi fare came to more
than the remainder, Clive would be there to make up the
difference. She had told him before she left that she would arrive
some time latish on this Saturday afternoon. There had been no
need to find out the exact time the boat-train arrived since he had
such a horror of railway stations that it was one of their
compacts he was never to be expected to meet her on her return.
But she knew she could count on finding him waiting for her at
Caroline Square; her saucer of milk and her basket ready to
welcome back a pussy-cat who, this time, had strayed so
alarmingly far from her master that she had dreaded she would
never find her way back to him. He himself might really have
believed her lost. She hadn't given him a sign since she left
Vienna, except for that one postcard the day after she had arrived
in Salzburg. His horror of writing letters far exceeded his horror
of railway stations so he had not expected her to write any,
though she had written him two quite long ones from Vienna,
knowing that he loved receiving them provided he was absolved

from answering them. But he did like, though he did not demand it – Clive never demanded anything – to get postcards at intervals, even if she only wrote 'Miaow' on them, to 'reassure him she was still in the realm of existence, however jostled by irrelevant events'. He had not received any more after her shameful flight from Salzburg, leaving nearly all the concerts he had so carefully chosen for her at the festival and for which she had bought expensive tickets in advance unattended, because she had felt too guilty to write any. However the fact that she had not written would make it all the more certain that he would be waiting for her at home and be all the more pleased to see her. Yet she knew very well that, even if he had been a little anxious, he would not leap up from his chair the moment he heard her key click in the lock and dash to the front door to welcome her. If he were reading, he would first insert one of those neat slips of paper, pencilled with notes in his exquisite handwriting to mark his place and lay the book down, mathematically straight, on the table. If he were listening to the gramophone, he would lift the needle very carefully from the groove of the record before he switched off the record. And, whatever he had been doing, he would pause, before he went out into the hall to 'verify his hair' in the Venetian mirror and if one red-gold strand seemed to him out of place, he would adjust it with his long thin fore-finger.

As she was adjusting her own hair before putting on her hat, combing her fringe to lie evenly over her high forehead and pulling one wave forward on either side to make a flat scallop over the cheekbone, she saw in the glass the reflection of two women on the other side of the wash-room who seemed to be staring at her. She could see them nudging each other and exchanging questioning glances, then one shook her head and the other murmured something in her ear which made her smile, put her finger to her lips and once more shake her head. Irritated by their behaviour, for now they were staring harder than ever in her direction and whispering together, obviously discussing her appearance, she stared icily back at their reflected faces. Only enough was visible under the cloche hats which no woman with any dress sense would dream of wearing nowadays to show that they were both about her own age and quite pretty in a common way. Two tufts of frizzy, peroxided hair showed below the brim of the royal blue cloche and two of natural auburn below the emerald-green one. Both wore long, dangling paste earrings and bright orange lipstick which clashed deplorably with their cloches, but the mouth under the emerald-green one was so wide and friendly it looked attractive in spite of it whereas the other was hard and tight-lipped. Clara had an odd feeling that she had seen both those mouths before and in conjunction. It must have been a long while ago for she could not recognise either of the young women, yet the way they kept peering at her, surreptitiously now, suggested they too saw something familiar about her face and, but for her forbidding expression, might have claimed her as an old acquaintance. Could they have been girls she had known at the drama school in her brief career on the stage? Yet the vivid cloches and gay – too gay – flowered silk dresses made them look more as if they hoped to be taken for actresses rather than as if they were really connected with the stage. They wore them with a slightly defiant, self-conscious air like schoolgirls flaunting their freedom to wear what they liked out of school and trying to appear daringly sophisticated. However, before she could decide when or where she had seen them before, if she ever had, to her great relief they gave a final dab to their already over-powdered noses and walked arm-in-arm out of the washroom. At the door, the one with the thin lips and peroxided hair, turned her head back over her shoulder and gave her a final stare.

She put on what Clive called her 'runcible hat', a casual felt as plain as a man's but broader-brimmed and so supple that she could manipulate it into any shape she fancied. Tilting it slightly forward over her right eyebrow, she pulled the brim down in front and moulded it into a flattering curve which threw a shadow over her eyes and the indigo smudges under them and swept up one side to reveal her hair. As she studied the effect from every angle, with the aid of the mirror in the Viennese handbag, she was struck more forcibly than usual by the discrepancy between her profile and her full face. Seen sideways, her features had a definite, clear-cut outline. The slightly arched nose and firm chin suggested a decisiveness of character of which there was no trace in her full face. Seen frontways, her features blunted and softened into contours which the extreme fairness of her skin made appear almost childish and which were so plastic that the least change of mood could alter not only her expression but the whole aspect of her face. It could compose into so many faces, some attractive and some repellent, that she seemed to herself to have no permanent reliable face that she could recognise as her own, for that rather handsome, even faintly masculine profile never seemed really to belong to her.

However, mainly owing to its colouring and the wavy golden hair that framed it, the general impression of her full face was that it was extremely feminine and a trifle above the average in prettiness.

It was considerably below the average, at the moment, she thought, surveying it with distaste. Her skin had lost the smooth, fine texture that make-up could emphasise but not replace. There were faint pincer lines round her mouth, accentuating the full, sensual lower lip she disliked. She looked not only jaded, and – with all too good reason, slightly coarsened – at least five years older than when she had left London three weeks ago. No one, seeing her face now, could possibly take her for under thirty.

However, as she left the wash-room, carrying her Vuitton suitcases, a glance in a long mirror showed that the rest of her appearance was well up to standard. She wished, as so often, that she were a couple of inches taller, but at least she was just slim enough not to look dumpy and she had very good legs. In her off-white coat and slouch hat, with her elegant accessories, she looked as if she must have strayed into the second-class quarters by accident.

A passing steward so obviously thought that she had that he let the rope down for her. For a moment she was tempted to follow him and go into the first-class restaurant. But remembering how little money there was in the beige Viennese handbag which so perfectly matched her Raoul shoes, she smiled and shook her head. She dared not risk it. Even though she could get back to her own class before landing, her cup of tea and sandwich would cost more there, not to mention the tip, and she had to husband every penny. She put down her cases and made her way to the cramped second-class one, which was so crowded that at first she could see no vacant seat. Then she saw one, but to her horror, seated at the same table were the two women in emerald and sapphire cloche hats. Searching vainly for another empty place and finding none, she had no choice but to take it. Her still aching head craved too violently for a cup of tea and her stomach for some food to be deprived of their last chance of them.

For a moment, they were too busy talking to notice that she had sat down opposite, but now that she could hear their voices, she could at last identify them. Having ordered her cup of tea and ham sandwich, she realised that she must show them that she had done so. Otherwise they might think she had been deliberately cutting them in the wash-room. At the first pause in their conversation, she said, as calmly as she could, though she could not keep a tremor out of her voice:

'Do forgive me for not recognising you just now, Nurse Smith and Nurse Jones. I've never seen you before out of uniform.'

The fair one nudged the red-haired one triumphantly.

'There! I was right, Jones. I could have sworn it was Clara – pardon me, I never could remember your other name – something posh and double-barrelled, wasn't it?' Without waiting for a reply, she went on: 'Jones was pretty sure, too, though you look very different from when we last saw you, *I* can tell you! But she thought, if we introduced ourselves, you might be a bit embarrassed.'

'Not in the least,' said Clara, with rather too bright a smile. 'How nice to see you again. Are you both still at Nazareth?'

'Yes, dear. Tomorrow we'll both be back in old Ward J.' She winked: 'Don't feel like coming with us for old times' sake?'

'Really, Smith, you are the limit,' said Jones. 'As if she wanted to be reminded of those days.' She gave Clara the wide, affectionate smile which had been such a comfort to her in 'those days'. Every time the cell door had opened, she had hoped it would be Jones' friendly, freckled face she would see, not Smith's contemptuous, pink and white, thin-lipped one.

'S'only my little joke,' said Smith. 'But I'm not sure I want her back. She could be a very naughty girl sometimes. I had to be a bit sharp with her sometimes.'

'Did you?' asked Clara, rather coldly, remembering how Smith had once hit her hard over the knuckles with the heavy key of the cell when she had pleaded not to be locked in.

'I never found her any trouble,' said Jones.

'Oh, *you* wouldn't. She always behaved herself with you. Anyway, you had a soft spot for her, like Doctor Bennett. If everyone was as soft with the patients as you, Jones, discipline would go to pot. You've got to be firm with them now and then otherwise they play you up.'

'Do stop talking shop, Smith. I'm sure it's the last thing Clara wants to hear. Anyway we're still on holiday. We've been having the spree of our lives, Clara – *do* pardon me for forgetting your last name – oh, wait a sec, I've got it. Hughes-Follett wasn't it?' Clara nodded. 'Well, as I was saying, this year we decided to save up and go a real bust. We've had a whole fortnight in Ostend. Neither of us have ever been "on the continong" before. Of course, we didn't let on we were nurses. Oh, my, what a time we had!'

'Couldn't walk a yard without getting our bottoms – pardon me, *derr-airs* – pinched. Really, those foreigners! I had to be firm with some of *those* lads, I can tell you. You been on holiday abroad too?'

'Yes.'

'Not *your* first time, I daresay?' said Jones.

'No. I go abroad most years. But this is the first time I've been to Austria. I usually go to France.'

'Fancy,' said Jones. 'I expect you know quite a lot of French by now, don't you?'

'Of course she does, fathead. Don't you remember how she was always gabbling French when she was delirious. Just like a native, Dr Bennett said.'

'Did I talk French?' asked Clara with interest.

'Oh yes, and all sorts of other things, including double Dutch. And you used to say prayers – in plain English at the top of your voice. Thought at one time you must have a spot of religious mania.'

Jones said fiercely: 'Shut up, Smith. It's so natural for a Catholic girl to say prayers. She doesn't forget them even when she's quite far gone. It just shows how a person's faith can stick to them through anything. I'm a Catholic too, you know, Clara.'

'I didn't know,' said Clara, feeling herself flush.

'Many a time I'd listen outside the door and hear you saying the Hail Mary. It was so wonderful that, when you were so ill you didn't remember your own name, you remembered every word of it perfectly. I'm sure it was due to Our Lady you made such a splendid recovery. Mind you, I was always sure you'd get better, but not all of a sudden like that. I can tell you now, you surprised the doctors. Of course they don't believe in miracles, but you and I do.'

Clara, who no longer believed in miracles, was in no mood to be reminded how much her sudden recovery had surprised the doctors. However she said politely, 'My father did tell me at one time I was considered to be a pretty hopeless case.'

'Oh, while there's life there's hope,' said Smith. 'All the same you were lucky. You had a pretty long spell in Ward J, you know, before they sent you up to Ward C. Sister Ware thought Dr B. had been a bit premature letting you out on parole.

Incidentally he got into hot water with the head for doing it behind his back.'

'But the minute he saw you again, the head discharged her for good on the spot, didn't he, Clara?'

'Yes.'

'Ah well, all's well that ends well,' grinned Smith. 'Kept fit ever since?'

'Yes, thank you.'

'You certainly look as if life had gone well with you.'

'You look simply marvellous,' said Jones affectionately. 'Oh, it *is* nice to see you again, Clara dear. You don't mind me calling you Clara and not Mrs Hughes-Follett?'

'Of course not. Anyway my name isn't Hughes-Follett any more. It's Heron.'

'Oh, so you've married again?' asked Smith, staring at her curiously and giving her a tight-lipped smile. 'That's ever so nice for you. Been married long?'

'Just over three years.'

'Any kiddies?'

'No.'

'Just as well. You don't want to risk any more trouble in the family. You didn't have any by your first, either, did you?'

'No.'

'Of course you didn't.' She tittered. 'I've just remembered something about your case that proved you couldn't have.'

'You lost your first hubby in the war, didn't you?' Jones asked with sympathy.

Clara shook her head.

'Funny, I always thought you were one of those young war widows. We had quite a few of them in those days. Still, you must have lost him very young. I mean before *we* knew you. If he'd been still alive, it'd have been him that the doctors reported to, not your Dad. And I know it was never anyone but your Dad who came on visiting days.'

Smith spared her from any more of Jones's speculations by exclaiming:

'That Dad of yours – I shall never forget him turning up in Ward D every Sunday, rain or shine, as regular as clockwork, just on the off-chance of being allowed to see you. Of course, lots of times he couldn't. And even when he could, you didn't know him from Adam. And even when we'd given you a little something to put you to sleep, he'd just go in and sit there looking at you. Talk about fond fathers!'

Clara's cheeks turned hot again, this time with anger. She hated Smith far more at this moment than when she had hit her with the door key.

'Oh, I used to feel so sorry for him,' said Jones. 'Such a nice man, he was too, Mr Batchelor – I've always remembered his name and his face. Rather stout but ever so nice looking, with such a fresh complexion. I could see where *you* got your lovely fair skin from. You've got quite a look of him you know, though he had such a round face and, of course, a typical man's one. I used to think what a cheery one it must be when he was happy. And however miserable you could see he was feeling, he'd always have a pleasant smile for us nurses and a pleasant word. Oh, he was a real gentleman, your Dad, Clara. It must have been awful for him having you in a place like that. You're his only child, aren't you?'

'I wonder he didn't send you to one of those private places,' said Smith. 'You know, those places that call themselves "The Cedars" or "Sunny Lodge" to give the idea they're just common or garden nursing homes. Our famous establishment isn't exactly the sort of place you'd expect a gentleman to send his darling only daughter. I bet you were ever so spoilt as a kid, like all only children.'

'Smith, you really are the limit. I'm sure he sent her to NRH because he knew she'd get the best medical treatment there. And I'm sure she wasn't spoilt as a child. I'd say he was one of those really good fathers who are ever so kind, but ever so firm. You could see he was that sort of man from his face.'

'Well, I bet he's spoilt her ever since he got his precious daughter back. And I bet her hubby spoils her too. Look at her, Jones, you can see she's used to the best of everything. Have you noticed that handbag? And did you see that posh luggage of hers in the Ladies? I'm surprised at you not travelling first-class, Clara. Or have you come back from the continong broke, like us?'

'Yes, quite broke.'

'Well accidents happen even in the best families, don't they, Clara?' Smith winked at her again under the royal-blue cloche. 'Bad luck running into a bit of your murky past through having to come home on the cheap.'

'But good luck for us,' said Jones eagerly. 'It *is* nice to see you again, Clara. I've so often thought about you and wondered what became of you.'

'Well, you don't have to wonder any more. She's fallen on her feet, like a cat. And I bet she's got a good home to go back to and a big saucer of cream waiting after being out on the tiles . . . That's a gorgeous ring you're wearing, Clara. Can I have a closer peep at it?'

Clara took off the square-cut sapphire and diamond ring and handed it to Smith who promptly slipped it on her own engagement finger. It was too small to go over the knuckle and she transferred it to her little one.

'What dainty hands you have. Anyone can see *you* don't have to work for your living. Ours get ruined with all those disinfectants. But I'm ever so particular about manicuring my nails. Look.' She spread out five blunt, thickly-jointed fingers. 'Aren't they pink and shiny?'

'Yes,' said Clara. She remembered those short, shiny pink nails very well. When she had walked round the asphalt square between Smith and Jones, Smith always seemed to be polishing her nails on the palm of her hand or with a little buffer she kept in her apron pocket.

Still examining Clara's hands, she said, 'I see you've got one of these new platinum wedding-rings. I've never seen one as thin as that. Doesn't look like a proper wedding-ring.'

'You have got a cheek, Smithy. Anyway, platinum wears for ever. It'll never get any thinner like a gold one.'

'It'd vanish altogether if it did,' Smith said, returning the other ring with a last envious glance at it. 'Look, Jones, now she's put on the gorgeous sapphire one you can't even see it. Anyone would think she wasn't married. If I were a man I'd want my wife to wear something a bit more conspicuous to warn other men off.'

'Her hubby can trust her. Clara's ever such a good Catholic. Is he a Catholic too?'

Clara shook her head.

'What a pity. Never mind. I daresay you'll convert him. Wives often do in mixed marriages. Is he travelling with you?'

Clara shook her head.

'You mean he lets you go off on a holiday on the continong all on your own? Well, he certainly must trust you. Or else he doesn't know what foreigners are like. They think every English girl's to be had for the asking.'

'They wouldn't dare try and get off with *her*. She looks much too cool and stand-offish.'

'Not when she smiles and shows those dimples. I bet lots of men did get off with you. Gentlemen prefer blondes, especially on the continong, don't they Clara? Your hair's a lovely shade still, but a bit darker than it was in the old days . . . you know where. I have a brightening rinse now and then to keep mine fair. You should try one.'

'I like the colour it is,' said Jones. 'But it seems almost a shame to shingle it. I always remember that mass of lovely, naturally wavy hair you had.'

'I'd call it a *mane*,' said Smith. 'I suppose it started off as a bob but by the time you left our tender care it was down to your shoulders. If I'd had my way, I'd have cut it all off, the business I had brushing and combing it.'

'Oh, that would have been a sin!' exclaimed Jones. 'I used to love doing it for her – you were too ill to do it yourself, dear. So fine, it was. Like silk.'

'Yes, dear. That sort of fine hair that goes into fine old tangles. *I'd* have given her an Eton crop. Whatever would her Daddy have said to that, I wonder?'

'He was so fond of her hair. I've often seen him sitting there, just stroking it.'

'Aren't you grateful to us, Clara, for leaving you your crowning glory? Not that you've much left of it yourself any more than we have of ours, but one's got to be in the fashion or die, hasn't one?' said Smith.

Clara said, with a faint aloof smile which abashed even Smith:

'I'm grateful you didn't sew it into a plait with a needle and thread as you did to some of the other patients.'

'Fancy you remembering that.' Her voice sounded disconcerted. 'I thought people didn't remember anything after . . . They all say not.'

'I remember a great deal. After all, it was a very interesting experience. And seeing you both has reminded me of things I'd forgotten.

'Interesting experience! Can't say I've ever heard it called that before.' Smith's eyes were round with amazement. 'Well, I suppose that's one way of looking at it. Anyway, you're obviously none the worse for it or you couldn't talk about it so calmly without turning a hair.'

'Of course she's none the worse for it,' said Jones. 'All the same, Clara dear, if I were you, I'd try to forget all about it. I'm ever so sorry if seeing Smithy and me again after all these years has brought it back again. Just put it right out of your mind and think how good life is for you now.'

'That's right, count your blessings. My goodness, you've

plenty to count, by the look of you. I'd be jolly glad to change places with you and be going back to the gay life I bet *you're* going back to. Tomorrow it'll be off with the glad rags and on with the old cap and apron and back to the old grindstone. No more being a couple of Bright Young Things on the loose.'

'It was ever so clever of you to recognise us out of uniform,' said Jones. 'We look a bit different since we last met, don't we? Almost as different as you! But we spotted you first, in the Ladies. Funny thing, I got the idea you guessed who we *might* be and didn't want to know us.'

'I did think I'd seen your faces somewhere before. But I certainly didn't realise it was in Nazareth.'

'Shh, dear. Someone might hear you. You don't want to noise it abroad.' Smith looked round. 'Goodness, there's hardly

A portrait taken around 1937. Antonia sat for an unusual number of portraits during the late thirties. These photographs offer a good opportunity to see how her appearance changed according to her frame of mind. Antonia was certainly describing herself in *Clara IV* when she wrote that 'the least change of mood could alter not only her expression but the whole aspect of her face. It could compose into so many faces . . . she seemed to have no permanent reliable face that she could recognise as her own . . .'

anyone left. 'We've been having such a good old chin wag, I never noticed the place emptying. We must be going to land soon.'

Clara had been aware for some time of the noise and bustle outside and overhead which meant the passengers were assembling on deck preparatory to landing. But, though she had been longing to get away from them both, she had not liked to hurt Jones' feelings by making the first move.

'I think we ought to go up on deck,' she said, rising. 'We must be getting into Dover.'

The nurses rose and picked up their cardboard suitcases. No sooner were the three of them outside, than they found themselves in a jostling mass of people. The ship was slowing down and a voice was shouting: 'Have your landing tickets ready.'

'I've got to collect my luggage,' said Clara. 'You go on up.'

'We'll wait for you.'

'No don't. It's suffocating in this crowd. I may be quite a while. I've just remembered I've left my landing card in a jacket I took off and put it in one of my cases.'

The landing ticket was safely in the pocket of the off-white mackintosh but she was determined to be well behind Smith and Jones in the queue for the gangway, so that they would lose sight of her in the crowd. For once, she was thankful for being short.

'I'll look out for you in the Customs,' she said. 'But you'll probably get through long before me. I'd better say goodbye now. It's been nice seeing you both again.'

She shook hands with them both.

'Ships that pass in the night,' said Smith. 'Well, orryvoir and cheerio in case we don't bump into you again.'

'Cheerio, and the best of luck, dear.' Jones squeezed her hand and gave her wide, friendly smile. 'You don't know what a thrill it's been to see you again and know that all's going fine for you.'

Clara smiled back, and, seeing that Smith had already moved away, she said:

'I've never forgotten how kind you were to me in there. Thank you.'

'Oh, go on with you! There's nothing to thank me for. I couldn't help being fond of you, you were such a sweet kid and it seemed such a shame. Now you just forget all about that and go on living happy ever after. Bless you, dear. Say a little prayer for me sometimes.'

'I will.' Clara had not the heart to say anything else.

'And I'll do the same for you.'

'Come *on*, Jones, we'll get separated,' called Smith who was being swept up the stairs, so that only her bobbing blue cloche was now visible above the crowd.

'I'll pray for your hubby's conversion.' She bent down and whispered hurriedly, 'Don't take any notice of Smithy's insinuations. It'd been quite safe for you to have a baby now. It was for your sake, not the kid's, Dr B. told you you shouldn't risk having one for a couple of years after you'd got well. He said there's never been any trouble in your family and it seems your particular kind isn't hereditary.'

'Thank you for telling me,' said Clara, who knew already.

'Just coming, Smithy,' she called loudly, then, turning back to Clara muttered in her ear: 'You don't think it cheeky of me to mention it? I know it's none of my business and as your hubby isn't a Catholic, he doesn't have to obey our rules. But I thought you might both be dying to have one and be a bit nervous, in case, well . . . *you* know. Well, you needn't be, dear. I bet it's the only thing missing from your happiness. And I bet that nice Dad of yours is dying to have a grandchild. You just go right ahead and have one. The sooner the better.'

She gave Clara an affectionate pat on the back, and, with a hearty 'Cheerio and God bless' she turned away and pushed her way through the crowd to join the now angrily gesticulating Smith.

Clara took care to be the last to leave the ship. By the time she was in the Customs shed, there was no sign of Smith or Jones. When her Vuitton suitcases had been chalked, the porter, who had prevented a rival from snatching them from her on the quay, asked her, with a confident smile:

'First-class on the train, Madam?'

When she had travelled out three weeks ago, the porters had said 'Miss'.

'No, third.'

The porter looked at her in pained surprise.

She kept close to his far side as he walked up the train trying to find a seat for her, hoping his bulk would conceal her if Smith and Jones were looking out of a window. The third-class was packed and she wished desperately she had enough to pay a supplement and travel first – her head had begun to ache badly again – but even second would be more than she could possibly manage. Though Clive would pay her taxi the other end, the price of her tea and ham sandwich had left her only just enough to tip this porter and the one at Victoria.

The porter said: 'Third's very full up.' He paused at one open door. 'There's room in there if those gentlemen will shove up a bit.' She saw with relief there was only one woman in the compartment and she was not wearing a blue or green cloche.

'Might be a bit more room further on.'

'No, no, this will do beautifully.'

He wedged her in between two stout men in check caps, both smoking foul-smelling pipes, and heaved the suitcases up on to the already overloaded rack. However, when she had tipped him, his gloomy expression vanished and he touched his cap as he said: '*Thank* you, Madam.'

A moment later he returned.

'I've found you a more comfortable place, Madam, in a non-smoker. Nothing like such a squash there and mostly ladies. I'll move your luggage along there.'

Clara shook her head.

'No, don't bother. I'd rather stay where I am.'

As the porter closed the door, he gave her a curious stare, as if to verify her sanity.

JULIAN TYE
(Unpublished: 1964?)

Julian Tye was written before *Clara IV*, although the events it describes, the meeting with Mark Mayhew, occurred a few months later in the marriage to Clive Heron. The manuscript was never sent to the typist and it is the only piece of my mother's post-war work I knew nothing of.

Also unknown is why Clara's name was changed to the adrogynous Julian. Certainly Antonia felt she had elements of a man in her make-up. In the short story 'Surprise Visit' (about a return to the old premises of the asylum) she changed Clara's name to Julia Tye. This story appeared in 1964.

Julian Tye was probably unfinished because it dealt with people who were still alive. The opening chapter describes a meeting with Mark Mayhew, who has usurped Julian's desk at the office. This young man was, in real life, Tom Hopkinson, whom Antonia married in 1930. Shortly to arrive on the scene was S.G., my father. Neither of these men would have welcomed revelations about their relations with Antonia.

These four chapters are not a shining example of Antonia's work. The office interchange with Mayhew needs tightening up. The picture of Julian's life with her second husband, Clive, is however vivid and very close to life. The conference at the advertising agency is also sharply and humorously observed.

1.

Julian Tye was, as usual, late for the office. But, since she had a room of her own, no one was likely to know. As she went up in the lift the porter grinned meaningly at his watch.

'Am I *frightfully* late, Bill?'

'It's quarter to three, Miss. Miss Evans asked me a little while back if you was in. I said maybe it was one of the days you didn't come in but, if not, no doubt you were in conference or out at a client's.'

'Bother.'

'I hope I didn't do wrong, Miss.'

'No, of course not, Bill. This new arrangement of having two jobs is rather confusing for everyone, including me. I'm quite likely to forget which one I'm supposed to be at. Still it's definitely Davidson's today and I'm definitely late.'

'Well, you're a privileged person, aren't you, Miss Tye?'

Julian smiled a privileged smile as Bill pulled open the gates and touched his cap in the way he kept for members of the staff whom he liked. But she hurried up the long passage to her room with the guilty tread of the unprivileged who have taken an unwarrantably long lunch hour. After six years of working full time at Davidson's Advertising Agency, she had not quite convinced herself that she really had got away with the greatest concession Davidson's had ever made to an employee. There were people in the firm who by merit, intrigue or falling in love in the right place had been promoted to large salaries or even directorships while still in their twenties. Julian's salary remained moderate and she had not the least ambition to be a director but she had achieved something unique and even preposterous. Thanks to her remarkable 'touch' in a certain type of women's copy, they had allowed her to work only four afternoons a week. The rest of the time she acted, at considerably less than half her Davidson's salary, as Assistant Editor and general factotum on a literary monthly. In order that her irregular hours should not cause scandals and jealousies among her colleagues, she was given a room to herself. A room to oneself was a very rare privilege, usually accorded only to directors. Only one other member of the ordinary staff had one; an abstract painter whom Jock Davidson, in a burst of enthusiasm for 'modern art' had lured into the firm by paying his debts and installing him in a large studio built to the painter's own design. Julian's room was not at all impressive and, as Miss Christian Campbell, one of the women directors had not failed to point out, it was given to her not to give her a 'guid conceit' of herself but in the nature of an isolation ward to prevent others from catching the infection of her irregularity. But in spite of Miss Campbell's fierce disapproval and assurance that 'this most unusual arrangement is to be regarded as strictly provisional' Julian clung to this room as a symbol of her independence. She had brought books and small objects from her own home to decorate it, she was extravagant with flowers for it, she kept private papers in the drawers of its desk and frequently, when she should have been thinking up 'new angles' on somebody's corsets or stockings or rejuvenating creams, she added passages to a certain notebook.

On this particular afternoon she threw open its door with unusual relief. She had had an extremely trying morning at *The Single Eye*. The editor had left her alone to cope with infuriated printers; somebody's proofs had been lost in the post owing to Cashel's habit of never telling her what he had done on private impulse; the same book had been sent to two people to review

and the reviewers, who fiercely despised each other, had arrived
at the same moment with their copy. A literary monthly, she
thought bitterly, had remarkably little to do with literatures as
far as she herself was concerned. At least here, in her small
room, she could have a little peace and privacy and, if there was
nothing urgent on her copy schedule, make a few notes on
something that was beginning, very dimly, to take shape in her
head.

But, no sooner had she opened the door, than she saw that
someone was sitting at her desk. This was outrageous enough,
but more outrageous still, the person did not even raise his head
when she came in but continued to write with diligent absorption, using *her* blotting pad and dipping his pen in *her* ink. The
intruder was so much at home that he had removed her vase of
tulips from the desk to the window sill and his pipe lay on the
Provençal saucer she used as an ashtray. She was so shocked and
indignant that for a moment she could only stare. What made
things worse was that the young man was not even one of the
regular old-time copywriters; he had been at Davidson's only a
month. Ordinarily she was kind to newcomers but from the first
week she had decided not to be kind to Miles Mayhew. Nearly
every other woman on the staff was already being far too kind to
him; it was impossible to wash one's hands in the cloakroom
without hearing a typist say, 'My dear, fancy such eyelashes
being wasted on a man,' or ' "Still waters run deep." He's so
frightfully polite and shy but, my hat, the way he *looks* at you,'
or 'He's *not* a mother's darling, Pam. Madge and her fiancé saw
him playing rugger at Twickenham last Saturday. He's terrific,'
or 'That story I typed for him in my spare time's been taken by
the *Manchester Guardian*. He stood me lunch on the strength of it.
I think he's a pet and I bet you he's famous one day,' or
'Davidson's is looking up, my dear. Our Miles took a degree at
Oxford and he's got two uncles in *Who's Who*.' And now this
tiresome young man whom she was quite certain needed taking
down several pegs was calmly sitting at her desk as if it were his
own and taking not the least notice of her.

Julian stared in furious silence at his brown hair, one end of
which stuck up from the crown like a schoolboy's and the two
crescents of downcast eyelashes, not only far too long for a man
but sweeping up in the way that her own, even with the help of
mascara, refused to do. By this time she was practically sure that
he was aware she had come in: no one wrote copy with such rapt
absorption as that. While she was trying to think of something

sufficiently cutting to say, the young man said, pausing in his writing, but not looking up –

'Sorry, Miss Tye isn't here this afternoon.'

'Oh, *isn't* she?' exploded Julian.

He looked up then. He certainly looked startled, even apologetic. Nevertheless his very large blue eyes, slightly bloodshot as if he had been walking in a high wind were too innocently surprised to be quite convincing. It was even possible that he blushed but he had such a high colour (another thing that she disliked in men) that it was difficult to tell. Julian was in no mood to give him the benefit of the doubt. She was trembling with irritation: the cool, cutting phrase she wanted would not come. All she could do was to burst out crudely:

'May I ask *what* you're doing in my room, Mr Mayhew? Your name *is* Mayhew, isn't it?'

Anger at her own anger made her more furious than ever. She was going to make a fool of herself and this intolerable young man would be responsible. Up to this moment she had merely mildly disliked him for no better reason than that she was tired with hearing the fuss the typists made about him. Now he suddenly became the embodiment of every insolent, conceited, contemptuous, ignorant man who did not instantly realise that Julian Tye was a very remarkable person indeed. She had the impression that several minutes went by during which the young man stared at her with impudent amusement.

'At least,' she said roughly, 'you might have the decency to answer when I speak to you.' The note in her voice appalled her. Was it her father working up to one of those scenes that used to paralyse her into idiocy or her mother screaming at a housemaid? She almost expected the young man to look shaken. Instead, he appeared calmer than ever. He said in a gentle, maddeningly reasonable voice:

'Which one do you want me to answer first? The second's easy: my name *is* Mayhew. Of course I've never been in doubt about yours. You're the celebrated Julian Tye. Julian Tye of *The Single Eye*.'

'You needn't be insulting.'

'Is it insulting to be called celebrated? I think *The Single Eye* is very good. I read your piece on Blake in the September number.'

'Oh, *that*,' she snarled. '*That* thing.' She spoke as if it were beneath contempt and at moments, indeed, thought so. Nevertheless she had put six weeks' hard work into it and there were moments when she thought it just possibly had a glimmering of something beyond competence.

'You mean you could do better if you tried as they used to say on one's reports? I've no doubt you could.'

'You're bloody patronising, aren't you?'

'I'm not bloody patronising, I'm bloody complimentary,' he said in a louder and much less polite voice. It occurred to Julian that perhaps he was getting angry too. For some reason, this slightly cooled her own temper. Her lip twisted in a sneer that could have easily been converted into a wry smile as she asked:

'Indeed? May I inquire how?'

'Isn't it obvious? If I think your Blake thing's extremely good . . . yes, seriously . . . if I'm convinced you can do lots better still, I'm convinced you're a real writer, aren't I? What more do you want?'

It was Julian's turn to stare. Her clenched face relaxed. She said guardedly; after all, this was only a young man just down from Oxford who probably had the shakiest critical standards:

'Nothing more, of course. If you could convince me, I mean. Still no one's been able to yet for more than a minute or two.'

'Do you despise other people as much as all that?'

'Despise?' She bristled. 'What nonsense. Far too much the other way. If people tell me something I've written is good, I long to believe them, but I can't. At least, not for more than a minute or two.'

'Does it work the same way if they tell you it's bad?'

'No. I usually believe them at the time and go on believing them.'

He jumped up.

'I say, I really ought to apologise. It's bad enough to be sitting at your desk but it's inexcusable to leave you standing in your own room.'

She did not sit down and they stood facing each other across her desk that was littered with his papers.

'You haven't told me yet what you're doing in my room.'

'You haven't given me much chance, have you?'

'You ought to have explained the minute I came in. Or at least said you were sorry.' Her anger was working up again. 'Why *are* you here? You know it's my private room, don't you?'

'Certainly. Your name is written quite clearly on the door.'

'Then why? You've got a desk of your own in the Copy Room, haven't you?'

'Oh yes. But I was told to use your room this afternoon.

There's a frightful din in there and I've got to rush out a pamphlet for a meeting tomorrow.'

'*Told* to? *Who* told you? No one's got the right to dispose of my room behind my back. You've only been here a month or two. I worked in that din for five years. You can really hardly expect a room to yourself at this stage.'

'I *don't* expect,' he groaned patiently. 'I tell you . . . I was *told* to use yours.'

Julian's voice rose.

'Who dared tell you? Of all the impertinence.'

'Miss Campbell.'

'Oh.' Julian knew better than he did that Miss Campbell could override everyone, including Jock Davidson himself.

'The whole thing's absurd,' she said indignantly. 'She must have known it was my afternoon in.'

'Perhaps she forgot,' he said with maddening meekness.

'I shall go straight to Miss Campbell and complain,' she raged.

'That really would be the most sensible thing to do, wouldn't it? I mean it would be fairer to curse her than to curse me.'

'It's intolerable,' said Julian, now long past any consideration of justice. 'I'm sure you asked her. You get round all the women here. It's disgusting. She would never have suggested it of her own accord. She *knew* . . .'

'That it was your day in? Well, she did think so but . . .'

'But you got round her. And trusted to getting round me. Well, as I'm neither a typist nor a spinster of forty-five, you won't.'

'I never supposed I could. If you could keep your temper for exactly fifty seconds . . .'

'I think you're the most insolent young man I've ever met.'

'I haven't the least intention of insulting you. And as you refuse to listen when I attempt to explain I'll just clear these things away and go.'

She stood speechless with anger at himself and her while he quietly and methodically collected his papers.

'That's where your blotter was,' he said. 'A shade to the left. I'm sorry I can't remember the exact spot where the tulips were. Is that more or less right?'

She bit her lip and controlled herself enough to mutter ungraciously, 'I'm sorry to have to turn you out. But you do see my point, don't you?'

'There were rather a lot to see all at once, weren't there? I'm sorry I was in your room when you wanted it.'

'Do you mean you've been in it before?'

He lowered his long eyelashes.

'Well . . . once or twice to be frank.'

This was more than Julian could bear.

'And I've never even been consulted. So anyone who thinks he's too superior to work in the Copy Room can come in and use my private room when my back's turned. Quite apart from everything else I've got personal things here. I've got very private things here. I've got private papers. They might at least have had the decency to tell me so that I could lock them up.' Her lips were trembling as if she were going to cry.

While she raged, she looked almost pleadingly at the young man, as if imploring him to sympathise with her at the monstrous injustice of it.

Suddenly he smiled. It was a very agreeable smile.

'Don't be so frightfully upset. I do see that it's maddening for you. I do agree they ought to have told you. But believe me, I don't make a habit of it. I only come here when I'm commanded to. And I swear I haven't looked at any of your private papers.'

She relented a little.

'No, I'm sure you haven't. All the same I shall go and clear up the whole thing with Miss Christian.'

'Now, this moment?'

'Yes.'

He said judicially, 'Of course you're absolutely justified. But there are moments – don't you agree? – that are better than other moments for doing these things. I know I've got no right to butt in . . . only I've caused you so much trouble already that . . .'

'What on earth do you mean?'

'Well, the fact is that today Miss Christian assumed *she'd* been wrong about it's being the day you came in. You see it was a little after two and seeing the room was empty . . .'

'Oh,' said Julian and gave up the struggle. She had enough sense left to realise that she must keep out of Miss Christian Campbell's way for the rest of the afternoon. Her privileged position that had seemed so secure as she soared up in the lift now seemed so shaky that she might have already been under notice to go. She had been trying for two years to leave – but she was as usual in debt and could not at the moment afford to take any risks.

'Thank you for warning me. Though of course I don't have to

keep absolute routine hours. I was kept late at *The Eye* and now I'll have to work late here.'

'Bad luck. And I've interrupted you by my disgusting intrusion. I hope my aura hasn't contaminated the room.'

'I'm afraid I lost my temper rather,' she said as he edged towards the door with his load of layouts and copy-pads.

'You lost it quite considerably. But don't apologise. At least it's given me the chance of meeting you. One day I shall be telling my grandchildren, "I once had the privilege of being cursed by Miss Julian Tye."'

There was something so odd in the contrast between the admiring, almost pleading stare of his blue eyes (she suspected he looked at all women like that) and the polite impudence of his voice that she had to smile.

'You win,' she said.

'Call it a draw. Now I can tell the little beasts that Miss Tye once condescended to smile at me. I shall also mention that at that moment I observed she had a remarkably attractive face.'

'Thank you. I suppose that's your technique for getting out of awkward situations with women.'

'I try not to get into them,' he said sweetly as he manoeuvred himself skilfully out of the door and closed it behind him almost without a sound.

2.

Julian did considerably less work than she had intended that afternoon. The campaign for Sally Severn's Rosedew Face Cream had not notably progressed when, having stayed late out of a guilty conscience, she tidied herself in the deserted cloakroom. Possibly because she had the mirror to herself for once, she combed and rearranged her fair hair more carefully than usual. She was tired and in the harsh spring sunlight she decided she looked every minute of twenty-nine, if not more. She was well-dressed and well made-up as Davidson's expected their 'charm specialist' to be but her looks were not of the type she herself admired. She had soft childish hair and a soft childish skin, the kind of skin that is admirable on its best days but reacts to every change of temperature, and is a barometer to the health and even the mood of its owner. Seen from the front, her features, except for her full, curved mouth were rather indeterminate but her profile was so definite that it came as a shock to anyone who troubled to observe her and sometimes even to herself. The high forehead, slightly arched nose and full round chin were typical of portraits of eighteenth-century women of the commanding type and they matched very oddly indeed with the front view of a face of which the most that could be said was that it was moderately pretty and almost too mobile. It was a considerable time since Julian had examined herself so carefully: though it took her several minutes to arrange her face in the mornings and repair it during the day, she had done this for some time as mechanically as one tidies a room. The fringe must be combed to lie all one way, rouge and lipstick neatly adjusted, nose powdered, lapels brushed. She was by nature untidy but constantly advising other women to be chic and soignée had had the effect of making her well groomed. It amused her to see how much she was influenced by what she wrote. She frequently took her own advice and while professing the cynical detachment common to copy-writers was liable to buy face creams and powders on her own impassioned recommendation.

Now she found herself considering her face from a more personal and critical angle and wondering how it might strike fresh eyes. Since it was impossible to come to any conclusion, she decided that her skin was 'winter-weary' as she had been warning thousands of other women that very afternoon. 'Can you face the spring sunlight with the confidence of a newly-opened flower?' Definitely, no, thought Julian. She decided to give herself a facial at home that night and to buy herself a new hat in the lunch hour tomorrow.

On the way down the liftman handed her a note in unfamiliar writing. She guessed it was from Miles Mayhew and waited till she was in the tube to read it. She had no idea what she expected to find in it but for some reason she was oddly excited. What she read, however, made her almost as angry as she had been that afternoon.

'After your magnanimous forgiveness, I must confess that I don't really deserve it. My conscience, usually so co-operative, will not let me rest until I disclose the horrid fact that, without exactly telling you a lie, I tampered with the truth. I have never even glanced at any private paper of yours but I *did* read something which I didn't think private since it was typed and obviously about to be sent to a publisher. I wouldn't confess it now, except for something you said about writing. I dare say it's impertinent of me but I thought you might possibly believe me when I say that you can write damn well if I said that you can also write damn badly. The Blake thing was grand. "The Masque of Love" is lousy.'

Julian spent the rest of the tube journey composing wounding replies to this note. This time Miles Mayhew really had insulted her and no charm could appease her. For 'The Masque of Love' was not hers: the manuscript had been sent to her for criticism by a man whom she had liked ten years ago. In those days, on the strength of his amusing letters and an occasional impromptu parody, his friends had supposed that he might become a writer. Now, in one of the dullest, most laboured first novels Julian had ever read – and she had read a great many – he had most definitely disproved this. How could this insufferable young man Mayhew dare to suppose for a moment that she could write anything so lamentable. His good opinion of her Blake article, which for a moment had genuinely pleased her, now appeared not only worthless but positively an insult. By the time she got home, she had almost decided on frigid silence as being more contemptuous than the cutting reply. But it was almost impossible to Julian, by nature and training, to leave even the baldest note unanswered. Moreover it was impossible to let Mayhew go on thinking, and very possibly telling other people, that she had written a disgracefully bad novel. As soon as she got in, she tore his note to shreds and, without removing her hat and coat, sat down and wrote with a hand that shook with annoyance:

'If you suppose I wrote "The Masque of Love", I'm afraid your criticism of my work, no doubt well intentioned, really isn't worth having. J.T.'

Usually her homecoming was the moment to which Julian looked forward all day. Tonight, perhaps because her husband, Clive Heron, was not there to welcome her as usual, she felt flat and restless. She lit a cigarette and wandered aimlessly about the tiny Chelsea house, still in her outdoor clothes. Usually the mere sight of the house refreshed her after the long office day. Her job at Davidson's she had undertaken when they married over four years ago purely and simply to supplement their income; she and Clive had always planned that she should leave it 'when they could afford it'. But though they had no children and Clive had long ago been put into a higher grade at the Home Office, they had acquired such a taste for small luxuries that both their salaries were always mortgaged well ahead and they were less able to afford it than when they first married. The Chelsea

Another photograph from 1937 showing the successful advertising copywriter and journalist. The coat was one that sold for thirty shillings. Antonia advertised it so successfully that it was given her. She wore it all through the war and long after.

house was one of those small luxuries. They had chosen its soft colour schemes and its charming, 'amusing' furniture with the greatest care: it had seemed absurd to both of them to save a few shillings a yard on curtains they would have to look at every day or to deny themselves expensive little odds and ends, a Bristol glass lamp, a Sèvres dish or a baroque statuette which looked so exactly right in the niche they adorned. The bills for the house were still not entirely paid off nor even the money Clive had borrowed from the family business to launch them. Sometimes Julian had qualms about the bills but she reasoned herself out of them by telling herself that her prestige at Davidson's was not unconnected with the house. Davidson's were snobbish about art and culture and the Heron's house, having been supervised by a fashionable elderly young man who did interior decorating, had been photographed in *Vogue*.

But tonight her home did not give her the usual pleasure. She even felt a faint distaste for its carefully thought out arrangements: the colour scheme of the living room built up round an early Vanessa Bell that had been one of their extravagances. Each small room was full of such conscious touches; a white cupboard picked out with a line of cobalt to match the blue edge of a crinkled bowl of opaque white glass, pieces of the Victorian bric-a-brac that was just coming into fashion, a mirror framed in shells, a papier maché table inlaid with mother of pearl, a case of brilliant stuffed birds made discreetly incongruous accents in the light coloured, sparsely furnished rooms that were as different as possible from their original setting. Charming in themselves, at this moment they struck Julian as almost too charming. When at length she arrived in her bedroom she was irritated at the sight of Clive's dressing-gown hanging on the door. She almost wished it were an ordinary shabby crimson or blue one instead of being made of the same material that covered their two beds, a Duncan Grant design of sepia scrawls and lemon-yellow dots on a ground of greyish-fawn.

Their cat Augustus was asleep as usual at this time on one of the beds. She went over and scratched his spine with particular affection. Augustus had a remarkable character but his appearance was not in the least exotic. He was a large plain alley cat whose black fur was just beginning to show rusty patches in the sunlight as if it had been hennaed. The setting called for a Siamese or a Russian Blue but Augustus tyrannised equally over the setting and his owners. He sharpened his claws on the elegant painted furniture, climbed up the curtains, pulled up the threads of the plain carpets into unsightly knots and left his adhesive black hairs all over the chair covers and their clothes. But neither Julian nor Clive ever reproved him or even complained. Augustus acknowledged her caresses by opening his yellow eyes, giving her a disapproving look and shutting them again; he seldom purred when it was expected of him. A moment later came the sound of Clive's key in the lock. Augustus, who had given the impression of not wishing to be disturbed for several hours, suddenly uncoiled himself, stretched his hind legs, rumpling the coverlet as he did so, bounded off the bed with surprising nimbleness for his weight and ran downstairs to meet his master. Julian followed more slowly. From the landing she could hear Clive talking to the cat as Augustus went through the evening ritual he had invented for himself of leaping on to Clive's shoulder and pulling off his hat.

'Well, how's my other pussy?' Clive said as Julian reached the passage. 'You look somewhat jaundiced. Offices more frightful than usual?'

Clive was thin and tall: the cat on his shoulder was within easy reach of the low ceiling of the passage. The mass of black fur against his cheek made his delicate face, half hidden by horn-rimmed glasses seem even smaller and paler than usual.

Julian nodded and made a face and he went on:

'I've had an appalling day myself. I had to see the Grand Panjandrum, that's why I'm so late. Let's go straight out and cram our bellies, shall we? I must just go and regulate my hair first.'

'Regulating' his hair was one of Clive's important rituals. During the day its fine reddish gold strands clung to his small neat head with the utmost precision but he lived in a state of constant anxiety in case one of them should be ever so slightly awry. If he had to take off his hat in a strange house, he was in a state of nervous misery until he was able to peer into a mirror and make his minute, often invisible adjustments. While she waited for him, Julian thought how many small rituals had established themselves in their four years of living together. There were moments when life with Clive seemed to be as prescribed and ceremonial as it had been at her convent school. She had adapted herself surprisingly well to Clive's peculiarities and considered this discipline a small price to pay for the extraordinary pleasure of living with Clive. From the moment she had met him, when she was only nineteen she had regarded him as the rarest of human beings and nothing had ever surprised and flattered her more than his asking her to marry him when she was twenty-five. The friends who had tried to dissuade both of them had had to admit that the experiment had been an astonishing success. The Herons were quoted as the perfect example of a modern marriage: they were unconventional without being messy, their home was equally free from quarrels and from boring domesticity and, though it was definitely understood that either could be invited alone without giving offence to the other, people usually preferred to ask them together because they shone in each other's company. Every year as Julian came to know Clive more intimately, she became more and more convinced of his uniqueness. Their life together was a kind of art: it involved suppressions and exclusions but it had its reward for Julian in an extraordinary delight that she knew she would never find with any other human being. They were not, in the ordinary sense, 'in love' with each other. There had been a short time, in their very early days, when they might have been but it had inexplicably passed and neither of them consciously regretted it. It seemed to both of them that the mysterious bond they had was something so much rarer and deeper that it was absurd to judge themselves by ordinary standards. 'We are both insane,' Clive often said, 'but I *really* can't see that it matters, can you?' They were completely dependent on each other, inhabiting a private world with its own language of allusions and catchwords, serious or completely nonsensical.

After the first two years, Julian had occasionally lapsed into a brief love affair. Against his own principles, Clive had shown a touch of jealousy over the first one. Julian had been remorseful to see that she had hurt him and Clive had been equally remorseful at having been so barbarous as to be hurt. After that, instead of jealousy he had shown amusement and even sympathy. One of the many endearing things about Clive and one which made him so unlike any other man she had ever known was his impersonal interest in a situation. At any moment he could detach himself from his own feelings (he was fond of assuring Julian that he had none though she knew this to be untrue) and examine any circumstance, a friend's deception, a lapse of Julian's, some piece of neurotic behaviour of his own with exactly the same quality of attention he gave to a book or a picture. While behaving with stoical calm in crises which would have driven the average man to frenzy, small things would exacerbate him into a state of nervous misery that was both tragic and comic. Here again he was unlike other men. The average man who is tortured by small mishaps, the lost collar-stud or the broken shoelace, is usually far too self-absorbed to pay any attention to other people's misadventures. But Clive was all eager sympathy when anything irritated Julian. He passionately acquiesced, he knew *exactly* how she must feel if she went out without her powder-puff or her hat blew off in a high wind. Tonight she could be certain that, however trying his own day had been he would appreciate every fine point of her annoyance at finding that intolerable young man sitting at her desk. Not the faintest shade of her frustration, or her mortifying behaviour would be lost on him. He would see more in it than she had, he would examine it from every angle until her ten minutes with Miles Mayhew had become an exquisitely intricate Henry James situation.

Clive's hair took longer than usual to reduce to order that night and he was not perfectly satisfied with the result. At the last moment Julian realised that she had forgotten to feed Augustus and Clive took advantage of the delay to slip up to the bathroom again for a further anxious inspection. When at last they were sitting in the little restaurant where they ordinarily had dinner, Julian knew better than to begin talking at once. It was another established ritual that Clive must be allowed to read his evening paper during the first part of the meal. He fairly gave Julian half of it, reserving the racing news for himself. One of the most unexpected things about Clive was his methodical interest in racing. Over breakfast he studied 'Form at a Glance' and most days he placed a small sagacious bet, occasionally bringing off a brilliant double. He rarely went to a meeting but he knew the form and pedigree of an enormous number of horses and had a shrewd notion of which entrant from any particular stable was really out to win. He treated racing as an intellectual pastime as other men treat bridge or chess. Though he was usually several pounds to the good at the end of a season, a run of bad luck did not tempt him either to lay off or to increase his stakes. He did not regard racing as a means of making money and there was nothing of the gambler in his temperament.

Tonight Julian was restless and unable to concentrate on her own share of the *Evening Standard*. Clive, perversely, took longer than usual over his. It was not till they reached the coffee stage that, having put the paper together and folded it neatly, he looked at her sharply through his glasses. Julian was still constantly struck by the freshness and clearness of those rather small blue eyes. It was as if the glasses which he had worn since he was a boy had kept them from tarnishing. At thirty-five, his delicate fair skin, tightly stretched over the small bones, was beginning to redden slightly and to parch into fine lines. But when he removed his glasses the area around the eyes was milk-white as a child's.

'Well . . . what's up with *you?*' he asked.

Julian knew that throughout his absorption in the paper he had been aware of every fidget and suppressed sigh.

'Nothing,' she said and proceeded to describe the Miles Mayhew episode.

He listened attentively. At the end he raised one pale eyebrow and gave a tragi-comic sigh.

'I presume that means you're off again.'

'Certainly not,' she said indignantly. 'I think he's an odious conceited young man and I haven't the least intention of seeing him again.'

'Doubtless. The fact remains he works in Davidson's so you obviously *will* see him again.'

'Well, I shan't speak to him. Or if I do, I shall be extremely offensive.'

'He sounds the handsome, hearty public school type.'

'Exactly. He's a shop girl's dream. For which reason he precisely isn't *my* type. You ought to know by now that I only like hopeless men.'

'Take care. You're protesting far too vehemently. He sounds exactly the kind of chap your father would have liked you to marry.'

'Yes, I admit that. Daddy would adore him. He plays rugger, he got a first in Greats, he's got sweet manners and he's literary in a nice gentlemanly way. Writes little pieces for the back page of the *Manchester Guardian*.'

'The combination sounds irresistible. Why don't you go to it?'

'Clive, you really are insufferable. Are you setting out to be a *Cocu Magnifique?*'

'Not in the least, my dear. But obviously you're blowing up for something. I suspected it from your distracted look when I came in. When you forgot to give Augustus his supper, I was certain. The sooner it's over the sooner to sleep, I say.'

'You're absolutely and utterly wrong. Even if I did find him attractive – which I don't – I wouldn't even consider it a possibility.'

'Why?'

'For one thing, he's years younger than I am.'

'So was your French boy.'

'That was different. Besides I was younger myself then.'

'I'm still unconvinced.'

'I'll give you two reasons out of at least a dozen. One, he's on the staff at Davidson's. Two, all the typists are in love with him.'

'Both quite irrelevant. Why not be honest and admit you're frightened.'

'Frightened,' she said indignantly. 'I never heard such nonsense. I think this is a stupid joke anyway. Can't we drop it?'

'Temper . . . temper.'

'Well, you deserve it. Why are you behaving like the devil's advocate? Anyone would think you were trying to provoke me into having an affair with this wretched young man.'

'On the contrary. But may I point out I'm behaving, not like the devil's advocate but like the devil himself. I'm shocked that you as a Catholic should fail to distinguish between the two.'

'You know perfectly well I'm not a Catholic any more.'

'Nonsense. Once a Catholic always a Catholic. I shall have to give you a refresher course in your own theology.'

'Sometimes I really think you *are* the devil, Clive. Who taught you all the theology you know?'

'You taught me a great deal. Not all. I've been fascinated by theology since I was thirteen. But I'm deeply indebted to you, I admit. You're always marvellous when you talk about Catholic dogma. I'm frequently tempted to become a Catholic myself.'

'And ever since we married, you've been steadily undermining my faith. Now you've completely succeeded, you browbeat me with the catechism.

He sighed and smiled at her with rueful affection.

'You've taught me the delights of Catholicism and I've attempted to teach you the delights of atheism. It's your only defect, dear Puss. You can't hold things in suspension and enjoy ideas for their own sake. You can see it perfectly well in art. It's the only thing I've never been able to teach you, to distinguish between poetical truth and literal truth. I suppose it's because you're a woman and all women are barbarians.'

'I'm stupid and cross tonight,' she said. 'I'm more of a barbarian than usual.'

'I won't torment you any more. Let's go home, and we'll have a little Mozart, shall we, to smooth your fur the right way again?'

Playing the gramophone was also a ritual. Clive always spent several minutes adjusting lamps so that the light should be of the softest and arranging their two chairs in the exact places where he was convinced the sound could be heard best. The EMG which they were still paying for was his special toy. Julian never dared to play it on her own: Clive fretted too much in case she forgot to dust a record or sharpened a needle badly. Nearly always it was Clive who chose what records they should play; he enjoyed building up a programme and did so with much skill. He knew her favourite records but he liked to spring them on her as a surprise or delay playing them until he had run through certain ones that suited his own mood. Sometimes he insisted on playing the gramophone when she would have preferred to read or talk: sometimes when she was longing for music he refused. But Julian, egotist as she was, did not resent this. It had become a pleasure to attune herself to his moods and since she herself was often so vague about what she wanted to do, it was a relief to have a lead to follow. It was Clive who decided what concerts and theatres they should go to and when. This did not cause friction either for they enjoyed the same things and whether they were enraptured or disappointed with a performance Clive was the one perfect companion with whom to share anything from a local music hall to the St Matthew Passion. There were times when Julian would have liked to do something on the spur of the moment but though Clive might have acquiesced his nervous anxiety would have spoilt the pleasure. Once she had asserted herself to the extent of beginning a piece of knitting but had abandoned it at the sight of his tormented face. 'I know I'm a monster,' he had said remorsefully, 'but I can't stand the click of the needles. It reminds me too much of my mother.'

Tonight Clive was evidently going to play the gramophone for her benefit so Julian could not hurt his feelings by retiring and giving herself the facial she had planned. When he had arranged the chairs and the lights, he put on, without announce-ment, one of the records she loved best and which had many associations for both of them: Mozart's D minor piano concerto. She tried to concentrate on this music that usually meant so much to her but her mind kept wandering. She found herself going over the absurd incident with Miles Mayhew and wondering how he would take her rude note. The conversation at dinner, instead of reducing the whole thing to triviality as she had hoped, had turned it into an obsession. When the record changed to the lovely slow movement, her attention was caught for a little while. But the music which had always represented for her utter serenity and a timeless world now seemed to her a nostalgic lament for something missed. There was a moment, when after long suspense the original theme returned, when she and Clive always caught each other's eye with mutual delight. Tonight she missed it. She was thinking not about Mozart but about the new hat she was almost certainly going to buy tomorrow.

Clive did something very unusual. He stopped the record before it was finished. Julian came to with a guilty start.

'Evidently not the right piece,' he said quietly.

'Oh, Clive *do* finish it,' she said, horrified at the falsity of her voice which she knew he was far too acute to miss.

'Not tonight. Miles away, weren't you?'

He was at the gramophone, with his back to her. Had he said 'miles' on purpose?

'Well . . . what do *you* feel like?'

'You choose. I warned you I was as stupid as an owl tonight.'

'Do you want to go to bed?'

'Not yet.'

He explored the record cabinet in silence. Then he exclaimed in gentle triumph – 'Ah, now I think I've hit it,' and put on *La ci darem la mano.*

He came over and sat beside her again. With a sad quizzical look, he sang very softly Zerlina's line: '*Vorrei . . . e non vorrei.*'

Then he turned his head away, giving the song over to her as it were, so that she could listen in private.

This time she did listen. It struck home to her as violently as if she were the girl whom Don Giovanni was soliciting. At the end she was on the edge of tears.

Clive went over and closed the gramophone remarking:

'Mrs Bloom's most celebrated rendering.'

'Yes,' Julian sighed, in harmony with him again.

He took it up, murmuring, 'Yes . . . I said yes.'

They were silent for some moments. Clive stayed over by the gramophone. Suddenly he said in a brisk voice, 'Any progress with the new work in hand?'

She shook her head sadly.

'Not a syllable. I'm stuck as usual. Worse than ever. It's no good, darling. I'll never be a writer and I don't deserve to be. I'm just a bitch.'

'Come, come, don't exaggerate.'

'I am,' she insisted, crying a little now. 'I've got no excuse.

I've got everything . . . no, much, much more than any human being could possibly expect. I don't know how you put up with me.'

'Nonsense. You know I'm devoted to my old puss. Come to that, how do you put up with *me*? No one else in the world would.'

'Idiot,' she sighed. 'You know perfectly well I couldn't manage without you.'

He said musingly, 'Yes, that's probably true. It's my fault. You ought to be able to manage without me. You'd probably be far happier.'

'That's not true. I've been happier with you these four years than I've been in the whole of the rest of my life.'

'Yes,' he sighed. 'Yes. The fact remains that you don't get on with your work, do you?'

'That's my fault. Absolutely and entirely my fault. I'm bloody lazy.'

'You are bloody lazy, but there's more to it than that. What is it you need and haven't got? If I can't give it to you, could anybody else?'

'No,' she said vehemently. 'No, no, no. It's me that's wrong, not you or anyone else. I'm always thinking what Martha Galt said to me . . . and she knew what she was talking about . . . "Are you a writer or a weeping woman?"'

'Well, she's a weeping woman herself.'

'Yes, but she's got the guts to be a writer too. And I haven't.'

'Possibly, you've hit it. *Auf meine tiefe tränen.*'

'Precisely. Another thing . . . I'm too comfortable. My tears aren't in the least *tief* nowadays. They're just wallowing in self-pity. I ask you . . . what *have* I got to cry about?'

'The old *lacrima rerum*. At least you're human enough to weep while these old eyes remain obstinately dry.'

'Oh Clive, I do love you,' she said impulsively. 'I really do.'

'I don't want you to love me,' he said sadly. 'I want you to love *it* . . . whatever *it* is. Nothing else matters in the end.'

'I know,' she said soberly.

His face brightened. He reached for a record which they played so often there was no need to search for it.

'Now I'm going to be your guardian angel and torment you,' he said.

She knew what he was going to play and submitted herself to it.

'By the waters of Bab-ylon,' sang the thin, true ancient voice of George Henschl, 'We sat down and we-ept When we remembered thee, O Si-ion.'

Her own tears were flowing now from a deeper source than the nervous one of a few minutes ago. The song ended.

Jerusalem, if I forget thee
May my right hand forget her cunning.

The record whirred into silence. The fact that Clive let it run down unchecked showed that he was greatly moved. He came over to her and pulled her gently to her feet, laying his thin cheek against her wet one.

'Poor Mrs Bloom,' he said. 'Poor Daedalus.'

'Oh, Clive,' she said, leaning against his shoulder. 'You terrify me sometimes. Is there *nothing* you don't understand?'

He laughed and said gaily:

'You're remarkably slow in the uptake, sometimes, aren't you? How often do I have to tell you that I am God?'

3.

The next day, being Friday, Julian did not go to Davidson's. She posted her note to Miles Mayhew on the way to *The Single Eye* and devoted two hours in the afternoon to buying a hat. During the week-end she continued to feel flat and restless: she found herself constantly wondering whether she would have been wiser not to have replied at all. On Monday morning there was a letter for her from Miles Mayhew. She read it hastily under Clive's eyes and said at once:

'I've had a letter from that young man.'

'Oh, indeed? I trust he's penitent.'

'Yes he is. It's all butter and dewdrops. He's even dug up that old short story of mine in *Miscellany* and seems quite excited about it.'

'So he should be.'

'He even asks me to go to tea with him next Saturday and bring a new story if I've got one. Of course I shan't go.'

'Why not?'

'I don't want to see him out of office hours. And anyway I haven't written a story for two years.'

'Then you'd better sit down and write one.'

'Don't be ridiculous. You ought to know by this time I can't just sit down and write a story like *that*.'

'It's probably what you need . . . someone to stand over you with a horsewhip and *make* you produce.'

'Well, I'm certainly not going to jump through hoops for Miles Mayhew. He's conceited enough as it is.'

'So you're definitely not going to tea with him on Saturday?'

'Certainly not.'

'Quite. By the way, I'm out myself on Saturday. Raymond's in London for the day and wants to hobnob with me.'

'Then I shall have a nice peaceful afternoon catching up on my mending.'

'Quite,' said Clive heartily.

There was very little to do at *The Single Eye* that Monday morning. Cashel had as usual taken a long week-end: no proofs had come in and none of the few letters could be answered without him. Julian had nothing better to do than glance through back numbers whose contents she already knew too well. Suddenly a sentence in one started up a train of thought. The train led to something she had meant to write about for seven years. During those years she had made several false starts. The experience was there; there was no likelihood of her forgeting any detail of it. But the raw material refused to crystallise into a form. It remained a shapeless, incoherent mass of details that she could not force into a whole. Idly, almost unconsciously, she scribbled a sentence on her desk pad; then another. Before she realised it, she had covered several pages. When she paused for a moment, she looked up and saw that she had been writing for three hours. She took the scribbled sheets with her to Davidson's, deliberately refraining from looking at them over her hurried lunch. By a stroke of luck there was a note on her desk telling her to do no more on the campaign for the moment as the client was considering a change of policy and Miss Campbell would discuss it with her at half-past four. Julian sat down without even taking off her hat and continued writing on the special green paper Davidson's provided for their copy staff. At half-past three a messenger brought her the cup of tea which was usually such a welcome interruption. She barely thanked him and let it get cold while she continued to write with a feverish absorption she had hardly ever known till her hand was cramped and shaking and her eyes ached. She wrote a sentence and sat back to think. Was that the right ending or should there be another paragraph? Then she noticed the time: it was twenty past four. However unwillingly, she must stop now. There was barely time to tidy herself up and collect the relevant papers on

Rosedew Face Cream for her conference with Miss Campbell.

At half-past four, feeling as if she were leaving a lover, she presented herself in Miss Campbell's office. Miss Campbell was not there but two or three other members of the staff were seated round the conference table. One of them, to her surprise and annoyance, was Miles Mayhew. He gave her a rather self-conscious smile. She returned the smile guardedly, saying, 'I didn't know you were working on this account.'

'I'm only standing in for Grayson who's had to go off on Baxton's Tea. They thought it would be good for my soul.'

'But Grayson's an executive. I thought you were a copy-writer.'

'Davidson's don't seem to have made up their mind whether I am or not. So they're trying me on a bit of everything.'

'I see.' The others were talking and Julian said, under the cover of the noise, 'I suppose they're planning to try out your charm on Sally Severn herself. I warn you, she's a tartar. She's broken three executives already. And poor Grayson definitely doesn't seem to be her type.'

At that moment everyone stood up as the door opened and Miss Christian Campbell entered, accompanied by a tremen-dous blonde in a mink coat. Sally Severn who made ten thou-sand a year out of a beauty salon and the famous Severn Aids to Loveliness was verging on sixty. She had let her figure go and left it to the sylphs in the salon to demonstrate the Severn Slimming Exercises but the skin of her vast face was blooming and unlined. She faithfully used her own preparations and reasonably prided herself on being an excellent advertisement for them. Miss Christian Campbell, the great feminine power behind the throne at Davidson's, looked more elegant than ever beside the fur-clad bulk of Sally Severn. Had it not been for her thin mouth, Miss Christian would have been a remarkably pretty woman. She had soft dark hair, carefully arranged so as to look both feminine and fashionable, but not outré and wide grey eyes that looked deceptively mild and a refined, gentle voice with only a trace of the Glasgow accent. She wore a modest pearl necklace round her white throat and her clothes, as always, were restrained and admirably cut. Miss Christian's ladylike mildness of manner hid, however, as everyone in Davidson's knew, a shrewd Scottish mind for business and an inflexible will. Jock Davidson, the nominal head of the firm, red-faced, loud-voiced and blustering might bully or cajole clients into spending large sums at the agency; it was Miss Christian who decided how those sums should be spent. Jock saw himself as a Napoleonic figure: he was fond of stopping his staff in the passages, tweaking their ears and promising them a rise in salary. These promises always carried the rider, 'Just step in and see Miss Christian and tell her I told ye to.' But if anyone were so rash as to do so, they would be met by Miss Christian's cool, mild stare and a little laugh like the tinkle of a spoon against a medicine glass. 'Mr Davidson's over-impulsive at times. He's so generous, he'd like to give the messengers a thousand a year. But I handle the finances of the firm and I know what they can stand and what they can't. Have you ever reckoned our overhead costs? I thought not and I'm not blaming you. It's none of your business. But it is mine. I'm no genius like Mr Davidson but if it weren't for me there'd be no Davidson's and there'd be no job for you, let alone a rise of salary.' Then, picking up the fountain pen she had laid down, as a sign that the interview was ended she would add with a gracious nod and a thin-lipped smile, 'I'm verra glad Mr Davidson's seen fit to commend your work. See that you continue to deserve his good words.'

The conference proceeded on the usual lines. Never had Julian found it harder to fix her mind on the interests of Sally Severn Aids to Loveliness. It was not part of her job to decide on the relative merits of a six-inch double in the *Telegraph* or a half-page in *Vogue* but she was expected to listen alertly. There was the usual protest from Miss Severn that the art charges were too high and the usual insistence that they should revive the old block of an Edwardian lady with a rose in her hair and a chiffon fichu.

'I sold twenty thousand pounds worth of Skin Food on it,' she asserted, 'and wrote the words myself. I'm sure it's very dainty and very good style. And it shows how long we've been going, not to mention that I've got blocks in every size that won't cost a penny. This Arden woman's a mere upstart compared to us.'

'Times have changed,' Miss Campbell assured her patiently. 'Your preparations have stood the test of time, of course, and you yourself are the most wonderful advertisement for them.'

'I certainly am,' said Miss Severn. Suddenly she grabbed Miles Mayhew's hand and held it against her copious, but firm and snowy chin. 'Feel that, young man. No flabbiness, eh? And smooth as a baby's bottom.'

A page from *Harrods News*, April 1934. Antonia worked briefly in the advertising department of Harrods writing just this sort of copy. She described working there as 'hell!'.

Three Unusual ways with Fur

'Damascus'   'Duverne'

'Damascus' The points to notice about this Coat are its colour—a most heavenly blue; the fur edging the short-ish wide sleeves; and the flattering collar which you tie stock-fashion. A soft Woollen Coat trimmed with full Flying Fox in a glorious Blue to match. Average sizes and large sizes. **6½ Gns**

'Duverne' Another of these charming '1934 Blues.' This formal Afternoon Coat is carried out in Wool Georgette with a sumptuous cape collar edged with Blue Flying Fox. The neck line is adaptable, with a long tie that can be worn in several ways. Small and average sizes. £.

6¼ Gns

Coats, First Floor.

'Dene' A clever new way to gain the smart cape line! This soft Woollen Coat for formal wear has a tucked cape coming barely shoulder-width and edged with lovely Beggar's Cloak Squirrel. Tuckings appear again on the tie scarf ends and the sleeves. Navy and Black. Small and average sizes. **7½ Gns**

'Dene'

Miss Christian coughed delicately. Miles Mayhew gazed at Sally Severn with impudent, enraptured eyes and said earnestly, '*Exquisite* texture, Miss Severn.'

'All built-up tissue,' she said proudly. 'I was using Severn Extra-Strong before you were born or even thought of, my boy.'

Miss Christian quietly turned to the attack. Severn Aids to Loveliness had a magnificent past and, with Davidson's co-operation a still more magnificent future. The fact remained that Elizabeth Arden was spending at least ten times as much on advertising as Sally Severn, that she had caught the modern fancy, that her preparations were charmingly packaged and that her distribution was phenomenal. In view of all this perhaps a stronger, more contemporary appeal was needed than Miss Severn's favourite slogan, 'Your grandmother used them and they're still the best'.

Some of Julian's copy was produced and Miss Severn scrutinised it through a lorgnette, bending her peroxide head at it till her large pearls were almost hidden in folds of built-up tissue.

'Some of the wording's really very nice, Miss Tye dear. But I'm afraid I don't care for the expression "ravishing". I've always understood "ravishing" was something no nice woman mentioned. Don't forget that Severn has always catered for *ladies*. When I started this business, I wouldn't treat anyone who hadn't been presented at court. And where's the piece about "Beauty in your own Boudoir"? You know I always insist on having that in.'

Julian said politely, 'Yes, I know, Miss Severn. Only, you see we were trying to appeal to a wider public . . . a new class of buyer. And I'm afraid most of them haven't got boudoirs and some of them don't even know what a boudoir is.'

'How shocking.' She pounced on a sketch that accompanied the copy. 'What's this? Got in by mistake, I suppose.'

'It's a suggestion for the kind of artwork we think we ought to use.'

'But it's not finished. The woman's only got one eye. My time's too valuable to come here and look at unfinished sketches.'

It was explained to her that this was modern art of the type the public was growing accustomed to in *Vogue* and *Harper's Bazaar*.

Miss Severn snorted.

'One-eyed women indeed. Whoever drew that should be told

to go and learn his job. Where's beauty gone, I should like to know? It's an insult to my preparations if any woman thinks that's how she's going to look after using 'em.'

Miss Severn was soothed with difficulty. The artwork, though modern, should be less extreme. The fear of rivalry was skilfully exploited. Miss Campbell assured her that in her private opinion Severn Aids to Loveliness were the finest in the world (she said the same to the two other beauty specialists whose accounts were handled by Davidson's), but that in the modern competitive world, upstart rivals must be fought with their own weapons. She herself did not greatly care for modern art but it had to be admitted that it sold luxury goods. The two women were well matched, but Miss Campbell held the winning card. The sales of Severn Aids had been steadily going down till she called in Davidson's. The conference dragged its interminable length until Miss Severn, temporarily defeated, signed an armistice and retired. She managed to knock twenty guineas off the bill for art charges and flushed with victory, conceded another £1000 to be spent on space. The word 'ravishing' was deleted: the artist was told to supply the lady with another eye. All this took up two and a half hours. Miles Mayhew occasionally interposed a modest and sensible remark: while appearing to agree eagerly with everything Miss Severn said he now and then maneouvred her into taking the line Davidson's wanted her to take. Once he caught Julian's eye in triumph and she had to smile. But apart from this there was nothing to lighten her boredom as she watched the hands of the clock move slowly round: her thoughts kept straying back to her story. What utter waste of time it all was. In another fortnight Miss Severn would be back again and the whole performance would be gone through again with exactly the same results until she either submitted to Davidson's methods or took her account to another agent.

As everyone stood up with suppressed sighs of relief to greet Miss Severn's departure, she suddenly turned and patted Mayhew's shoulder with a fat white hand.

'I haven't seen this young man before,' she said to Christian Campbell. 'Is he taking over Mr Grayson's work?'

'Not taking over. Maybe he'll be assisting,' said Miss Campbell with her thin smile. 'Mr Grayson is one of our most experienced executives: that's why we've allocated him to the Severn account. Mr Mayhew is a very junior member of the firm. He only left the University very recently.'

'University, eh?' said Miss Severn. 'That's a new departure isn't it? Oxford or Cambridge, my boy?'

'Oxford.'

Miss Severn beamed, 'My boy went to Oxford. Tell me . . . did you know my son . . . his name's not Severn of course . . . Laurence Dale he is?'

'Certainly I did,' said Mayhew. 'Big, handsome fair man. Rowed for New College in my first year. Quite a famous character.'

Sally Severn was radiant.

'There, you see! Miss Campbell, why don't you let this nice boy work for me? Mr Grayson and I don't see eye-to-eye about many things. I feel Severn needs a bit of *je ne sais quoi* that he hasn't got. I don't want to hurt anyone's feelings but, well, Oxford's Oxford and you can't deny it.'

'I'm afraid that would need a great deal of discussion, Miss Severn. It would be a verra big responsibility. In any case I should have to consult Mr Davidson. Mr Mayhew has a great deal . . . a great deal to learn.'

'Well he's at the age when one *can* learn. And he appears to have some sense, not to mention some manners. Mr Grayson looks at me sometimes as if he thought I'd escaped from Colney Hatch. I'm sure he doesn't bother even to listen to what I say and I've run this business single-handed for twenty years.'

'I'm sure we're only too anxious to meet your wishes. But you must realise that I have no authority in this matter.'

And with this stupendous lie, Miss Campbell finally steered the beauty specialist out. As the door closed, someone gave a low whistle and said:

'You're for it, Mayhew. I wish you joy of the old bitch.'

4.

Things continued to be so peaceful that week at *The Single Eye* that Julian was able to spend several hours typing out her story on the office typewriter. She had merely meant to make a legible draft to work on. To her surprise she found few obvious changes to make. This was so unlike her usual method of writing anything serious that she was even more suspicious than surprised. Usually she worked slowly, with pauses of weeks and even months; sometimes spending hours over one paragraph, incessantly revising and altering. Very often she tore up the whole thing half way and it was a long time before she recovered her nerve to start again: often she would put away the thing that had begun well and unaccountably taken a wrong turning and not look at it again for years. Occasionally, clearing out a drawer, she would come across an abandoned piece that she had entirely forgotten and read it, fascinated. Sometimes she would find a sentence or two that struck her as so good she could hardly believe she had written them. When this happened, she usually fell straight from pleasure to despair, telling herself how much she must have deteriorated since she was sure she could not write anything as good as that now. She also managed to torment herself when the reverse happened. When she found something absolutely flat or false, she had barely thought, 'At least I wouldn't let *that* pass now,' before the automatic reaction set in: 'Anyone who could put down and preserve anything as awful as that can never possibly hope to be a writer.'

Never, as far as she could remember, had anything come straight out like this. Certainly she had brooded on it for seven years; she had known that some day she would have to write it. She had only time to read the draft once through before Cashel came in with some proofs to be sent off. But from that first reading, though no doubt she was suffering from delusions and seeing words which weren't actually there, it struck her as surprisingly good.

On the way back to Chelsea in the tube she could not resist fishing out the typescript and reading it through once more, slowly and critically. Now she saw clearly that she had been suffering from delusions. She looked at all the solid 'real' men and women sitting behind their newspapers or swaying from straps. What would they make of this attempt to penetrate such an unreal world as the one she tried to suggest in her story? It had been real enough to her at the time she lived in it, far more real than this tube train. To have convinced them she should have used some burning power, words with the impact of poetry, a cold, nightmare touch that would have convinced them against their will that such things happen. And what had she made of this sharp experience, given to few and remembered by fewer still? Something unutterably scrappy, feeble and flat.

When she got home she was so disgusted with herself she could hardly manage to smile at Clive.

'What's up with you?' he asked amiably as she collapsed into a chair, too dispirited even to light the cigarette he offered her.

She told him.

'You're a foolish pussy, aren't you? You'd better let me read it. I'll tell you at once if it's all right or not. You know I'm infallible.'

At once she brightened.

'Will you really, Clive?' she said anxiously. 'I know you can't bear reading things in manuscript. But it *is* quite decently typed. It's either frightfully good or utter nonsense.'

'Being this particular thing, you're probably right for once. We always knew it fairly bristled with pitfalls.'

'I've got it here in my case.' She pulled it out. 'Will you read it now . . . at once? . . . I'll go upstairs and leave you to it.'

He shrank back in his chair.

'What . . . before dinner? Now, be reasonable, there's a good girl. You know perfectly well I can't do anything immediately, ever. I couldn't read the most immortal work before I've had my dinner.'

'Then I'll tear the beastly thing up,' she said frantically.

He snatched the pages out of her hand and sat on them.

'Now, now darling. Try to be reasonable. I promise to read it in the course of the evening. But *after* dinner. Be a good girl: powder your nose and give Augustus his fish while I finish my sherry and rehabilitate my locks.'

If it had been any other man but Clive she would have worked up a scene, accusing him of caring nothing about her work and therefore about herself and ending with bitter self-contempt. Once, within a few weeks of their marriage she had attempted the preliminaries of a scene with Clive. He had merely watched and listened with such an air of respectful interest that she had had to laugh and the scene had collapsed. They sometimes referred proudly to 'our celebrated scene' and Julian occasionally reconstructed it before their friends, impersonating herself with candid malice. There was no danger of a repetition of it tonight. She knew what a huge concession he was making in reading it at all that night: he suffered intensely when he was forced to do anything unexpected or at short notice. In gratitude – and also in fear that he might be simply unable to bring himself to keep his promise which would add still more to his load of guilt at not being like 'ordinary, decent, sensible people' – she did not mention the subject while they dined, did not fidget when she had finished her share of the *Evening Standard* and drew him on to prolong a dissertation on Shakespeare's theory of kingship which was uppermost in his mind at the moment.

At last they returned home and, still without mentioning her own preoccupation, she left him alone in the sitting-room.

Twice she crept downstairs to listen at the door to hear if he had settled down. Both times she could hear him moving about. The third time there was silence except for the creak of his chair. She counted out a quarter of an hour and crept down again. Still silence. Many more minutes passed and she became anxious. By now he must have had time to read it, though he read everything very slowly and carefully. She climbed dejectedly back to her room and waited again. By now she was convinced what had happened. He had read it and found it awful. Now he would be sitting smoking, wondering how best to break it to her. She could trust him not to lie but she would see the look on his face as he worked out a formula that would convince her that bad though this was he still believed in her. She was on the point of going down to him to put him out of his misery when she heard him call her.

He waited till she was in the room, then stood up from his chair still holding her manuscript and looked down at her, sighing, shaking his head slowly.

'Awful?' she said in a detached voice. 'Yes. I *did* realise that the second time I read it. I just wanted you to confirm it.'

'Awful?' he continued to shake his head and sigh. 'I suppose all writers are mad. Do you mean to say you don't really *know*?'

'Know what?'

'When you bring it off? Because this time, my dear, you most definitely *have*.'

'Clive, you don't mean it . . . you really think it's all right?'

'It's a great deal more than all right. Not a foot wrong. I tell you it nearly . . . no, quite, brought tears to these arid eyes. *Not* for your sufferings – just sheer pleasure in seeing you do the real right thing at last. My old pussy cat.'

He let her fling her arms round his neck but he would not listen to her excited questions about this and that point.

'Don't mess about with it. You'll spoil it.' He considered her almost with irritation. 'How is it you can do it and not *know*?' he groaned.

'I *did* think . . . at first . . .' she said timidly. 'Then I didn't.'

'Because *you'd* written it, of course.' He looked at her with loving contempt. 'I suppose it's because you're a woman. I admit it's all very rum. Rosedew Face Cream and so on. Now you've produced one small masterpiece you'd better go on and produce several more. I've always suspected it was merely a matter of habit. Why not a slightly longer one next time?'

'Cheese it, mate,' she said and kissed him. Then she stood away, asking earnestly, 'Seriously . . . no criticisms?'

'I've corrected one or two of your maddening typing errors. Also two places where I venture to suggest semi-colons instead of commas.'

'Oh, Clive, you can't imagine how excited I am.'

'Oh yes, I can.' He threw the manuscript at her. 'Now sit down like a sensible girl and read it again with a less jaundiced eye. You don't mind if I just finish my chapter before bed.'

She was too happy to mind. After all Clive was Clive and it was useless to expect him to go over it word by word, reading out a sentence sometimes, comparing troubles and triumphs as she had so often longed to do with another writer.

As he opened his book on Shakespeare's view of kingship, neatly marked with slips of paper for cross-reference, he shot her a look.

'Why don't you try it out on this new young man? If he's any sense of what's what, he'll treat you with proper respect after that. If he hasn't, he's not worth bothering about.'

'I've told you at least ten times that I'm not bothering about him.'

'So you've definitely refused to go to tea with him on Saturday?'

'I'm certainly not going. But I forgot to tell him so when I ran into him at the office. *That* shows how little I bother.'

'Quite,' said Clive, attending to his book.

She thought he was absorbed, but as he turned his first page he glanced at her again.

'It seems rather a pity. He would probably be tremendously excited. After all, he writes himself, you say. Also you've left it rather late to back out. This is Thursday.'

'Then I shall be very apologetic. But I'm definitely not going.'

'If you're afraid he'll get too uppish, there's no need to let him know you wrote the story after receiving his invitation.'

'You'll never finish your chapter at this rate.'

'Quite. I admit that, since you're not going, this discussion is jejune.'

'Totally jejune.'

He returned to his book and she to her own story. Now she read it with a kind of intoxication. It seemed remote from her and magical, like a discovery she would like to share with someone, someone to whom it would be a revelation, someone unlike Clive who knew everything and was incapable of surprise. The wonderful surprise that she had produced something good had been hers, not his. Once or twice, mentally reading it aloud, very quietly, with no dramatic emphasis, she looked across at Clive. He was impregnably absorbed in Shakespeare's theory of kingship. At that moment she knew that she was going to read that story to Miles Mayhew the day after tomorrow.

5.

'That's all,' said Julian in a flat, breathless voice. Miles Mayhew, in the opposite armchair, gave a deep sigh and said very softly:
'Yes.'
Looking not at her but into the fire, he said after a pause, still in that quiet voice, 'You don't expect me to say anything, do you?'
'No . . . perhaps not . . . I don't know.' Her voice was shaky. The effort of reading the story aloud had left her giddy and weak. She was trembling a little and in spite of the fire her hands and feet had gone cold.
He looked at her then with a face she had not seen before.
'You should know,' he said more loudly. 'About *that* you should know. You've said it all, haven't you?'
'I've left out lots. Then I wondered if I'd left out enough.' He interrupted the nervous, voluble explanations she was beginning.
'Don't *say* anything more. Read it again to me from beginning to end if you like, but don't *talk*.'
'All right,' she said uncertainly and was silent. This time it was she who looked into the fire, drawing jerkily on her cigarette and aware of his eyes on her. She no longer minded that he was staring at her: she had given herself away too much in the story to care at all about the body of which she was usually so nervously aware.
He said after a moment, 'It's rather frightening, you know.'
'Frightening?' She considered. 'Yes, I suppose so. It frightened me of course. But it doesn't any more now.'
'I don't mean the thing. I mean you're having written it.'
'Because one should keep quiet about such things?'
'I don't mean that at all,' he said almost roughly. 'You know perfectly well what I mean.'
'Do I?' She shook her head slowly. 'No. I think not. You might mean a lot of things.'
'I mean simply that it's right beyond – not just my range . . .

but . . . forgive me . . . anything I conceivably imagined as yours. You'd be perfectly entitled to die now if you wanted to.'

She looked at him suspiciously. Finding he was still wearing this different face, serious, alert and excited, and that she could see neither flattery nor impudence in his large shining eyes, Julian relaxed and even smiled.

'So you think it *has* come off? Clive did too.'

'Clive?'

'My husband.'

Mayhew frowned. 'Yes. I remember now; they said you were married.'

'I didn't read it *to* him, of course. If you knew Clive, you'd realise that was impossible. In fact, you're the first person I've ever read anything to.'

He looked pleased. 'Am I? Why?'

'Nobody ever asked me to before. Now it's your turn.'

'No. Not after that.'

'But that was in the contract.'

'I daresay. I didn't know you were going to produce . . . well . . . anything like that. Another day, perhaps. But not now.'

Seeing that he meant it, she did not press. But for the first time she felt curious about his own work.

He stood up, smiling.

'I'm not usually modest. Some time, if I ever get to know you better, I'd like to read you things. At the moment I'm sure a drink is what you need.'

As he moved about the room, opening cupboards, Julian leant back in her chair, at ease for the first time. She studied the room itself, wondering whether it was one of those that were going to become familiar. There was not much in it but each modest piece of furniture was carefully placed. It was singularly tidy for a young man's room and had the air of being always kept so and not hastily cleaned up for the occasion. The cupboards he was opening were as orderly as Clive's; the light oak table and sideboard looked as if they were polished every day; the daffodils in the lustre jug had evidently been planted one by one with care. The comfortable chairs by the fire were an ugly shape (she guessed they had come from his home) but he had had them covered in a pleasant material. There were only three pictures on the cream walls; photographs of a rugger team and a ship's figurehead and a summery landscape by a painter she did not know. The fire burned clearly on its swept hearth and when he drew the curtains, he did so gently and expertly, reminding her again of Clive.

'I like your room,' she said, sipping her sherry. 'Is it always as tidy as this?'

'I'm afraid so. I'm horribly tidy by nature. I've tried for the good of my soul to be deliberately untidy but it's hopeless. Everything persists in arranging itself with spinsterish neatness.'

'I'm exactly the opposite. I just naturally create chaos. It isn't that I like untidiness – I loathe it – I just can't control objects. I nearly drive my husband mad. He's naturally tidy, like you. Morbidly so, he says.'

'You're very tidy in your looks,' said Miles. 'I've noticed that at the office. You're one of the few women at the office whose stocking seams are always straight.'

'It's a daily struggle. It took me years to get that far. When I was young I was the worst groomed creature imaginable. And even now, on bad days, a devil gets into everything; hair, clothes . . . everything. Things just conspire against me. Half the times I'm late at Davidson's it's the conspiracy.'

He laughed. 'You talk as if you weren't young.'

'Because I'm not. Twenty-nine isn't young.'

'Twenty-nine,' he said thoughtfully. 'I've often tried to guess. Sometimes you look much less. And sometimes . . .'

'Much more. Yes, I know. It's always been like that since I was a child. Now and then in my teens I used to be taken for thirty.'

'I'm getting on twenty-four.'

'Exactly what you look.'

'You must find me a very dull dog. Nothing unexpected. No skeletons in my cupboards.'

'My cupboards are rather too full of skeletons,' said Julian. She sighed. 'Yet you know I wanted everything to be so simple and straightforward. I never wanted to be anything but respectable.'

'Aren't you respectable?'

'No.'

'You're lucky. You probably wouldn't be able to write so well if you were. That's what the matter with me. I'm too bloody respectable. My writing's bloody respectable too.'

'I'm sure that's a fallacy,' said Julian with conviction. 'If you'd met as many people as I have who think you can't be an artist unless you live in squalor and sleep around – or who think that living in squalor and sleeping around *makes* you an artist.'

'It suits you to be a little angry.'

'Beast,' said Julian with a smile.

'I said a *little* angry,' he said, smiling too.

'You're rather good at dealing with infuriated women. When I think what I let you get away with . . . a man six years younger than I am . . .'

He looked at her with his old polite impudence.

'How much, I wonder, if it came to the point? You're rather intimidating, you know.'

'Am I?' sighed Julian. 'People tell me that. I don't feel it. I know I have a horrible temper. But I'm sure I'm much more frightened of people than they are of me.'

'So you get in first.' He filled her glass and his own. 'To your story. That's the right kind of intimidation. The other kind . . . well . . . it doesn't become you.'

'People always begin by saying they're frightened of me. Then they promptly proceed to lecture me.'

'I warned you I always did the expected thing.'

They sat silent for a little, measuring each other up.

'Well . . . Julian?' he said smiling.

'Well?' she said thoughtfully. 'Yes . . . I think it is well. Better than could be expected.'

'From two people who took a violent dislike to each other at first sight?'

'*Did* you take a violent dislike to me at first sight?'

'You fell into that trap, didn't you? As a matter of fact I didn't. The first time I set eyes on you . . . I thought . . .'

Julian suppressed her curiosity and said nothing. He stared away from her into the fire with a brooding look that made him seem much older and went on in a quiet voice.

'I had a very strong impression. Perhaps it was nonsense. I'll know in time.'

'Will you tell me?'

He tightened his lips, still not looking at her. 'Some day, perhaps. But only if I was wrong.'

'Then it was bad?'

He shook his head.

'No. Bad is the wrong word. Incidentally it was nothing to do with one silly scene in your room. It was months ago . . . when I first came to Davidson's. You didn't see *me* and I hadn't the remotest idea who you were.' He turned his head to her again and said in a changed voice

'Anyway I know you a hundred years better since this afternoon.'

She said hesitantly, 'Because of the story? Yes . . . it's a give-away.'

'Certainly. But not in the way you're meaning me to think.'

'It happened.' Her voice was dry and defiant.

He said with extreme gentleness, 'So I supposed. That's not

LOW-DOWN

By Antonia White

What a Woman Does when She is Alone

She hopes he'll come. so she:—

Puts on something attractive.

Makes up carefully.

'Phones for drinks and cigarettes in case she misses him by going out for them.

Removes all traces of everyday occupations from her room.

Hides the books and magazines she thinks he'll laugh at.

Displays the ones she thinks will impress him.

Puts on his favourite records, and leaves the door open in case she doesn't hear him ring.

Looks in the glass every quarter of an hour in case her nose is shiny.

Plays the piano, if she's got one, carefully dodging the bits she's not quite sure of.

Flies to the door when the bell rings and finds herself saying "Darling, I never expected you" to the man selling tickets for the Orphanage fête.

Tries to settle down to the book he lent her, finds it hard going.

Looks at the clock; decides it's slow.

Rings up TIM and finds it isn't.

Wishes she could get on with that dress she's half cut out but daren't . . . it makes such a frightful litter.

Rings him up so that she can know definitely if he's coming.

Finds he's out. Decides it means he's on the way.

Thinks she'll ring up a friend for a chat.

Decides she won't in case he 'phones her and can't get through.

Tells herself she'll do twenty rows of her jumper and if he's not come by then she'll give up expecting him.

Does forty, rings him up again. Still no reply.

Thinks of all the possible places where he might be.

Is tempted to try some of them

410

Facsimile of the first page of a humorous article for *Lilliput*, written in 1945. Antonia produced several articles of this type at the time, some of them for *Punch* and the *Spectator*.

the point. It might happen to anyone. Only they wouldn't be able to make *that* out of it.'

Julian's eyes were a little wild. She said fiercely, 'Such things happen, yes. But not to the people one meets. And if they do, decent people keep quiet about them.'

He said, as fiercely as she, 'Decent people! Are you *ashamed* of being a writer?'

'A writer,' she groaned. 'God knows if I am. The thing was a present. I didn't even work at it.'

'How long ago did this happen to you?'

'Seven years.'

'You must have been working at it in your mind.'

'Oh yes. And of course I've made notes and hopeless beginnings and all that. But it came straight out the way you heard it. I've hardly changed a word.'

'Hasn't that ever happened before?'

'Never in my life. Or, if it has, it's been bad.'

'So as this obviously is anything but bad, you feel you've cheated?'

'Exactly. All the more because there's no imagination in it. It's nothing but a piece of reporting.'

'I don't agree. Some part of you imagined these things.'

'You could say the same about dreams.'

'Possibly. Yet don't you think the kind of dream a person has might depend on the quality of that person's imagination?'

'Ye-es. But –'

'Let me go on. Anyone might have a marvellous dream. But it takes something to perceive that the dream is marvellous and something more still to re-create the dream in a way that other people can share it. You *must* see that this isn't just reporting. If you'd kept a literal day-to-day diary of what . . . what happened to you, it would have been as boring as hell to anyone but a doctor. But in a few pages you've extracted the essence of the thing. It's all the difference between a poem and a clinical report.'

'You're very comforting.'

'It's absurd that you should need comfort. When and where are you going to publish this?'

'Publish? I don't know . . . I hadn't thought about that. I've only just done it. You and Clive are the only people who've seen it.'

'Clive? Oh, your husband. Well, doesn't he agree?'

'He likes it. That means a lot from Clive.'

'Is he a writer?'

'No. But he knows all about it. Almost too much. I mean, when a thing's done, he knows. But he doesn't want to know how it's done. He really hates seeing anything till it's printed.'

'What about *The Single Eye* man?'

'Cashel? He just says "Yes" or "No" about printing anything. He doesn't say why it's right or wrong.'

'Well, he'd presumably fall over himself to print this. And I'll buy *The Single Eye* the day it comes out.'

'Cashel? I don't think I could show it to Cashel. It's too personal.'

'Nonsense. It isn't personal any more. It's a work of art.'

She made a face. 'That awful word.'

'Yes. That bloody awful word. Artwork – Art Department – art charges.'

Julian suddenly laughed.

'Do you know where I finished this thing?'

'Where?'

'In my room at Davidson's. Waiting for the Sally Severn conference on Wednesday.'

He laughed too.

'They ought to put a plaque on the wall.'

'In *our* room?'

'I shall intrigue to use that room again as soon as possible. You might have left an aura or something.' He stared at her. 'Of all the queer places for you to work . . . Davidson's.'

Cashel thinks it's abominable. But I like keeping things separate. You can't deceive yourself when you're writing copy to sell face creams. Anyway you work in Davidson's yourself.'

'I've got to make a living.'

'So have I,' she said defensively.

'Hard luck. I thought perhaps . . . as you were married.'

'We can't manage on Clive's salary. At least . . . we couldn't do the things we like doing. I suppose we're extravagant.

'I should like to be extravagant. I've every intention of being so one day. But being north country, I'm not going to begin till I can afford to.'

'We can't afford to be as extravagant as we are. Yes, I admit it. Don't look so disapproving.'

'Actually I was looking admiring. I wish I could be rash instead of being so damned prudent. You've got a dreadfully suspicious nature, haven't you?'

'Or a dreadfully guilty conscience.'

'Have you got a conscience? I implore you, don't let it get the better of you. You see, I've really gone into the subject. My father is a parson and my mother does every known kind of good work. When we were children they used to assure us: "If you don't listen to that still small voice it will get fainter and fainter until one day you won't be able to hear it at all." I always though how wonderful it would be if one could reduce that voice to total silence. And ever since my first year at Oxford I've been working really hard on those lines.'

'How are you getting on?'

'Not too badly. I warn you, it's a long job. Often for a considerable period, I don't hear the horrid little thing at all. Then it suddenly pipes up quite loudly and I have to exercise the severest self-control to ignore it. In fact sometimes, on bad days when I've given in to the temptation of listening to it, I wonder whether my parents were right.'

'I don't suppose they ever tried the experiment.'

'Certainly not. They've hoed and watered and manured their consciences till they're as big as giant marrows and as sensitive as sea anemones. They can even detect a moral difference between milk chocolate and plain.'

'Milk chocolate being a shade more immoral?'

'Of course. But the odd thing is that now and then those hyper-sensitive consciences can swallow a camel that would choke my partly anaesthetised one.'

Julian noticed that his face changed as he talked of his family. It took on an absorbed, slightly clouded look. Though he seemed to be speaking lightly and freely, she felt the faintest possible chill in the atmosphere. Up to that moment she had been growing more and more conscious of the two of them as individuals, of the familiar excitement of discovering a new human being. Now, his attention was no longer focused entirely on her. It was as if, in the middle of an intimate conversation, people she did not know had come into the room. She asked:

'Do your family approve of your writing?'

'They approve of my having little stories printed in the *Manchester Guardian*. And they approve in the abstract of writers. They're not altogether happy about my being at Davidson's because they think it is wrong to induce people to spend money on luxuries. But they do like my having a regular job because it is a barrier against a dreadful menace called "just drifting". And they're terrified in case some day I might write something immoral.'

'Have you ever?'

'I wrote a long satirical piece at Oxford . . . don't worry . . . I shan't ever show it to *you*. But I made the fatal mistake of showing it to my father.'

'He was angry?'

'My father is never angry. He is something much worse. He is "inexpressibly pained".'

'Did that . . . have any effect on you? I mean did it make you stop writing for a time?'

He opened his large eyes still wider. 'Good heavens, no. It simply made me stop showing anything to my father unless I was quite sure he would approve of it.'

Julian said nothing. She frowned a little as she finished her sherry and lit a cigarette. He said after a moment, 'What's suddenly made you look so stern and remote? Have I been a bore, talking so much about my family?'

She shook her head. 'Not a bore at all. You reminded me of something about my own father.'

'I somehow can't imagine you with parents . . . not the kind that would worry you, anyway. Surely you keep them in their place.'

'I hardly ever see them. But I was thinking how terrified I used to be of my father. I was wondering if I still am. Because I don't feel it any more. He's so kind to me nowadays that I feel a hypocritical beast. Once the mere thought of his being angry or even disapproving would have frightened me into giving up anything . . . or *not* giving up something . . .'

'It's worse when they're kind, isn't it? Mine's never said a harsh word to me . . . or any of us. He ruled us with a rod of butter.'

'Mine was terribly kind when he wasn't violently angry. But *when* he was angry . . .'

'Do you know you've gone quite white? Are you remembering something special?'

'Yes. It was your talking about *your* father's being shocked at what you wrote. When I was fifteen . . .' Julian's throat suddenly and unexpectedly went dry.

'Yes?' he encouraged gently. 'Unless, of course, you'd rather not.'

'It's too silly. I can see now that it was extremely funny.'

'You don't look as if you saw anything of the kind.'

'It's simply that when I was fifteen, I began writing a novel. I meant it to be a present for him. I used to write little books of stories and things for his birthday sometimes. He used to like that.' Again her voice went dry.

'Please go on,' Miles said very softly.

'Well . . . I did a few chapters of this novel and I was so awfully pleased with myself . . . it looked so exactly like a *real* novel . . . that, though it was months before his birthday, I couldn't resist showing them to him.'

'And?'

'And he was so shocked that he put them straight in the fire,' said Julian in a high, flat voice.

Miles said nothing.

'You do admit it was funny?' she asked anxiously.

After a moment he said angrily, 'I think it's one of the most tragic things I ever heard.'

'Oh that's an exaggeration.'

'It isn't.' His voice was almost bullying. 'It's a beastly little story.'

'That's what he thinks . . . thought, I mean.'

'You've never got over it, have you?'

'I've never written another novel, if that's what you mean. Probably a very good thing. Far too many women write novels anyway.'

'Shut up, Julian. You're not talking. You're just screaming to distract my attention. And I'm not going to let you distract it.'

She looked at him as if she were going either to laugh or to be angry. Instead she threw her half-smoked cigarette at the fire, missed it, and said with false detachment, 'As a matter of fact, I'm exaggerating now. I must have started at least three novels since then. But luckily I always realised they were hopelessly bad and destroyed them.'

'Precisely,' he said with irony. 'Bad. Not badly written. But wrong. Wicked.'

Julian sat up.

'I wonder,' she said, 'I wonder if you've got hold of something. It's terribly interesting, what you say.'

'I should have thought it was obvious. You tell me you have awful qualms of guilt about everything you write. Then you tell me this. One doesn't have to be a psychoanalyst to spot some connection.'

'What amazes me is that Clive never spotted it. It's so exactly the sort of thing he does spot.'

'Not knowing him I can't say. Perhaps he needs analysing himself.'

'Of course he does. No one knows it better than he. He's a perfect compendium of all the case histories. But he says it would take away his greatest pleasure in life . . . studying the absurd and fascinating spectacle of himself in action. Or rather, in inaction.'

'What's your husband like? Does he do anything?'

'He's like no one I've ever met. As to doing anything . . . well, he's a civil servant.'

'Good Lord. A typical one?'

'I shouldn't think so. I hardly know any others.'

'Does he loathe it?'

'Not in the least. He says it's the only thing which stops him from flying into a thousand pieces. You see, he's never quite convinced that he really exists.'

'I'm not sure that I'm convinced either. I can't imagine you with a husband any more than I can with parents. Or children, for that matter.'

'Am I as unreal as all that?'

'No. Not unreal at all. And most certainly not disembodied. I just can't fit you in to any ordinary framework. At Davidson's you give a very convincing performance of a smart young woman in business. But it's obviously only a performance. And, forgive me, you don't look in the least like my idea of a woman writer. It's a compliment really,' he added hastily. 'You look as if you never thought about anything but clothes and you produce that story. I like to be able to pigeon-hole people.'

Julian sighed. 'If you only knew how desperately I want to be like other people. Ever since I was at school. I wanted to have exactly the same kind of home and parents as everybody else. I wanted to have brothers and sisters because everyone else had them. I was at a convent, you see. I wanted to be able to play games. I was miserable if my mother sent me a pair of shoes that wasn't exactly like all my friends' shoes. I'd go on beautifully for months, thinking I'd really brought it off this time. And then I'd go and do or say something that spoilt it all.'

He laughed. 'And I'm the exact opposite. I've suffered from being a Mayhew all my life. My family has lived in the same part of Cumberland for about a century. My father married a second cousin so I'm a Mayhew on both sides. They're all parsons or barristers or professors in provincial universities. They marry safe women they've known from childhood. There's a Mayhew face and a Mayhew voice and a Mayhew point of view. I was the fourth brother to go to the same school. However hard I try to be original, I instinctively react like a Mayhew to any situation. God, what wouldn't I give to have been born an orphan.'

'I believe you're extremely fond of your family.'

'Yes. That's the trouble. I can't get them out of my hair as you seem to have done. Tell me about yours. Were you ever fond of them?'

'I was awfully fond of my father. I still am.'

'Of course. Women always are. And you wouldn't have minded so much about what he did otherwise, would you? But your mother . . . what's she like?'

'Oh, she's crazy. I don't mean officially crazy. Don't think that had anything to do with her . . . what I read to you, I mean.'

'You don't like her, do you?'

'I don't either like her or dislike her. She just embarrasses me. She always has. But Clive thinks she's marvellous. He much prefers her to my father. I can't understand anyone doing that. It's just part of Clive's general perversity.'

'What sort of person is she? What does she look like?'

'She's extremely good-looking.'

'I can believe that.'

'Don't worry. I'm not in the least like her. At least, not in the only way I'd like to be. And yet we are alike, even physically. Strangers come up to me in the street and say, "Excuse me . . . aren't you Cynthea Tye's daughter?" My father says he can't tell our voices apart.'

'And that infuriates you even more,' he said with a smile.

'It certainly does. The maddening thing is that I wouldn't mind if my face was like hers. She's very pale, very dark with what they call "exquisitely chiselled features" and enormous soulful brown eyes . . . exactly the sort of looks I'd have liked to have.'

Ignoring Miles' steady gaze, Julian went on volubly:

'I can't bear brown eyes. No. When they're pressed to say where the likeness is, they say, "It's something in your expression," or, worse still, "You've got you dear mother's little ways." If there's one thing I can't stand about my dear mother, it's her "little ways". They admit we haven't got a feature in common except our hands.'

Antonia's wedding to R.G.W. in 1921 when she was twenty-two.

'Very lovely hands too,' said Miles, too loudly this time to be ignored.

'Oh, they're all right of their *kind*,' said Julian contemptuously. 'They just don't happen to be the kind I admire.'

Actually, though Julian was speaking the truth and longed for those thin long fingers that are supposed to be artistic, she had had so many compliments about her hands that she had come to be a little vain of them. Like a piece of furniture that is admired by one's friends, they had acquired a certain prestige in her own eyes, especially since Davidson's kept her in free manicures in order that they could be photographed sewing up haddocks or handling jars of face cream in advertisements. They were small and smooth and white with voluptuous palms and full, but tapering fingers.

'I like them,' said Miles. 'They look so beautifully useless. Like the hands of ladies in Victorian books of beauty. They might just manage to do a little tatting perhaps or offer a lump of sugar to a pet canary.' He leant forwards and took one of them. 'Let me look at it closer.'

Julian withdrew her hand though his manner was carefully ambiguous. He might have been making a faint advance or merely examining an object with impersonal curiosity.

'They have been used,' she said dispassionately 'to hit people quite hard.'

His answer was to take them both and hold them firmly.

'I think I could defend myself,' he said, looking into her eyes with some of his old polite impertinence.

Julian flushed with annoyance. She felt she had handled the situation clumsily.

'How shy you are,' he went on, without letting go her hands, 'in spite of looking so extremely sophisticated.'

She frowned. She had frankly not expected things to take this turn. In spite of considerable experience she realised that she was at this moment shy. There was nothing to do but leave her hands where they were, aware, to her own annoyance, that she liked the feeling of his warm, strong grip on them. Their minds for the last half hour had been running so easily together that it was a shock to her to know that their bodies too might have something to say to each other. In spite of herself, she felt her hands relaxing and yielding to his. She smiled aloofly and asked:

'Are you as conventional as all that?'

'What does that mean? That any young man left alone with you wants to make love to you?'

'Or feels he ought to,' she said bitterly.

'I don't feel I ought to. I feel I'd like to.'

'Why?' she said dispassionately.

'I don't quite know. I've had it in mind ever since you raged at me in your room.'

'Revenge?'

'It might have been then. Not now. Actually, I've been fighting the idea. And evidently you don't want me to.' He kissed her hands, laid them gently in her lap and returned to his chair.

Julian looked at him thoughtfully.

He asked, 'Are you annoyed?' She smiled. 'No. I'm too vain for that. Only . . .'

'This is so sudden?'

'Yes. It really didn't enter my head.'

'But people do make love to you, don't they?'

'They have, yes.'

'You don't mind my asking?'

She was perfectly detached now. 'Not in the least.'

'You are the strangest creature,' he said, looking at her. 'At one minute so violently personal and the next so violently impersonal. Now you look as if you could examine yourself like a purely abstract proposition.'

'I've caught that from Clive, I expect.'

'This Clive,' he said with a shade of annoyance, 'he keeps haunting us. Oh, I know you're married. Then why don't you *look* married? It's not fair.'

She said with false naïveté, 'Is there a married look?'

'You know perfectly well there is,' he said angrily. 'And the way you're looking at me now . . . that lost vague innocent expression . . . I swear that's one of your mother's.'

'Beast,' she said and laughed. 'Of course you're perfectly right. You're hideously observant.'

'Isn't it a writer's job to be?' he said complacently.

'Not all the time, I think. One has to go to sleep sometimes, surely?'

'Does one?' he said eagerly. 'Is that what's wrong with me?'

'How can I tell? I haven't seen a thing of yours.' She was relieved, yet faintly disappointed that they had changed their ground again.

'Yes . . . *you* slept,' he said frowning. 'And look at the dreams you had. I'm not a poet. I'm a reporter.'

'This conversation is entirely in the air,' said Julian, 'if you refuse to show me anything you've written. It isn't fair. You've made *me* give myself away. In fact, if you won't, I'm going.'

'No, no. You're staying and having supper with me. Didn't you know?'

'I thought I was asked to tea.'

'I didn't want to overdo it. I was afraid you mightn't come at all.'

'I must go soon, all the same.'

'Nonsense. Ring up your husband and say you've been unavoidably detained. I've been shopping all the morning. I couldn't possibly eat all that food alone. Please, Julian.'

She laughed. 'I thought you said you never did anything rash.'

'And you said I had a knack of getting my own way. It would be shocking manners to prove you were wrong. Besides I've been looking forward so much to showing off my cooking.'

'You're very clever at setting traps, aren't you?'

'Of course, I know I'm being awfully presumptuous,' he said, dropping his eyelashes. 'I'm sure that hat has got a much more interesting date for this evening.'

'As a matter of fact,' said Julian with a burst of frankness, 'it hasn't got a date at all. Clive is dining at his club. Of course I've got stockings to darn and letters to write . . . things I really *should* be doing.'

'Of course. That's settled then,' he said pleasantly. 'Will you prove it by taking off your hat? Just as a gesture.'

'Very well.' She put up her hands to it, then suddenly dropped them and said with dismay . . .

'Augustus . . . who's going to feed him?'

'Who on earth's Augustus?'

'Our cat. No, I can't – I'm sorry – I'll have to go home.'

'You don't mean to say you're thinking of leaving me for a *cat*?'

'You don't understand. He's not an ordinary cat. Clive would be furious.'

'Don't tell me you're the slave of some great petted Persian?'

Julian frowned. 'I wonder if I dare. I did leave him an extra big saucer at lunchtime.'

'Nothing better than fasting for them,' he said. 'If you studied the mortality figures of petted Persians as I do, you'd realise that 85.326 per cent die premature of over-eating.'

Julian laughed. 'Well, I'll risk it for once. But Augustus isn't a Persian. We only like common cats – common in looks, that is. And he's not petted. He wouldn't permit it.'

'I'm sure he's a horrible tyrant. I'm delighted I've deprived him of his supper.'

'It's entirely our own fault if he tyrannises. We like it. I suppose it's because Clive and I are both awfully selfish. We need to have someone to put ourselves out for.'

'Is that why rich old ladies let themselves be trampled on by Pekingese? Are you suggesting that unselfishness is one of those fierce natural instincts that get back on you if you suppress them? That is a most alarming thought.'

'Are you wondering if you ought to let the still small voice have its way more often?'

'I am indeed. Only in small ways of course. Do you think otherwise it might betray me into some heroic and undesirable act of self-sacrifice?'

MON PAYS C'EST LA MARTINIQUE

(Unpublished: 1922?)

This unpublished story is of special interest because it appears to be Antonia White's first work of fiction (apart from the two chapters of *Frost in May* which she wrote when she was sixteen).

The typescript bears no date but it was found among other papers dated 1922. It recounts a holiday love affair between Sabine, a young English girl, and a boy from Martinique. Sabine bears a resemblance to Antonia as she was in her early twenties, but the lover and the Provençal setting are almost certainly imagined.

Although the story is obviously the work of a young and somewhat romantic writer, it is well written. It is surprising that its author did not succeed in selling it to a magazine.

Patiently, over and over again, Sabine rang the iron bell of the Hotel Excelsior. There was no sound, no light in the windows, though it was barely midnight. The iron grill, the faded palm trees, the shutters on the moonlit wall might have guarded an empty house.

'It is no use, Mademoiselle,' said the man who had driven her over from Marseilles. 'They have all gone to the fête.'

He gave the bell one last furious tug and stooped over his car.

'Mademoiselle understands?' he said, as he started the engine. 'I must be getting back.'

Sabine was on the verge of begging him to take her with him when a light kindled behind one of the shutters. Presently, someone with a lantern, stepping very lightly and quickly, came along the terrace. It was a young man in white shirt and trousers.

'What do you want, Mademoiselle?' he asked with a brilliant smile.

'I wrote for a room a week ago,' she explained impatiently. 'Miss Loring.'

'Ah, yes,' he hissed gently. 'Tomorrow there will be a room. But tonight it is too late.'

Sabine protested.

'Very well,' he said, jerking his white shoulders, 'I will ask Madame. But no room is prepared.'

He arched his hand over his mouth and called softly in the direction of the lighted shutter: 'Aglaya.'

A woman's voice answered. There was a short dialogue in a language which sounded like Russian; then the young man said, with another of his dazzling smiles, 'You may come this way, Mademoiselle.'

Half an hour later, Sabine lay down in an unmade bed in a room lit only by the moon shining through the uncurtained window. She was too tired and too grateful to have found a bed of any kind to complain. She was already half asleep, lulled by the rustling sea and the ghostly music of the roundabouts at the fête, when her door opened, and someone, whose feet made a slithering noise on the tiled floor, came in. Sabine opened her eyes. Standing in the doorway was a woman in a long white nightgown. The woman was broad-hipped and handsome, with blue eyes and a skin the colour of deep yellow wax. Her hair hung in two long, untidy plaits over her shoulders, and there was a smile on her lips, a smile at once ancient and weary and unutterably beautiful. She did not speak, but stood smiling and poising her lantern, as if she drank up her own richness and beauty from its beam. After a long minute, she laid a finger on her mouth, and moved softly away on her bare feet. '*Dormez bien, mon enfant,*' she whispered and was gone.

Sabine woke quickly and completely and was out of bed almost as soon as she had opened her eyes. The sunlit tiles were warm to her feet and the very air had a new softness as it closed round her like water. But even before she went to the window for her first glimpse of the Mediterranean, she stooped at the looking-glass and peered anxiously into its green depths as if she expected to find herself changed during the night. But, no, it was the same Sabine. There was her thin haughty nose, there were her very dark blue eyes looking out from their arched lids and fine-spun lashes, there was her reddish hair, damp from sleep and parting on her too-high forehead. A face too bony, too sharply drawn for a girl of twenty-three. But Sabine had only to laugh, to turn her head this way and that for the harsh lines to melt, for her pearly skin with its even flush of rose to weave a veil of loveliness over cheek and neck and temple. 'Sabine,' she whispered to the girl in the glass, and 'Sabine' the other girl shaped with thin, smooth lips. But suddenly, as if the real Sabine hated the other girl, she stripped off her nightdress and hung it over the mirror.

She dressed quickly, in a dress of yellow silk, thrust her bare feet into sandals, and went out on to the terrace. The young man in the white shirt and trousers was lounging against the wall. At the sight of her, he gave his brilliant smile and she noticed the surprising evenness of his teeth. She watched him as he walked

into the house with his quick, light, deliberate step and thought
he was more like a cat than any human being she had ever seen.
All his muscles seemed elastic and padded like a cat's, even his
dark hair grew in a thick, short cap like fur. 'He is attractive,' she
admitted to herself, 'then why does he repel me so?'

But before she could decide, he was at her elbow again with
coffee and crescent-shaped rolls and a bowl of tiny green grapes.

Who was he? Obviously not a waiter. The proprietor
perhaps? But the Excelsior belonged to Madame Demidoff.
Madame's husband? No, he was too young . . . not more than
twenty-five at the most. In an open doorway she could see the
Russian woman, forty-years-old at least in the sunlight, all her
Demetrian beauty of the night before gone. She was just a big,
comely, slatternly creature in a crumpled grey cotton dress. But
even this morning Sabine had to look at her twice. The strange-
ness of her blue, black-lashed eyes in her honey-coloured face
was still rare and lovely. The young man in white was looking at
her too. Very slowly, the Russian woman turned on him,
narrowed her blue eyes, settled her hands on her wide hips, and
gave him that ancient, suffering, exquisite smile of hers. He said
something Sabine could not understand which made her laugh.
She disappeared indoors, and the young man followed hot on
her tracks like a small black and white cat after a large grey one.

'He is her lover,' thought Sabine, with a little thrill of distaste
that she couldn't understand. For why should she mind? If she
hadn't a lover herself yet it was just because she didn't want one.
No, it wasn't the idea of a lover that worried her. She liked the
idea, in the abstract. But whenever a young man presented
himself, she felt this very same little tremor of distaste. She
would like him well enough until he came too close, and then, as
if her eyes were distorting mirrors, he would appear ridiculous
and even horrible and she would shake her head and sigh and tell
him, no, no, it was quite impossible.

Pondering over this, she took a cigarette from a pale tortoiseshell case, and began to smoke very deliberately, almost
wearily as if she were too old to be in a hurry about anything ever
again. Below her in twos and threes, the bathers were beginning
to saunter up the white road to the sea. Ribbon-bound heads
bobbed, brown legs kicked up a powder of dust, bracelets slid
and glittered on bare arms as the groups of boys and girls swept
past, laughing and chattering like a flock of starlings. Last of all
came a boy of about twenty, walking by himself with his eyes
fixed on the toes of his canvas shoes. He wore a sailor's vest and a

pair of faded red canvas trousers. Sabine could see a crest of rough dark hair, oddly tipped with gilt as if someone had splashed it with a brushful of gold paint, and a foreshortened chin and a mouth, too small for a man's, and thin bright lips like her own. As the boy passed under the fading mimosa of the balcony, he stopped and looked up at Sabine. His face was only a foot or so below her. She met the intent look of two black-rimmed eyes, and smiled. The boy did not smile, but watched her with the same intentness while he pulled a dead dusty spray from the hedge. Then he dropped his lashes, lashes so thick that they made two solid little crescents on his cheeks, beat the dead twig of mimosa against his knee, then bowed and walked on. Sabine watched him till he disappeared by the cactus tree at the corner, but he did not look back.

Soon, with a big peasant hat tied across her shoulders and a striped cloak over her green bathing dress, she too was struggling up the steep, sun-bleached road to the sea. The *plage* was a tiny, semi-circular, almost shadeless beach, with an umbrella pine at one end, and a booth for mineral waters at the other. Every summer visitor seemed to be on the beach, splashing at the edge of the waveless sea or lying half-naked on the rocks, sunning himself or herself to a richer brown. Sabine was very conscious of the paleness of her own limbs among these sun worshippers, whose skins ranged from deep gold to a chocolate that was almost black. A young man, naked but for a bright blue loin cloth, with seal-wet hair bound in a sort of hair-net, was taking snapshots of a lovely creature, slim as a birch in her black woollen bathing dress. A little gold medal swung against her long brown neck. A rich lazy voice called '*Viens ici, Marie Esther, viens ici-i-i.*' And the lovely creature screamed back, '*Sois tranquille, ma belle.*'

Leaving her cloak on the warm stones, Sabine stepped into the water. Too lazy to swim, she lay floating like a green flag. Through her lashes shone the dazzling sky and the orange headland across the bay; a brown-sailed boat passed a hundred yards away and rocked her with its swell. She lay warm and happy, feeling the rich water clasping its hands under her chin. The shrill voices sounded fainter and fainter; she felt her body spreading, dissolving into the sun-shot Mediterranean that gloomed from turquoise to sapphire, from sapphire to indigo as she watched. She came out of her trance and waded to the clear green foamless edge. Turning over, with the sun on her back, she leaned on the thick water that held her up, and stared down through it at the pebbles on the bottom. There were stones like bird's eggs, dull green, slate blue, creamy or speckled, all exquisitely clean and rounded and smooth to touch. Suddenly a voice asked, 'Have you seen this one, Mademoiselle?' and the boy who had looked at her over the mimosa hedge was kneeling by Sabine in the sea. In his brown hand was a perfect little stone, oval, milky-white, and marbled with coral streaks.

'Oh, what a beauty,' breathed Sabine.

Together they trampled out of the water and lay side by side on the hot stones. The water peeled from their bodies in the bright heat as quickly as the drops dry on an eggshell. The visitors had flocked away to their *déjeuner*; the little *plage* was empty but for the two of them. Sabine, her chin on her bare knees, gazed at a castle of ashy-white rock, naked but for its dark bosses of pine trees. The boy lay with his head turned towards her, a cigarette in his thin bright lips, playing with her pale tortoiseshell case.

'I never thought you could be English,' he said, 'I did not think English women were ever beautiful.'

There was something sulky and defiant in his voice. She did not answer, and he looked away, proudly and mournfully, at the gilded headland. Sabine watched him lazily and drew the outline of his naked back on a stone, with a wet finger. His body was slender and small boned, like the body of a very young girl. There was no harshness in it, no broken line, no sudden angle. With his smooth, darkly golden limbs, and his black brows he looked like a Spaniard.

'Give me my case,' she said lazily. He turned the pale square of tortoiseshell in his dark fingers. There was a pencilling of hair between the knuckles, a thing she usually hated, but for some reason it did not repel her.

'It is like you, this blonde tortoiseshell,' he said. 'In my country the women wear combs of it in their hair. You would look well like that.'

Sabine put out her hand for the case. But instead of taking a cigarette, she jumped up abruptly and said, 'Let's go.'

'But you haven't told me your name.'

'Sabine.'

'And I am Yvon. Goodbye, Sabine.'

'Goodbye, Yvon.'

After lunch, when the sun had grown unbearably hot, and shutters were closing everywhere on white walls, Sabine went and lay down on her bed. The walls of her little room were

On holiday at Les Baux, an historic village overlooking the Val d'Enfer near Arles. Antonia and E.E.S. were living at Paulton's Square, Chelsea. She was head woman copywriter at Crawfords'.

painted green, the colour of a pistachio ice; it looked cool and bare as a nun's cell with its tiled floor and the crucifix on the wall. Outside, in spite of the noonday heat, some workmen were swinging their picks and calling to each other in a patois she could only half understand. Peering between the slats of shutters Sabine could make out three bodies stripped to the waist, with huge muscles shifting up and down under skins brown and glossy as leather. Every time a pick struck the ground, a chalky dust flew up and covered the backs with a white powder. One of the workmen stopped, leaned on the handle and looked up at Sabine's window. He must have seen her through the bars, for he smiled, threw back his head and began to sing something. He was short and swarthy as a sweep and his voice grated on the ear as harsh red Provençal wine grates on the tongue. Whatever he said seemed to amuse the other two, for they stopped work to laugh. Sabine, feeling suddenly shy and ashamed, tip-toed away from the window.

A wind, hardly more than a slow shifting of air, was softening the fierce edge of the heat when she went out again. Her body felt cool and light under the thin silk; a patch at the back of her neck burned and stung; her insteps were already beginning to turn a faint eggshell brown. Down on the quay of the tiny harbour she found Yvon.

'I have been waiting for you,' he said. 'I have a boat here. Will you come?'

In the boat were two sailors. One was old and wrinkled, with gold rings in his ears, and feet so gnarled and knotted that you could never believe they had ever been mere tender flesh. The other, a beautiful wild boy of sixteen, barefooted too, and amazingly dirty, lay on his belly in the bows and neither moved nor spoke.

Sabine and Yvon sat in the stern while the old man rowed and talked incessantly in the patois that seemed to bear no relation to French. Yvon talked to him, but Sabine gave up trying to understand and contented herself with watching the sea. Never had she imagined a sea like that, so dark, so nearly black that it shone like a lake of tar under a sky that still burnt a pale and perfect blue. Only by the rocks did the water pale to bright rusty patches or rims of frosty green.

They anchored on one of the narrow bays, a mere tongue of sea spanned by the shadow of enormous cliffs. When Sabine looked up she could see a tiny city with turrets and roofs and walls carved on the grey face of the cliff among the dark fur of the pines. But it was better still to stare over the side of the boat through water as clear as faintly-tinted glass at anemones and long spongy weeds trailing their garlands over the white floor. When Sabine put her hand in the sea that felt warm and a little sticky she disturbed a whole shoal of small transparent fish.

'Ah, beautiful,' said Yvon. '*C'est comme dans mon pays.*'

There was something in the way he said '*Mon pays*', drawing the words out, that made Sabine look at him kindly.

'Where is your country?' she asked.

And Yvon answered, in a voice deep and melancholy and nostalgic like a bell under the waves. '*Mon pays, c'est la Martinique.*'

Sabine said nothing, but she suddenly saw quite clearly a street of small square white houses, a palm tree, a flamingo and a negress with a yellow handkerchief.

'Martinique,' she mused. 'It's a lovely word.'

'If you could only see my Martinique,' he sighed.

The old fisherman had joined his son in the bows and was

sitting, silent at last, stuffing his short black pipe.

'Tell me about it,' said Sabine.

'There is one place I think of all the time.'

'Tell me.'

'It is a stream, a stream that runs through volcanic rocks. No matter how high the sun is, it is always in shadow, always cold as ice. It comes out of a cave. I used to bathe there every day when I was a boy. And there are reeds there . . . bamboos . . . as tall as a man – that never stop rustling all day long. There is no other sound at all.' His voice was dreamy and he looked darkly at the sea as if he had forgotten her.

'Are there earthquakes?' Sabine asked like a child.

'Yes. Only the other day my mother wrote to me that she looked out of the window and there was a fine powder all over the leaves, like sand or dust. That means a volcano may break out any day.'

'But isn't she afraid?' asked Sabine.

'Why should she be? There is a curse on my family. One may as well die by fire as by water. My sister was drowned. My elder brother was struck by lightning. He was a soldier in Africa. My mother cares for nothing now. Maurice was her favourite son. She would be glad to die.'

'But you . . . you must go back to Martinique?'

'Not yet. Perhaps never. I have no money, and, besides, next year I am due for my military service. What does it matter?'

'Where do you live?'

'In Paris, in a filthy little hotel in the rue de Clignancourt. Oh, yes . . . I am poor. You English do not understand that. I have my back bedroom on the fifth floor and my chessboard and my map of Martinique. What more can you expect at my age?'

'I wonder why you spoke to me,' said Sabine idly.

'Perhaps I wonder too. I had been thinking very hard as I walked and then I looked up and saw your face. It was like the answer to a question. Is that ridiculous?'

'I don't think so,' mused Sabine. 'But you're rather odd, all the same. When I meet new people I want to find out all about them . . . what they like . . . their pet words . . . oh, everything. And you haven't asked me a single question. I've been asking *you* all the time.'

He smiled and shook his head. 'What does it matter? You are as I see you. I don't want to know any more.'

He did not speak as they rowed back. Sabine sat quiet, too, trying to remember the exact tone of Yvon's voice as he said

'*Mon pays*'. For she said to herself, if she could remember that, she would have this hour perfect, enclosed in a crystal globe, to the end of her life.

She smiled and her beauty awoke and cast its pearly shadow over her face and neck. The boy watched her with bright, brooding eyes. The old fisherman saw it too, and grinned appreciatively at Yvon.

'*Je voudrais bien être marin,*' said Yvon suddenly to the sailor. '*C'est un beau métier.*'

And Sabine imagined herself in a pink-washed cottage on the coast of Brittany, hanging out a lantern night after night, and looking out to sea for a glimpse of Yvon's ship.

Yvon held her hand close for a minute as he pulled her up on to the quay.

'Have you been happy?' he asked, almost roughly, looking her straight in the eyes. His own were a bright hazel, with dark specks in them; in the sun they were very nearly golden.

'Happy?' she said vaguely, 'Oh, yes!'

She was still in her trance.

She met him again after sunset and they ate beautiful tasteless gold and silver fish in a workman's café down by the harbour. A film seemed to have been laid over Sabine's eyes, through which everything gleamed, swam, composed itself into exquisite shapes and colours. The dusty festoons on the awning were gilded with rich light, the same light that soaked through coppery skins and lingered in the bright syrups, green and garnet and purple, in the bottles behind the counter. In a doorway across the road squatted a monkey-like man playing a harsh concertina. Sailors and their black-dressed, bright-shawled girls swung to and fro across the little cobbled square under the stony approving eyes of Mistral, who gleamed tartly white from his pedestal under the plane trees. And each separate thing seemed to fill Sabine with a separate ecstasy . . . the sickle-shapes of the melon on their plates, the red fez of an African soldier against the darkening blue, the coins of phosphorescence that spangled the edge of the sea. She pressed her fingers to her temples, as if she could never hold so much beauty safe; she gave Yvon a lovely blind look which was not for him but for the summer night. Yvon mistook the look, and leaned across the table to catch her hand, talking low and quickly. But she did not want to be touched, to be made love to. If anyone touched her, all her burden of beauty would be spoilt.

'I must go,' she said and stood up. The harsh and haughty

lines were in her face again. The boy understood and did not
follow her. She paused at the corner of the path that led up to the
hotel and looked back at him. He was sitting very still, with his
chin in his hands, staring in her direction, but making no sign.

Sabine went straight to her room and undressed in the dark, as
if a light would break the spell. She lay, feeling not sleepy but
very wide awake, watching through the open window the broad
band of moonlight wavering over the sea. She had brought her
cup of beauty safely home; not a drop was spilled. An hour
passed. The last footsteps had lisped down the passage outside.
She turned to the window and saw a head outlined in the square.

'Yvon,' she said softly.

But he did not answer, only jumped lightly through the
window and came and knelt beside her and put his face against
her shoulder. She meant to be angry, but her calm was too deep
to be shaken. He did not move and presently her hand began to
stray through his hair that was harsh and springy yet somehow
pleasant to touch. Still he did not move, though a kind of
shudder went through him and he pressed his face deeper against
her neck.

A crack of light ran round the door; someone was outside.
Sabine checked an impulse to speak as the door slowly pushed
open. It was the Russian woman, lamp in hand and finger on lip.
Her deep beauty had come back with the night; her eyes were
black-pupilled and shadowy in her golden face. As she raised the
lamp, it shot a beam on to the white shoulder and the dark head
buried in its hollow. Slowly, as if it were the very crown and
secret of this southern night, her ancient, suffering, exquisite
smile dawned again.

'*Dormez bien, mes enfants,*' she whispered, and went out.

THE PAINTER'S WIFE

(Unpublished: 1931?)

This second unpublished story is also set in the Midi. It tells how Sylvia, the too-perfect painter's wife, is brought low by a difficult confinement.

The exact date of the story is uncertain, but the first line tells us that it could not have been written earlier than the early thirties. The account of pregnancy suggests that the author had experienced the condition herself, and as her second child, Lyndall, was born in 1931, this might be the date of the story.

'The Painter's Wife' has autobiographical elements, as did almost everything that Antonia wrote, Antonia was always fascinated by painters and their studios. Courbeille-les-Anges, the imaginary French fishing port of the story, was typical of the places she and Tom Hopkinson chose for their holidays, places that she admits were 'practically an annexe of Chelsea and Bloomsbury'.

The harrowing account of Sylvia's labour may well have been based on the death at this time of someone very close to Antonia, as the result of a backstreet abortion.

The author had gained a good eight years in worldly wisdom since she wrote the previous story, and had become familiar with the Chelsea scene of the twenties. Although the subject of the tale was something of a stereotype, her story was told with grace. Again, it is surprising that it did not get into print.

It was at Courbeille-les-Anges, in the late twenties, that we first met Sylvia and Simon Frant. At that time, when the coast of Provence was practically an annexe of Chelsea and Bloomsbury, Courbeille was only just beginning to be discovered. Cassis, Bandol, La Ciotât were full of familiar faces from the Fitzroy and the Café Royal but the only method of staying at Courbeille-les-Anges was to buy, rent or build yourself a house there.

John and I would not have been there ourselves had we not been invited by a friend, a retired actor, who had brought himself a small vineyard in the hills behind the port. After dinner on the first night, he suggested that we went down in his car to the fisherman's café on the quay.

'There won't be any other English people except possibly the Frants,' Max said.

'Who are the Frants?'

'Simon Frant and his new wife. He's a painter. Haven't you heard of him?'

'Not a *painter*. We know Cyril Frant the sculptor, of course.'

'Second cousin or something. Better not harp on him if those two turn up. Simon doesn't mind but it makes Sylvia rabid. She thinks Simon is far more important. "Significant" is her word.'

The café was hardly more than a bistro with a zinc bar and a few iron tables. Through the open door we could see the harbour with the boats riding at anchor and the dark blue sky hung with yellow stars that seemed so much brighter and nearer the earth than in England. Inside the bistro, lit only by oil lamps, the air was marbled with smoke: the other customers looked as if they had been models for Cézanne and Van Gogh: in one corner a sailor was playing a concertina. The whole interior was so 'authentic' that it had the air of a stage set. After we had been sitting there drinking bocks for half an hour, the Frants came in. To be exact, they did not come in; they made an entrance. They advanced slowly into the oblong of light flung from our door-way on to the quay; then they stopped, turned and stared at us like two inhabitants of another world trying to get their bearings in this. They were both striking to look at; the woman almost as tall as the man and silvery fair against his sunburnt darkness. Their clothes were as carefully harmonised as those of a pair in a ballet. Simon wore an open shirt of strong blue and fishermen's trousers of faded terra cotta canvas. Sylvia's tight-bodiced, full-skirted dress was a subtle grey-blue – a Picasso blue – with a lemon scarf draped with considerable art. For a moment they held their interlocked pose, the woman with her head thrown back against the man's shoulder, exposing her long slim neck. Then, loosening their entwined arms, they moved slowly towards us as if magnetised by the light, pacing with slow, perfectly matched steps in their espadrilles which were so like ballet-shoes.

'The picture of the year,' murmured John. 'Paolo and Francesca. School . . . New English Art Club.'

Max giggled.

'Or "The Second Honeymoon". They both had a try-out in the provinces with understudies so they've had time to polish up the show.'

I merely noted that, though at the time Augustus John smocks were almost a uniform for painters' wives and mistresses, Sylvia Frant's was the first I had seen with a properly darted bodice and evenly distributed gathers.

No sooner had the two entered the café than they came out of their lovers' trance and behaved like any Chelsea couple in the village pub. They greeted the drinkers with '*Soir*' and '*Ça va, hein?*' and a great many shrugs of Sylvia's thin shoulders. After a talk with the proprietor in which she did the talking for both the Frants and made a very small vocabulary go a long way, they drifted over to our table.

In the distance, her extreme slimness and her narrow face had suggested that she was hardly more than a child. Close to, I saw that she must be about thirty. There were dark channels under her blue eyes and the texture of her skin under the powder was dry and coarse. At first I thought I must have seen her before; then I realised that it was simply that she was the perfect type of modern art. Her high cheekbones, her long eyes and the grooves under them looked as if they had been carved; her head, her neck and her whole body were elongated almost to the point of distortion. I should hardly have been surprised if she had been as bald as a Modigliani sculpture but she had flaxen hair worn in a Trilby fringe with a chignon low on her neck. I was just deciding that anyone so self-consciously arranged must be extremely tiresome when the decorative mask broke into a frank, almost homely smile. She stretched out both hands, crying:

'*Tiens, Max! Quelle chance!*'

'Speak English if you can remember any, dear,' said Max. 'These are the Verralls. Marion . . . John.'

She nodded at us.

'Was I speaking French? I keep doing it without noticing. We've been here such ages. Simon darling, get three more *fines*.'

'Not for me,' I said.

'A *porto* then? But the *fine's* the safest. There's not much choice, I'm afraid.'

'I'd rather have another *bock*. A small one.'

'Are you off drink or something?'

Max explained. 'It's Marion's blessed baby. It's up at the villa. It seems to prefer beer to wine or spirits. Very British and bourgeois.'

Sylvia raised her well-drawn eyebrows. For a moment she looked genuinely puzzled. Then she said:

'You don't mean you feed the brat yourself? How marvellous and primitive of you. Have you got masses of them, like Dorelia?'

'Only one up to now.'

Simon came over with the drinks.

'How many infants did Milly have, darling?' Sylvia asked. 'Three? Or was it four?'

'Three,' he said gloomily. Unlike his wife, Simon looked younger at close quarters. He was remarkably handsome but he glowered as shy, good-looking adolescents do when anyone glances at them with interest.

'He spent all his youth in an aura of bibs and nappies,' she explained. 'But he's not like Augustus. He found it *far* from stimulating. Didn't you, *cher*?' She turned to John. 'What do you *do*? I'm sure I ought to know but we've been out of touch so long.'

'Architect,' said Max. 'You'd better be nice to him: he might let you decorate for him.'

'Perhaps it's not so bad for an *architect*,' said Sylvia. 'But for a painter like Simon . . . *absolutely* the wrong atmosphere. Imagine, they actually lived in *Putney*.'

'Of course I see now it was a ghastly little house,' said Simon. 'Funny I didn't notice it at the time. But that's the extraordinary thing about Sylvia. She keeps making me see things I never saw before. It's terrific.'

'Do I, darling? I've only made you see that the *mise-en-scène* of one's ordinary life is important. Everything one looks at or wears or handles. John Verrall, I'm sure you agree. As long as they build poky little houses in Putney and people *like* living in them . . . life will never be beautiful or significant or . . .'

'She dress-designs as well as interior-decorates,' put in Max.

'Ah, now I understand,' I said.

Her long eyes rested on me for the first time.

'Understand what?' Her voice was patronising but not unkindly.

'The way your frock's cut. And those two colours. They're wonderful together.'

Her face lit up.

'Ah! Then you're not completely swamped in domesticity. You notice things. Would it bore you to come and see our house one day when your infant gives you time off? It's *minute*, the merest Provençal cottage, but we've made it quite amusing.'

'Sylvia's got a terrific eye for colour,' said Simon. He spoke rather slowly and heavily and there was something in his voice which convinced me that, in spite of his perfect Chelsea exterior, he had not been brought up among intellectuals. 'She's taught me no end. I used to draw mostly in the old days. But now I'm painting like anything. Of course she's an ideal (it was almost, but not quite 'ideel') model.'

She laid her long pale hands over his brown one.

'I've turned out quite a practical investment, haven't I?' She laughed. It was a soft, controlled laugh but there was a note of uncertainty in it, almost of sadness.

During the rest of our stay at Courbeille I saw a good deal of Sylvia Frant. At first inclined to patronise John and myself as intruders in a place she looked on as her discovery, she thawed to our frank admiration of her little house. Enchanting in itself, she had 'done' it with extreme skill. There were old Provençal cupboards and *panetières* of silvery-brown wood; bedspreads and cushions made of the quilted Paisley-like material the peasant women still wore on feast days; crude pictures of ships in shells or beads, made by sailors. She had the knack of making the oddest things look right together; a Victorian pincushion and a Braque; a carved, ornate Spanish chest and a piece of mathematical modern sculpture called 'Quadratic in crystal'. When it was too hot to be out of doors, I used to spend hours in her room that seemed as cool as a dairy with its white walls and red-tiled floor. White muslin curtains tempered the heat and filtered the sunlight; Sylvia would wear a negligée of the same cloudy whiteness or one of her Augustus John dresses in some colour never obvious, but perfectly attuned to the colours of her background.

In the large room on the top floor which she had arranged as a studio for Simon, several portraits of herself hung on the walls or leant against them. There were also racks of sketches and studies of Sylvia or some part of her, drawn from innumerable angles.

'I'm excellent for his anatomy,' she said with her sad smile, showing me a charcoal drawing of her, stepping into a bath, 'but he needs a good blowsy Renoir type as well for his nudes, don't you agree? The local girls refuse to oblige as models. They just can't grasp the idea that it's only the mass and volume of the female shape that interests him.'

'They might grasp it better if he weren't so good-looking.'

'Perhaps. Some of them, naturally, would be only too willing to oblige him in other ways. Simon's so *naïf*, he doesn't even notice. If black eyes could kill, I'd have been stabbed in the back a dozen times.'

'You're never tempted to be jealous?'

'Tempted?' She frowned. 'I wouldn't *let* myself even if I were. Jealousy's inadmissible among civilised people. Don't you agree? It would be sheer self-deception to pretend I don't delight in Simon's physical beauty. But it's the artist I love. That's why I hold him and why Milly couldn't. I feel genuinely sorry for Milly.'

'I suppose she didn't marry again?'

'No, poor thing. Everyone advised her to. There was a bank manager hovering, only waiting for her to flutter an eyelash. The *perfect* solution. But Milly has the complete *Home Notes* mentality about marriage. I hate seeing people wretched. I'd do anything to help her. But, like all people with one track minds, she's fantastically vindictive. In Putney I'm just the Scarlet Woman who stole her husband and wrecked her home. *Totally* irrational.'

I risked asking: 'Was your first husband irrational too?'

'Oh no. Super-rational, my dear. He's as dessicated as Milly's mushy with sentiment. He promptly married a research statistician and lives in abstract bliss. I hear they're going to produce a little digit or cipher.'

'If Simon doesn't worry about Milly, why do you?'

'It's a question of design. I don't like ragged ends.'

'You're much more human than you like to admit.'

'I admit I'm not an utter bitch. She and I might have had quite a civilised relationship if she'd only be honest and face facts.'

'What facts?'

'That she and Simon *couldn't* have lasted. She'd have suffered ten times more if he'd stayed.'

'Is she attractive?'

'Quite. In a soft, cushiony kind of way. No *line* and she dresses quite disastrously. But she's probably rather charming without her clothes. Like a middle period Renoir before they got so *pathologically* pneumatic.'

'I should never have thought that Simon . . .' I began and stopped. After all, I knew practically nothing about Simon.

'They were *babies* when they married. He's a late developer. In fact, he's only just beginning to mature. I assure you it's not all been plain sailing. I've had to adjust myself and be patient. Stand back and wait for him to catch up . . .'

'With you?'

'No, no. With his own genius. With his *real* self.'

The lines on her strange young-old face deepened. I suddenly perceived that she loved him. Averting my eyes, I began to turn over some of Simon's drawings in the portfolio on my knee.

Two chalk sketches of babies' heads slipped out on to the floor. She made a grab at them and a dull red ran over the skin whose coarse pores showed even under the careful ivory cake.

'I didn't know he'd kept these.'

I said nothing and continued to look through the other drawings, making vague, admiring noises. When I looked at her again, she had recovered and was studying the sketches at arm's length.

'Technically they're interesting, aren't they? He was quite right to keep them. He burnt all the other drawings of his children as soon as he realised that too much unsublimated feeling had got into them. But these . . . yes, they're *decidedly* interesting. Look how he's suggested the plastic volume at the back of the head. And in this other, the recession of planes is stunning. Don't you agree?'

'Quite marvellous,' I said fervently.

I did not see Sylvia Frant again till a year later. I was walking down King's Road, Chelsea when I saw her approaching. She was wearing a grey-green cloak which added so much volume to the elongated slimness I remembered that, for a moment, I did not recognise her. When she came close her face too seemed different and not merely because she looked tired and the grooves under her eyes were deeper. Something in the eyes themselves no longer quite conformed to the modern sculpture design of her features.

It was Sylvia who spoke first, with a breathless catch in her voice that was oddly like relief.

'Marion! The one person I'd most like to run into. Come back and have a cup of tea, there's an angel.'

I hesitated, mainly from surprise. This note of urgency was new in Sylvia.

She caught my arm. 'No, you must. It won't take a minute. We're just round the corner.'

We went back to a great white studio. Simon was not there. While Sylvia, without even taking off her cloak, was hurriedly making tea on the stove in the corner, I looked about the place. Though the effect was quite unlike the little house at Courbeille, I recognised Sylvia's touch in everything. It was all that a studio should be: workmanlike, decoratively untidy, full of paintable objects, of which Sylvia, tall and pale in her lichen-coloured cloak was obviously the most paintable of all. However, I searched in vain for any portrait of her, old or new. On the easels and leaning against the walls were only abstract landscapes and geometrical patterns.

'How's Simon?' I asked.

'He's away at the moment,' she said rather hurriedly. 'His eye was out and he felt like looking at some scenery. So I packed him off to a country pub.'

When she had made the tea and put out two charming French coffee bowls to drink it from, she at last threw off her cloak. I saw then the reason for the change in her. She said with her sad smile:

'Surprised? *You* at least won't be shocked. Most of my friends are.'

I could only say: 'I'm delighted, naturally. And how wonderful you look.'

She did indeed look wonderful. She wore a medieval dress of fine wool that hung in Gothic folds from a high girdle.

She reverted to her Courbeille manner. 'It's a problem of design to be treated like any other. I believe in making a feature of being pregnant instead of being coy and treasure-cot about it. I adapted this dress from that Van Eyck. You know . . . Arnolfini's wife.'

'Magnificent. Simon ought to paint you like that. You knock spots off Mrs Arnolfini.'

She sank into a carved chair, remembering to manage her new weight gracefully but with a momentary sag that showed how glad she was to sit down.

'Didn't you find getting your balance one of the major problems?' she asked.

'Yes. When is it due?'

'About six weeks. Less, perhaps.'

'You're awfully strong-minded,' I said. 'I was such a coward, I hardly let John out of my sight the last weeks before Monica. I was terrified the baby would suddenly arrive and I'd be alone. I hope I'll be more reasonable this time.'

'You mean you've started *another*?'

'Yes, but only just.'

'Poor pet. But I was forgetting . . . you two are Roman Catholics, aren't you?' She frowned. 'All the same . . . I can't understand . . . *My* one fear is that I mightn't be alone. I certainly don't intend Simon to be there for the final horrors.'

'I'm a primitive female. We agreed that at Courbeille.'

'It isn't offensive in you. I suppose because you're *fundamentally* intelligent.'

I laughed. 'Not intellectual enough to suppose you'd ever want a child.'

Her face stiffened. 'Who said *want*? For myself, I mean. It was obvious that Simon needed some new experience . . . shock, if you like. Something's gone wrong with his painting. It's lost that marvellous plastic quality. Look at those new things. They're only two-dimensional.'

I agreed guardedly that something did seem to have gone wrong.

'He was developing so marvellously at Courbeille,' Sylvia went on. 'Then suddenly his painting got stuck. Naturally *he* got bored and restless. *Enfin* . . .' She shrugged her shoulders. '*Il lui fallait un déplacement.*'

'So you came back to Chelsea and even that didn't work?' I said innocently.

'No. I was *au bout.* Then one day it came to me. What he needed was a child. A child deliberately *willed.* A positive, creative experience. To show him it could be something beauti-ful . . . significant, like the work of art. Something *totally* unlike poor Milly's haphazard breeding, all mess and muddle.'

'I see. Don't *your* feelings come into this at all?'

'Oh, I'm finding it a *definitely* valuable experience. For one thing it's so amusing seeing how the atavistic instincts crop up and putting them firmly in their place. One's reactions are very odd sometimes, aren't they?'

'Very.'

'I suppose, once the physical upheaval's over, one *does* get it back? One's self, I mean. One's essential, undistorted, civilised self?'

Three weeks after that conversation I had a telephone call from a Nursing Home asking me to come and see Mrs Frant. It was after visiting hours but Mrs Frant was a 'bit nervy' and had asked to see me.

I found Sylvia huddled up against her pillows and almost unrecognisable. The pains had started so suddenly that she had had no time to collect her own clothes and they had put her into a white flannel hospital nightdress. Trickles of sweat had washed away most of her make up; patches of powder stood out on the darker natural tone of the skin, her fair hair poured in a lustreless tangle over her thin, flannel-clad shoulders and swollen body. All this I noticed later: at first I saw only her eyes, blue, expanded and staring with a wild brightness.

At first she could not speak: but lay with her knees drawn up, biting her pale lips. I took her hand and waited till the spasm passed. When I felt her fingers relax, I asked:

'They've got in touch with Simon of course?'

Her hand stiffened again. 'Simon,' she said savagely. 'Don't mention Simon's name to me.'

I waited. It came out in gasps between the sobs she choked back with a self-control more painful to watch than any hysteria.

'The doctor said it was starting. I didn't want to phone Simon in the country. He stood over me till I did. They said he was out. They said *Mrs* Frant was in,' she said with unspeakable bitterness. 'So I spoke to *Mrs* Frant. Who do you suppose *that* was?'

I said in a whisper –

'Milly?'

'Yes. Poor dear, deserted Milly.' She gave a terrible giggle which turned into a moan. A nurse appeared round the door and beckoned me away. I asked if I could stay the night and they made me up a bed on the floor of the waiting-room. I did not sleep. At intervals a nurse came in to tell me how things were going.

About four in the morning a sister came yawning behind fingers roughened with disinfectant. Your friend's having a bad time I'm afraid,' she said. Doctor and Matron are with her now. These thin fashion-plates . . . they pay for it good and hard when it comes to having a baby.'

'Is she going to be all right?'

'We've never lost a mother yet and I hope we're not going to blot our copy-book tonight. Cheer up – I've seen Dr Sykes pull off far worse cases than this. As to the baby . . . well . . . I must warn you, dear . . . that your friend may be unlucky.'

'It's not dead?'

'It wasn't five minutes ago. If I'd been her I'd have wished it was. Will she take on if she loses it?'

'I don't know . . . She had a terrible shock before she came in.'

'Hubby trouble, eh?' She winked behind her glasses. 'I guessed as much. Cheerio – I'll pop in again as soon as there's any news.'

I had been lying down in my slip. Now I got up and put my shoes and dress on. It was a warm night but I shivered. I took off my shoes again so that I could walk about the small bare room without making a noise. After what seemed hours the red-faced sister came in again.

'Your friend's got pluck,' she said. 'Dr Sykes said it might be either or . . . You're married so you know what I mean. But she said she'd risk it. Not R.C. is she?'

'No,' I said. My teeth were chattering.

'They're funny that way. What I say is she's only got one life and there are more babies where that one came from. Here . . . what's come over *you*?' She pushed my head down between my knees. 'Steady on, now. We've got no beds to spare in the wards.'

I spent the rest of the night in the nurse's kitchen. I don't remember much except cups of hot tea and white aprons bustling in and out. I believe I talked quite a lot and even laughed. I heard a church bell ring and realised it was Sunday and wondered vaguely if I should be able to get to Mass. Then Sister came in. Nearly all the red had gone out of her face, leaving only a network of veins. But she was smiling.

'Cheer up, dear. We've pulled 'em both through. Dr Sykes deserves a medal. In all my days of midwifery I never saw nicer work. And your friend, she deserves a medal too. I said to her just now, "Wherever did a nice girl like you learn such language?"'

It was several hours before they let me see Sylvia. She was lying back, a strangely flattened shape under the bedclothes, her face the same greyish-white as the flannel nightdress. I stood in silence till she opened her eyes, shrunk again to their normal size but very bright under the haggard lids. She gave me a wry, triumphant smile and said in a croaking whisper:

'I've brought it off, Marion.'

'You're the world's wonder. Boy or girl?'

'Boy. Forgot to ask. Nurse so shocked. Didn't realise . . . only important thing . . .*get* . . . *my* . . . *baby*.' Her eyes closed after the effort of speaking.

'And now, my girl, get some sleep.'

As I tiptoed over to the door, I heard the hoarse whisper again. 'Marion!'

'Yes, darling?'

'Civ . . . civilised self . . . *Utter* . . . nonsense . . . Pure ration . . . rationalis . . . ation.'

PART TWO
EPHEMERA

A CHILD OF THE FIVE WOUNDS

(Published in The Old School*, edited by Graham Greene, Jonathan Cape, 1934)*

'A Child of the Five Wounds' gives us a unique opportunity to explore the creative process, for it provides the material about life in a convent from which *Frost in May* was woven. *Frost* is often described as an autobiographical novel, but of course there is no such thing. This piece provides facts about the convent that are nowhere to be found in the novel, just as the novel contains imaginative interpretations that are nowhere to be found in this piece.

   The anthology from which 'A Child of the Five Wounds' is taken is a collection of personal memories of schools published a year after *Frost in May*. It includes a piece about his old school by Graham Greene who also edited the book. He was an old friend of Antonia, and she admired his work. She even wrote a 5,000 word article in French comparing *The Power and the Glory* favourably with Huxley's *Time Must Have a Stop*.

1.

Soon after my book *Frost in May* had appeared, I received two letters from 'old children' of Lippington. One of the writers had left in 1883; the other in 1927; both were quite certain, from my description of the convent, that I must have been their contemporary. The fact that actually I left in 1914 is irrelevant; Lippington does not change. Reverend Mothers and Mistresses of Discipline may come and go, but their characters affect the school very little. The real ruler is an invisible one – the French saint who, in the early part of the nineteenth century, founded the Order of the Five Wounds and laid down, once and for all, its code of manners and morals.

2.

I went to Lippington when I was eight. My first few weeks were miserable as I expected them to be. I had to adapt myself to another new element besides that of a boarding-school – the difficult, rarefied element of the Catholic faith. For I was a very raw Catholic indeed. My father had been received into the Church only six months before, and, although I had learnt my catechism and made my first Confession, I had none of the Catholic manners and graces. I wore neither scapulars nor miraculous medals under my serge uniform; I could not boast of having been dedicated to Our Lady and dressed exclusively in blue and white for my first seven years; I had not even a patron saint. Worse than that, I made mistakes which, for years after, caused me to turn cold with shame when I remembered them. I often made the Sign of the Cross with the wrong hand, forgot to genuflect to the Blessed Sacrament or bow my head at the Holy Name, and even finished the Lord's Prayer with the Protestant tag of 'for Thine is the kingdom, the power and the glory' instead of stopping short, as Catholics do, at 'deliver us from evil'. In fact, I was far more of an outsider than any of the foreign children. Spanish, Austrian, French and Polish girls, who could not speak a word of English, found their level at once. They might be inarticulate but the very way their trunks were packed, with a crucifix folded in tissue paper among the dozen regulation calico nightgowns, was proof of 'a good Catholic home' in the background.

3.

Every day at Lippington was punctuated, at brief intervals, by bells and prayers. At half-past six the rising bell clanged through the corridors and was followed by the tinkle of the 'sonnette' of the nun in charge. Her voice declaimed 'Precious Blood of Our Lord Jesus Christ' and from behind the white curtains of our cubicles we answered sleepily 'wash away our sins'.

I soon learnt to leap from my warm, narrow bed at the first clamour, for there was a tradition that such an act might help to release a soul from purgatory. In winter, if we put our wash-basins outside our cubicles, we received a meagre allowance of tepid water, but it was considered more in the spirit of the order to wash in cold. Baths we had twice a week, but they were no ordinary baths. Before we stepped into them, although we bathed separately and behind locked doors, we had to envelop ourselves in huge calico cloaks which tied round our necks and hung in heavy folds to our feet. They protected us from the scandalising sight of our naked bodies but they made washing difficult. Personally I never attempted to soap more than my face and hands and was contented to lie in the hot water, with my cloak swelling round me like an inflated balloon, until the bell rang 'Out of your baths, children'.

Dressing was conducted behind closed curtains and on the same principles of modesty. We were taught to tie the sleeves of our nightgowns round our waists while we slipped on our vests so that, at no time, should we be entirely naked. A quarter of an hour after the rising bell, another tinkle warned us to emerge from our cubicles, in our flannel petticoats and dressing-gowns to brush our hair in public. Looking glasses were, of course, forbidden, but we were allowed to make signs (never to speak) to a neighbour to find out whether our partings were straight. Hair was obliged to be worn plaited and strained back so stiffly from our foreheads that it drew our eyes up at the corners, Chinese fashion. And, once a week, a Lay-Sister went over our heads with a fine tooth-comb and drenched them with a vile-smelling yellow wash. Once a month, rather surprisingly, a young man came to shampoo us. We looked forward to this, not because of the young man (all of us, except a few foreigners, had a proper contempt for the other sex), but because we got off preparation for an hour and were allowed, during the drying process, to loosen the high starched collars that scored red rings round our necks.

Early Mass was at 7.15 and breakfast, a French breakfast of bread and butter and coffee, at eight. Except during Lent we were allowed to talk at meals (the only time we *could* talk, apart from recreation), but if we made too much noise, as we usually did, another bell commanded silence. The food was not calculated to make us greedy, but every morsel of hated fat and vinegar-soaked cabbage had to be eaten on pain of the whole table being kept in from games.

After breakfast, we made our beds and proceeded, always in orderly files, to the big study room for morning preparation. During this hour a curious custom was observed. If a child wished to go to the lavatory, she handed an orange card marked 'study' to the mistress in charge. The nun, having collected perhaps sixty of these cards, distributed them as she chose and, until you had received back your card, you might not leave the room.

For the rest of the day, major and minor bells announced classes, meals, recreations and prayers. Each hour of study began with an invocation to the Holy Ghost and ended with a recommendation to Our Lady. Three times a day we recited the Angelus and, at half-past six, the whole school assembled for the Rosary and for prayers to the patron saints of hygiene, St Philomena and St Roch. After supper came a brief indoor recreation, then night prayers in the chapel and bed. We undressed with another ritual of bells and our last spoken words, like our first, were 'Wash away my sins'.

At first I used to curl up in bed for warmth as I did at home but I was cured of this evil habit by an old French nun.

'Suppose, my child,' she said gently, 'that you died in the night. Would that be a becoming posture in which to meet Our dear Lord?'

And she taught me to lie on my back 'like a Christian' with my feet thrust well down into the cold sheets and my hands crossed on my chest. She taught me, too, to imitate St Teresa by letting my last thoughts dwell on the Agony in the Garden, and to murmur the name of Jesus before I fell asleep.

4.

It is a great mistake to suppose that children in a school like Lippington are unhappy, or even that their spirits are crushed. Up to a point high spirits were encouraged and, during my first term I was often teased by the nuns for not showing sufficient 'natural healthy naughtiness'. One thing, however, was severely stamped out of us – any tendency towards a dangerous in-dependence of mind. Through years of training, the nuns had learnt to recognise the faintest signs of such an attitude, and it was severely repressed. They could detect it in the slightest thing – a straying curl, an inclination to 'answer back' and, most of all, in the faintest hint of speculation in matters of faith. The world was waiting for us outside with its Satan-set traps of heresy, free thought and easy morals, and the whole object of our education was to arm us against its snares. Mental pride and physical vanity were considered the most dangerous of all our temp-tations and our mistresses were always on the watch for their appearance. I do not agree that their sharp way of dealing with them was due to any sadistic impulse. Given the Catholic way of looking at things, there was no more personal cruelty in it than in the drawing of a poisoned tooth.

Nor, though we lived in perpetual consciousness of religion, were we often worried by the thought of hell-fire. During retreats there were certainly some harrowing sermons on eternal punishment but, after all, we knew very well how to avoid it. No one goes to hell who does not die in mortal sin and we were all firmly resolved never to commit such a thing. Indeed, in

The Sports Committee for 1913 poses for its picture at the Convent of the Sacred Heart, Roehampton. Antonia (front left) holds neither racquet, bat nor ball, which is not surprising as she excelled at one sport only, croquet.

A class photograph at St Paul's, 1914. Antonia (second from the right at the front) never took her day school as seriously as her convent and, much to her father's disappointment, she failed to win a place at Cambridge from it.

those days, a mortal sin would have presented itself not merely as an imprudence but as an actual difficulty. In my nightly 'examination of conscience', I could always discover two of the main ingredients in the day's faults, full knowledge and full consent, but never the third and most important one, grave matter.

In the Junior School, especially, we were encouraged to look on the bright side of Catholic theology. Our Lady, the saints and the angels were real people to us to whom we looked for sympathy and encouragement, whom we could even reverently tease. I soon learnt to pray to St Anthony when I lost my pencil or my hair-ribbon, to seek the aid of Our Lady of Good Success in the weekly examinations, to promise extra piano practice to St Cecilia if she got me into the choir.

Every night I confided the day's troubles to my guardian angel and smoothed a place for him on my pillow so that he could watch over me in comfort. I began to recognise all round me the signs of heaven on earth. The cross on the donkey's back was a reminder of the Entry into Jerusalem; the cock at the farm crowed '*Christus natus est*', the cows lowed '*Ubi . . . ubi?*' and the sheep bleated 'Be-e-ethlehem'.

Any genuine attempt at neatness or diligence brought its recompense – a sweet wrapped in paper, permission to read *Little Folks*, visit the bakery (where the beetles so often got baked into the bread), pick flowers for the altar or dress the statue of the Holy Child in His best tinsel robe and crown for a feast day. We were not bullied, but coaxed, into virtue. At intervals, if there had been a notable falling off in manners, silence or obedience, we would have a special 'practice' to strengthen us in it. We would be enrolled as Knights of Our Lady wearing silver shields inscribed with '*Noblesse Oblige*'; as medieval champions tracking down the dreadful dragon of disobedience; as English martyrs practising the heroic virtue of silence on the rack.

5.

Each term had its own special character. The autumn one began badly, after the long summer holidays, when we had got a little out of training and were inclined to be rebellious and homesick. But it warmed up as Christmas approached (we began to look forward to it about the first of October) and towards the end of it came one of the pleasantest feasts of the year, the Immaculate Conception. The 'old children' came back in full force for this and, with their worldly clothes and unrepressed chatter and shrill '*do* you remembers', they were an exciting element. All of us, at least all who did not intend to become nuns, looked forward to the day when we could sweep about the corridors in long skirts and spotted veils and sable muffs, and we could not understand their passion for dressing up in old uniforms whenever they had the chance. The stone passages were decorated for the 'eighth' with garlands of evergreen and Chinese lanterns, and the smell of laurel and burning candles for once overcame the typical Lippington smell of beeswax, tea-leaves and incense. At the close of the tea we filed two by two past the picture of Mater Admirabilis in the Lady Chapel, saying 'Oh, Mary, I give you the lily of my heart, be thou its guardian for ever'. The lilies symbolised our Purity, but I think we were all a little hazy as to what Purity really meant. We knew that it was very important but that it was not *convenable* to talk about it.

The Spring Term was always a wretched one, for it brought Lent and, for us, Lent was a depressing reality. We did not fast, of course, but we ate a greal deal of boiled cod which tasted no better for being eaten in silence. The nuns, we knew, not only fasted for the full six weeks, but endured all sorts of penances as well. What these were we could only guess; there were rumours of hair shirts and spiked belts. Once I saw a nun reach up to take a book from a high shelf; her sleeve fell back and I noticed small chains bound tightly round her arms. There was a gloomy, penitential air about all those weeks and many of us prayed quite frankly for an epidemic to break the monotony. Our prayers were usually answered.

But the summer months almost made up for Lent. The term was thickly strewn with major feasts and there were glorious holidays when we played hide-and-seek with the novices up and down the lime-shaded alleys, and when we were allowed to read thrilling secular books instead of the usual lives of the saints – such books as *Carrots*, *Jan of the Windmill* and, rather surprisingly, Fr Rolfe's *Stories Toto Told Me*. There would be chocolates and weak currant wine for dinner and the day would end up with some dazzling entertainment; fireworks by the lake, charades, performing dogs hired from Whiteleys, or, best of all, a ghost story told, in pitch darkness, by one of the nuns. Ghost stories were a great feature of Lippington and there were at least five born storytellers in the community. The fact that there was always a moral attached, such as that one must never miss Sunday Mass or become a Freemason, did not prevent them from being larded with good sound horrors. Huddling close together on the floor and even, under cover of the darkness, daring to disobey a strict rule by clutching a friend's hand, we listened breathlessly to tales of tortures, murders, skeleton hands and lost brides crumbling to dust in cellars. We enjoyed them immensely and thought them well worth an occasional nightmare.

6.

The Order, as I have said before, was founded by a saint. But she was a French saint and a woman of the world. The first object of the Five Wounds had been to provide a good education for the daughters of the French aristocracy. Certain formal graces still clung to our manners. Nuns in the higher positions had to be greeted, whenever we met them, with a deep curtsey. When we saw our parents in the parlour on Sundays and Thursdays we had to wear our lisle thread gloves. The parlour had once been a ballroom in the big, eighteenth-century house, and a certain faded elegance still clung to its parquet floor and stiff lace curtains. On entering it, we made no less than three curtseys – one to our own relatives, one to the other children's, and a third to the *surveillante* in charge.

At the back of our Mother Foundress' mind had been the idea that many of us would one day marry. She had great faith in the influence of good wives and mothers and a great sense of social dignity. Though personal vanity was sternly discouraged, neatness of hair and clothes and grace of movement were respected. I wonder in how many secular schools in 1914 deportment was still being taught as an art? We went further than that; we even had several backboards in the study-room, and anyone suspected of a round back had to recline on their slippery surface for half an hour a day.

Once a week we were visited by the deportment mistress, an elderly Frenchwoman with a brassy wig and the smallest black satin shod feet I have ever seen. Clapping her fat little hands together and crying 'Graces, Graces, to your places', or 'Alack, alack, what a deplorable back' she would shepherd us through the motions of the *grande révérence*, the minuet, entering and leaving a room, greeting a friend at a soirée, performing an introduction and gracefully ignoring an unwanted acquaintance.

We learnt a little dancing, mainly mazurkas and quadrilles,

but in response to the demands of some of the more worldly parents, Reverend Mother reluctantly allowed the elder ones to learn the *valse*. It was a rigid affair, that *valse*. We danced it, not in silk frocks, but in our clumsy serge uniforms and cotton gloves and thick black stockings, and, as in no circumstances were we allowed to encircle each other's waist, each girl held her partner stiffly at arm's length, as, a full yard apart, the couples gyrated slowly round the room.

The mazurkas were more fun. I can still see a fierce, blue-eyed girl from Warsaw, who was always declaring that she would wade through seas of blood to restore the freedom of Poland, stamping her heels and shaking her long fair plait, in a perfect fury of abandon to Chopin's music.

7.

Lippington was, officially, an English school. But the old French tradition was stronger than any new-fangled British notion about 'leaving girls on their honour'. True, the nuns talked about 'honour' but they were too wise to trust so frail a reed. We were kept under the most rigid *surveillance* and, even when we believed ourselves alone, a nun would appear from nowhere, in her noiseless list slippers, to make sure that we were not getting into mischief. On the assumption that 'when two are together, the devil makes a third' we never walked in pairs but always in trios. Outgoing and incoming letters were opened and censored; desks, pockets and workboxes were liable to inspection at any moment. When I took my weekly piano lesson with my old music master, it was always with an open door and in the presence of a *surveillante*.

We were not allowed to possess any book without permission. In my first term, my father gave me a Bible. But, although it was the orthodox Douay version, it was promptly banished to my trunk. The reason was simple. The nuns said, quite rightly, that the Bible contains many passages quite unsuitable for the eyes of any girl under eighteen and, to this day, I have never read the whole of the Old Testament. Even our school poetry books, chosen by the authorities themselves, had several pages cut out of them. I remember that Browning's 'Last Ride Together', Shelley's 'I Arise from Dreams of Thee', and the fourth canto of Dante's Inferno were among the suppressions. The National Song Book was another trap; it was not actually mutilated, but there were several apparently innocent songs, of which we were never allowed to sing more than the first verse. One day we were given 'The Little Red Lark' to read at sight but the mistress stopped us after a few bars.

'I am sorry, children,' she said, 'I had only looked at the music of this song, not the words. Will you please turn immediately to another page?'

And I remember a child in the Junior School (she came from a blameless Catholic home) who was given *The Water Babies* for a birthday present. It was burnt, but no shame attached to the recipient. Her parents had obviously forgotten that it was on the Index.

8.

Most people laugh at a Convent education. In my own experience it was at least as good as, if not better than, the one which I received later at 'the best type of English High School'. At Lippington it was hoped that none of us would ever fall into such dire necessity as to be forced to earn our living, so we competed for no public examinations. We were educated, purely and simply, for a civilised and leisured life. The curriculum may have been narrow, the outlook biased, but the teaching was admirable and there was no lesson at Lippington that I did not thoroughly enjoy. The excellent digests of other people's books which were later crammed into me at St Paul's and which enabled me to pass Cambridge Higher Local have left no impression whatever on my mind, but I have never forgotten anything I learnt at Lippington. Languages, music, and the history of painting were taught with far more intelligence and efficiency at the Five Wounds than at any ordinary secular school and we also learnt such old-fashioned, but useful accomplishments as reading aloud and writing tolerable letters. Literature, it is true, was taught with many reservations, but well enough to give us a genuine love of it and the elements of a respectable taste. In the matter of writing I owe a great deal to that education and I may as well admit it. I have not used my pen for purposes of which the Lippington authorities would approve but, were it not for them, I should probably never have used it at all.

9.

The Lippington system, in all but a few cases, produced its intended effect. We were expected to leave at eighteen or nineteen, with strong convictions and still stronger habits of mind, to marry young and hand on the Catholic tradition to a large family. I often wondered what would have happened to me if I had run the full course of the Five Wounds training. But, on my fourteenth birthday, a terrible disaster befell me. For some months before that I had been a puzzle to the nuns and to myself. Outwardly I had behaved quite well, even to the point of being awarded the coveted green ribbon for good conduct. But, deep inside me, a tough little core of rebelliousness was growing. I was hardly aware of it myself, but the nuns, with their infallible eyes, knew all about it and watched me with suspicion. The saints began to have less and less attraction for me, and the poets more and more. I soaked myself in Francis Thompson, wrote passionate essays, and, in the Christmas holidays read *Dorian Gray*, which lit in me an uncontrollable desire to write a novel. A convenient epidemic in the spring term gave me my chance. Isolated in the Retreat House I wrote three burning chapters. It was meant to have an extremely moral ending in which the heroine became a Carmelite and the hero a Jesuit, but I thought it would be more exciting if I made them all very bad at first. Accordingly, the hero (remembering *Dorian Gray*) wrapped himself in a yellow dressing-gown 'of some subtle Levantine silk, wrought with strange embroidery', and the heroine, who had lips 'like a scarlet geranium', kissed a total stranger on a balcony, 'to the wild, throbbing strains of a Hungarian band'.

Vanity was my downfall. I could not resist showing the three chapters to my best friend. Next day there was one of those sudden, secret inspections of desks and the manuscript disappeared. But nothing was said. For a week of torturing suspense I waited. It was Holy Week and never had the ceremonies seemed so interminable. The catastrophe did not come until Easter Sunday which coincided that year with my birthday. I was actually lighting the candles on my cake when I was summoned to the parlour, not the ordinary friendly parlour, but the gloomy Community one, with its dark serge hangings and forbidding portraits. The interview with my father was one which, after twenty years, I don't care to remember. I was given no chance to explain the magnificent conversions I had arranged for the later chapters; I was accused of perversity, corruption and indecency. And I was told that, though I was not officially expelled, I must leave the school at once.

After my parents had left and I still sat on, battered and weeping, the nun who had been responsible for my disgrace came and talked to me. She explained, quite kindly, that I needed a humiliation of this kind. The fact that I had written something silly and vulgar was almost irrelevant; the real fault lay in my essential vanity and stubbornness. As she put it, 'Our own wills can do nothing but harm unless they are humbly united to the will of God. And your will, my dear child, little by little, has been growing away from Him. Spiritual pride is the greatest of all sins and it must be rooted out, however much it hurts us. Your will had to be broken and re-set in God's own way.'

10.

I went on, not to another house of the Five Wounds, as the nuns had suggested, but to St Paul's Girls' School. After Lippington it was difficult to take any school very seriously. The gentle social pressure of 'good form' and 'loyalty' meant absolutely nothing to me; in a mild way I behaved outrageously. The relief of getting away from uniform was such that I never wore a 'gym tunic' unless compelled to and burst out into the brightest colours and the most unsuitable clothes. Although I was only fourteen, I felt far older than any of the prefects. I refused to play games, did very little work, patronised everybody and generally made a nuisance of myself. In spite of this, everyone treated me with the kindness English people show to lunatics, and I had a rather good time.

But, if I had no loyalty to my new school, my loyalty to the Church was more fervent than ever. I became more Catholic than the Pope; carved my desk with pious mottoes and festooned myself with scapulars. My history essays had a Catholic bias which would have shocked even Mr Belloc; I invariably wrote Protestant with a small 'p' and always spoke of 'Good Queen Mary' and 'Bloody Bess'. But, at heart, I felt *declassée* and an exile. I had forfeited the rights of a child of the Five Wounds. I went back at intervals to see the nuns, and watched other children, in dark blue uniforms, walking about under the plane trees and munching their *gouter* of bread and jam as they listened to the old stories about their Mother Foundress. But, though they received me very kindly, the situation was false and strained. It was a relief when the heavy door shut behind me and I was back again in the suburban lane, in the world to which I, an outsider from first to last, really belonged.

THE FIRST TIME I WENT ON TOUR

(Unpublished: 1934?)

This piece was probably written in the middle thirties, about the same time as *A Child of the Five Wounds*. Readers of *The Sugar House* will recognise much of it, particularly the character Trixie, whose name in fiction was Maidie. The fictional name of the play was *A Clerical Error*.

Antonia trained at the Academy of Dramatic Art (now RADA) and at the age of twenty-one, while engaged to R.G.W., landed a job with the touring company of *the Private Secretary*. After that, she only acted privately, in satirical sketches she wrote for her friends.

Antonia refers to two members of the company as Jews, one a homosexual and the other a rather over-vigorous heterosexual. Perhaps it should be pointed out that in the mid-thirties it was still acceptable to single out people as Jews. Needless to say many of Antonia's best friends, and almost all her father's private pupils, were Jewish.

Strictly speaking I had no business to go on tour at all. I had still two terms to run at the Academy of Dramatic Art (in those days it was not yet 'Royal') before I could consider myself a trained actress, instructed, if not proficient in elocution, miming, fencing, ballet dancing, voice production, make-up and the actual impersonation of characters in Shakespeare and Modern Drama.

But, having heard that a certain manager was looking for a girl to play the small part of Eva in *The Private Secretary* to replace another who had fallen ill, the temptation to apply for it was too violent to resist. I do not think I ever had any illusions about the part itself. Let me state once and for all that I am a singularly poor actress, feeble of voice and constrained of gesture. I doubt very much if Bernhardt, Duse or Mrs Siddons could have shaken the world to its foundations with Eva. But in those days I had ambitions, ambitions not to play any particular part, but simply to *be* an actress. I think what chiefly tempted me about Eva was that her lines, meagre as they were, would be spoken by me and me alone throughout all three acts.

If this does not seem to you dazzling bait, you have not been to a dramatic school. At the Academy, owing to the preponderance of male parts and the equal preponderance of female students, the heroines were always played piecemeal. A young man might strut through a whole play as Hamlet or Sidney Carton. But a young woman, fortunate enough to play Ophelia or Lucie Manette in Act I, by the end of the play would find herself degraded to Second Clown or Assistant Executioner, a proceeding very galling to all but true-born actresses and vastly confusing to one's relatives in the audience.

So, with my knees trembling under my best frock and my head whirling under my best hat, I went to interview my first manager. As I sat in the agent's office, waiting to be summoned through the dirty, glass-topped door into the fearful presence of Mr B., I could take no pleasure in the thought that one day my own photograph, dusty, curled at the edges and lavishly signed, might be impaled with a drawing-pin to that faded green baize board. Should I confess that I had no experience? Or should I bluff, as I had been advised to do, and refer brazenly to half a dozen imaginary engagements?

Fortunately the question never arose. Somehow, like Alice pushing through the looking-glass, I found myself on the other side of the door, and a neat, melancholy man with a large cigar, instead of asking me searching questions, was running a tape measure round my waist and hips. Still without speaking, the melancholy man removed my hat, the hat to which I had pinned so many hopes. I thought at first he was going to measure my head too, but he contented himself with pulling my hair, turning my face to the light and examining my teeth.

He then seated himself at a desk, wrote down some figures, compared them with other figures on a block in front of him, sighed deeply, and said, 'I *think* you could wear Miss Davidson's clothing.'

A long pause followed during which I remained standing and Mr B., swivelling round on his chair, pulled sadly at his cigar with an air of utter abstraction. At last, turning his back on me completely, he said, 'I'll give you a try-out. Three pounds a week and find your own shoes and stockings.'

Repressing an impulse to cry, 'Oh, *thank you*, Mr B . . . !' I managed a careless, 'That's settled then?'

I was tiptoeing towards the door when Mr B. suddenly swivelled round again and shouted, 'One minute, young lady. This is a flapper part, you know. Short skirts. Come here and let me look at your legs.'

From his pocket he produced three sixpences, and pulling up my frock, inserted one between my knees, one between my calves and one between my ankles. By this time I was shaking all over, but mercifully the sixpences held firm.

'They *seem* straight,' he said sceptically, lapsing once more

into deep sadness. After a few more minutes of smoking medi-
tation, it was obvious he could bear my presence no longer.
Savagely pressing his bell he cried, 'Rehearse King's Theatre
Monday ten sharp. Send your contract on to-night.'

Impelled by the sheer pressure of his hatred, I dashed for the
door. It was actually swinging to behind me when I heard his
voice, suave and melancholy once again, murmur, 'By the way,
what's your name?'

We assembled on the night train to York where we were to open
on Bank Holiday. After three weeks of rehearsal we had come to
know each other's faces, but for the next six months we were to
be indissolubly bound up in each other's lives. In London we had
been individuals; from the moment the train left King's Cross
we became a Company – an oddly assorted company too. There
was the elderly lead, aloof yet gracious, sitting in the third-class
compartment with the air of disguised royalty mingling with
the common people. He was, he told us, giving Mr B. his
services for the beggarly sum of eight pounds a week, a mere
fraction of his usual salary. But then, he confided, he was like
that. If a part amused him, he did not mind roughing it. In fact,
though five London managers were after him, he preferred the
provinces. As for money, it was nothing to him. He was like
that. The rest of us, who were not 'like that' and to whom eight
pounds a week seemed a fortune, looked impressed. All of us,
that is, except the old actor with the wide hairy nostrils and the
face which looked so naked without its greasepaint (there was
always a rim of number nine round his collar) who played 'Mr
Cattermole'. 'Mr Cattermole' was fond of taking us aside and
telling us how bravely the lead clung to his vanishing middle
age, how every night he annointed his scalp with bear's grease
and smeared white of egg on his wrinkles. 'Mark you, I'm not
saying anything against G.,' he would say in his fruity voice.
'He's a nice old chap: a *thoroughly* nice old chap. But you can't
fight against *anno domini*. B. said to me when poor old G. was
begging with tears in his eyes for the part, "G's a steady worker,
but he's getting a bit long in the tooth. What about it?" and I
said, "Give the old boy one more chance B." Now – if G. would
only have the guts to play character parts he might go on for
another ten years. Still it takes more than *guts* to play character, it
takes *talent*, my dear.' And he would inhale deeply, spreading his
hairy nostrils still wider, and throwing back his grizzled head.

Violet Delancey always nodded vehemently when 'Mr Cattermole' talked about the talent required for character parts. Vi, a voluptuous frizzy blonde of twenty-two, played the comic old housekeeper, and had, much to her annoyance, to hide her yellow bob under a grey wig and mar her smooth cheek with a web of pencilled wrinkles. She had applied for the more important of the two girl's parts and been refused on the grounds that she was too fat to make a convincing flapper. The very sight of Trixie Dawson, the successful applicant with the thirty-one-inch bust and the long slim legs, brought tears of rage to Violet's blue eyes.

Since, for economy's sake, we were to 'room' in twos, Mr Logan, the disillusioned manager with the hairy tweeds and the gnarled pipe, had originally suggested that Trixie and Violet should pair off together. 'Oh, *no*, if you *don't* mind, Mr Logan,' Trixie had answered sweetly, dropping her long lashes, 'I'm such a little thing. I shouldn't care to be rolled on in my sleep. I'd rather room with White if you *don't* mind.' Whereupon Vi, who had designs on Mr Logan as being the most promising, as well as the most useful male in the company, whispered audibly to the ASM, 'We all know whose room *someone* would like to share. But of course no *man* looks twice at those skinny little wurzits of women.' Aloud she said, 'Please yourself, I'm sure, Miss Dawson. I'm very particular too who I share with.' And, arching her big bosom, she smiled at Mr Logan, who promptly allotted her to the venerable Miss Potter.

Miss Potter, who played our chaperone on the stage and off, looked as if her only likely connection with the theatre might be selling tickets for charity performances. A seasoned, competent actress, she indulged in no stage gossip and no back-biting, and did her job as she might have done nursing, dressmaking or typewriting, simply in order to make a living. Only two things did Miss Potter really care for – gardening (though in her nomadic life she can rarely have owned so much as a window box) and the Catholic Church. She invariably wore a Liberty hat trimmed with raffia bluebells and an ebony crucifix on a black cord. On the long train journeys while the rest of us knitted jumpers or played nap, she would sit saying her rosary or marking a seedsman's catalogue.

The rest of the company consisted of two ambiguous young men in suede shoes who played the juvenile lead and the juvenile

Antonia aged sixteen. While at St Paul's she became keenly interested in dress and make-up. For this picture she brushed her newly shingled hair over her forehead and bound it with knicker elastic.

lead's best friend, an elderly young man whose face was permanently contorted in a spasm of fright (I remember neither his name, nor his part, but only a peculiar episode in which he figured in Edinburgh) and the Assistant Stage Manager, a young Jew who had an uncomfortable way of looking first at one's ankles and then running his eyes very slowly up one's body until at last they met one's own, and who wrote poetry in his spare time. I only remember one of his poems, which he thrust into my hand one wet Monday morning at Gainsborough station. It ran:

Dearest, you have my heart,
Dearest, why must we part?
I long thee to enfold
On a bed of gold.

Seeing my look of surprise, he hastily explained, 'There's nothing personal in it. I understand you're interested in literature, Miss White. I just want your opinion – from a *purely* literary point of view.'

The train journey through the stuffy August night was long and uncomfortable. I had not yet become hardened to hours of night travel, sitting, if one was lucky, in a smoke-hazed compartment; if one was unlucky, on one's suitcase in the corridor.

At six o'clock in the morning we arrived at York. My skin was taut and creeping with weariness, my powder caked with soot, my skirt rumpled and my hair like unravelled string. Moreover, it was raining. Never had the stage seemed less glamorous as I surveyed the pouched, relaxed faces; the unshaven chins; the filmed eyes of the actors. Violet's lipstick was smeared and her mascara streaked on her lids. Miss Potter's face showed yellow under the raffia bluebells. Only Trixie retained her porcelain neatness; her straight flaxen hair as smooth as if it had been painted on her head and her mouth mathematically outlined with modest pink. She looked as if you had only to wipe her with a damp sponge for her to 'come up' as immaculately rose and white as ever. Her travelling costume would have been frowned on by *Vogue* – a flax-blue suit of flimsy serge, a frilly blouse, a large black lace hat and patent shoes with conspicuous paste buckles – but in my eyes at the moment she was the very *nonpareil* of well-dressed women.

'Come along, White,' said Trixie briskly, while I was still marvelling at her. 'You and me are rooming together, so we'd better go and hunt for digs. I've got three good addresses from a boy who was with me in the 'Aunt'.

In my ignorance I had supposed that the management would have arranged about rooms for us in each town, and that all we had to do was to inhabit them and pay for them. I rashly told her so.

'God,' said Trixie, whose language sometimes fell rather oddly from her small, prim mouth, 'you do have some bloody odd ideas about life on tour. Still you're only a kid beginner. Lucky I don't have to depend on you for ads, or we'd be sleeping in the police station.'

Trixie was a seasoned old-timer of twenty, with two-and-a-half years' experience 'on the road' behind her. As we walked along the wet streets, tired, rain-sodden and hideously inconvenienced by our high heels and heavy suitcases, I suggested a taxi. Trixie was withering.

'Suppose you think you're a bloody millionairess on three quid a week? You wait till you've paid your room and your washing and tipped the call-boy and the dresser and the baggage man every Friday and you'll have a fat lot left over for taxis.'

I fell back into silence, only muttering when I stepped in a puddle and shifted my suitcase from one aching wrist to the other.

'All the same,' declared Trixie generously, two endless streets further on, 'I'm glad I'm rooming with you, White. You're mad, but you *are* a lady. And that bloody fat cow Delancey definitely is *not*. And you're a Catholic too. Funny all the women in the company are Catholics except her. Say what you like, religion *does* make a difference.'

The first landlady was full up. The second had decided that never again would she take in actresses.

'I'm fed up with your professionals,' she said, crossing her arms and eyeing us with great distaste, 'smoking in bed and wanting hot water all hours of the night for what purpose I don't know.'

But the third would take us in. My head was aching and I wanted sleep, nothing but sleep. Could I go to bed at once?'

'You'll 'ave to wait a bit, dear,' she said. 'The beds isn't made yet. The two young ladies in *Chu Chin Chow* Number Three only went off by the early train. Sit down and make yourselves at 'ome and Florrie'll get you a nice cup of tea.'

While we gratefully drank the strong, leaf-speckled Indian tea, I took in my surroundings. They were to become very familiar for, though we moved once and sometimes twice a week, digs varied very little. Always, except in Scotland, there were aspidistras, red serge tablecloths and photographs of sea-side towns in plush frames. The great excitement was whether there would be a yellow-keyed and tinny piano for Trixie's singing exercises and whether the landlady would give us butter or margarine.

'Not used to this sort of thing, are you, White?' said Trixie, assuming the aristocratic manner, the most genteel thing I ever hope to see. 'I'm sure you come from a nice home. So do I. My mother would be *horrified* if she saw the places we have to live in. We have some really beautiful furniture. Antique. And my mother always dusts it herself. She says you can't trust the maids, though we've got three and she need never lift a finger. She's very particular, my mother. I take after her in that. D'you know I simply couldn't *dream* of sending my stockings and handkerchiefs to the laundry? I think there's something *disgusting* in the idea of strangers handling anything so *intimate*. I *always* wash them myself. Perhaps I'm funny that way. But you're sort of sensitive. Not like that bitch Delancey. I feel you'd understand.'

I did not understand then, or ever, Trixie's peculiar refine-ments of conduct, but I nodded sleepily. At last the landlady appeared and showed us into a dingy bedroom. As an only child who had always slept by herself I was relieved to find there were two beds. The sheets looked suspiciously grey, the mattress sagged like a hammock, but it *was* a bed and I was free to sleep in it.

'Give us a knock at 12.30 and a spot of lunch at one, will you?' cried Trixie to the retreating landlady. 'We've a call for rehearsal at two.'

I dragged off my clothes, flung them in a heap on the floor and plunged into bed. But through my half-closed eyes I could see Trixie's pink mouth pursed in disapproval as she carefully folded each of her own garments, shook out her skirt and brushed her coat, before donning a virginal nightdress of white lawn.

'I didn't *think* you'd be so untidy, White,' she said reproach-fully. 'Still, I'll forgive you this once. You look bloody tired, poor kid. Got that fed-up, far-from-home feeling?'

'Mmm.'

'Ah, well, it'll all come out in the wash, as the monkey said. Nighty-night.' She was half in bed when she suddenly jumped out again and fell on her knees.

'Oh, damn!' she exclaimed, 'I forgot to say my night prayers. S'pose they count when you go to bed in the morning.'

Exhausted as I was, I opened my eyes to watch the spectacle of Trixie at prayer. In her long white nightgown, with her fair hair in a plait and her eyes closed in an expression of unspeakable innocence, she looked exactly like Little Eva. Uncomfortably I remembered that my own prayers were not said. But before I could make up my mind to imitate her, I was asleep.

I woke a little later with the feeling that at least five people were simultaneously running pins into me. As I sat up, more pins jabbed my shrinking flesh.

'Trixie,' I cried.

'What the *hell's* the matter with you?'

'Trixie, I'm being *bitten*.'

Trixie was out of bed in a moment, pulling back my sheets.

'If it's bugs,' she said practically, 'we'll move. If it's fleas, wet soap's the thing.'

We spent a quarter of an hour catching fleas with a cake of wet soap.

As the weeks went by I grew accustomed to all sorts of uncomfortable things. I grew acclimatised to a diet of sausages, strong tea and grilled herrings, to living 'in my suitcase', to having a perpetual smear of blue on my eyelids, to never feeling properly washed or dressed or groomed (Trixie was all these things, but I never could catch up with her), to sitting up all night in trains and playing nap at dawn in station waiting-rooms. At first I was interested in each new town we came to, would explore its streets and even the surrounding country, but soon, like Trixie and the rest, I would hardly bother to notice its name and remember only the address of that week's digs and the theatre we were playing in.

Ten people cannot be constantly in each other's company without a constant shifting of feuds and friendships. Firm alliances struck up in Macclesfield would dissolve acrimoniously in Nottingham; people who cut each other dead in Liverpool would be found rooming together in Aberdeen. One friendship remained constant; the partnership between the two ambiguous young men, Derek and Jimmy. Occasionally Jimmy would complain that Derek had been 'really rather beastly, dear,' or Derek would sulk because Jimmy had snatched the corner seat twice-running on night journeys, but on the whole they were a most peaceful pair. In their way, too, they were considerate. In a touring company you soon learn not to expect preferential treatment from the male members of the company. You may be the most ravishing or appealing woman in the world, but you will carry your own suitcase, fetch your own coffee from the buffet, and, if one of your fellow-actors has taken the last seat, ride from Aberdeen to Coventry in the corridor. But Derek and Jimmy, though they would not, of course, give up a corner to Trixie and myself, would hold seats for us against other claimants and, when they had quenched their own thirst, give us the dregs from their thermos flask. Sometimes the four of us would spend Sunday morning at their digs and while Jimmy played patience and Derek embroidered cushion-covers with sprays of almond blossom, Trixie (if it happened to be a piano week) would sing. She had a surprisingly good voice, high, sweet and true with a violin-like tone to it. When she was not singing indecent songs, she preferred 'classical' music. Sitting very upright, like a schoolgirl practising, before the head-mistress and breathing very conscientiously, she would sing in her pure, sad impersonal voice:

One fine day you'll notice
A ship – a ship arriving

occasionally breaking off to snap, 'For God's sake, turn over, White,' or 'Damn that bloody Wurzit of a chord'. We would all feel a little sentimental, and tears would come into Derek's bloodshot eyes. He was an odd creature, Derek, fond of telling dirty stories in a voice as cold and greasy as congealed bacon fat, but extremely sensitive. I found him once sitting in the wings after the show was over, still wearing the faded hunting pink get-up he assumed in the last act, with the tears running down his cheeks. He was weeping because his landlady's little boy had caught his finger in the mangle. Next day he spent half his salary on toys for the child.

Once, on a Sunday journey, I found myself marooned in a carriage with Jimmy. Jimmy was a stocky little Jew with a straight nose and yellow hair. Once you had heard the story of his life, how he had been born in the East End and worked in a hat factory, his conversation lapsed into a pale imitation of Derek's. So, after I had giggled politely at a few well-worn stories, I returned to my crochet and Jimmy to his laborious spelling out of 'Le Jardin des Supplices', borrowed from and annotated by Derek.

After about half an hour I became aware that Jimmy had closed his book and was looking at me wistfully.

Then, sighing and clearing his throat he said earnestly, 'Eva . . . I should like to ask you something.'

'Yes, Jimmy?' I said, pausing in the middle of a 'treble'.

'Well, it's something rather personal. I don't hardly like to ask you.'

My curiosity was now well aroused and I laid down my work.

'You've always,' said Jimmy, still eyeing me with the same hungry wistfulness, 'seemed to me different from other girls, Eva. More understanding, if you know what I mean.'

Feeling just a little apprehensive, I murmured, 'What is it you want to ask me, Jimmy?'

'I've always had an ambition, Eva. But I've been afraid to mention it to anyone in case they'd laugh.'

Feeling on safer ground and flattered, as anyone is, by a confidence, I said eagerly, '*Do* tell me, Jimmy.'

Jimmy clenched his little ringed hands and out it came with a rush.

'I've always been so envious of Derek. He's such a wonderfully cultured chap. And he's so artistic. Look at those marvellous cushion-covers he makes. Oh, I wish I could do something like that. Eva – I hate to bother you – but *could* you, would you teach me to *crochet*?'

But it was Trixie who made my first and only tour so memorable. I have never met anyone like Trixie, and I probably never shall again. I should have found it difficult to live with anyone, being bookish, moody, impractical and accustomed to being as untidy as I liked in a bedroom of my own. But to adjust myself to Trixie was a severe strain. I could neither rise to her heights of old-maidish refinement nor follow her in her moods of rollicking relaxation. We shocked each other profoundly, we quarrelled bitterly, we went for days without speaking beyond a withering, 'May I trouble you for the sugar, Miss White,' or 'I *believe* that's my number five, Miss Dawson,' yet we continued to share bed and board.

On her refined days, Trixie was a stern moralist. We would shake our heads together over the deplorable excesses of Violet Delancey who was now pursuing the stage manager so openly that, not content with tramping for miles after him in high-heeled shoes round the golf-course, she followed him home every night to his lodgings and had been found at two o'clock one morning by 'Mr Cattermole' weeping and cursing on

Logan's doorstep. Yet whenever we had a free Sunday, Trixie would disappear to spend the day and a considerable part of the night with 'an old friend of my mother's, dear', and arrive at the station, just in time to catch the train, in a large blue Bentley. I never saw the occupant of the Bentley, but occasionally Trixie would remark reverently, 'You ought to meet my friend, White. He's really well educated,' or flippantly, 'Pots of money, dear, and *does* he know how to spend it. Still, all is not gold that glitters, as the monkey said.' But when she returned about eleven one Sunday night and found me sitting over the gas ring with a highly respectable cousin who had driven over from Brighton, she refused to speak to me for twenty-four hours.

Feeling unjustly treated, I taxed her as we were dressing for the show.

'Why so surly, Trixie? We were only talking and reading.'

'It's the principle of the thing,' she said primly, pursing up her mouth as she dipped a hairpin in a heated spoon of eyeblack and applied a blob to each long lash of her right eye. 'Where's your *religion*, White? You know we ought to avoid the occasions of sin and to be alone with a man after dark *is* an occasion of sin.'

'Well, there wasn't any sin,' I retorted, 'unless reading Herrick over a gas fire is a sin.'

To my amazement, Trixie burst into tears. But practical to the last, she carefully held the lids of the made-up eye apart with her fingers so that the black should not smear.

'You and your bloody education,' she sobbed furiously. 'Thinking you can come it over everyone just because you went to some bloody rotten school and can read poetry.'

The next day she presented me with a shilling copy of John Oxenham's *Bees in Amber*.

Trixie was very devout. She went to early Mass and Communion every Sunday, even when it meant a three-mile walk before breakfast, and she wore a Miraculous Medal and three scapulars under her clothes. These last often caused her a good deal of trouble during her quick-change into evening dress in the second act. It was difficult to pin them out of sight, and she would curse them volubly, ending up with an apologetic, 'Sorry, God.'

One Sunday, in Edinburgh, Trixie surpassed herself in devotion. It was too far for 'my mother's friend' to come, even in the Bentley, and she had the day to herself. She went, not only to early Mass, but High Mass, Benediction and Vespers as well.

But, by supper time she felt ready for a little worldliness. We were in very superior digs that week, and the elderly young man with the terror-stricken face, whose part I have forgotten and whom I will call Lloyd, had a bedroom in the same house and shared our sitting-room.

On her way home from Benediction Trixie bought several bottles of Guinness. After supper she grew very merry, and dashing into our bedroom reappeared clad only in a pair of black silk stockings and a short pink chemise.

The elderly young man looked more terrified than ever, but he was not going to be driven out of his comfortable sitting-room.

'I feel like dancing,' announced Trixie gaily. 'I haven't practised for months. Wonder if I can still get up on my points.'

After one or two unsuccessful attempts, she balanced on the tips of her toes, a slender, charming figure. In spite of the pink chemise, her face was a study in angelic innocence.

'Wonder if I can remember a routine.' She skipped a few steps, then stopped. 'Damn,' she said sweetly. 'I'm as stiff as a poker. Can't get my leg up. Come here, Lloyd – hold my foot.'

Very gingerly, as if it had been a live shell, Lloyd took hold of the small black-stockinged foot.

'That's right. Now lift it up. No . . . higher. Hell, man, don't look so frightened. Haven't you ever seen a girl's leg before? Well, you're bloody well going to now.' She whipped her foot out of his hand and sent it flying up in a head-high kick. 'And again – *and* again,' she panted, '*now* you've got something to write home about.'

The sight of Lloyd's panic-stricken face sent her into peals of delighted giggles. Then she relented.

'Poor lamb,' she pouted. 'Was he shocked then. Did naughty Trixie commit a *faux pas*? Well, it'll all come out in the wash as the monkey said.'

Averting his eyes, the unhappy Lloyd collapsed in a chair. Trixie sat down at the piano and, regaining her most virginal expression, began to sing:

Hark, hark, my soul,
Angelic songs are swelling.

'You sing beautifully,' said the frightened man, 'but aren't you a little cold, Miss Dawson?'

'Trixie to you, and I'm not as cold as I look,' cried my

room-mate, taking a flying leap from the piano stool and landing on Lloyd's knee. 'I bet you don't know the difference between a man and a woman, Lloyd,' she said, winding her slim arms round his neck. 'Sweet thirty-five and never been kissed.' And she pressed her lips to his recoiling mouth.

After he had, with some difficulty, unwound her, Trixie rushed once more into her bedroom and returned with an empty Guinness bottle and a rosary. Flinging herself on the floor and waving the bottle in one hand and the rosary in the other, she proceeded to pour out alternate strings of 'Hail Mary's' and curses. The elderly young man, now pale and sweating with fear, dashed out of the room and I heard the key turn in his bedroom door. After much persuasion, I induced Trixie to come to bed. Once in the bedroom, she became completely sober, did the rest of her undressing in her usual methodical way, cleaned her teeth, plaited her hair and in her long schoolgirl nightgown, knelt down to say her prayers.

When she had finished, she opened her limpid blue eyes and looked at me reproachfully.

'You're a good sort, White,' she said, 'but I wish you'd take your religion more seriously. You ought to go to Communion more often.

After six months the tour came to an end. We had gradually declined from week-long runs in first-class towns to three nights in obscure ones. Not one of us, except the lead, was sorry when Mr B. wrote and said that, for the present, he had no further use for our services. We broke up one Sunday morning at Euston, with warm expressions of mutual affection and passionate promises to write. But I never set eyes on Trixie or any of them again.

THE MOST UNFORGETTABLE CHARACTERS I'VE MET

(Unpublished: 1948)

The Misses Jeffery were Antonia's great aunts on her father's side, being the sisters of his mother, Ada. Their cottage, Binesfield, stood back from the road on Bines Common, near Ashurst in Sussex. My sister and I also spent holidays at Binesfield but knew only Aunt Agnes, by then a frail old lady with her white hair piled on her head. She had become bedridden but was still cheerful. She liked us to sing *Jesus Bids us Shine* in bed before we went to sleep, as her bedroom was above ours.

The aunts figure both in the *Autobiography* and in *The Lost Traveller*. In the latter book they were renamed Leah and Sophie and lived at 'Paget's Fold'.

In the course of my life I have met examples of almost everything that makes human beings admirable to each other. I have known brilliant people, wise people, people of outstanding talent, even genius. I have known people who have devoted their whole lives to a cause or an ideal and could be reasonably called heroic or saintly. Yet the two people whose characters have most impressed me were a pair of country spinsters, my own great-aunts.

The Misses Jeffery, were they alive today, would be respectively 103 and 102. Both of them lived to be over eighty and died in the house where they were born, a centuries-old Sussex cottage which had once been a small farmhouse. Their ancestors, yeomen and village craftsmen, had bought the place in 1720 and slowly acquired here a field, there a labourer's cottage until the family owned a small, scattered property bringing in rent of something over one hundred pounds a year. The lion's share of this belonged to my Grandmother, the eldest. When she married she let her spinster sisters stay on rent free in the house with its half acre of garden. My great-aunts' joint unearned income could not have been more than forty pounds a year. They supplemented this by very meagre earnings of their own.

In her youth, Aunt Agnes, the elder had taught the children of the better-off farmers but the advent of the State School had put her out of business. In any case her lessons had more often been paid for in eggs and butter than in cash. Had she been educated and certificated (a good education was the only thing I have ever heard her mildly envy in others) she would have made a first-class schoolmistress. As it was she continued to teach in

Sunday School, for which of course she was paid nothing, till she was eighty-two. Aunt Clara's dressmaking was a little more profitable. She had such a knack of fitting the clumsiest figures that her reputation spread far beyond their own village and even when cheap readymades began to appear in the nearest country town, the older women remained loyal to Aunt Clara. Her buttonholes never frayed, her gathers never came adrift and her seams were so beautifully finished that I've heard farmers' wives say, 'You could wear one of Miss Jeffery's dresses inside out without shame.' Each of these dresses took her long hours of hard work, mainly at night for she shared the housework with Aunt Agnes and did all the gardening. Every stitch was done by hand: she had no faith in machines though my father had implored her to let him buy her one. I can see her now, sewing by the feeble light of an oil lamp, with the steel-rimmed spectacles she had bought from a travelling pedlar giving a false air of severity to a sweet plump face like an apple that has just begun to shrivel. But as her clients rarely afforded more than one dress a year and as she refused to charge more than four and six pence even for making the most elaborate, her earnings, though steady, must have been remarkably small.

My father was only too willing to help the 'little aunts' but it was almost impossible to make them accept money which they had not earned. Only by threatening never to go to the cottage at all, did he blackmail them into letting him pay them for our spending our summer holidays there. During our stay they provided us with such wonderful cakes and pies and roast chickens (all cooked in an oven the size of a biscuit tin over a tiny kerosene stove) that I doubt if they made a penny profit. Our only comfort was that, for two months every year, we could be sure that the aunts had really good meals.

Though in those days the pound went very much further than it does today, my great-aunts were poor, even by the standards of an old-fashioned village community. They considered themselves however as very comfortably off and even, compared to those who did not own a few cottages let at two and six a week, ladies of property with social responsibilities. I never heard either complain of any affliction of their own but other people's troubles aroused their immediate passionate sympathy. The sympathy was always practical. My plump, impetuous Aunt Clara would ask her thin, thoughtful elder sister whom she venerated as an oracle, 'Agnes, isn't there some little thing we could *do*?' Aunt Agnes's forehead would wrinkle under the soft flaxen silver hair while she examined the problem from every angle. But the 'little thing' was always done, whether it were letting a hard-luck tenant off a month's rent, confecting broth richer than they ever allowed themselves for a sick woman or even producing a silver coin from the tin box which contained their tiny provision for a 'rainy day'.

I think the greatest charm of my 'little aunts' was the way they turned the thrift so desperately necessary to them into a kind of fascinating game. Though it was almost impossible to make them accept money, they would receive with delight any object, however worn, old or apparently useless. After repeated enquiries, 'Are you quite sure you may not need it again some day?' and repeated assurances that one never would, they would pounce on it with the twittering excitement of nest-building birds. Nothing could have equalled their dazzling and sometimes comic ingenuity; they found a use for the humblest and most unpromising objects. Old cotton reels were painted and converted into blind-cord tassels; corrugated paper was cut into strips, varnished and stuck round the walls as a dado or made into frames for pictures cut from old Christmas annuals. Even corks were given gay crochet jackets and converted into decorative wasp-crushers. When we gave them boxes of chocolates at Christmas, the chocolates themselves (eaten at the rate of two a day) were only part of the pleasure. Each piece of tinfoil was smoothed out to be used later to adorn a mirror-frame or hair-tidy, the paper shavings were kept for packing flowers, the ribbon trimmed their hats or tied back their lace curtains while the box itself did duty for years.

My mother's and my own old clothes and hats were of course transformed by Aunt Clara into things which they considered suitable for their own wear. I doubt if they bought anything ready-made all their lives except their shoes, gloves and the black cotton stockings they wore in summer. Aunt Clara even made their stays on the pattern that had been popular in their girlhood; stiffly boned over the bosom and tight at the waist but allowing nature a certain revenging latitude in the parts intended to be hidden by the crinoline. Even frail Aunt Agnes presented a slightly bow-fronted line while Aunt Clara's figure was a perfect cottage loaf; a small sphere balanced on a larger one. Though their workaday clothes were old and much worn, the Misses Jeffery never relapsed into the dowdy sloppiness some much wealthier women who live in the country allow themselves nowadays. Not for them the wispy hair escaping from a wool scarf, the baggy jumper and skirt and muddy rubber boots. If a visitor arrived while they were baking or hanging out their washing or digging up their potatoes, they would whip off their alpaca aprons and wooden clogs and receive the caller in their tiny parlour, looking as neat as any ladies of leisure.

On Sundays they achieved a certain old-fashioned elegance. They wore their best home-made mantles and the hats Aunt Clara re-trimmed twice a year, not to impress their neighbours but as a mark of respect to the Lord. Church going was no convention to them but an act of love and worship. Rain or snow never deterred them from walking well over a mile of rough fields and muddy lanes, their mantles protected by ancient waterproof capes and their hats by huge cotton umbrellas. Occasionally illness would keep one or the other at home. If, some Sunday, neither of the Misses Jeffery had appeared at church, there would have been alarmed speculation in the village.

When I was very small, Aunt Agnes used to give me Scripture lessons on Sundays. There can be few people nowadays who know the Bible as well as she did. Ever since she had been confirmed at fifteen she had read a chapter every night in rotation and a series of vicars had learned to respect and even fear her astonishingly accurate memory. I fear my thoughts sometimes wandered during these lessons to trying to guess the origins of Aunt Agnes's Sunday blouse. My parents had warned me never to comment, however admiringly, on the transfigured remains of my mother's silk petticoats and velvet teagowns. But once I was so dazzled by a certain cream lace creation that I thoughtlessly exclaimed, 'What a pretty pattern. Just like those curtains we used to have in the drawing-room.' My Aunt Agnes said mildly, 'Shall we keep that as a little family secret, dear?' I know now that this was not because my great-aunts had any false shame about wearing other people's cast-off curtains but only in case their cherished independence might seem to reflect on my father. They knew how gladly he would have added to their income and they loved him for understanding that money, even expensive presents would have made them feel like poor relations and destroyed their pleasure in contriving.

Aunt Agnes was the brain of the partnership. She loved to read what the more frivolous Aunt Clara called 'old dry things'. Her mind was stored with neat snippets of information as miscellaneous and unrelated as the pieces in their patchwork quilts. She would have loved to travel though she had never been further from her home than Devonshire. There when she was twenty she had once spent three weeks which had remained her most glorious memory. But in her reading and imagination she had travelled far; she would come out with surprising information about the orchids of Borneo or the habits of headhunters. Whenever I went to a new town or country I always sent Aunt Agnes a picture postcard. After her death I found every one pasted into an album, many of them annotated in her large clear writing. Her small thin body retained its nervous energy till she was over eighty; it was indeed this energy which brought about the cruel crippling of her last three years. Dashing into the kitchen with a tray, she slipped on the flags still wet from her scrubbing and broke her thighbone. The bone was too brittle to mend and she was bedridden to her death. It was a comfort to her that Aunt Clara had died before the accident: 'Dear Clara would have fretted so and fancied I suffered much more than I do.' But she did suffer and the nurse-companion whom my father insisted on installing said she had never had a patient so gay and uncomplaining. Her mind remained energetic to the end but after Aunt Clara's death her slight severity relaxed and she seemed to take over some of her sister's more light-hearted nature. We gave her a radio which was an endless source of pleasure to her. She listened eagerly and critically to every-thing from serious talks to variety and once electrified me by telling me that what I was wearing 'though very becoming, I'm sure dear, is not quite what I understand to be the new vogue in Paris.' But when the hour for reading her Bible chapter came, the radio was turned off, even if it were in the middle of the most exciting play. My aunt's religion was part of the very fibre of her being. But she and Aunt Clara were rare examples of Christian charity, in thought and word as well as deed. But Aunt Clara was temperamentally a Martha and Aunt Agnes a Mary. There was a depth of fire and zeal in her which her restricted life never called out. Once, as she lay in bed during those last years, she spoke to me with unusual intimacy for she was delicately reserved about her deepest feelings. 'God has given me such a happy and easy life,' she said, 'I know I must not complain. But how dearly I should have loved to have been called to do *difficult* things in His service. How I should have liked to be a mission-ary, even a martyr if it had been His will.'

Aunt Agnes would never, I think, have wished to marry. But Aunt Clara was cut out by nature to be the sweetest of wives and mothers. In her youth she and a young farmer had had a great 'liking' for one another but both had been so shy that the decisive word had never been spoken and the farmer had let himself be married by an aggressive shrew. No one would ever have guessed that anything was lacking in her life; she adored and was adored by generations of other people's children. But on her deathbed, when she lay unconscious and delirious, her hands were busy snipping bits of paper with her old dressmaking scissors. At first we thought her mind was wandering to the days when she cut paper patterns. Then we saw that she was cutting out paper dolls. Looking at my mother, she said with a sudden return of her natural look and voice, 'My children. Aren't they pretty, my little children?'

UBI SUNT GAUDIA?

(New Statesman: 15 December 1952)

This sad little poem resulted from the desertion of Lyndall and myself. Lyndall had settled permanently in Italy and I had married. 'In Dulci Jubilo' was always her favourite carol and she liked us to sing it beside the Christmas crib.

In dulci jubilo . . .
Once in the candleglow
Two faces seraph-bright
Opened round mouths to sing
'*Ubi sunt gaudia*
If that they be not there?'

Wild solstice: all the caked snow of the year
Iron to summer, melted to that sound.
The winter heart awoke; the curtained eye
Couched of its cataract let in the light.

Christmas returns and other children cry
Alpha et O! pursing as sweet mouths round:
Shuttered and dark beneath the clotted snow
No star, no angel penetrates my night.

Though as *celesta*-clear
As any other year
The crystal bells may ring
In regis curia
Two mouths no longer sing
Ubi sunt gaudia.

Ubi sunt gaudia
If these two be not here?
Only I blindly know
Tu Alpha es et O.

PART THREE
AUTOBIOGRAPHY

AUTOBIOGRAPHY
(Unpublished)

The autobiography is the longest and the last of Antonia White's 'superb collection of beginnings'. She worked on it for the last fifteen years of her life. The paper of the early pages turned yellow while she was at work on the later ones, and in several places in the typescript 'sixty years ago' was amended to 'seventy years' ago.

Chapters two and three, describing the youth of Antonia's parents, were incomplete at the time of her death. My task was to select from a mass of often almost identical handwritten sheets and add linking passages which are indicated by square brackets. Sadly, in her last years, Antonia would sometimes revise a paragraph she had written ten years earlier. In many cases (such as the description of her father's terrier Socrates) the revised paragraph was of inferior quality and in these cases I have let the original stand.

It is ironical that it was a case of 'writers block' that brought the autobiography to an end, for it was intended as a 'blockbuster'. Antonia had been working ineffectually for years on *Clara IV* and had become so frustrated that her friends suggested she should write the story of her own life, starting at the beginning. The idea appealed to her, for in the last years of her life she wished chiefly to contemplate the first.

The method worked well at first. For fourteen chapters she described her home, her family and herself up to the age of four. But Eirene could not stay four forever. When Antonia attempted to describe her more worldly adventures as a five and six year-old, the magic fled and, approaching eighty, she laid down her pen for the last time.

1.

When my father, Cecil Botting, a Classics master at St Paul's School married Christine White on 18 April 1898, he had been engaged to her for over four years and in love with her for even longer. After their brief honeymoon in Paris, he brought her back, not to a new home but to the house in West Kensington where he had been living with his parents since his promotion, in 1896, from Colet Court, the preparatory school to St Paul's, to St Paul's itself. In order that he and his wife should have the house to themselves, he had installed his parents in a small flat not far away – in the case of my grandmother, much too near for my mother's comfort – but he had not been able to afford more than the minimum of redecoration and most of the furniture consisted of what my grandparents had left behind when they moved. That house, 22 Perham Road, was to be my parents' home for twenty-eight of the thirty-one years of their married life and they were not to leave it till my father retired from St Paul's in 1926, three years before his death.

I was born there on 31 March 1899, shortly before the first anniversary of their wedding. Much as my father had hoped for a boy, he was too relieved that my mother had been safely delivered after a long and agonising labour (because she had bronchitis at the time, the doctor had refused to give her chloroform) to mind too much that it was a girl. Moreover, once he had got over his initial disappointment, he decided that the ambitions he had cherished for a son might be equally fulfilled by a daughter. He did not believe that a woman's brain was *ipso facto* inferior to a man's. If a girl was intelligent, there was no reason why, if she were educated on the right lines, she should not become a good classical scholar, possibly even a female don, like his friend, Melian Stawell. He would begin educating her himself as soon as she was capable of learning anything and see to it that, from her earliest years, she was sound on the unity of Homer and fore-armed against the lamentable heresies of the pluralists.

My mother wanted me to be called Cynthia. My father pointed out that such a romantic name would sound absurd with such a prosaic surname as Botting. My mother urged that Botting might not always be my surname; in the normal course of things one expects a daughter to get married. My father argued that one could not count on this. Indeed, in view of his private ambitions for me, the odds were heavily against it. Who, in 1899, could envisage a married female don or even a married Classics mistress? However, as my mother had to admit, even if I was not fated to remain a spinster for life, I was unlikely to change my surname for some twenty more years, she agreed that something less glamorous than Cynthia might be a wiser choice with my present one. In the end I was given a name which at that time was universally spelt Irene but which my father insisted on being spelt, as in Greek, Eirene.

Had I fulfilled his hopes for me, I might have appreciated this classical spelling. As it was, it caused me considerable embarrassment, especially at school where all the Irenes who spelt their names normally regarded it as not merely unorthodox but 'frightfully affected' – one of the most withering accusations one schoolgirl could bring against another. I grew to dread having to dictate it letter by letter in front of the whole class to some new mistress and explaining it was spelt E-I-R-E-N-E. But, however laboriously I spelt it out, they more often than not transposed the two letters when they wrote it down and it appeared on my report, much to my father's fury, as IERENE.

However, my Christian name was a minor affliction compared to my surname which naturally inspired school wits to refer to me as 'Blotting Paper' or 'Bottom'. That fatal 'o' caused me much more embarrassment than the superfluous 'e' in my Christian name. Batting, Betting, Bitting or Butting were not

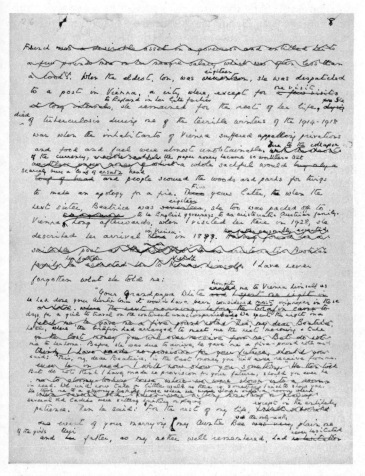

Facsimile page from chapter 3 of the *Autobiography* and an example of Antonia's writer's block. A barely legible page such as this might be all she would have to show for a morning's work.

attractive surnames but at least they were inoffensive and any one of them would have been preferable to Botting.

In addition to Eirene, I was given my paternal grandmother's name, Adeline. This must have been entirely my father's decision, for my mother not only disliked the name but disliked her mother-in-law even more. I disliked the name myself, but at least it was normally spelt and seldom had to be revealed. But I did not dislike my grandmother; on the contrary I found her most agreeable. She thought I was perfect in every way, 'the very image of your Daddy', her idolised only son. She refused to see any resemblance either in my looks or in my disposition to her son's wife whom she considered entirely unworthy of him, but was too frightened of his displeasure to criticise openly. I learnt very young that any grievance I had against my mother would be listened top with the utmost sympathy by my grandmother.

How often I was to hear – and not only from my grandmother – what an unsuitable wife she was for him. Nevertheless she was the wife he wanted and was determined to have almost from the moment he set eyes on her. He had been fascinated by her because she was unlike any woman he had ever met and every year of their engagement and marriage must have strengthened his conviction. Nothing about my mother, even her beauty, fitted into any conventional category. Up to a point, her behaviour was predictable, but it was governed by laws impenetrable not only to my father's logical mind but to everyone else's. Since to herself she appeared sublimely reasonable, she was genuinely aggrieved that anyone, especially anyone as intelligent as my father, could be so obtuse as not to perceive this. As both were equally self-willed and equally convinced they were in the right, arguments between my parents, though frequent and passionate, never succeeded in changing the other's opinion by one iota. If my mother gave in to my father on the surface, she had subterranean means of getting her own way. At least theirs never degenerated into a humdrum marriage. However many quarrels they had, they celebrated every anniversary of it like lovers.

In looks, as in so many other ways, they could hardly have been more different. My father was unusually fair, even for an Anglo-Saxon. He had golden hair, flax-blue eyes and an extraordinarily pink and white complexion which made people describe his broad, rather too plump face as cherubic. This was a superficial impression for his features were boldly and emphatically cast and though, when he was in a good temper, his face positively radiated geniality, when he was angry, it could set in a mould of implacable sternness. When he thrust out his heavy, obstinate jaw, compressed his lips under his golden waxed moustache and drew his brows down over eyes blazing with wrath like two blue electric sparks between their screwed-up lids his face was truly intimidating. However, few people besides his pupils and his family ever saw that aspect of it and normally his expression was kindly and humorous. He was stockily built and, though of average height, looked shorter than he was because of the size of his head and the breadth of his shoulders. Though he was not a vain man and was only too conscious that the best tailor could not give him an elegant figure, he was something of a dandy. He was meticulously careful to wear exactly the right clothes for the occasion and every outfit had to be accompanied by the right accessories down to the correct type of gloves and walking-stick. If he had had a valet, he could not have been more immaculately groomed. His trousers were always well-pressed, his tie perfect-ly knotted and his umbrella so impeccably rolled that it looked as if it had never been unfurled since he bought it. To this day I can never roll – or rather attempt to roll – an umbrella (for I justified his conviction that this was something no woman could do properly) without remembering the ritual process involved when my father rolled his. Each fold had to be shaken out, smoothed of creases, then lapped one over the other as neatly as fish scales before, taking a firm grip with his strong white hands, he worked them slowly upwards in a spiral movement, squeez-ing the folds together as ruthlessly as if he were wringing the umbrella's neck. Then, keeping a tight hold on the victim with one hand, he deftly slipped the elastic noose round it with the other and finally throttled it. If there was so much as a faint wrinkle in one of those folds, the whole process had to be repeated until perfect smoothness and symmetry were achieved. That irreproachably-rolled umbrella symbolised two outstand-ing traits in my father's character: his perfectionism which demanded that everything he did, from his work to giving a dinner-party, should be done as well as possible and his refusal to be frustrated by any obstacle which could be overcome by sheer force of will. As will be seen later, he had had to overcome a great many before he moulded himself, like his umbrella, into the shape he set out to achieve.

If my father could not have looked more typically English, my mother looked so exotic that she was often assumed to be partly foreign. In fact, both her parents had been English and, as far as I know, she had no foreign blood though there were rumours, unconfirmed, of a French ancestress and even of some remote descent from the Bourbons. She had huge brown eyes, a sallow, almost olive complexion and such an unusual face that it was hard to decide if she was an exotic beauty or an exotic *belle laide*. Her hair, which, as a child, had been a vivid corn-gold, had darkened to a dull light bronze without losing its childishly fine texture and her faint brown eyelashes were so fine as to be almost invisible which gave her eyes a naked, vulnerable look. They were peculiar eyes, with very large, clearly defined eyeballs in which the amber-brown irises were set so low and under such deep upper lids that, even when they were wide open, they still looked hooded. Set high above them were two symmetrical golden-brown eyebrows whose hairline stopped abruptly on a rising arc midway, leaving a bare space between her temples and the outer half of her eye-sockets. These unfinished eyebrows gave her high round forehead a naïvely childish look which contrasted oddly with the decisive chiselling of the rest of her features. Her most remarkable one was her nose of which she was very proud and which my father admired as much as she did. It was a straight, thin, rather arrogant nose, flawlessly cut from its high narrow bridge to its high narrow nostrils. Her pale lips, too, were exquisitely chiselled but with a feminine softness that contradicted the austere severity of her nose. They had a faint droop at the corners which, when her eyes were set, as they so often were, in a dreamy stare under their drooping lids, gave her an expression of romantic melancholy. When her face wore this expression, it made my father's robust pink-and-white, normally cheerful one seem almost ludicrously stolid and unromantic.

Unlike him, she had an elegant figure, so well proportioned that she gave the impression of being taller than she was just as my father's stocky build made him seem shorter. Before her marriage she had been too thin by fashionable standards, but after it her body developed the most admired contemporary shape for a woman, full-bosomed and slender-waisted, with well-rounded arms and wax-smooth shoulders. She looked her best in evening dress and ultra-feminine laces and chiffons, and she resisted my father's attempts to make her wear the stiff tailor-mades and severe shirt blouses which were then the correct morning uniform for a self-respecting Englishwoman. Having none of his rigid sense of sartorial propriety, it did not worry her in the least if her clothes were gloriously unsuited to the occasion, provided she looked charming in them. She would go for a country walk in a lace frock and high-heeled shoes and carrying a parasol or make the morning round of the West Kensington shops dressed as if for an afternoon round of calling, wearing a feather boa and an ostrich-plumed hat. I was often embarrassed by my mother's eccentricities and wished she would look and behave more like other people's mothers. However my father compared more than favourably with other people's fathers so I was thankful I had one parent who was not only reassuringly normal but of whom I could feel positively proud.

2.

My parents came from very different family backgrounds. I never knew my White grandparents, for my mother's mother died only two months after giving birth to her, and her father while I was still a baby. However, when I come to describe my mother's life before she met my father, it will be seen that they were very unlike my Botting ones.

Botting is a Sussex name and both my father's parents came from families who had been settled for generations in one small area of West Sussex between Horsham and the Downs; the Bottings as farmers and his mother's family, the Jefferys, as village carpenters and blacksmiths.

My grandfather, George Frederick Botting (always known as 'Fred'), was the third of four sons of a prosperous tenant farmer who leased a large farm called Upper Chancton at Washington, a downland village a few miles from the much larger one of Storrington. Chancton Farm belonged to the chief landowners in that part of Sussex, the Gorings of Wiston, one of whom planted the trees of Chanctonbury Ring, in order to prevent archaeologists from excavating what was believed to be the site of a neolithic settlement. Upper Chancton Farm was situated at the foot of the Downs on the border of three parishes, Washington, Ashington and Wiston, to all of which tithes had to be paid. The Manor Chancton was an ancient Saxon one (it is named in the Domesday Book as Cengeltune) belonging to King Harold's brother Gurth, who, like him, was killed at the Battle of Hastings. In 1866, when my grandfather's eldest brother Charles had succeeded his father as tenant of Upper Chancton, a great hoard of Anglo-Saxon coins was discovered in one of the fields, in which a very old building had been cleared away and the ground was being ploughed up. To quote the West Sussex Gazette of 3 January 1867: 'The farming men were at plough and struck upon what has been described to us as a large crock, which broke and out fell a quantity of bright coins which their ignorance at first thought were only pieces of tin.' My cousin Zillah Tickner, Charles Botting's grand-daughter, who still possesses some of these coins, tells me that the farm labourers had been changing coins for a quart of beer at the Frankland Arms before their value was realised and her grandfather got in touch with the authorities and they were declared Treasure Trove. Nearly 2,000 of these coins were sent to the British Museum and discovered to be silver pennies of Edward the Confessor and King Harold, coined at four local mints: Lewes, Chichester, Hastings and Steyning, the last of which had not till then been known to have a mint. It was presumed that the crock had been buried there by some Anglo-Saxon who went off to fight the invading Normans and was killed, like his lord of the manor, Gurth, at the Battle of Hastings. There was a story that the spot had long been haunted by a ghost, often known locally as 'the old Saxon', who was never seen again after the coins were found.

Storrington has more of the characteristics of a small country town than a village for it was the market and shipping centre of the district. When their father died, the eldest son Charles took over the tenancy of Upper Chancton but, before his death, he had arranged a different future for my grandfather and his five-year-old brother Edgar. The repeal of the Corn Laws in 1846, two years after my grandfather's birth, had hit the farming industry so badly that he had decided to put them into commerce. He and his wife were on friendly terms with a Mr and Mrs Carter who owned a grocery and drapery business in Storrington and had done so well out of it that they had bought the best house in the Square, Mulberry House, as their private residence. Thomas Carter died at the age of forty-one, leaving no son to inherit the business. After running it on her own for a year, his widow Zillah decided to sell it and retire in comfort to Mulberry House. The Carter's only child, Sarah, who was then seventeen, some years later married Charles Botting, my grand-father's eldest brother.

When their father bought the Carter's business for them in 1859, Edgar was twenty-one and my grandfather barely sixteen. Presumably he hoped that, with the help of an older employee and the advice of Zillah Carter herself, they would be able to run it successfully. He was perhaps over-optimistic for, though Edgar had probably served some kind of apprenticeship under the Carters, my grandfather had only just left school and had no commercial qualifications beyond the ability to write a beautiful copperplate hand and being 'good at figures'. Moreover, he suffered the handicap of being almost stone deaf. When he was a schoolboy a brutal master had slammed his head down on a desk and dealt him such a savage blow, first on one ear and then on the other that he had been deafened for life. He could not take part in any general conversation and could only hear what people said if they came very close to him and almost shouted in his ear. His deafness made it difficult for him to deal with customers over the counter, so his part in running the shop consisted mainly in keeping the books and delivering goods to outlying districts.

The shop itself occupied the ground floor of one of the three-storied, stucco-fronted Regency-style houses which, about 1830, had replaced the old half-timbered ones in the market square and made Storrington High Street look almost like a street in Worthing or Brighton. However, apart from this built-up centre, whose architecture contrasted oddly with the low, two-storied houses and cottages of weathered brick in the country lanes leading into it, Storrington had gone in for no further urban development and remained a village no different from its neighbours, except that it straggled over a much wider area and had a much larger population. The only other grocer's and draper's shop was such an inferior establishment that it offered no serious competition. All the best customers both in Storrington itself and in the outlying villages had always patron- ised Carter's and they continued to patronise Botting's. The new proprietors found they did not have to exert themselves unduly to keep the business running on an even keel and devoted no more time to it than was strictly necessary. They were, after all, two young bachelors with no family cares, and, though it was not possible to lead a life of riotous gaiety in Storrington, they spent a good deal of their time drinking at the White Horse Inn, conveniently next door to the shop, and playing billiards in the local saloon. Sussex was traditionally a betting county. Everyone from the Squire to the farm-labourer indulged in it. My grandfather and his brother were no exceptions. Whenever they could, they attended the race-meetings at Brighton and Goodwood and, as there was a bookmaker's office in Storring- ton, they did plenty of off-course betting.

In 1864, five years after Carter's became Botting's, Edgar got married. In the same year the other grocer's and draper's, Andrews, housed in shabby, old-fashioned premises round the corner from their own handsome one in the High Street, changed hands. A printed handbill announced that John Andrews 'has let his Business to Mr James Greenfield, whom he recommends with the greatest confidence' and that 'James Greenfield, having taken the above business, trusts by strict attention to Business and moderate charges, to merit the increasing support of the public'. The Botting brothers probably attached no importance to this change of proprietorship. But, in James Greenfield, who, unlike themselves had served a long apprenticeship to the trade and had had years of practical experience in it, these two amateurs who had merely stepped into a flourishing, ready-made business were to find themselves up against the most formidable of rivals. How serious the menace was did not become apparent for some years, so that when Edgar and, later, my grandfather got married, their shop was still not doing too badly though not nearly as well as under the Carters.

Edgar married a young woman from Brighton, Ellen Blaker, who, unlike himself, had a good brain and a remarkably strong character. She needed her admirable, if somewhat formidable strength of character, for a hard life lay ahead of her, bolstering up her weak, feckless husband, working in the shop and bringing up six children on an ever-diminishing income. My grandfather did not much relish the arrival of his sister-in-law. He and Edgar had got along very pleasantly as bachelors in their rooms over the shop and he found this domineering young woman, who promptly set about trying to reform Edgar's character and who strongly disapproved of drinking and gambling, a far from welcome addition to the household. Soon it was increased to five for Ellen produced the first two of her six children in quick succession. My grandfather, who by then was twenty-four, decided it was time he got married and set up a home of his own.

In 1858, he married Adeline Jeffery, the eldest of three daughters who lived with their widowed mother in Ashurst, a small village some ten or twelve miles from Storrington. The Jefferys had been settled in Ashurst since the reign of Charles II and for some hundred and fifty years my grandmother's branch of the family had lived in a small Elizabethan farmhouse not much larger than a cottage which, when her great-great-great-grandfather John Jeffery bought it, was called Rook's Garden, but, presumably because it stood on Bines Green, was later named Binesfield. Like John Jeffery, her father, grandfather, great-grandfather and great-great-grandfather had all been village carpenters and, as all were called William, I will refer to my grandmother's father as William Jeffery IV and her grandfather as William Jeffery III.

Early in the eighteenth century this family of hereditary carpenters, having acquired 'gardinum et septem acros vocat Rookes Garden et duos agros vocat Sex Berries' for £190.12.0, began to acquire a little more property. As and when they could afford it, they bought parcels of good arable land and pasture which each in turn left to his eldest son. In 1817 William Jeffery II bought several fields for £1,151 so that by the time William Jeffery III inherited it in 1835 the property comprised forty-one acres of land in Ashurst, leased to a tenant-farmer and henceforth known as Bines Green Farm, and several labourer's cottages, not only in Ashurst but some miles further away in Cowfold and West Grinstead. He was sixty-one when he inherited it and, though he had not married till he was forty-five, his wife, who was a good twenty years his junior, was already dead. She had borne him four children; two sons, William and James, and two daughters, Elizabeth and Anne. It was this elder son, whom I refer to as William Jeffery IV, who was my grandfather's father. William Jeffery III seems to have been a somewhat rakish character for his daughter Anne was so shocked by her father's addiction to gambling that when she married, she and her husband vowed never to keep a pack of cards in the house. She married a farmer at West Grinstead named Benjamin Boniface and their grandchildren have told me that they rigorously kept their promise. Perhaps her father resented her disapproval of his way of life for, though he left an annuity to his other married daughter, Elizabeth Batchelor and his unmarried son James, there is no mention in his will of any bequest to Anne Boniface.

His elder son and presumptive heir, William, married a young woman from Washington, Anne Rice, who was a friend of my grandfather's parents at Upper Chancton. They were married in Washington church in 1844, the year my grandfather was born, and a year later Anne gave birth to the first of their three daughters, his future wife.

William brought his bride back to live in Ashurst at a house called Bats. According to my grandmother and my great-aunts it deserved its name for there was one cupboard they could never open without finding a bat in it. Country women in those days had a peculiar abhorrence of bats for they believed they attacked women's hair and that their claws were coated with some sticky substance so that once they were hooked in it they could not be extricated and the hair had to be cut off. Apart from the bat-haunted cupboard, it was a pleasant little house and William and Anne were very happy in it for the whole of their brief married life. It lasted only seven years for, when William was thirty-two, he died of consumption, leaving Anne with three small children of whom the eldest, Adeline (always called 'Ada') was six and Agnes and Clara respectively five and two.

William Jeffery III, who was seventy-seven when the son who would normally have succeeded to his property died at the age of thirty-two, lived to be eighty-six. Ever since his daughters had married and left home he had employed a housekeeper to look after his comforts at Binesfield. A few years before his death he engaged a new one, a young woman named Sarah Sayers, who soon acquired an influence over him which neither his daughters nor his daughter-in-law had ever exerted. The result was that he made a will appointing her the principal trustee of his estate, the other two being one Richard Newman, who later retired from his trusteeship, and Edward Cripps, a solicitor in Steyning. When he died in 1860, he left 'all his freehold, copyhold and leasehold land and houses in the parish of Ashurst' on trust to them on the following conditions. Sarah Sayers was to receive all the rents and profits from the property, after paying certain annuities to his son James Jeffery and his daughter Elizabeth Batchelor, and to retain the residue for the maintenance of his grand-daughter, Adeline Ramsden Jeffery until she was twenty-four. Thereafter she was to be paid all the rents and profits for the rest of her natural life for her own absolute benefit without coverture, i.e. without her rights to them being transferred to her husband if she married. If she had a 'lawfully begotten son' who lived to be twenty-one, the whole of the property was to go to him. If she died without leaving such a son, the property was to be sold and the proceeds divided among her first cousins on her late father's side.

As Ada Jeffery was only fourteen when her grandfather died, she had to wait another ten years before she was entitled to draw the income from his property. The immediate difference it made to her situation was that Sarah Sayers now became her legal guardian. As Miss Sayers had always been very fond of her, and had almost certainly been responsible for the terms of William Jeffery IV's will, she wished her to come and live with her at Binesfield, which, whether she was legally entitled to or not, she continued to occupy after her employer's death. Ada, though she was fond of Miss Sayers, did not want to be separated from her mother and sisters, so it was finally arranged that the whole family should move from Bats to Binesfield. This meant that Anne Jeffery was no longer mistress of her own home as she had been at Bats but had to live in a house ruled over by Sarah Sayers. Her second daughter, Agnes, who had always disliked Miss Sayers, keenly resented her mother's being submitted to the domination of their grandfather's former housekeeper, was thankful when Sarah married a Mr Ansell and went to live in Steyning. However, this did not wholly relieve them of her presence, for she was constantly coming over to Binesfield to collect the rents from the property and see to the repairs to the cottages and barns for which she was responsible as trustee. And when her husband died only a year or two after their marriage, she came back to live at Binesfield, so that it was not till her beloved Ada married and she moved to Storrington to be near her that Anne Jeffery and her other daughters, Agnes and Clara, were left in peaceful occupation of the house they were to live in for the rest of their lives. Ada's sisters never married and when she herself married she was twenty-three and had only a year to wait before she inherited the rents from the property.

The fact that Ada Jeffery would soon inherit an income of some hundred pounds a year – quite a considerable sum in those days – must have been a decided attraction to my grandfather, but it would be unfair to assume, as my mother did, that it was his only reason for marrying her. Admittedly my grandmother, even as a girl when she was said to have had a blooming complexion and beautiful chestnut hair can never have been good-looking. She was very short, barely five foot tall ('the same height as Queen Victoria' she used to say proudly), and, unlike her sister Clara, who had the same dumpy figure, hers was not redeemed by a pretty face. Nevertheless, though she was no beauty, she had qualities my grandfather thought more important in a wife. She was kind-hearted and good-tempered, and above all, the sort of girl who could be trusted, now that he had decided to get married and set up a home of his own, to make that home a cheerful and pleasant place, and, unlike his domineering sister-in-law, allow him to be master in it. As for Ada herself, it must have been the happiest moment of her life when 'Fred' Botting proposed to her. She had fallen in love with him on his first visit to Binesfield for he was not only the handsomest young man she had ever seen but utterly unlike the burly, red-faced young farmers who were all that Ashurst had to offer in the way of male society. He was tall and slim, with chiselled features, large blue eyes and a very white skin and, what charmed her most of all, he looked 'every inch a gentleman'. Even my mother, who, in moments of particular grievance against my father, bemoaned the fact that she married a 'peasant' conceded that her father-in-law looked surprisingly aristocratic considering his origins. In fact, she was really fond of him and could forgive him for everything except for marrying my grandmother. The mere sight of her pudgy face and dumpy figure and the sound of her accent irritated her like a hair-shirt and provoked her to a spitefulness which, hot-tempered as she was, I never knew her display to anyone else. But I doubt if my grandmother had looked as presentable as her husband and spoken as impeccable English as her son, my father's mother and my father's wife would ever have been anything but mutually hostile. Neither could tolerate the other's determination to retain exclusive rights in him.

My grandparents were married in Washington parish church and spent their honeymoon in the Isle of Wight. This excursion to the Isle of Wight was to be their one and only experience of foreign travel and the souvenir they brought back from it, a glass model of the lighthouse filled with multi-coloured sands, was still as proudly displayed on the mantelpiece in their flat in West Kensington as it had been in their first home in Storrington.

This was a pleasant small brownstone house then known as Rose Cottage, but nowadays as Stone House, conveniently situated in West Street, just round the corner from Botting's Stores. It had a tiny garden in front and a sizeable one at the back, beyond which lay open fields. My grandmother was delighted with her new home. It had amenities she had never known at Binesfield; not only running water and indoor sanitation but the wonderful new form of lighting – gas. Gas had only recently been introduced into Storrington and Rose Cottage was one of the few houses that had it laid on. In the others, as in all houses great and small in the outlying villages there was no form of lighting other than oil lamps and candles. What pleased her even more than these amenities was the smart new furniture that had been installed in it. All the furniture at Binesfield, most of it made by her carpenter forebears, had been sadly old-fashioned, not to be compared with the modern plush-upholstered walnut suite in the parlour of Rose Cottage or the brass bedstead and veneered wardrobe and dressing-table in the best bedroom. She settled down happily to married life, proud of her home and even prouder of her handsome husband. If her beloved 'Fred' had a somewhat irascible temper, she found every excuse for it in his cruel affliction of deafness.

Their first child, a girl, was born within a year of their marriage and christened Alice. Both of them loved her dearly; my grandfather, I think, even more than my grandmother. Eighteen months later, on 25 September 1870, my father was born, but it was an occasion more of sorrow than rejoicing for his parents for on the very day of his birth little Alice died of croup. They never quite got over her loss and one of the first things I remember their showing me was a photograph of her tombstone. It grieved them very much that they had never 'had her likeness taken' and this was their only memento of her. I think one reason why they were so fond of me was that their own daughter had died in infancy.

Shortly before the birth of their second and last child, my grandfather had backed the winner of the St Leger, a horse called Cecil. So he decided, if the child was a boy, to name him after the horse. He was baptised on 20 November by the same rector who had baptised and buried his sister, the Rev. J. Scott Whiting, and entered in the Storrington parish register as Cecil George, son of George Frederick and Adeline Ramsden Botting, his father's occupation being described as 'draper etc.'. The last thing his parents could have envisaged was what his own occupation would be.

3.

Having lost her first child, his mother was so terrified of losing her second that even when little Cecil had survived infancy and grown into a sturdy small boy, she continued to worry incessantly about his health and safety. In her anxiety to preserve him from every possible hazard to life and limb she discouraged him from playing with his boy cousins outside the precincts of Rose Cottage in case he should be lured into such dangerous activities as climbing trees or sliding on frozen ponds.

His main amusement was reading. Once he had learned to read, which he did phenomenally early, he became so passionately fond of reading that, in spite of her fears that he would damage his eyesight, his mother had not the heart to restrain him from doing something which gave him such intense pleasure and kept him happily occupied for hours when she was busy in the kitchen or over at the shop. Another amusement was playing croquet against himself on the small bumpy lawn in the back garden. In those days croquet was played (and was still being played in country gardens in my own childhood) with hoops a good foot wide and shiny wooden balls no bigger than cricket balls. Instead of being four, coloured blue, yellow, red and black, there were eight, which allowed Cecil a wide choice of pieces with which to manoeuvre.

His mother was of course terrified of exposing him to the hazards of school (after Fred's terrible misfortune). She must have wished he had been born in her grandfather's day, before the rough county schools of those times, when it was not considered necessary for the sons of small farmers and village tradesmen to be sent for a few terms to some 'Young Gentlemen's Academy' to have a little book-learning that would be useless to them in after life, beaten into them by men almost as ignorant as their pupils. But by now it was a hall-mark of gentility like the lace-curtained parlour and the best tea-service, never used except on state occasions. A few generations ago it had been no disgrace for a wealthy farmer to be able to do no more than 'make his mark' on the legal documents that give him freehold possession of another fifty acres. But by the middle of the nineteenth century there were labourers who could shakily scrawl their name on a marriage certificate and some who could, with great difficulty, decipher one.

Cecil was a precocious boy. At the age of seven he bought a Greek and a Latin grammar from a stall at Storrington market, took them home, and taught himself both Latin and Greek. [Fred and Ada could not ignore such aptitude in the child who was evidently to be their only son, and it seems they employed a tutor to coach Cecil for an assisted place at a public school.] At the age of thirteen he won a scholarship to Dulwich College.

Cecil worked hard at Dulwich, hard enough to win another scholarship, this time a classical one to Emmanuel College, Cambridge in 1889, but throughout his schooldays he was plagued by a sense of social inferiority. To be near their son and to spare him the terrors of boarding, his parents sold the shop at Storrington and bought one in a back street of Dulwich. On Saturdays Cecil had to deliver groceries at the backdoors of the homes of his school friends. It was a humiliation he never forgot.

[At Cambridge he enjoyed the only four years (1889–1892) of leisure and extravagance in the whole of his working life. He made friends with young men whose background verged on the aristocratic, he learned to appreciate good wine and good clothes and he ran up the usual debts.]

Just before his twenty-second birthday Cecil began his career as a schoolmaster at Colet Court, the preparatory school to St Paul's at a salary of £120 a year. During his first term, he was recommended by the headmaster to give some private coaching in Greek to an extremely intelligent boy of nine whose father was anxious for him to win a scholarship to St Paul's. That boy was Compton Mackenzie, who must have been the first, as well as subsequently the most famous, of my father's innumerable private pupils. In Octave Two of *My Life and Times*, Sir Compton, on whose photographic memory I have the utmost reliance, describes him thus:

Mr Cecil Botting . . . was at this date a very plump young man with a pink face and a small fair waxed moustache; as I remember, he was living with his parents in Dulwich, where he had been at school. Every time he came to 54 Avonmore Road he seemed to hang up in the hall a different greatcoat.

'I never knew any young man with so many greatcoats,' I once heard Miss Stawell observe. 'Does he ever wear the same one?'

I am really not exaggerating when I say that Botting had at least eight greatcoats, of which I recall with particular wonder a dark one with astrakhan collar and cuffs with which he wore a top-hat; and a fawn Newmarket coat, skirted and waisted, with which he wore a brown bowler. I can see him divesting himself of those greatcoats and hanging them up in our hall seventy years ago as clearly as I can see the words I am writing on the page before me.

I suspect that this extraordinary abundance of greatcoats was partly responsible for a gloomy passage in a letter my father wrote in his first term at Colet Court (which he referred to as 'St Paul's Purgatory School') to Nevinson – always known as Toby – de Courcy, the man who had been his best friend at Cambridge and who was to remain so till de Courcy's death in 1919.

Life is not all beer and skittles with me just now in more ways than one. The Cambridge tradesman, and for me his name is legion, is

pursuing me with a fury as keen as it is impotent. I bore up like a man
for some time; but when it came to having thirteen letters in one
week, I caved in: and one half-holiday, I put my Life Insurance Policy
under my arm and went and interviewed some of 'our conquerors' in
that formidable locality E.C. demanding the loan of One Hundred
Sterling, offering as security my 'note of hand' and the Insurance
Policy, which however is too young as yet to have any Real Existence,
or in City dialect any 'Surrender Value'. And the City men laughed at
me and the Bank referred me to 'some respectable Solicitor' and every
respectable solicitor referred me to 'some Bank'. But as yet the only
offer I have had is the hundred pounds at eight or nine per cent for
which I would have to pay the lender a premium down of twenty-five
pounds!!!

How my father survived that particular financial crisis, I do
not know. It was the first of an endless series for though he
worked harder than anyone I ever knew, he never managed to
live within his income. However, he had other things to depress
him even more than his money troubles during his first term at
Colet Court. He had just spent the three happiest years of his life
at Cambridge – and now he saw nothing ahead but boredom and
drudgery. In time to come he was to love his profession, as well
as being outstandingly good at it, but in that letter to de Courcy,
written two months after he had launched on it, he wrote:

I forget whether I have written to you since I began schoolmastering
or not. In any case, I am quite tired of giving gallery accounts of it:
enough that I am pretty sick of it! I think the present methods of
education utterly wrong, though I have not the faintest idea of how
they can be improved: and that I consider the profession of the usher★
the most soul-destroying possible. Of course the boys bore me
horribly: but happily they have done what the dentist does when he
bores a tooth: they have *killed the nerve*, and I am now so thoroughly
blasé of the whole thing that I care but little for anything. I only make
three stipulations concerning the boys:
  1. That they play some game
  2. That they read Scott
  3. That they *never*, under any circumstances, put the Dative after a
     verb of motion.
The Masters are, some of them, nice men, but I know scarcely
anything of them, and am not likely to. I don't know how it is, but I
really don't wish to make any more friends. I made friendships up at

★ Schoolteacher.

A caricature of Cecil Botting printed in *The Pauline*, St Paul's school magazine,
1924.

Cambridge which nothing will ever destroy, and which no new friendships can ever equal.

    A year later, on Christmas Day 1893, he wrote an immensely long letter to Toby, in which he describes, not only his current financial situation but a situation of a very different kind in which he had just become involved. The letter, which covers sixteen of the double sheets of writing paper of the period, and which did not come into my hands till some seventy years after it was written, describes, early on, one of the straits to which he was reduced to the end of his fourth term at Colet Court.

Thank you very much indeed for the design.★ It does you credit, though to my poor mind it is quite unintelligible. Up to the present it has not gone to a carpenter for execution; you will understand when I tell you that for days the water has entered into my boots, even as the iron has entered into my soul, because I couldn't afford to get them . . . oh, I swear, on my honour, that I was not leading up to a very cheap pun, believe me: – moreoever my watch has lain motionless and inert, because I couldn't have a new spring put in: I was in fact only saved from Parish Relief by the temporary loan of the family spoons, for a purpose obvious: and also by a rather ingenious idea – if you can possibly credit me with such a thing. But poverty makes even a Botting brilliant. I had the photograph of my form taken, and requested payment in advance from the boys for all photos ordered. With this I managed to get through the last week of the term; but for many weeks I have had to be reduced to the 'Beth Bun' and . . . no, no – *not* a 'Battle of Milk' for my lunch on half-holidays when I usually do not go home till the evening. Toby, hear it with befitting horror: but there is a Railway Station Refreshment Room – far be it from me to name its name – where I can never enter now but that the goddess of the bar will begin putting new Bath Buns out on the counter! And this for one who in the old days, like Hector's hopeless child etc. 'nought but marrow and the rich fat of sheep – or (in the modern equivalent) – *vol-au-vent au financier & ris-de-veau aux champignons en caisses*'.

    ★ This was for a frame for a plaque of Sir Walter Scott, an author for whom both he and 'Toby' had an admiration second only to their passion for Meredith. It did get executed in the end – in olive green plush – and the plaque still hung on the walls of my father's study in 1926 more than thirty years after 'Toby' gave it to him.

An extract from his next letter to de Courcy, dated 10 January 1893, records the failure of another attempt to recoup his fortunes by entering for one of those newspaper competitions which in those days were the equivalent of the Football Pools.

I am surprised, Toby, to find in your letters no mention of our latest 'modern malady' – the Missing Word, or of that valuable contribution to modern literature – *Pearson's Weekly*. Can it be that to you too the subject is fraught with memories all too painful. Or can it be that you went through the fire unsinged or escaped it altogether? To me, sitting in the sackcloth of a bitter repentance, amid the ashes of blighted hopes and crumbled ambitions, the subject is well-nigh too terrible to record in words. Fortunately I did not hear of the Missing Word Competitions till a few weeks before they were stopped. But no sooner did I hear of them than I saw therein a relief for my shattered fortunes. Like all whom the Gods intend to destroy, I was haunted by a Scheme which seemed as unerring as it was original. Now I know that it was neither. I communicated the Scheme to my colleagues in misery at Colet Court. A memorable scene ensued. The Purgatory School was in a blaze of excitement. Every member of the staff was infected by the contagion: several sent in their resignation on the spot. Younger men made wild promises of fizzy dinners; married men who had grown old in servitude stood on forms and swore by the Latin Arnold that their wives and children should suffer want no more. For days our whole life seemed to turn on the pivot of *Pearson's Weekly*: for days a column of *Pearson's Weekly* was the regulation thing to set for Impositions: and men who took an interest in their work offered bound volumes of *Pearson's Weekly* as special prizes. As for me, visions of airy magnificence floated before my eyes: mentally I compared myself with the Man that broke the Bank at Monte Carlo: as I walked along the streets I saw in anticipation flaming placards with such devices as –

MISSING WORD COMPETITION
Repeated Success of the Schoolmaster
or
ANOTHER HAUL FOR THE USHER
or again
Strand Magazine
Interview with Mr Botting, the Pearson Plunger

But alas for the vanity of ambition. Though I formed a Syndicate at school and joined several Syndicates at home besides sending up several words on my own account, only once did I get the word and then, owing to some mistake, it was not sent up. Let us close the subject: but when you see on the placards 'More about the £44,000' you may remember that your unhappy friend's little all forms no inconsiderably portion of that sum.

Two months later he was feeling slightly more resigned.

Yes, I think I am gradually settling down to this sort of thing. I find there are lots of things one can get keen on at school, and my boys are really almost without exception very nice chaps. I always talk to them as far as possible as if I were a boy myself and I have never found my authority suffer from it a bit as yet. So long as a man does not look on boys as a separate creation, mainly of the devil, there is some chance of his not crystallising. I am getting into a groove, too, in everything and the unpleasant jolts of this rough world are less noticeable. Of course you must expect me to break into a gallery talk about Usherdom. For I must occasionally beat against the walls of my coffin to make sure of my own existence.

But now things are looking up. I have received my screw, and, rejoice with me, the promise of a ten pound rise next term. This last delights me muchly, as we usually never get a rise at the charnel house till we have been there two years, and many men have been there four to five years without a single penny being added to their original £120.

After that he devotes several sheets to describing pictures he has been seeing and books he had been reading (I hear the Master is writing a new novel, to be entitled *An Amazing Marriage*) and it is not till almost the last one that he finally brings himself to mention a subject which obviously required all his courage to mention for fear of how his friend would react to the news.

Toby . . . I have a great confession to make to you in the most sacred and inviolate confidence. I did not intend to make it to you till I could do so by word of mouth. A letter is not the best means of transmission of thought. But I am unwilling to have this secret from you, and I hope you will receive it with sympathy and forbearance. You have probably guessed what it is by this time, and I can hear you murmuring 'silly fool' and 'weak idiot' but I must put up with that. You will remember that in a very desponding letter that I wrote at the beginning of this year, I said that I had met a charming girl who had just returned from Germany, who condescended to dance with me and who talked Pessimism. And . . . well, I am not engaged at present; but we have an understanding with each other which will, I think, be binding on both sides. Whether I shall become openly engaged or not soon I don't know. My resources are so very small and my responsibilities (people) are so great. I certainly shall have to work for years and years, but I don't mind that, for *I* think the prize is well worth working for. You must not think me too weak. If I have been unwise in some ways from the worldly point of view, in others I have not. This has given me an incentive to work which nothing else could have given: it has revived in me all the fiery energy that I had as a boy at school when I was still ambitious: it has done away with all the morbid view of life which I developed at Cambridge, and much of which was not mere literary exercise but bitter fact. I have now an object in life which I shall not count ten years of hard work too high a price to pay. It was a case of 'Love at First Sight' quite, and I don't think I shall ever repent it . . . Oh please forgive this very sentimental talk – inspired I suppose by the influence of Christmas (today in Christmas Day) which I am not yet sufficiently the New Young Man to escape from. I do hope you will like her. I will not attempt any description. It could only bore you and could only, I suppose, be grossly exaggerated. I will only tell you her name – Christine White – and ask you not to take too hard a view of me. If you have any affection for me, you will be pleased that anything has come to make life a little brighter than it was when I came down. I don't think you can ever realise how utterly wretched I was during my first term after coming down. All that time I had not one single person with whom I could exchange an idea, with whom I had one idea in common, and at that time I expected that I had nothing any better to look forward to throughout my life – that too after all the pleasant time I had had at Cambridge, surrounded by men that I loved.

And whom I shall continue to love. Do not think that this that I have told you will ever make any difference in that respect. 'True love in this differs from common clay / when you divide you do not take away.' So the Poet, and I do not think we shall refute his theory.

A few days later he became engaged to Christine White, though they kept their engagement secret for a month or two. Of the next year, during which he had taken on all the private coaching he could get in the holidays as well as in term time, he could report to de Courcy: 'In the year of grace 1894, I find I made a little over £200, which, considering that my salary is still on £130, I don't consider so bad.' Not bad for a young man of twenty-four in those days but hardly enough for one whose parents were partly dependent on him.

However, in 1896 his prospects brightened. So many of his pupils had won scholarships to St Paul's that he was invited to join the staff as a junior Classics master. He was to remain at St Paul's till he retired as Senior Greek Master thirty years later.

4.

Unlike my father, whose sister had died so young that he can be reckoned an only child, my mother was one of a large family.

She was the youngest of her father, Henry White's six children by his second wife, one of whom, her immediate predecessor had died in infancy. Besides her own brother and three sisters, she had a much older half-brother and half-sister, their father's children by his first wife. Her mother, who was fifteen years younger than her husband, died ten weeks after giving birth to her, so the only parent she knew was a father who was nearly fifty when she was born and had very firm ideas about the bringing up of his children. The basic one was that his duty to them must never be allowed to take precedence of his duty to himself and he took care to ensure that it never did.

Though the Whites were far from well off, they could, unlike the Bottings and Jefferys, be called an upper-middle-class family. But because they had a coat-of-arms and could reasonably claim descent from one Robert White, Keeper of the Parks of Farnham, who died in 1467 and whose great-grandson, John White, Bishop of Winchester, preached the funeral sermon of Queen Mary I, my mother regarded herself as an aristocrat. This conviction, which amounted at times to a kind of *folie de grandeur*, gave her a comforting sense of superiority to whatever company she was in, most of all, of course, to my father's relatives.

Her own family was in some ways a peculiar one. Their twice-married father, Henry White, had lost both parents by the time he was eight, and though his second wife, Clementine Sears, was his cousin, her children seem to have had no contact with their mother's relatives after her death. In fact, all they knew about their mother's family was that her father Thomas Sears had been a gentleman farmer who lived at Fulwich House near Dartford and owned three large farms, Fulwich, Wilmington and Temple and that her younger sister, Isabel, had married a successful surgeon named Victor Bonney. Whether Henry White had quarrelled with the Searses or merely drifted apart from them after Clementine's death, the result was that the children had a strangely isolated home life. Not only were they a 'one-parent family' but they lacked any of the grown-up relatives, grandparents, aunts and uncles, who are normally part of people's childhood. Even their only cousin, their mother's niece Violet Bonney, they did not meet till she was grown-up.

Although I never knew my Grandfather White (he died before I was two) I knew enough about him to be sure I should have found him a very formidable old gentleman. His own family background was so unusual that, if there were not documentary evidence to prove it, it would seem incredible. His father, Henry Barbour White, who was born in 1734, was presumably a man of some wealth; rich enough at any rate to own a large country house in still rural Fulham, and to have his portrait painted by Lawrence. No one seems to know exactly what he did, but in all probability he was a city merchant. He married twice, but had no children by his first wife, Ann Rogers, who came from Little Nasse, Shropshire. She died in 1811, at the age of seventy-three, and the following year, when he himself was seventy-eight, he was married again, at St George's, Hanover Square, to Sophia Taylor, who was only thirty. Three years after the wedding, against all probability, the couple had a child. More surprisingly still, this son, James, born in 1815 when his father was eighty-one, was not to be their only child. Seven years later they had another. This son, Harry, born on 13 October 1822, when his father was eighty-eight, was my mother's father. Soon after his younger son's fourth birthday, on 23 November 1826, Henry Barbour White died, aged ninety-two. There was a tradition that he died of shock, after discovering that he had lost all his fortune in a rash speculation. Whatever the cause, he died a poor man. He was buried in the family vault in Bunhill Fields, the burial place of John Bunyan, Daniel Defoe and William Blake.

His widow, who was said to have been devoted to her old husband (the Lawrence portrait, probably painted at the time of their marriage, shows a handsome man with fine dark eyes and firmly-cut features), survived him by only four years. She died in 1830, at the age of forty-eight, leaving her orphan sons homeless and unprovided for. As the elder, James, was by then fifteen, his father's friends probably found him some kind of employment. All that is known of him is that he never married and died when he was thirty-two. The younger, Henry, who was only eight when his mother died, was sent to a Masonic orphanage, which suggests that his father had been a Freemason. The Freemasons were well known for their charity towards impoverished widows and orphans of 'the Brethren' and the education given to the boys in their orphanages was equivalent to that of a grammar school.

What Henry White did when he left the orphanage is unknown, but in 1845, when he was twenty-three, he married a Miss Louisa Sawkins, of whom nothing is known except that she was twenty-one when he married her at St Pancras Church, Bloomsbury, and thirty-one when she died and was buried in the 'new' family vault, of which she was the first and last occupant. She bore him two children; the first, Louise Elizabeth (always known as 'Louie') born four years after their marriage in Dublin; the second, Henry Victor (always known as 'Vic') two years later, in Paddington. Judging by my Aunt Louie's looks, her mother must have been extremely pretty, though the second wife's children were probably right in surmising that she came from a lower class than their father. My mother's (unsupported) theory was that Louisa Sawkins had been the pretty daughter of the landlady of some house in which he had been a lodger, and, like many a lonely young man in such circumstances, he had let himself be lured into marriage.

Two years after Louisa's death, he married his twenty-year-old cousin, Clementina Sears. I have already said what little I know about her family and I have no idea whether she was a cousin on his father's side or his mother's or whether her parents disapproved of her marrying a widower of thirty-five with two children and very little money. If they did, it might account for the apparent rift between the two families. Clementina, however, cared nothing for such drawbacks. She was passionately in love with Henry White, as some letters written to him during their courtship show, and she was an adoring wife throughout the fourteen years of their marriage. When they married in 1857, her husband was presumably settled in the only definite post he was known to have held and which he held for thirty years – that of Secretary to the Warehousemen and Clerks' School. Where the school was and whether it still exists under another name, like so many other things about my Grandfather White, is unknown, including why at some stage in his career he received the rather unusual honour of being made a Freeman of the City of London. Probably his children were too concerned with the side of his life which directly affected them, the domestic one, to bother about any other. What mattered to them was his personality and there was nothing hazy about their recollections of that.

The house to which he moved on his second marriage, and where he lived for the rest of his life, was in Palace Road, Upper Norwood, near the new site of the Crystal Palace, the vast glass and steel building which had housed the Great Exhibition of 1851 in Hyde Park. Norwood was then still almost rural and very unlike the vast sprawling suburb it has since become. Though they were married in 1857, Clementina did not produce her first child, a daughter, till 1860. Constance was followed by their only son, my much-loved Uncle Howard, in 1862, then by four more daughters, Beatrice (1865), Alice (1868), Edith (1869), who died in infancy, and lastly, on 24 April 1871, by Christine Julia. Clementina was left very weak after the birth of her last child, but her husband, who had never known a day's illness in his life, insisted, like Mr Dombey, that she should 'rouse herself' and accompany him to a Handel concert at the Crystal Palace. Like a dutiful wife, she obeyed, but with fatal results. She caught a severe chill at the concert, which developed into pneumonia and two and a half months after my mother's birth, she died at the age of thirty-four. I have a tinted photograph of her as a young, still childless married woman of twenty-two though her Victorian dress of sober brown silk, smoothly braided hair and composed expression made her seem much older. She has an oval face and the same straight, finely-chiselled nose as my mother's, also the same large deep-lidded brown eyes, with the same curiously modelled sockets and half-finished eyebrows. A photograph of her taken some years later with her two eldest children, Constance and Howard, aged about four and two, when she could not have been more than twenty-seven or -eight, shows her face looking careworn and already a little lined between the drooping braids.

By the time she died in 1871, leaving five motherless children of whom the eldest was only eleven and the youngest a ten-week-old baby, her husband's two by his first wife were grown-up and off his hands. Louie was twenty-two and acting as companion to a rich old lady. She was to fill similar posts for the rest of her life for, though she was very pretty and, according to her, had had numerous admirers, she never married. Victor, who was twenty, had settled his own future by running away from home when he was fifteen and working his passage to America, where he had taken a job as a lumberjack. After spending many years as a lumberjack he founded a timber company of his own and became a successful business man in Omaha, Nebraska.

After Clementine's death, Henry White did not marry again though there were two ladies in Norwood who would have been only too willing to take her place. Presumably he engaged a housekeeper to run his home and a nurse to look after three-year-old Alice and baby Christine but my mother seemed to have no recollection of any such female figures in her childhood, only of the all-dominating male one of 'Papa'. Although 'Papa' was an authoritative parent, he allowed his daughters more freedom when they were children than most Victorian little girls. My mother and her sisters were allowed to run wild in the grounds of the Crystal Palace and indulge in all kinds of 'unladylike' activities. The great delight of herself and her favourite sister Alice, the nearest to her in age, and the most 'tomboyish' was to climb inside the great hollow models of prehistoric monsters in the Palace grounds and roar to frighten the passers-by. She and Alice (always known as 'Jan') were their father's favourites, 'Jan' because she was the cleverest and most spirited of the four girls, 'Chrissie' because she was the prettiest.

Their father had no intention of supporting his four daughters indefinitely. It was made very clear to them that, as soon as they were old enough, they would have to earn their own living. Having provided for his own future by buying himself a life-annuity, he considered he had made sufficient provision for theirs by giving them an education that would fit them for almost the only employment considered suitable for young women of their class, that of governess in an English or foreign family. Accordingly, they were sent first to a then famous day-school for girls – Miss Wordsworth's – (one of my mother's contemporaries there was the actress Lilian Braithwaite) and then to a boarding-school in France. The ability to teach French was a desirable asset in a governess and entitled her to demand a slightly higher salary. Even with the addition of these few extra pounds, it was almost invariably less than a cook's.

When the eldest, Con, was eighteen, she was despatched to a post in Vienna, a city where, except for one visit to England in her late forties, she remained for the rest of her life. She died of tuberculosis during one of the terrible winters of the 1914–1918 war when the inhabitants of Vienna suffered appalling privations and food and fuel were almost unobtainable. Due to the collapse of the currency, banknotes became so worthless that a whole sackful would scarcely buy a loaf of *ersatz* bread and people scoured the woods and parks for twigs to make an apology for a fire. Five years later, when the next sister, Beatrice, was eighteen, she too was packed off to Vienna to be English governess to an aristocratic Austrian family. Long afterwards, when I visited her there in 1928, she described her arrival in Vienna in 1883. I have never forgotten what she told me:

Your Grandpapa White brought me to Vienna himself as he had done your Auntie Con. It would have been considered *most* improper in those days for a girl to travel on the continent unaccompanied. We spent the night in a hotel, where the *Gräfin* had arranged to meet me the next morning and take me to her home. Before she was due to arrive, he gave me a five pound note and said: 'This, my dear Beatrice, is the last money you will ever receive from me. But do not think I have made no provision for your future, should you ever be in need. We will now take a little walk as there is something I wish to show you.' He took me to a gloomy looking house where we were shown into a room where several old ladies were sitting knitting or playing patience. Then he said: 'For the rest of my life except in the unlikely event of your marrying' (my Auntie Bee was the only really plain one of the girls and their father, as my mother well remembered, had never hesitated to tell her so) 'I shall subscribe a guinea a year to this excellent institution which provides a home for governesses when they are too old for employment. So you will have the satisfaction of knowing that, whatever happens you will always have a roof over your head.' I am afraid that, at eighteen, it was not much satisfaction to *me*.

Alice, besides being the cleverest of the four girls, was less in awe of 'Papa' than any of them. Without waiting for him to find her a 'suitable situation' she took matters into her own hands and found herself a post, not as a governess but as a teacher in a girl's school. Much as my mother admired 'Jan's' independent spirit, she saw no hope for herself of avoiding the fate of Constance and Beatrice. However, there was one member of her family who was determined that she should not have to become a governess if she did not want to. Her brother Howard, who was ten years her senior, had a very special affection for his youngest sister and had been her staunch ally and protector ever since she was a small child. It was he who suggested she should try to get into the Post Office. The Post Office employed a certain number of women on its clerical staff and, being part of the Civil Service, offered securities of a kind particularly attractive to middle-class parents in search of a respectable career for their daughters. Once a girl got into the Post Office she could stay until she reached retiring age when she was entitled to a government pension. If she married she was automatically retired but received a gratuity. The entry was by examination and every year there were far more candidates competing than there were vacancies to fill. Howard had no difficulty in persuading 'Papa' to let my mother sit for the examination but, to her bitter disappointment, she failed to get a place by only one mark. To have failed by only one mark seemed to her such a cruel injustice of fate that it rankled all her life. To anyone else it might have

seemed fate would have been much crueller had she been one of
the successful candidates for I cannot imagine anyone more
temperamentally unsuited to the routine work of a Civil Service
clerk than my mother. But the grievance remained and, like
certain other of her pet grievances – in particular the fact that
once, in the first year of their marriage, my father had spent a
convivial evening with some old Cambridge friends and come
home drunk – it would flare up at intervals and blaze with as
fierce a flame of resentment as if the injury had been inflicted
only yesterday.

Howard was as disappointed as she was at her failure to get
into the Post Office but he knew it was hopeless to try to
persuade their father to give her another chance to take the
exam. 'Chrissie' might be Papa's favourite daughter but he had
no intention of keeping her at home any longer at this expense.
Howard himself, who had done brilliantly at school, had tried
vainly to be allowed to sit for a University scholarship. He was
by nature an intellectual and his one real ambition had been to
become an historian. But 'Papa' had stubbornly refused to
listen. Instead of sitting for that University scholarship he had
been forced to take the examination for the Bank of England. He
had passed top of all the candidates, much to 'Papa's' satisfaction
but little to his own, for though he worked hard and conscientiously, he was never happy in the Bank of England.

Henry White now proposed to conduct Christine to Germany
and place her in a family in Hamburg as a governess. She soon
discovered that in Prussia at that time the ruling class was the
officer class. Any girl who managed to get engaged to an officer
was the envy of her friends and the pride of her parents, who did
not mind in the least the scant courtesy with which their future
son-in-law treated them. The eldest daughter of my mother's
employers brought off this triumph while she was there and was
in a state of sentimental rapture about her *leutnant*. All Prussian
officers of that time wore the spiked, upturned moustaches, so
familiar in the portraits of Kaiser Wilhelm II, and to keep them
trained upwards they wore a contraption at night. One of the
ways in which Lisa showed her devotion to her *Leutnant* was to
make these contraptions for him and embroidered them with
forget-me-nots. Other girls in her position would even stuff
pincushions for their fiancés with their own hair. My mother
was shocked by the slavish attitude of German women towards
men and even more so by the German husband's calm assumption that a wife should devote herself entirely to ministering to

his wants and have no interests beyond the famous three K's – *Kirche, Kuche und Kinder*. She was also shocked by the vast quantities of food and drink consumed by the Germans. On Sundays so many courses were served at the family lunch that the meal often lasted three hours and she found it almost unbearable to sit through. Her employers were distressed that she ate so little. They found their 'English Miss' alarmingly thin and were anxious to fatten her up. They hoped that the good nourishing German food would fill out her slender figure to the plumpness proper to a healthy young woman. However, she had no desire to resemble the stout German *Mädchen*, who stuffed themselves even between meals with cream cakes and *apfelstrüdel*, and she returned to England as slim as she had left it. All the same, her life with the Hamburg family had many compensations, one of which was that it greatly increased her self-confidence. Her employers treated her with the greatest kindness and respect and were much impressed by the speed with which she learnt to speak fluent German. She was naturally a good linguist and, rather to her surprise, found she was a good teacher. Besides managing to instil some English and French into the heads of the daughters, she successfully coached Karli, the student son of the house, for his English examination. Karli, a gentle, intelligent boy, developed a *schwarmerei* for her and, though she did not return his passion, she liked him very much and enjoyed being admired. All her life, my mother frankly admitted that there was nothing she liked more than admiration and she had quite an agreeable amount of it in Hamburg, for Karli was not the only young man who fell romantically in love with her and wrote poems to her. One rather curious result of living in Germany was that she became interested in philosophy and took to reading Schopenhauer. As a result she went through a phase of Pessimism, which, rather amusingly, was to prove one of the things that attracted my father when he met her for the first time. I think it must have been in Hamburg that she had her remarkable nightmare about eternity. She went to bed speculating about the nature of eternity and dreamt that she was tied to a great wheel perpetually revolving in empty space. 'It depressed me so dreadfully, darling,' she told me, 'that the next morning I went straight out and bought a new hat.'

She returned to England in the late summer of 1893. It was the first time she had seen her family for nearly four years, and not only Howard and Alice but 'Papa' himself urged her to stay at home for several months. She joined a local tennis club which my father, who was living nearby in Dulwich, had recently joined. He had just completed his first year as a junior master at Colet Court and, feeling the need for some form of physical exercise, he had taken up tennis. He played very badly, but, after meeting my mother, he suddenly decided that 'tennis was a very nice game'. He told me afterwards that what most impressed him at that first meeting was the 'charming little continental bow' she gave him when they were introduced. They were soon deeply in love and by Christmas had reached a secret 'understanding' for my father did not feel it fair to tie her down to a positive engagement, since it might be years before he was in a position to marry her. But in January 1894 he could no longer endure the uncertainty of a mere 'understanding'. Early one morning he rushed over to the house in Palace Road and finding her alone, proposed to her. My mother needed no persuasion to accept him, for, as she frequently told me later, 'Daddy must really have been truly in love to propose to me at that moment for I had a bad cold and was looking my worst. And as I wasn't expecting visitors at that time of day I was wearing a hideous old pink blouse I'd made myself and hadn't even done my hair properly.'

For the time being they decided to keep their engagement secret from their respective parents. But, after a few weeks, they felt they had to be told of it. 'Papa' took the news surprisingly well and even congratulated my father on having chosen 'the pick of the bunch'; the latter's own parents could hardly object, though his mother would have done so if she dared. In her opinion Christine White was much too vain and selfish to make her beloved Cecil a good wife. Her only consolation was that, as the engagement was bound to be a long one, he might come to realise this for himself or, better still, Christine would get tired of waiting and break it off.

However, neither of them even considered breaking it off, though it was over four years before they were able to marry. Since my mother had to earn her living in the meantime she took a post as governess with an English family named Garrard who lived in a large country house in Berkshire. The Garrards were 'horsey' people. Their grown-up children, Claude and Elsie, would ride miles to attend a meet and Elsie had spent so much time on horseback since her childhood, that she had permanently displaced one hip as a result of riding side-saddle, as was *de rigueur* for women in those days, and walked with a limp. But my mother's pupil, their younger daughter Nina, suffered from a far worse physical disability than a limp, for she had only one arm. The other had been bitten off by a donkey.

[One of the surprising things about my mother was that, impatient and quick tempered as she was, she showed remarkable tolerance towards Nina who, although an apt pupil, was also a difficult one. As she said: 'You couldn't blame Nina for being bad tempered at times.'

Christine Barbour White resigned her post without regret in order to become Christine Botting on 15 March, 1897.]

5.

I cannot say at what point I became conscious of myself, as it were, as a going concern, surrounded with familiar objects and people and firmly established in my own identity. I think I was probably getting on for four when this consciousness became continuous. Before that, there are of course flashes of momentary perception, lucid intervals in which I was perfectly aware of myself and my surroundings, but between them is a blank which I can only fill up from hearsay.

The first lucid interval must have occurred when I was a baby. I 'came to' suddenly out of nowhere, and saw as clearly as if I were seeing them now, black rails above me and, suspended from them, white hangings. I can even remember that the white draperies hung unevenly and were tied at the rail with tape and that there was a scorch mark on them. It puzzles me how they could have left such a definite imprint on my mind when I could have no concept of such things as 'rails' and 'hangings'.

Long afterward, my parents corroborated that I did sleep in such a cot, but only during the first year of my life after which I, at any rate, never saw it again.

'Of course it may have been described to you later,' said my father. 'Still it sounds like a genuine infantile memory. That scorch mark is very circumstantial.'

'If you can remember being in your cot, can you remember my coming in and tucking you up and kissing you goodnight?' asked my mother.

'No, I'm afraid I can't.'

'But I used to every single night when you were a baby. Didn't I, Cecil? Once you were so cross with me because we were going out to dinner and the cab was waiting at the door and I insisted on going in to say goodnight to Eirene first. You were in a vile temper all the way to the restaurant.'

'More likely because you'd taken such an unconscionable time dressing.'

'Oh no, that time it was definitely because I wouldn't leave the house till I'd said goodnight to her. I can tell you exactly what I was wearing that night . . . my black chiffon with the pink satin chou and nothing over the shoulders but two velvet straps. And I had a sequin dragon-fly in my hair.'

'I can't remember that particular instance of my brutality.' He smiled at her. 'But I do remember that particular dress. To my mind, one of the most becoming you ever had.'

'I believe *you* thought I looked rather nice in it,' she said, turning to me. 'At any rate, whenever I was wearing it when I tucked you up in your cot you used to stare at me very attentively and then suddenly give me the sweetest smile as if you decidedly approved of your mother's looks. As for that dragon-fly – it fascinated you so much, I suppose because it glittered – that you used to put up your little hand and try to pull it out of my hair. I'm sure you *could* remember if you tried.'

But, try as I would, I could not conjure up the required memory of my beautiful mother in a black chiffon evening dress with a sequin dragon-fly in her hair bending lovingly over my cot. It consoled her a little that I could not remember my father doing so either though apparently he did it quite often. However it seems he was nervous of kissing me as I was apt to cry at the contact of his spiky waxed moustache.

As my mother's mother had died when she was two months old and her only married sister had gone to America before I was born, there was no one to advise her how to cope with a young baby but the person whose advice she had no intention of taking on anything; her mother-in-law. I have no doubt that a great deal was offered and that its rejection increased my grandmother's grievances against her son's wife. In my grandmother's opinion her daughter-in-law was a shockingly selfish and neglectful mother. However I grew into a remarkably healthy child in spite of it. My mother was, in fact, very fond of me, but she was not the kind of woman who finds deep

Portrait with her mother at the age of seven. At her own insistence, and to her mother's chagrin, Antonia wears her Froebel school tunic and a hussar's cap. Her mother wears a hat adapted from one that had been Antonia's as a bridesmaid, a piece of pilfering that Antonia resented.

Inset: Antonia feeding the chickens at the age of three. The occasion was a country holiday with the relatives of Connie, one of her mother's two servants. Antonia always claimed to have forgotten the visit.

satisfaction in ministering to the physical needs of her baby. She was only too thankful to leave all that side to someone else and be free to enjoy a social life and the more romantic aspects of motherhood. Since my parents could not afford a nurse one of the current cooks or housemaids did duty as my 'nannie'.

There was another lucid moment which must have occurred when I was still a baby, for I know that I was in a pram. It is impossible to convey how I knew this and I have no image of the pram itself. It must either have had no hood or the hood must have been down, for I could see what was happening behind me. Perhaps I was sitting up in it for I was able to turn my head and see whoever was pushing me along. I cannot possibly describe her but it seems to me that I did at the time recognise her as some presence and voice with which I was familiar and that there was some kind of communication between us. Not enough, however, for me to convey to her that I strongly objected to something she was doing to the pram and wished she would stop. Every now and then she would give it a shove, take her hands off the handle, and let it run forward a little way on its own momentum before catching up with it again and checking it. Each time I felt the pram running away with me, I was paralysed with terror and convinced that she would never be able to catch it again. I do not suppose that I was in any real danger. Whoever was in charge of me was probably in complete control of the situation but how was I to know that? Perhaps she thought I enjoyed these sudden bursts of speed and was exerting herself to amuse me. However, for me it was a most alarming experience and my first awareness of fear, insecurity and what I can almost describe as moral indignation. For each time she repeated the proceeding some intuition told me that she *ought* not to be doing it and that some greater authority would be angry if she knew. But the greater authority was not there to intervene on my behalf and I felt utterly helpless, unjustly abandoned to malevolent forces beyond my control and powerless to make any protest.

My second lucid moment lasted longer than my first and this time I was not a placid neutral spectator unaware of any emotions, pleasant or unpleasant, but a sentient being, involved in a situation and conscious of complex feelings and even a rudimentary ability to think, though unable to express its thoughts. But the 'coming to' was very brief. Like a patient momentarily emerging from an anaesthetic, I found myself there in the pram and then relapsed into unconsciousness again. I have no more notion how the pram ride ended than how it began. Obviously it did not end in any disaster, for in the accounts of various accidents which befell me in infancy there was no mention of one connected with a pram. But I think it was a traumatic experience for all my life I have had an irrational terror of the sensation of being 'out of control'. I have never been able to learn to skate or ride a bicycle. As soon as I find myself unsupported, abandoned to a dizzy momentum I cannot check, I lose my nerve and fall and am too cowardly to persevere. It is not the fall I dread so much as the sense of panic-stricken helplessness that preceded it.

Perversely, I have no recollection of something my father took great pains to impress on my memory. I suppose, as I was getting on for two at the time, he thought there was a hope that something connected with the occasion would linger in my mind, so that I would be able to say in after life that I remembered Queen Victoria's funeral. But all the trouble he took was wasted. However much I would have liked to be able to say I remembered being held up in his arms to watch the procession, my mind remained obstinately blank and he had to be satisfied with the knowledge that he had done his best to provide me with a historic memory.

It surprised me more that I cannot remember Socrates, my father's Manchester terrier whom he had at Cambridge. He was quite an old dog when I was born and so attached to his master that it was feared he might be jealous of the new arrival. On the contrary, he took a great liking to me, constituted himself my guardian and growled at any stranger who approached me – sometimes, even, at my parents. I was evidently as devoted to Sock as he was to me and could hardly bear to be separated from him. The only photograph of me as a baby, taken when I was one year old, shows a plump solemn infant in a lace-trimmed frock with one hand resting on the collar of a large black and white dog. It seems that no sooner had I been propped up on a chair to face the camera than Sock seated himself at my feet in his position of watchdog and reassured me by his comforting presence. I faced it with stoical calm. I was about two when he had to be put down and I am told that for several days I missed him so badly that I seldom stopped crying and refused to be comforted. Although I cannot remember him, my friendship with him must certainly have been responsible for the irresistible fascination all dogs possessed for me in my childhood. I had such a passionate fondness for them and such absolute confidence in their goodwill towards myself that I had only to see a dog to make enthusiastic advances. No grown-up warnings – 'Don't touch him dear, he may bite' – could deter me from accosting strange dogs in the street and caressing them. I was convinced they would never bite *me*, and, in fact they never did. At home, the most boring visitor would suddenly become a delightfully exciting one if she turned up accompanied by a dog. This sometimes led to embarrassing situations for my parents, as the whispered injunction 'Now go and say how d'you do nicely to Mr and Mrs So-and-so' was apt to be met by a very audible, 'Please need I? They haven't brought their dog.' After Sock we never again had a dog of our own in London. But sometimes my parents would look after a friend's dog while its owner was away and of course I became so attached to the visiting dog that I wanted it to stay for ever. Still, the ecstasy of taking it out on a lead and pretending it was mine almost made up for the pain of parting with it.

There is a human being whom I am surprised I do not remember more clearly, for she looked after me all through my infancy and did not leave till I was over three. This was Lizzie the cook who replaced the legendary Emily, my parents' first servant. I do not know whether it was before or after my birth that the memorable episode occurred which resulted in Emily's dismissal. She was apparently a very handsome girl and a wonderful worker, but she had a fiery temper and she drank. One day she got violently drunk and chased my mother, who was alone in the house, all the way upstairs, brandishing a rolling pin and threatening to kill her. My mother had just time to get into her bedroom and lock the door. There she stood, trembling, behind a wardrobe while Emily battered on the door with the rolling pin, shouting drunken menaces. My father returned from school to find Emily lying senseless on the landing and my mother still locked in the bedroom, too terrified to emerge.

Lizzie, unlike Emily, was plain and middle-aged. If I remember rightly, she was a gaunt woman with a thin face, red complexion and frizzy dark hair. But she too had a temper. It was never aroused against me, only against anyone whom she thought was being unkind to me. Apparently she idolised me so much that she could not bear to hear me scolded and there were constant clashes between her and my parents over questions of discipline. In her opinion they were far too strict with me and she actually dared to say so.

'Such impertinence!' my mother said indignantly one day,

reminiscing to me about my early childhood. 'We were *never* unkind to you, only determined you shouldn't be spoilt. If Lizzie had had her way, she'd have ruined you. I'm sure we couldn't have been more doting parents but we weren't going to let you turn into one of those odious children who expect to get their own way in everything and scream if they don't. Sweet little thing as you were, you could be very self-willed. Every bit as obstinate as your father.' She smiled. 'You took after him in *every* way, but most of all in that. Really, I had to laugh sometimes, you were so absurdly alike.' She added, after a moment, 'I did think *he* was too hard on you sometimes when you were little. But luckily you weren't a sensitive child as I was. Such a good thing you weren't. I was such an *absurdly* sensitive creature always. I've *always* felt things more than other people.' She sighed. 'I believe I was *literally* born with a skin too few.' Then she smiled again. 'Daddy used to tell me when we were engaged that I was like the princess who could feel a pea under seven mattresses.'

The classic example of my obstinacy occurred in connection with Lizzie. I have no recollection whatever of the incident, though I was nearly three at the time and, as will be seen, very decidedly 'walking and talking'. I find it hard to believe it really happened, but my mother described it to me so often and so circumstantially as one of the few times I was sensationally naughty when I was little that it probably did. It must be the only recorded instance of my openly defying my father.

As soon as I was able to sit up on a chair piled with cushions and eat fairly tidily, I had my midday meal with my parents. My father came home from St Paul's for lunch and it was almost the only time I saw him during the week, for when he returned from afternoon school there was always a private pupil waiting in the study and by dinner time I had long been in bed in the night nursery which I shared with Lizzie. It was during these lunches that I probably made good progress in speech and still better in understanding grown-up conversation. My father never addressed me in baby talk and disapproved strongly of anyone else's doing so. From the first, I was made to give things their right names and not prattle about 'gee-gees' and 'bow-wows'. I was also made to pronounce my words properly and not lisp or slur my syllables. I was allowed to speak only when spoken to but I was quite often invited to have my say, interrupted only by my mother's eternal exhortations. 'Sit up straight', 'Stop fidgeting with your spoon' and 'Wipe your mouth', or my father's

correcting my pronunciation. Then would come another inter-
lude of the dialogue from which I was excluded in which the
participants addressed each other as Cecil and Christine and
became, from my point of view, two mysterious characters who
had no connection with Daddy and Mummy. The conversation was equally mysterious but, as I was fascinated by words,
I acquired a great many new ones and gradually pieced together
their meaning.

The ringing of the bell for the removal of the sweet course was
also the signal for Lizzie to come and remove me, so that my
parents could enjoy their coffee in peace. One day when she
came in, as usual, to take me off to the nursery, it seems I spoke
very rudely to her. My father, enraged, thundered: 'Apologise
at once to Elizabeth. At *once*, do you hear?' Astonishingly, I
refused. Whereupon, he picked me up and carried me off, not to
my nursery, but right up to the very top of the house and locked
me in his dressing-room. Then he stood outside the door and
informed me that I should not be let out until I said I was sorry.
But I still refused to apologise so he went downstairs again,
leaving me in solitary confinement to come to my senses. Lizzie,
now in tears at having been the cause of my terrible punishment,
was banished to the kitchen and forbidden to go upstairs. My
mother was told not to interfere. This was a matter in which the
master of the house was 'for *once*' going to exert his authority.
Not only had I been rude to a servant but I had wilfully
disobeyed his orders. He then proceeded to drink his coffee in
peace. Or rather to try to, for my mother thought the punishment was too severe for a child of under three, however
disgracefully it had behaved. My father insisted that I was old
enough to know what I was doing and to deserve a sharp lesson
in obedience. The first and foremost thing a child had to learn
was to obey and this could not be too firmly impressed on it.
However, my mother worried so much at the thought of me
locked up alone in a room at the top of the house, too far away
for my cries to be heard and by now perhaps really frightened,
that eventually she persuaded him to come upstairs with her and
listen outside the dressing-room door. But what they heard was
not terrified sobbing. Their daughter was stamping about the
room and shouting lustily: 'Shan't apologise, shan't, shan't,
shan't.'

When I was told this story I was so lost in admiration of my
reckless spirit that I forgot to inquire whether I was finally
brought to repentance.

The relations between Lizzie and my parents finally became so strained that she was given notice. She wept bitter tears at parting from me, but, ungratefully, I seem to have accepted her going quite calmly and not mourned her disappearance as I had mourned the disappearance of Socrates. It seems hard that, after all the fierce devotion she lavished on me, she should have left so little impression. What surprised me most is that I have no recollection of what must have been at the time an ecstatic experience: staying with Lizzie at her home in the country. Yet I remember detail after detail of what I myself could have sworn was my first visit to the country; the holiday I spent with my grandparents at Binesfield when I was four.

In the summer of 1902 when I was three, my parents took the first of a series of holidays abroad, leaving me behind in England. This year it was decided that I should have a holiday too and Lizzie was allowed to take me to stay with her parents who lived in the country – I do not know in what county. Apparently it was a great success and what delighted me most was being allowed to feed the chickens. She had a snapshot of me doing so and I have it to this day. But stare as I will at that child, recognisably myself, in a sunbonnet, earnestly concentrated on the responsible task of feeding the chickens, not the faintest memory stirs. What I do remember of that summer is the present my mother brought me back from Paris. Perhaps my joy in that swamped every other joy and I forgot even the baby chickens. After all they were not *mine*. For this was my toy black poodle, my cherished companion for years, at once dog and super-human, Mr Dash.

I know for certain that I was three when my father decided once again to try and impress something on my memory. This time his effort was not wasted as it had been over Queen Victoria's funeral. I could not forget the first line of the *Iliad* if I tried or the circumstances in which I learnt it.

He must have been longing from my birth for the day when he could begin my classical education.

One Sunday evening he decided to teach me by ear the first line of the *Iliad*. It must have been late autumn or winter for there was a fire in the study grate under the black marble mantelpiece with its row of framed photographs, including the one of myself and Socrates, and the gilt and black marble clock in the shape of the Parthenon. I stood on the hearthrug, close by my father's desk, at which he was seated in his high-backed Windsor chair. He was wearing his red waistcoat with the brass buttons which I greatly admired and which my mother called his 'robin red-breast'. First he intoned several times, with the emotion which always came into his voice when he quoted a Greek or Latin poet:

μηυιγ αειδε, θεα, Πηληϊδεω ᾿Αχιληος

He used the old pronunciation, as I think he continued to do all his life. Then, syllable by syllable, he taught me the incomprehensible words till at last I could recite in a solemn sing-song: 'Mee-nin ay-i-de Pee-lee-i ad-yo Ak-il-ee-os.'

Then I had to learn by heart in the same parrot fashion the incomprehensible words of the translation: 'Sing, oh Goddess, the wrath of Achilles, the son of Peleus.' It was not till some months later when I had begun my regular Sunday lessons in Greek mythology, that I realised that the goddess was not being invited to sing the wrath of 'a kill-ease'.

After a time my attention began to wander and, as a result, I tripped more often, now over a Greek word, now over an English one. The hands of the marble clock were pointing nearer and nearer to six, an hour I knew very well because it was the easiest to read and it was also my bedtime. I also knew that my grandparents were coming over for Sunday supper and that they were due to arrive at six. When they came over to Sunday supper, I was allowed to stay up a little later than usual because they came so early expressly to see me before I was put to bed. It was my treat to run out into the hall the moment I heard the doorbell, hide behind the big oak chest and, as soon as the maid had let them in, jump out and surprise them. They were always delightfully surprised and I think they enjoyed this ritual game as much as I did. With one ear cocked for the doorbell, I was no longer making much effort to get my lines right and my father was becoming impatient.

'Come along, Eirene, you can say it perfectly well if you try.'

I knew that note in his voice and concentrated again on 'mee-nin ay-i-de thee-ay'. I had managed for the first time to get both lines right when I heard the door-bell.

'Can I go now? That's Granny and Grandpa!' I exclaimed, already on the move. It was essential to get into my hiding place behind the oak chest before the maid answered the door.

'Stay where you are,' he commanded.

'But I always go and . . .'

'Stand still and don't fidget,' he interrupted. I realised it was useless to protest. I was not allowed to stir from that hearthrug until I had repeated my piece three times without a fault. He gave me an approving nod and smiled.

'Good. I think you've got it well in your head now. You can run along now and meet Granny and Grandpa.'

But from my point of view it was too late. My grandparents were already outside the study door and I had been deprived of the treat of lying in ambush in the hall and springing out and surprising them. I think my wrath against Homer at that moment exceeded the wrath of Achilles. But at least I never forgot the first line of the *Iliad*. I only know that I was three when I learnt it because my father told me so.

That episode is the first vivid personal memory I have of him. All the earlier ones are blurred into the haze from which I did not emerge permanently till I was four, when, without quite know-ing how it had come about, I found myself established in a solid, continuous world and very much aware of everyone and every-thing, including myself, contained in it.

6.

I think one reason why everything came into focus when I was four was that by then I could read and write. I do not know when my mother gave me my first lessons from that classic primer *Reading without Tears*. I know that they took place in the drawing-room and I can still see the book in its blue and gold cover and the hyphenated words and little black and white drawings on its yellow pages. It more than justified its title, for I learnt to read so quickly and pleasurably that there seemed to be hardly any transition between being able to decipher 'The cat sat on the mat' and finding myself literate. Another primer helped me to learn quickly: the enamelled tin advertisements on the omni-buses. My mother sometimes took me shopping with her in Kensington High Street or, as an occasional treat, to Kensington Gardens. The journey in the green, horse-drawn omnibus gave me a wonderful opportunity to exercise my new skill by de-ciphering the names of various commodities such as Monkey Brand, Sapolio, Van Houten's Cocoa and Mazawattee Tea. I developed strong feelings for or against certain goods, depend-ing sometimes on their names, sometimes on the pictures and trademarks associated with them. I would gladly have obeyed the injunction 'Always use Sapolio' because Sapolio was such a beautiful word, unlike Mazawattee which I thought both silly and ugly and, for some reason, rather vulgar, perhaps because it rhymed with 'potty'. The one I disliked most was Mellin's Food which had a personal and embarrassing significance for me. The first time I spelt it out, my mother informed me that I had been reared on it and added with a smile: 'I think you're quite a good advertisement for Mellin's Food.' The bus was crowded and though my mother's high-pitched voice was soft, it was a voice that carried. Several passengers stared and grinned at me. I turned hot with shame because I thought they were identifying me with the bloated baby in the picture. Ever afterwards, if we travelled in a bus containing a Mellin's Food advertisement, I averted my eyes from it. Naturally my favourite was Nestlé's Milk with its Louis Wain cats, the fat contented white one and the poor lean ginger one. I was never tired of looking at the pictures and reading the story which ended so happily with the thin one becoming as fat as the white one after he had persuaded his owners to give him rich, full-cream Nestlé's instead of skim milk.

The legend under the little-curly-haired boy blowing soap bubbles who advertised Pear's Soap presented a problem. It said 'Matchless for the complexion'. I had not realised before that Pear's was the only soap that had no matches in it and thought how much safer it must be than the kind we used at home. For a long time I supposed that the burning sensation when soap got in my eyes was due to the matches in it.

Although my mother's nickname for me was Madam Why-Why, I was often too proud to ask questions and preferred to puzzle out my own interpretations of a word rather than show my ignorance. Very often, as in the case of 'matchless', I caused myself a great deal of unnecessary anxiety but I did at least exercise my mind. By the time I was four, I was a confirmed bookworm and, in some ways, I suppose, precocious. Being the only child in a house full of grown-up people and having no companions of my own age, I had so much time, whether alone or in the company of my elders, to reflect on everything I saw and heard and read that my brain developed a good deal ahead of the rest of me. In feelings and behaviour I was still a child and very conscious of my utter dependence on the adults who ruled my life but in my mind, apart from lack of knowledge and experience, I think I was very little different at four from what I am now, over seventy years later. At any rate if I reached the 'age of reason' before the official age of seven, I doubt if I am any more rational now than I was then.

Now that I could read, my own life often seemed depressingly uneventful. I could, and did, pretend to be many people other than myself, some out of books, some of my own invention. I acted out a great many dramas alone in my nursery, with a supporting cast of dolls and toy animals who were also transformed into different characters. As they could not talk, I had to act their parts as well as my own. But the imaginary adventures in which I involved them and myself, however exciting, were not the same as real ones. However thoroughly I threw myself into my various rôles, I knew that I was only *pretending* to be a witch or a princess or a shipwrecked mariner. The nursery door had only to open and some grown-up voice say: 'Come and wash your hands' or announce that it was time to get ready for my walk, or worse still, bed – 'Come along now, don't dawdle', and once again I was just Eirene, involved in a life I had no power to change.

Nevertheless, I did not always want to change it. Very often I was quite satisfied with it as it was. If in bored or rebellious moments I sometimes thought of running away from home, as children so often did in books, I always ended by deciding not to, at any rate not just yet. When Daddy was not being stern, I could not imagine a nicer father, and though I would have preferred Aunt Edith for a mother, my own could be very pleasant when she liked and I could overlook many of her irritating ways when I remembered that she had given me Mr Dash. And I should miss Bessie the cook and Millie the housemaid, both of whom were very kind to me, and our tabby cat Sunny. Even if Sunny sometimes scratched me and strongly objected to being put in a doll's cradle, with a handkerchief tied round his head to impersonate the wolf in Red Riding Hood, I loved him dearly because he was a real live animal. However, he usually eluded capture when I tried to carry him off from the kitchen premises where he lived and imprison him in the nursery. Even when I succeeded, the moment someone opened the door he escaped with unflattering speed back to his own territory in the basement and the only two members of the household to whom he was really attached, Bessie and Millie. I knew that I would never be able to persuade Sunny to accompany me on my travels in search of adventure, though he would have been a great asset, for he was as expert a mouser as Dick Whittington's cat. Of course I should take Mr Dash with me. He had been my inseparable companion ever since the day he arrived and I loved him more than anything in the world.

I had always preferred toy animals to dolls; the few dolls I possessed had no personalities of their own, only the ones I assigned to them in my dramas. Even my biggest and most lifelike one, Cynthia, who had real flaxen hair, could open and shut her brown eyes and be dressed and undressed, ceased to interest me once I had stripped her a few times of her shot-silk frock, lace-edged petticoat and muslin drawers and reclothed her. I admired her looks but I had no personal affection for her. I much preferred a small shabby yellow velvet cat called Tiger Tim who had lost one eye and had a tail. He had started life as a pincushion and was peppered all over with pinpricks but, although ugly, he had an engaging grin and a cheerful nature which had survived many indignities and misfortunes, from being thrown away as rubbish to being clawed and chewed by Sammy who used him as a dummy for mousing practice. Fond as I was of Tiger Tim and of other more presentable animals, I could have borne parting with all of them provided I could keep Mr Dash.

He looked exactly like a real black poodle. His coat was of real fleece and he was perfect in every detail from his top-knot to his tufted tail. When my mother first put him into my arms, I could not believe that this glorious creature was really mine to keep. Assured that he was and that Mummy had brought him all the way from Paris as a lovely surprise for me, I was too over-whelmed to thank her. I could only clutch him tight and bury my face in his silky fleece.

'Aren't you going to kiss Mummy too? Haven't you missed her all these weeks she's been away?'

I had not even noticed her absence, but I gave her a kiss of passionate gratitude. At that moment I truly loved her. But not as much as the black poodle.

'What's his name, you must name him yourself? As he's a French poodle, you might call him "Toutou".'

I thought it a silly name for so noble a dog, but my mind was a blank and I could only shake my head at that and all the other names she suggested. Finally she produced 'Dash'. I liked that much better. I stroked back his long silky ears and gazed questioningly into his intelligent brown eyes. After a moment I nodded.

'He says yes. Only, please it's *Mister Dash*.'

Later I gave him a Christian name as well, Bruce, after a dog my father had had when he was a little boy and of whom I could never hear enough, either from him or my grandparents. But he only used his full name when he signed letters or official proclamations to his subjects. From the moment he arrived, all dolls and animals accepted him as their rightful ruler and did homage to him.

Naturally he was the principal hero of all my nursery dramas but I never had to invent another personality for him, only speeches noble enough to express his own. His courage was, of course, dauntless but bravery was only one of his superficial qualities. He had other deeper sides to his nature which I respected even more. He was sage and reflective, something of a philosopher, in his way, and always ready with comfort and advice when I was in difficulties. I looked up to him as a being older and wiser than myself with whom I could be more intimate than with any grown-up. Yet for me Mr Dash was always a dog, though a magic one. He was a true familiar, like Puss-in-Boots, not a fairy prince disguised as a toy black poodle. He had a very noble character and exquisite, slightly formal manners and he always expressed himself in very dignified language, both in speech and writing. Though often gay, he was by nature serious and he had a touch of reflective melancholy in his disposition which made him wonderfully sympathetic when I was in low spirits myself. There were times, especially when we lay awake together in the dark, when Mr Dash confided to me that he too found many problems insoluble and was sometimes overwhelmed by the complexities of life.

Nevertheless, if home seemed dull at times, it had its compensations. And now and then quite exciting things happened to me, such as Father Christmas coming down the chimney and leaving me a pillow-case full of presents. Next time – if Christmas *ever* came again – was any day ever so long in coming? – I might manage to stay awake long enough to catch him and ask him to take me for a ride in his sleigh over the roofs of the houses. Perhaps he would even let me drive the reindeer. If I were not still at 22 Perham Road, West Kensington, London, Middlesex, England, he might not know where to find me.

That was our full address and now that I could write I sometimes put the whole of it on the folded pieces of paper directed to Miss Eirene Botting, with a stamp drawn in red pencil which I occasionally slipped among the real letters on the oak chest in the hall so that when my parents opened theirs at breakfast, I too had a letter to read. It took a long time to write out, but it made them look more important as if they came from 'abroad'. 'Abroad' had acquired great prestige for me since Mr

Dash had come from there. Occasionally I had real postcards from 'abroad' for my mother's sisters, Auntie Bee and Auntie Connie, whom I had never met, actually lived there in a place called Vienna. Its name had a glamour for me – for some reason I always pictured it as a very smart lady in evening dress dashing off gay tunes on a golden piano – but nothing like the glamour of the name Paris. I had no mental image of Paris. To me it was simply an incantatory word which, when I closed my eyes, I could see flashing in letters of dazzling white light. But Auntie Connie's and Auntie Bee's treasured postcards written in purple ink and adorned with pictures of Easter hares and children dressed like Hansel and Gretel arrived seldom and they were not signed 'Eirene'. Sometimes they came from a fairy or from a character in a book but my most frequent correspondent was Mr Dash. One of his has survived. I found it among my mother's papers after her death. It is inscribed in her own handwriting: 'Written entirely by herself by Eirene aged four.' It reads as follows:

The waves are drifting High alas. Our ship is sinking Alas now we must die

Yours truely
Bruce Dash esq.

7.

Outwardly, Perham Road has changed little since I first remember it over seventy years ago. Its brown brick is dingier, its stucco more scabrous and one or two more of the stone urns shaped like policemen's helmets have fallen off the balustrade which surmounts its tall, narrow houses. Nevertheless its character has altered. It has the forlorn, unkempt look of a street that has gone down in the world. I doubt if one of those houses, rising three stories above their basements, is now inhabited by a single family and not let off in flats or furnished 'bedsitters'. Dirty curtains hang at the windows and lines of washing on their balconies; their doorsteps are uncleaned and the paint of their front-doors cracked and peeling. No. 22 is one of the shabbiest. When I stood gazing at it a few months ago, its front door was wide open and I could see down a passage covered with worn linoleum to the room next to my father's study that had once been my nursery and now appeared to be a kitchen. I was half tempted to walk down the passage – it would have been easy to find some pretext for entering a house obviously occupied by several tenants – but at that moment a grubby child sucking a lolly emerged on to the chipped, dirty steps of the stucco porch.

I lost my nerve and hurried away up the street to the far and 'better' end of Perham Road where the houses are of red brick and some of their windows look out on the grounds of Queen's Club. From there I made my way back to West Kensington station by another route. Now that I had verified that the house was still there, I did not want to see it again in its decrepit shabbiness. I had instinctively looked for its red front door, its polished brass knocker and well-hearthstoned steps instead of its number and gone well past it before I realised that the dark brown door and the dirty steps belonged to No. 22. I had stood for a while staring at its bleared front windows, the basement one belonging to the servants' bedroom, the drawing-room ones above and the two smaller ones of my parents' bedroom on the top floor, with an odd sensation that the house was staring back at me, with an expression at once blank and defiant, as if it were deliberately disclaiming any remembrance of me, like an old acquaintance who has gone down in the world and cuts former friends out of pride. I shall not go and look at it again. I prefer to remember it as it was when for twenty-seven years it was the home of my family.

Each room had its own particular character and atmosphere. When I was a child, it seemed to me that people's personalities changed according to the room they were in. For instance, my parents tended to be more irritable with me and with each other in the dining-room, whereas they were always gay and good-tempered in the drawing-room. And Bessie and Millie were quite different in the kitchen from what they were 'upstairs'. As for myself, the mere words, 'The Master wants to see you in his study, Miss Eirene,' made me hastily examine my conscience as I removed my pinafore, whereas if I was summoned to the drawing-room I knew there was nothing to fear. Not that my father was invariably stern in the study: he often welcomed me with his most genial smile. But enthroned in his high-backed Windsor chair at his great double desk, half-veiled in clouds of blue smoke from his pipe, I was more conscious of him in the study as the Zeus who ruled our domestic Olympus than in any other room in the house. I knew quite a lot about the gods of Olympus by now for every Sunday after tea he gave me a lesson on them. Unlike my first introduction to Homer, I thoroughly enjoyed these lessons and because I was really interested, I learnt quickly. He had made out a list for me of the Greek and Latin names of all the gods and goddesses in his exquisitely clear and legible writing, the Greek names in one column in red ink and the corresponding Latin ones in green so that now I knew them all by heart and who was the god or goddess of what. I also knew what each looked like for he showed me pictures of their statues and he would test me by putting his hand over the name beneath to see if I could get it right. The first I learnt to identify was Athene, the goddess of war and wisdom, for there was a plaster bust of her wearing her helmet engraved with the owl's face on the tall bookcase opposite his desk. Poe's 'pallid bust of Pallas' in *The Raven* will always be for me the one on the top of the bookcase in my father's study. In fact I still instinctively see the whole poem in that setting as I did when I first had it read to me. The raven steps in through the big window to the left of my father's desk and perches on his dusty cast of Athene and the cushioned seat that 'the lamplight gloated o'er' is lined, not with violet velvet, but with the faded green plush of his great 'Duke of Norfolk' armchair.

The study is always the first room I think of when I remember 22 Perham Road. Not only has it more potent associations for me than any other, but it was also the one room that never changed in the twenty-odd years I lived there. Minor alterations took place in others. Pieces of furniture were added or removed, curtains and chair-covers were renewed, occasionally a wallpaper that was not the exact replica of its predecessor made a room look different until one got used to it. But the study remained unchanged, sacred to my father and so impregnated with his aura that even when it was empty one could feel his presence there. Though, with that constant stream of pupils, more people came and went in it than any other room in the house, its atmosphere was impervious to the imprint of any personality but his. It blotted out all trace of any other as completely as its permanent smell of dusty books and stale tobacco smoke blotted out all trace of my mother's scent.

When I last saw my father in his study in 1926, it still looked the same as it did when he taught me the first line of the *Iliad* in 1902. And I am sure it looked the same in that autumn of 1899

22 Perham Road, the house in West Kensington where Antonia spent her childhood. It is mentioned in each of the novels that make up the 'Frost in May' quartet, and a return visit to it in its present decay is touchingly described in the *Autobiography*. Its name in fiction was Valetta Road.

when Compton Mackenzie, then aged sixteen, used to come over twice a week from 54 Avonmore Road on the other side of West Kensington to be coached by him. I cannot resist quoting the whole passage in 'Octave Two' of *My Life and Times* in which Sir Compton refers to this. Not only does it conjure up my father's presence so vividly but something of his character too. Some years earlier Compton Mackenzie had been in my father's form at Colet Court and he had a great affection for 'dear Botting', as my father had for him. Now both master and pupil were at St Paul's but Compton Mackenzie was not in his form. In that Michaelmas term of 1899 there was a financial crisis in his father's affairs and there was even talk of cutting short his brilliant sixteen-year-old son's academic career and articling him to a firm of solicitors.

Gloom had descended upon 54 Avonmore Road . . . As for going to Oxford, that was out of the question unless I won a scholarship. I consulted Botting, who suggested I should keep up my Classics and generously offered to set me composition and unseens twice a week: he said that, even if I decided finally to go in for a history scholarship, a good Latin prose or a facile translation of an unseen would help.

Botting lived at 22 Perham Road and I think by now had just been married. He was plumper than ever and always smoked Guards Mixture, which was the strongest of the Carreras mixtures . . . There was always a quarter-pound tin of Guards Mixture standing by Botting's side on his desk in that small study at the back of the dining-room and Botting used to puff away incessantly at one of half-a-dozen large curved pipes. The wall opposite his desk was lined with books and to my surprise one evening I noticed the green volume of Oscar Wilde's *Intentions*. Out of some ridiculous schoolboy embarrassment I did not like to ask Botting to lend me the book; but I managed to slip it under my coat that evening and took it home with me to read. I was rather taken aback, on turning up again for my coaching a couple of evenings later, when Botting asked me if I had enjoyed reading *Intentions* and if I had finished with it yet. I had in fact revelled in it and I thought it the *ne plus ultra* of sophisticated wit. I apologised for borrowing the book without asking his leave to borrow it.

'That's all right,' he said, 'I quite understand.' I remember thinking that if I had done such a thing to Cholmeley or Cook★ they would have indulged in heavy-handed sarcasm.

★ R. F. Cholmeley and A. M. Cook – two assistant masters at St Paul's at that time.

Perhaps my father was still smoking Guards Mixture when I first remember that study but I think it must soon have been replaced by what he claimed to be his one contribution to the happiness of mankind – Botting's Mixture. This blend of his own invention was made up for him by Lewis, the tobacconist on Addison Bridge and the name Botting's Mixture was not only printed on the pink label on the tin but stencilled in large letters on a card over the brass pan containing a sample of it on Mr Lewis' counter. I used to feel half-proud, half-embarrassed when I went with my mother and later, when I was old enough, by myself to collect his weekly supply. I was proud that my father had his own special tobacco named after him but I wished it were not such an ugly name as Botting. I felt acutely self-conscious seeing it publicly displayed in a shop and imagined that all the other customers were laughing at it and at me, for of course Mr Lewis knew us well and always addressed us by name. I do not know what ingredients besides Latakia 'Botting's Mixture' contained but I do know that it was a powerful blend. In his later years it was too strong for his heart and to his great regret he had to give up smoking it.

The tin of tobacco stood on the right of one of the twin mahogany office desks, placed back to back to form one huge one, which took up half the study. They were pushed up against the far wall, the only one not lined with bookshelves, and my father sat at the one nearest the window so that what little light there was fell on his work. Even on bright days it always seemed gloomy in the study. One window looked out over the back-yard on to high brick walls, so that no sun ever penetrated it. The room seemed darker still for what little wall space was clear of rows of shelves housing books in dull neutral bindings and black cardboard files was covered in deep crimson wallpaper and the heavy serge curtains at the window had once been olive green and had faded in streaks to the colour of liquorice powder. The only cheerful colour in the room was the red Turkey carpet, of which only small sections were visible and the only light piece of furniture a small natural oak coffee table whose top was inlaid with blue tiles. Though it was a solid little table, its pale wood and gleaming blue tiles looked as incongruous among all the rest of the study furniture as my mother looked in her light, frilly dresses sitting in the great 'Duke of Norfolk' armchair.

On the desk under the window, other objects besides the tin of Botting's mixture and the large box of wax vestas were aligned. Two black cardboard 'nests of drawers' with each drawer neatly labelled flanked the blotter and the ornamental brass inkstand. I think the latter must have been a wedding present which he felt it his duty to display – perhaps his form had clubbed together to buy it – for its ink-wells were never filled and he always used Onoto fountain pens. There were four of these, two filled with black ink, one with red and one with green, stuck in a bowl of lead shot beside the inkstand. To the left of the blotter lay the huge dark-red tome of Liddell & Scott's Greek dictionary. The objects on his desk never varied in all the years I remember that study.

The further one was usually empty except when he was making copies of exam papers or special notes on the 'jelly-graph', a mysterious gadget which consisted of a tray filled with some gelatinous substance which had to be boiled up and then allowed to cool and which smelt like fish-glue. The original, written in copying ink, was pressed firmly against the jelly. When it was removed it left an imprint in purple looking-glass writing, from which a series of fainter and fainter duplicates could be peeled off. It was a fascinating process to watch but very trying to the temper of the manipulator. My father prefer-red to wrestle with the 'jellygraph' alone so that he could swear uninhibitedly when he got copying ink on his shirt cuffs or peeled off a duplicate peppered with blank spaces.

My father's high, spoke-backed wooden armchair was never shifted from its place at his desk. There was so little space behind it that when he got up and pushed back his chair, it knocked loudly against the big bookcase filled with Delphic Classics. The sound of it could be heard outside in the passage and in my nursery next door, signalling the arrival or departure of a pupil. The pupil sat on his right in a small ebony armchair, un-cushioned like his own. When there was no pupil in it, it lived on the other side of the black marble mantelpiece in an angle between two bookcases. Facing the fireplace and pushed up against the double desk was a vast armchair known as the 'Duke of Norfolk'. It was upholstered in faded green plush and was as luxuriously comfortable as the other three chairs were austere. It had been in his rooms at Cambridge and he always blamed it for his getting a second instead of a first. Once you sank into its cushioned depths it required a heroic effort of will to get out of it. If he idled at Cambridge, my father made up for it by overworking for the rest of his life. It was very seldom indeed that I ever saw him relax in that huge green armchair. It is always sitting bolt upright in the hard Windsor chair that I envisage him in the study.

The 'Duke of Norfolk' was not the only relic of his under-graduate days. The sepia reproduction of the Mona Lisa over the mantelpiece, the framed photographs of Meredith and Wagner, the china plaque of Sir Walter Scott framed in green plush, had all been acquired, like the shield bearing the blue lion of Em-manuel, in the intoxication of his first year at Cambridge. The Mona Lisa was there for the sake of Pater who remained, like Meredith and Wagner, among his idols. He could quote the whole passage by heart. For him it was one of the greatest pieces of English prose ever written. He loved to declaim it, gloating over every cadence from, 'She is older than the rocks among which she sits', to the final, 'the eyelids are a little weary', spoken softly and *rallentando*. But though my father continued to re-read Pater and Meredith to the end of his life, I never saw him re-read Scott, though he professed a great admiration for him and forced his novels on me too early so that I 'took against' Scott till I was getting on for thirty.

I think the plaque was a tribute to the donor's love of Scott rather than his own. It had been given him by his dearest friend at Cambridge and ever after, an Irishman named Nevinson de Courcy. Their great common passion, however, was Meredith whom they always referred to as the Master. 'Toby' as my father always called him, was my godfather. I had never met 'Uncle Toby' – he was in the Egyptian Civil Service and lived in Cairo – but I had heard a great deal about him and I knew what he looked like. There was a photograph of him on the study mantelpiece, beside the one of myself and Socrates. He had an attractive, quizzical face, distinguished rather than handsome, with droop-ing eyelids that looked wearier than La Gioconda's and a long drooping moustache. What fascinated me about my godfather was his glamorous surname. I could not help wishing some-times that, as so often happened in books, I should discover one day that my parents were not my real parents and that I was his long-lost daughter. I would be quite content to go on living with my adopted parents provided everyone knew that my rightful name was Eirene de Courcy.

Had it not been for de Courcy, my father might have got a better degree, but he would not have had such a happy time at Cambridge. Even if Cambridge was more democratic than Oxford in the 1890s, a grocer's son coming up from Dulwich on a scholarship might well have been cold-shouldered by his fellow-undergraduates. De Courcy came up with the right credentials to open all doors to him. The de Courcys were a very old family and 'Toby' was fairly close in succession to the hereditary title of Lord Kinsale; in addition he was witty, charming and extremely sociable. Perhaps, being Irish, he was less conscious of the rigorous class distinctions that obtained in England or perhaps it amused him to defy them. At any rate, he befriended my father from the first, steered him through all the pitfalls of his freshman year, taught him what to drink, what to wear and generally acted as his mentor. As a result my father came down from Cambridge a much more sophisticated and polished young man than he went up, having acquired a social education which was to be more useful to him in after life than a first in the Classical Tripos.

When I was older, I recognised de Courcy as a type of man to whom my father was instinctively attracted: sophisticated, amusing, something of a dandy and a man about town and above all well-born and well-bred. My father's reverence for aristocracy was too innocent and romantic to be called snobbish. His attitude towards people better born than himself was the reverse of my mother's. Having no pretensions to blue blood himself, he could admire it in others as he might have admired any natural advantage he did not possess. My mother, on the contrary, refused to acknowledge any social superiors, royalty not excepted. The White coat of arms and crest, combined with a conjectural descent from a fourteenth century ancestor and that still more conjectural connection with the Bourbons, justified her in her own eyes as the equal of anyone in Burke or Debrett. This conviction of her own noble birth had given her moral support in the days when she was a governess. She needed the support even more now that she was married and had exchanged the surname of White for the unromantic and plebeian one of Botting. On the fly-leaf of any book she acquired she always wrote

Christine Julia Botting
(née Barbour White)

In her later years she frequently added a hyphen and, after my father's death, she had a seal made with the White coat of arms and sealed all her letters with it.

The study was next door to the dining-room and beyond it and at right angles to it was my day nursery. The dining-room was nearly twice the size of the study and though its bay window faced south, by day it was almost as sombre, for the three lower panes were obscured by removable screens made of squares of stained glass to prevent people staring in at us from the street. The walls were covered with a dark red patterned wallpaper, the curtains were greenish-brown plush, and the furniture mahogany. In the intervals between meals, the dinner table was covered with a plush cloth that matched the curtains. Over the centre of it hung a gas chandelier, surrounded by a crimson silk flounce, which could be raised or lowered by a pulley. The black marble mantelpiece was larger and more ornate than the one in the study and inset with panels of green marble. It was backed by a big, black-framed wall mirror that almost reached the ceiling. On the sideboard stood the locked Tantalus with its three cut-glass decanters, only one of which was filled with whisky, and above it hung two head and shoulder portraits, one of my father and one of my grandmother painted by my mother's sister-in-law, Edith White.

There were two other pictures in the dining-room, both Arundel prints. One of them of someone called, I think, Aeneas Piccolomini, receiving the Cardinal's hat, the other of St Anthony of Padua healing the foot of a young man. The second was the only one that interested me. It showed a brown-haired man who looked rather like my Uncle Howard, dressed in a long olive-green robe with a kind of white Toby frill round the neck, pointing down at a young man who lay on the ground. One of the young man's feet had been chopped off and the severed foot was still standing upright in front of the bleeding stump. It had been chopped off so cleanly just above the ankle that you could see how neatly it would fit on to the bleeding stump if it were stuck on again. Since I was first fascinated by this picture before I could read what was written under it I assumed that the person pointing down at the poor young man who had had such a terrible accident was a doctor and for some time the word 'doctor' conjured up the image of a brown-haired man in an olive-green robe and a white Toby frill. Later the word 'God' was to conjure up the same image, though why I cannot conceive. All I know is that to this day it still does.

The dining-room was the scene of my first deliberate crime, as it had been of my refusal to apologise to Lizzie. That earlier crime, which I do not remember, had obviously been committed in the heat of the moment, but there was no such excuse for this one. Scribbling on the walls, even of my own nursery, was strictly forbidden. Left alone one day in the dining-room, in possession of a pencil, I calmly decided to ignore the prohibition. There was so much furniture in the room that it took a moment to find a blank space on its crimson wall-paper on which to scribble. Then I perceived a nice large one between the sideboard and the door. After making a few tentative squiggles and finding it a most delectable surface to draw on, I decided to do something more ambitious. I drew an enormous noughts and crosses plan and proceeded to fill it in. I had just finished and was standing back surveying my handiwork when the door opened and both my parents came in. As the open door momentarily screened it, it was not till my father shut it that he exclaimed wrathfully:

'Good God, Christine, just look at this infernal mess on the wall.'

My mother stared at the huge scrawl and said in a horrified voice:

'I can't believe my own eyes. I can't believe *Eirene* would have dared to do anything so naughty. She knows perfectly well she's not allowed to scribble on walls.'

My father interrupted her to demand in his sternest voice:

'*Did* you do this, Eirene?'

I knew as well as he did that he knew I was guilty. I also knew that if anything infuriated him more than my being disobedient, it was my telling lies. In spite of this, I was foolhardy enough to say, 'No'.

'You impudent little liar!' he thundered. Grabbing me roughly by the arm, he dragged me towards the door.

'What are you going to go with her, Cecil?' asked my mother. 'Goodness knows she deserves to be punished for being so disgracefully naughty and telling such a wicked fib but . . .'

'Don't argue with me, Christine. And stay where you are.'

He dragged me into the study and shut the door behind us. Then, pushing me into the narrow space between the spare desk and the bookcase surmounted by the bust of Athene, he stationed himself in front of me, blocking me in. He picked up a ruler from the desk and fingered it. His face was flushed and his eyes glinted with anger yet he was wearing a curious one-sided smile as if he were in some way pleased, as well as angry. When he spoke, his voice was unexpectedly quiet.

'This time you've gone rather too far, Eirene. There are limits to what I am prepared to put up with in the way of shameless disobedience and even more shameless lying. This time I'm not going to waste my breath scolding you.'

He held up the ruler. 'You see this ruler?'

I nodded. It was a stout yellow wooden one, with spots of red ink on it.

'Turn round and bend over that desk. I'm going to take down your knickers and beat you with it.'

I was too horror-struck to obey. What horrified me was not the idea of being beaten though, as I had never been beaten before, I imagined it would be extremely painful, but those dreadful words, 'I'm going to take down your knickers.' No one except the maid who acted as my nurse ever saw me naked. I should have been shy of being seen with nothing on even by my mother. Certain parts of my body I knew were 'rude' and must always be kept covered up, except in my bath, by my knickers. The thought of these most secret and shameful areas being exposed bare to the person I most revered, and not even accidentally, but by his own hand, was so shocking that I felt I should never survive such shame.

After that, my mind is a blank. Perhaps my look of horror softened his heart, perhaps my mother intervened, perhaps the doorbell rang announcing the arrival of a pupil. All I know is that he did not carry out his dreadful threat. Indeed, I cannot remember receiving any further punishment for my crime. However, I never scribbled on walls again and it was several years before I committed my next crime, a much more serious one, but which, since by then I had established a reputation for truthfulness, remained undetected.

8.

The drawing-room was the pleasantest room in the house. It ran the whole width of the first floor of the front of the house and besides a bay window had a french one opening onto a balcony, so that it was always light. In contrast to the heavy dark furniture and sombre hues of the dining-room and study, everything in the drawing-room seemed gay and elegant. Even going into it was a treat for me for I was not allowed in there on my own. There was always some ritual preparation before entering it. If there were visitors, I was changed into my best frock, but even if my parents were alone, I had to be washed, brushed and combed and have my pinafore removed before I presented myself. These formal preparations seemed to have a good effect on my conduct, for I was never even tempted to behave badly in the drawing-room. The idea of scrawling noughts and crosses on its white, satin-striped wallpaper (where they would have shown up so much better than on the dull crimson one in the dining-room) would never so much as occurred to me. I admired everything too much in what seemed to me an apartment worthy of a princess to want to spoil it.

It was the one room in the house in which my mother had been allowed to have her own way. Every single piece of furniture, however solid and durable, which had come from my grandparents' house in Dulwich was banished from it. Every colour and stuff in the drawing-room was a defiance of my grandmother's two main criteria of interior decoration: 'Will it wear well?' and 'Will it show the dirt?' Looped back by day over the white lace window curtains were long curtains of a turquoise blue Liberty fabric with a pattern of tiny formalised green tulips, the armchair and sofa had loose covers of gay flowered chintz, the carpet was dove-grey bordered with garlands of faint pink roses and faint green ribbons, and the satin-striped wallpaper and the paintwork were a muted creamy white. The furniture was much lighter and more elegant than in any other room. There were two lute-backed chairs with velvet seats and two fragile-looking straw ones with lacquer backs depicting Chinese scenes which were drawn up to the card-table for bridge or strewn about the room on my mother's 'At Home' days, the first Monday of every month. In the centre of the room stood a small ebony table with slim curved legs. On it were displayed various silver and china knick-knacks which I was careful never to touch. I was perfectly content merely to look at these objects which I believed to be priceless. The only really precious one was a blue Dresden basket ornamented with exquisite minute china flowers, in full relief and almost as thin as eggshells which had belonged to my maternal grandmother and which my mother allowed no one to dust and wash but herself. Much as I admired it, I preferred the human interest of the china figures of a gentleman in knee breeches playing the flute and a lady in hoops and panniers playing the piano. The lady and gentleman were attached to their chairs but the piano was a separate piece. It was a miniature white and gold grand adorned with forget-me-nots. I admired it more than any of the other objects on the table. The silver filigree *bonbonnieres* and ivory *netsuke* left me cold, but I greatly coveted an inch square silver box with a lapis lazuli top.

It would be just the thing to keep a magic ring in if I ever acquired one.

A glass-fronted rosewood and gilt cabinet held other treasures, some of which I was allowed to handle under supervision. Four of them actually belonged to me; two tiny dolls, a boy and a girl, dressed in Tyrolese costume, sent me by my aunts in Vienna, a slightly larger Swiss doll with a stiffened lace headdress, white bodice, red skirt and black satin apron and a Japanese one in a long-sleeved flowered kimono. But though they were officially mine, they were considered too delicate and precious for the rough life of the nursery and I myself regarded them as *objets d'art* rather than toys. Frankly I found other objects in the cabinet more interesting, enormous bronze coins with raised edges, so heavy I could hardly hold them which were George IV pennies; a wrought-iron key, said to be a private key to Kensington Gardens which had belonged to some ancestor of my mother's; snuff boxes, ivory fans, a faded silk purse embroidered all over with tiny cut steel beads and one or two miniatures of dead ladies and children belonging to the White family. One object fascinated me most of all, though it was modern and entirely frivolous and really had no place among these ancestral relics. I suppose it commemorated some gay dinner party my parents had once attended. It was a miniature champagne bottle and when you pulled the cork, out sprang a pleated paper fan, bigger than the bottle itself. When the cork was pushed in again, the fan vanished – but where to? I was not allowed to operate this magic toy myself, but I never wearied of watching a grown-up doing so. Though the grown-up wearied first of the performance, he or she seemed to enjoy it almost as much as I did.

Everything about the drawing-room seemed to me so rare, so removed from dull everyday life, that I could quite easily see it as a room in a fairy palace. With only a slight effort of imagination, I could translate it into one of those splendid apartments into which mortals were introduced when they entered an enchanted castle. All the ingredients were there: 'White marble' (the mantelpiece), 'rich hangings' (the Liberty curtains), 'costly inlaid woods' (the coffee table and the what-not), 'fine silks and sumptuous velvets' (the cushions), 'ornaments of gold and silver' (the gilt clock and the silver vases and *bonbonnières*) as well as the 'delicate porcelain' and 'profusion of precious objects' already mentioned. Nor was it difficult to see my mother as 'Queen Christine', her favourite character in the games we sometimes played together, when she sat enthroned in the draw-

ing-room on 'At Home' days, wearing her most elegant afternoon frock and her garnet necklace. I was of an age now to be
summoned in for a few minutes on these occasions which
seemed to me quite dazzling. Dressed in my best frock, with a
hair-ribbon to match my sash and wearing my white kid shoes, I
would enter, carrying Mr Dash, the only other inhabitant of the
nursery allowed in the drawing-room, and make the round of
the guests, saying 'how d'ye do' politely to each. They were
mostly ladies, all in *their* most elegant clothes but there was
always a sprinkling of men, sometimes young and very good-
looking ones, and all wearing morning coats and striped trousers.
My father was never among them for he was downstairs in
the study taking pupils. The ladies kept their hats on, mostly
large ornate hats bristling with so many hatpins that I was
nervous of getting pricked when they swooped down to kiss
me. But some, especially the older ones, wore toques with
tight-fitting spotted veils which they had to roll up on the bridge
of their noses in order to be able to drink their tea and eat the
dainty little cakes and sandwiches handed round by Millie, one
of the two servants who had succeeded Elizabeth, in her best
muslin cap and apron, or smoke my mother's fawn-coloured
Russian cigarettes which were half cardboard holder. The men
were bareheaded and sometimes there was a silk hat upside
down beside their chair, with a pair of grey suede gloves draped
over it. I tried not to look at all the tempting food displayed on
the doileyed plates and bamboo cake-stands, wafer thin bread
and butter and cucumber sandwiches, iced cakes, meringues and
chocolate fingers, the mere sight of which made my mouth
water since such rich and delicate fare only appeared at 'At
Homes' and bridge parties. However, I could not quite keep my
eyes off it and occasionally a kind grown-up, usually a man,
would offer me a sugared cake and, if the person was really nice,
one for Mr Dash.

It was extraordinary how differently everyone, including
myself, behaved in the drawing-room. It seemed to cast a
benevolent spell over all who entered it, most noticeably on my
father. I rarely saw him in it except on Sundays, the only day he
was free from school and pupils, and whether he was alone or

A studio portrait taken at the age of seventeen, probably to celebrate putting her
hair up. She was still living at home. It was her father's favourite picture of her,
no doubt because in the modest Quaker collar she could have been taken for a
school mistress. Both of Antonia's daughters have a look of her: this one very
much resembles her eldest daughter, Susan.

with my mother, he was quite unlike his weekday self. He was
so gay, so good-humoured, so easy-going that it seemed impossible one could ever be afraid of him. Such a halcyon calm
reigned over Sunday tea in the drawing-room with my parents
that we seemed, all three, to achieve a harmony that we never
achieved in any other place or any other time. How different that
Sunday teatime was from our communal meals in the dining-
room, in particular, lunchtime. The atmosphere at breakfast
varied; my parents' mood depended a good deal on what letters
they received by the morning post. If they read out bits to each
other, the meal would be quite interesting for them, but I was
almost totally ignored. If my father ripped open certain en-
velopes with a peculiar fierceness and frowned as he read the
contents, my mother behaved in a peculiar way. She began to
address a series of remarks to me in a nervous, excited voice,
paying no attention whatever to my father, and keeping one eye
on me and the other on the clock. Every time he attempted to
interrupt her flow of meaningless chatter she pretended not to
hear. Then quite suddenly, perhaps in the middle of a sentence,
she would break off, stare with both eyes at the clock, then turn
to my father and say urgently:

'It's a quarter-past, Cecil. Oughtn't you to be getting off to
school?'

To which he would reply, grimly, that he was as aware of this
as she was and that he would now take his departure, no doubt to
her relief. My mother would sometimes open her great eyes
very wide, sometimes almost close them as she told him not to
be so horrid and sarcastic. When he had gone, sometimes
without even kissing her goodbye and quite often slamming
both the dining-room and the front door behind him, my
mother would sigh heavily and, turning to me, tell me how
lucky I was to be only a child and not to have to worry about
hateful things like bills. This was always a tricky moment, for if
I did not commiserate at once with some such remark as, 'Poor
Mummy, horrid old bills', she was liable to turn on me and
accuse me of a rising scale of crimes, beginning with not
listening to a word she was saying and mounting up through not
caring whether Mummy looked pretty or not, not caring for
Mummy as much as Daddy, not caring for Mummy at all to the
grand climax, 'I don't believe you'd care if I was dead and you
were looked after by your grandmother. I daresay you'd prefer
it. I daresay Daddy would too. At least he couldn't accuse *her* of
spending too much money on clothes.'

However, this breakfast scene only recurred once or twice a month and I found it infinitely preferable to the atmosphere of etchy irritability which prevailed at lunchtime on weekdays, particularly on Mondays. Luncheon was the meal I most disliked in any case and Monday's was my pet aversion. It consisted invariably of Sunday's cold joint (why was cold fat even more repellent than hot fat?) served with lumpy mashed potato and beetroot salad, and was followed by milk pudding, usually the most detestable of all, tapioca. My father would often bolt his food so fast to finish his meal before his lunch hour pupil arrived that he would get up and ring the bell for the pudding before my mother had finished her first course. One Monday, seeing him about to do so, my mother said querulously:

'Really, Cecil, I must ask you not to ring the bell before I've finished.'

At which he leapt to his feet and thundered:

'So now I'm not even permitted to ring the bell in my own dining-room? I shall ring the bell when I choose. I *shall* and I *will*.' In two strides he was at the wall, wrenching the lever of the bell to and fro so furiously that we could hear it ringing like an alarm clock in the kitchen below until, with one final wrench, he broke the wire. I watched and listened, half-fascinated, half-shocked, wondering what would have happened to me if I had dared to display such temper and trying vainly to establish any connection between this furious, bellowing man and this peevish, shrill-voiced woman and the charming, affectionate couple with whom I had had tea only yesterday in the drawing-room.

I have omitted to mention the most important piece of furniture in the drawing-room: the piano. It was a walnut upright with an open-work front that revealed a panel of dark green silk. Attached to the front was a pair of brass candle-holders which jangled if anyone sounded a loud chord on its yellowing ivory keys. Its tone was thin, but sweet, and at intervals a man came to tune it. Several of my parents' friends played and sang and were always asked to do so at evening parties and sometimes on 'At Home' days. As my night nursery was on the landing below the drawing-room I lay awake, listening entranced to these performances. My parents were too modest to play or sing in public, not being talented enough to be recognised as people who were asked to 'bring their music' though I am sure my father sang quite as well as some of the gentlemen who were. However, they played and sang at home to amuse themselves and each other and on Sundays I was often their admiring audience. I enjoyed my father's performances better than my mother's, because I preferred songs to 'pieces'. She could read music and he could not, but though I thought it very clever of her to decipher all those clotted masses of black dots, I was always glad when she accompanied my father's songs instead of playing solos. Her repertoire was small and consisted of Weber's 'Invitation to the Waltz' and the shortest of Chopin's preludes, and three other selections from Chopin, a waltz, the first part of the 'Berceuse' before the tempo quickens, and the second 'Nocturne' with runs and trills omitted.

Though my father could not read music, he had quite a good ear and could vamp up some kind of accompaniment to his songs. This was usually more successful than my mother's attempts to accompany him from the score, for she would seldom keep up with him and was constantly beseeching him as he turned over a page – 'Wait, Cecil, I'm not *there* yet!' He had a very pleasant light baritone voice and it was amazing how many songs he could sing quite effectively. He was particularly fond of Gilbert and Sullivan and knew the libretto of their operas almost by heart. One of my favourites was the nightmare song from 'Iolanthe' and I was never tired of hearing him perform that breathless feat and wondering if he would hold out to the last gasp, which he sometimes managed to do. But I liked even better two comic songs, 'Abdul the Bul-bul Da Meer' (I have to guess at the spelling), and 'The Baby on the Shore'. Its tune was as mournful as Abdul's was lively and I would join in the last line of every verse which was repeated as a refrain. All I can remember is three of them:

> The sun was setting, slowly setting
> Was setting as it never set before
> We were feeling weary, very weary
> And we left the baby on the shore.

> We left the baby on the shore
> A thing that we had never done before
> Go get the pipes and whisky ready
> And we'll feed the baby on the shore.

> The baby's sleeping, quietly sleeping
> A thing that it has never done before
> So after all perhaps it's better
> To leave the baby on the shore.

Sometimes, to my great amusement, my father would substitute 'Eirene' for 'the baby'.

My mother, of course, did not sing comic songs. She had hardly any voice at all, a tiny breathless mezzo-soprano but quite sweet. She was fond of singing German songs which I could not understand but which had charming tunes. Her English songs were usually very sad ones, such as 'On the banks of Allan Water' and Thomas Moore's 'Vale of Avoca' and she sang them with much expression. I liked them as much as my father's comic ones, for their melancholy seemed to give the happiness of these Sunday afternoons all the keener an edge. There was one which they used to sing in unison which moved me almost to tears. I think it is originally a German song but they sang it in English. They knew it so well that my mother could look up from the keyboard and into my father's eyes as he bent down over her while they sang, half smiling, because the song was about old lovers and they were not old yet:

Lay by my side your bunch of purple heather
The last red asters of an autumn day
And let us sit and talk of love together
As once in May
As once in May.

Whatever I felt about either of my parents on weekdays or in any other rooms at 22 Perham Road, I most certainly loved them both on Sunday afternoons in the drawing-room.

9.

Judging by the number of things that I can remember having done or experienced for the first time when I was four, it must have been a crucial age for me. Yet it is only in retrospect that I can appreciate what an eventful year it was and how many new discoveries I made about the world in general and my own in particular in the course of it. At the time, I was far more conscious of the interminably long intervals during which nothing significantly pleasant or unpleasant interrupted the daily routine of my life.

I was usually awake long before Millie, the housemaid, came to get me up. If it was summer, I could while away the time reading in bed, but in winter the night nursery where I now slept alone, except for Mr Dash, in a full-size iron bedstead, was dark. As yet, we had not got electric light, so I had to entertain myself with my own thoughts until Millie came in and lit the gas. The room it illuminated was uninspiring. There was nothing in its décor to amuse or interest a child, not even a picture on the wall. It contained, beside my iron bedstead, a white painted wardrobe and chest-of-drawers that had done duty in other rooms and a straw-seated chair that had also come down in the world because its straw seat was frayed away on one side and was no longer up to a grown-up's weight. Its curtains and wallpaper were equally uninteresting, so much so that I cannot even remember them. I have an impression that the paper was pale, as in all the bedrooms, and that the curtains were of some cotton material whose pattern has faded from repeated washings. The floor was covered with the same yellow straw-matting with a design of green leaves on it that covered the floor of my day nursery and that of the servants' big double bedroom in the basement. By no stretch of the imagination could I glamorise the night-nursery into the bedchamber of a fairy princess.

Having been given what Millie called 'a lick and a promise' in the way of a wash and been dressed in my dull everyday dress and pinafore, I descended the fourteen stairs from my night nursery to the ground floor and went into the dining-room to have breakfast with my parents. Sometimes I was down before them and would amuse myself by looking out of the window. I was not tall enough to see above the stained glass screen but Perham Road was magically transformed by being looked at through it. The screen was composed of small squares of glass of four different colours and according to which square I gazed through the world outside was blue, mauve, pink or yellow. At will I could change the postman's face from a rosy to a jaundiced hue or turn sunlight into moonlight.

However, my father was usually down before me, looking very brisk and fresh in his dark suit and stiff white collar, with his pink cheeks newly shaved and often adorned with a black court-plaster beauty-spot where he had cut himself. My mother was invariably last, and came down to breakfast in a tea-gown, looking languid and sallow, with her soft brown hair sketchily pinned up and not yet arranged in puffs over a 'pompadour'.

When my father had gone off to school, she would ring for Bessie the cook to come up from the kitchen for her 'orders'. Bessie, in her morning dress of pink print, wearing a big white apron, but with no cap, would appear with a block and pencil and stand beside my mother's chair wearing her demure 'upstairs' expression and adding 'Madam' to every sentence as they arranged the day's meals and my mother made out her shopping list. I would avoid Bessie's eye and she mine. My mother little knew that '*Her* giving orders' was one of her best turns in the kitchen and made Millie laugh 'fit to split her sides'. Sometimes I nearly laughed fit to split my own sides when Bessie mimicked my mother's high-pitched voice, exaggerating her drawl and the way she sometimes swallowed her Rs.

'Oh dear! Cook, are we out of b'own sugah again? How agg'avating! You must have been d'eadfully ext'avagant with it.'

To which she would reply in her own character, giving some fantastic reason why it had run out so quickly such as: 'The cat's took to having it on his porridge, Madam.'

'It's the black beetles, Madam. They gets into the tin when my back's turned and helps themselves.'

When her interview with Bessie was over, my mother would retire to her bedroom at the top of the house to finish dressing. Often she would take me upstairs with her and I would play with her possessions while she did her hair, using curling-tongs heated over a spirit lamp to roll the front into sausage curls which were then back-combed and pinned over pads to form puffs. In those days women wore their hair piled up in elaborate coiffures on the top of which they skewered elaborate hats. Only women with very luxuriant, rather coarse hair could build up this structure without an underpinning of pads of some substance like matted wool, called 'rats', or silk-covered wire frames known as 'pompadours'. My mother's hair needed a great deal of building up to achieve the fashionable effect. It was limp and very fine and, when down, barely reached her shoulders. Millie, on her afternoon out, could produce a much more imposing structure without any artificial aids. Her thick mane of hair was so long that, by tilting her head back, she could perform the much-admired feat of sitting on it. I had seen her do it 'for a dare' when there was male company in the kitchen and it was as much of a success with her audience as Bessie's imitations of my mother.

Up in my mother's bedroom, her favourite game with me was to pretend that I was her lady's maid, 'little maid Marie'. I can still smell the smell of scorched paper as she tested the tongs – and occasionally a whiff of scorched hair – mingled with the scent of her *Trèfle-Incarnat* face-powder as I hovered about the dressing-table with its lace doilies and silver-topped jars, offering her hairpins or 'doing her up'. 'Doing her up' was a rather alarming process, for there was a lining as well as the blouse or dress itself furnished with closely spaced hooks and eyes which my small, clumsy fingers usually managed to fasten awry or worse still, pinch 'Madame's' flesh between them so that 'Maid Marie' came in for some genuine scoldings, as well as histrionic ones. I much preferred searching in 'Madame's' jewel-box for 'my diamonds, Marie' (a gold-bar-brooch set with three very small ones) or 'my opals' (her engagement ring mounted with five).

Though I knew that my father slept beside my mother at night in the big brass bedstead, I never thought of the bedroom as anyone's but hers. Millie had made the bed while we were having breakfast so there was no sign of his occupation. All his clothes were kept in his dressing-room next door and his shaving tackle in the bathroom. Outwardly the big bedroom looked fairly tidy, but if one pulled open any drawer in its mahogany furniture, it was stuffed with heterogeneous feminine litter, torn lace scarves, unmended stockings, broken fans, and wilted artificial flowers all jumbled together with articles still fit to wear, so that it was no wonder that my mother took so long dressing. She often had to rummage through drawer after drawer to find the one of a pair of gloves or two matching stockings without holes in them. She was as untidy with her possessions as my father was almost pathologically tidy with his. On the rare occasions I went into his dressing-room – never of course when he was in it but Millie sometimes let me go in with her when she was dusting it – I used to marvel at its immaculate order. Outwardly, there was nothing visible but a trouser-press, a pair of military hair-brushes, two leather boxes, in one of which he kept his studs and in the other starched collars, and a bottle of Jaborandi hair tonic. Even his dressing-gown and slippers were stowed away in the wardrobe, along with a row of suits hung on solid wooden coat-hangers and the shoes and boots stuffed with solid wooden trees, made in three separate sections. If my father was safely out of the house, I would get Millie to open the drawers of the chest-of-drawers and the tall-boy and together we would admire the exquisite neatness of everything, the separate drawers for evening and day shirts, for silk and lisle and woollen socks, for day and evening waistcoats, scarves, gloves, handkerchiefs and even braces and sock suspenders. Sometimes, if she was quite sure the house was empty, Millie would do something very daring which both delighted me and filled me with agonising apprehension. She would take from its shelf my father's opera hat or 'gibus', the most fascinating of all his possessions. It resembled a top hat, except that its crown was of corded silk and had springs inside so that it could be crushed flat and put under a theatre seat. The crown could also be partly bashed down on one side or the other. This concertina effect made Millie look very rakish when she put on the gibus, tilted it over one eyebrow and screwed a penny in her eye as a monocle. But much as I enjoyed it when she announced that she was Vesta Tilley and pranced about the dressing-room singing 'I'm Burlington Bertie from Bow' I was always terrified in case she permanently damaged my father's precious hat. Sometimes she frightened herself too and would exclaim: 'Oh Law, I believe this time I've really been and gone and done it.' But after a little anxious manipulating, the crown would spring up to its full height again with a pop like the opening of a champagne bottle.

If my mother had nothing as fascinating as the gibus, her untidy drawers often offered rich plunder, scraps of ribbon and veiling and all kinds of odds and ends I was allowed to carry off to my nursery to dress up myself and the animals. There were two bits of treasure trove I valued particularly and cherished for years, a pair of silver sequin wings that had once adorned my mother's hair and a piece of cut blue glass, half an inch square, which had once topped a hatpin. With the wings fastened to a brown paper helmet I became a Viking chief and with them tucked into the back of my shoes I became Hermes. As for the blue glass hatpin-top which, for me, was a magnificent sapphire, I put it reverently away in a box. I was quite sure it possessed some kind of magic though I could not guess what kind. It was not until I was getting on for six and Hans Andersen had become my Bible that I decided that my sapphire was nothing less than the most precious jewel in the world – the Philosopher's Stone in the story of that name. It was one of those mysterious stories I could only dimly understand but which fascinated me all the more for that reason. But I grasped enough to realise that the Philosopher's Stone which enabled one to discover the truth was in some strange way a more desirable possession than a magic wishing-ring.

When my mother was at last ready to go out, I too was dressed in my street clothes and went out with her to do the shopping. There is a record of what was obviously my best outdoor ensemble in that memorable summer when I was four. It is a photograph on ivory, very cunningly hand-coloured to look like a genuine miniature and shows my face framed in a vast, very becoming muslin bonnet and my shoulders clad in a pale blue-caped coat. I remember that coat very well, it had tiny flecks of white on its pale blue ground and I was very proud of it. That particular bonnet I cannot recall but I can remember the scratchy feel of starched muslin strings being tied under my chin and the disagreeable noise it made in my ears. However, I am sure I did not object to wearing it, for I was beginning to be interested in clothes and was vain enough to like being seen in my best ones. I had certainly improved in looks in the three years since I had been photographed as a pudgy-faced baby with Socrates. My face had acquired some kind of shape, with a small, but definite cleft chin and my colouring could not have been more Anglo-Saxon and less like my mother's – pink and white cheeks, blue eyes, and a fringe of authentic gold hair covering my forehead. As my grandmother said triumphantly: 'Every inch *Daddy's* girl!'

However, I am sure I was not dressed in my best for the morning shopping round. I know that I detested being dressed for outdoors in winter because of the misery of having my gaiters put on. Buttoning them up was a painful process and, even if Millie was not in a hurry, the button-hook would dig into my chubby legs and occasionally pinch a morsel of flesh into the buttonhole.

I quite enjoyed these almost daily shopping expeditions with my mother. On the walk to North End Road where most of the shops were, my mother and I relieved the tedium of the streets of grey houses by travelling through them on horseback. Oddly enough I cannot remember the name of my pony, but my mother's horse was a spirited light chestnut called Cyprian. When we reached North End Road we usually dismounted and left our horses in charge of the groom, after patting them and giving them lumps of sugar. Sometimes if we were having a particularly pleasant ride, we did all the shopping on horseback. But not very often as Cyprian was very temperamental and apt to shy at the traffic.

My father never played 'let's pretend' games with me. It is as impossible to imagine him doing so as to imagine him calling me 'Reeny-ree' or 'Madam Why-Why' as my mother did, but only when we were alone. He had such a loathing of pet names and abbreviations that he could hardly bear to hear my Uncle Howard call his sister 'Chrissy' as he had done all her life. If my uncle asked him 'How's Chrissy?' he would reply firmly:

'*Christine* is quite well, thank you.' I suppose that neither of his parents, both of whom were very literal-minded, had ever played such games with him when he was a small boy and that, having no brothers and sisters, no one else had either. Or perhaps his precocious intelligence had developed so fast that, unlike normal children, he had very early found the 'real' world more interesting than any imaginary one. One of the many differences between my parents was that my father was quite incapable of impersonating anybody but himself and always pleaded successfully not to be included in any charade and that my mother, even in ordinary life, was nearly always seeing herself in a part. My father, though very well disposed towards small children, found it so impossible to come down to their level that he might never have been a child himself. My mother, in many ways, remained a child all her life. As a result she got on very well with young children but was not so popular with older ones and still less with adolescents whereas my father was a failure with infants but an outstanding success with 'young people', girls as well as boys.

I suppose my happiest relation with my mother was between the ages of four and seven, before I had grown into a critical little prig of a schoolgirl terrified of the impression she might make on my friends. The prouder I grew of my father, who could not have been a more presentable parent, the more embarrassing I found her refusal to look or behave like other people's mothers. Even as a small child I was critical of her and realised that many other women, besides my grandmother, were critical of her too. All these women who adored my father thought that my mother was unworthy of him and pitied him for having married a capricious, affected, extravagant woman with no sense of wifely duty. I came in for some of the pity too, naturally most of all from my grandmother, but also from others who considered that she was as unsatisfactory as a mother as a wife. As regards my physical needs she was not so much neglectful as sublimely unaware of them. Someone else always had to point out to her that I had outgrown my shoes or needed new underclothes. Nor did she normally devote any time to me except in the mornings. Once luncheon was over she disappeared upstairs to the drawing-room to lie down on the sofa before dressing for the afternoon's calls or bridge-party or, if she had no social engagements, to read her latest Mudie* novel (she averaged nearly one a day) and strum on the piano.

* Mudie, the famous lending library.

Nevertheless, in her own way she was fond of me and, in mine, I was fond of her. She often took my side against my father, and I sometimes took hers against my grandmother. But our great bond was that we both found everyday life very hundrum and longed for exciting things to happen. We longed even more to be very rich so that I could have a real pony and buy all the toys I coveted and she could have a carriage and pair and any amount of exquisite dresses and furs and jewels. In each other's company we went in for orgies of wishful thinking which neither of us would have dared to indulge in in my father's presence. Of course I did not revere her as I did my father but neither was I frightened of her. Though she flew into rages much more often than he did I was never intimidated by them. There was something childish about her sudden bursts of temper so that I sometimes felt a certain superior amusement when she flared up, especially if I was not the target of them. Even if I was, they did not worry me much; I merely waited for them to pass over my head, leaving me undamaged. But if my father was even moderately angry with me, I was miserable till I was restored to favour.

The morning shopping round, if confined to West Kensington, did not tempt either my mother or myself too severely to spend our imaginary wealth. Nevertheless, I sympathised with her for having to part with real golden sovereigns to pay the weekly bills at the dairy and the butcher's and the grocer's when she could have bought far more exciting things with them, even in the North End Road. Some of our local shops had their allurements though not to be compared with those of the big stores in Kensington High Street, Barker's and Derry & Toms. My mother could never pass the florist without gazing longingly into its window.

'It seems such a waste to have to spend money on prosaic things like beef and mutton when one thinks of all the lovely flowers one could buy for the same amount,' she would sigh. I heartily agreed with her, not only as regards beef and mutton, but almost every kind of food except scrambled eggs, sausages, chocolate blanc-mange, treacle tart and, of course, cakes, sweets and ice-cream. It puzzled me that grown-ups who could eat what they liked wasted any money at all on such revolting things as meat and cabbage and milk pudding. However I should not have spent the resulting saving on lilac and mimosa but on toys and books. My twopence a week pocket money bought me one green *Tim Pippin* or one pink volume of *Stead's Books for the*

Bairns, neither of which lasted me more than a day. The stationer's shop, Gomms', where I bought them sold quite a number of fat, enticing books in stiff covers at prices well beyond my range – a shilling or more – as well as cheap, but quite attractive toys. There was a fair selection of these at twopence, but not alluring enough to seduce me from the weekly addition to my library. Some of the fourpenny toys might well have seduced me if I had had as much as fourpence to spend but, not having it, I was spared the temptation. Sometimes when my mother took a half-sovereign from her purse to pay for some dull purchase, I would speculate on all the delightful things I could buy at Gomms' if I had had such riches. Ten whole shillings – more than an entire year of my pocket money – represented untold wealth to me. A sovereign was too regal and grown-up for me to aspire to; the limit of my financial ambitions was to possess one of those magical little coins that looked like golden sixpences and could buy as much as twenty silver ones. However the prospect was so unlikely that what I would buy with it was too abstract a speculation to dwell on for long.

I had, of course, my preferences among the West Kensington shops and shopkeepers. I liked Floyd's the dairy as much as I hated Sendall's the butchers. The diary was cool and pleasant, with its tiled walls representing rural scenes and its china milkmaid in the window with her yoke and pails. On the counter was another interesting piece of sculpture, a china stork with a green china frog in its mouth surmounting a china bowl filled with real cream into which Mrs Floyd would dip one of the graded metal cups hooked over the rim of the bowl and dredge up 'two-penn'orth' or 'four penn'orth' for the humbler customers who came in carrying jugs. Mrs Floyd, presiding over the bowl of cream, always reminded me of the fat white cat in the Nestlé's advertisement. She looked as sleek as if she fed on nothing but cream and she had not only a purring voice but a ribbon round her plump white neck tied in a pussy-cat bow. The pussy-cat bow was fastened with a brooch I greatly admired, an oval gold one with 'Annie' printed on it in little diamonds. I also had a brooch with my name on it but not nearly such an impressive one, a squiggly affair of gold wire which could just be deciphered as 'Eirene'. This brooch was a bone of contention between my parents. It was a christening present from my grandmother and my father was constantly insisting I should wear it and my mother removing it the moment his back was turned.

Both my mother and I hated our weekly call at Sendall's the butcher's. My father frequently grumbled about the quality of our Sunday joint.

'How is it that my mother gets admirable meat from Sendall's and what we get is often hardly edible? At the price he has the impudence to charge for this piece of horseflesh he has the impudence to call beef, it's bare-faced robbery!'

To which my own mother would retort that perhaps he would prefer his mother to do the housekeeping, adding meaningly, 'I'm sure she's much better at dealing with *tradesmen.* After all, it's only natural, isn't it?'

Since I did not yet know that my grandparents had kept a grocer's shop, I was puzzled why this kind of remark always silenced my father. He would frown and clench his heavy jaw, but he stopped complaining about the meat.

The truth was that my mother was as revolted as I was by the sight and smell of raw meat and spent as little time as possible in Sendall's horrible shop with its blood-stained sawdust and, even worse than the flayed carcases, hares and rabbits still with their fur on hung up by their hind legs with tin cups fixed under their noses to catch the garnet drops that still dripped from them. Nothing would have induced her to inspect a joint or piece of steak and prod it as my grandmother did before she ordered it. Without deigning even to look at Mr Sendall in his striped blue apron with his great steel dangling from a leather belt like a sword, she would read out her week's commands from her shopping list, and gathering up her long skirt to avoid the tainted sawdust, sweep out of the shop. As a result, the sirloin or mutton or liver Mr Sendall's errand boy brought round on the wooden tray strapped to his tricycle to the back door of No. 22 Perham Road was always inferior to the meat my grandmother took home in her string bag to 13 Owen Mansions. My grand-mother always insisted on carrying her purchases home herself. She had a profound and perhaps professional distrust of errand boys. 'If I take it myself,' she would say, 'at least I can be sure I've got what I paid for.' My mother, needless to say, had everything sent, with the exception of flowers. She had the knack of carrying a sixpenny bunch of daffodils as if she were a royal personage who had been presented with a bouquet.

Beyond Sendall's were two much pleasanter shops, Wilkinson's the chemist's and Evans the jeweller's. Wilkinson's was smaller than Pickard's, the chemists opposite West Kensington station, but my mother preferred it because it stocked perfume

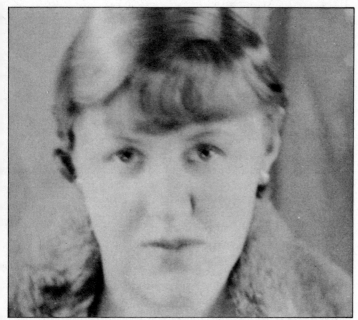

A studio portrait taken around 1928, not long before the birth of her first daughter, Susan, although in the portrait she strongly resembles her second daughter, Lyndall.

and powder as well as drugs. Mr Wilkinson was a gentle, dark-haired man with an air of fragility; he was slightly built and had pale, hollow cheeks and rather sad brown eyes behind rimless glasses. His eyes would brighten when my mother entered the shop. She was, I think, his favourite customer and he delighted in making up special lotions and face-creams for her. She often preferred to buy his own fresh, light flower scents to the heavier, 'oriental' bouquets such as Phul-Nana and Shem-el-Nessim. On a shelf behind the counter stood a row of stoppered glass jars labelled Lily-of-the-Valley, Rose, Heliotrope, Jockey Club and so on, and Mr Wilkinson would take them down in turn for her to sample. The one she nearly always selected in the end was Night-Scented Stock, which was wonderfully true to the flower and which I have never seen on sale anywhere else. Before he corked up the small medicine bottle into which he decanted it, she would dab a little on her upper lip and mine so that we could inhale the delicious smell and get the reek of the butcher's shop out of our nostrils. The process of sampling scent usually took a long time, but I was quite happy studying the various contents of Mr Wilkinson's shop and watching his thin white hands deftly wrapping up our purchases in pale blue paper and sealing them with red sealing wax from a lighted taper on a little brass stand. Now that I had read *Rosamund and the Purple Jar*,★ the great carboys in the window, filled with red, green and purple fluid, in which people in the street were reflected upside-down, inevitably reminded me of the hapless Rosamund. Much as I hated that moral story, as my mother did too, I loved the little old-fashioned book with its brown print and s's that looked like f's which contained it. It had belonged to my mother when she was a little girl and perhaps it had been *her* mother's. In case you do not know the story, Rosamund was a foolish little girl who invariably chose what would give immediate pleasure as opposed to what was solidly useful. She had a priggish elder sister who always did the reverse and a Mamma whom both my mother and myself regarded as a horrible woman. Rosamund took a violent fancy to the purple carboy in a chemist's window. Her Mamma told her that it was a useless object and gave her daughters the choice between the purple jar and a new pair of shoes. The elder sister, of course, chose the new pair of shoes. When Rosamund brought her purple jar home in triumph, she emptied it of what she thought was water, only to find that her jar was no longer purple, but just plain glass. The next time she was taken for a long walk she came home limping for her shoes were too tight. Her Mama told her it was her own fault, since she had chosen a 'foolish bauble' instead of new shoes. Later the girls were offered the choice between a stone plum, so realistic that it deceived the eye, and a housewife. Rosamund of course chose the plum, but found the pleasure of tricking people soon palled. She and her sister were invited to a desirable party. As they were dressing for it, she tore a rent in her party frock. But her Mama refused to let her sister lend her a needle and cotton from her housewife, so poor Rosamund was left weeping at home. As far as I remember she never succeeded in making a 'sensible' choice. My mother and I agreed in profoundly sympathising with Rosamund who was 'idle and wilful' and detesting her elder sister who was so industrious that she 'drew nearly the whole of Mamma's bedroom, in perspective, before breakfast'.

Almost next door to Mr Wilkinson's was Mr Evans the jeweller. Officially we only visited Mr Evans to take a clock or

★ A novel by Maria Edgeworth (1767–1849).

watch to be mended but we often paid him surreptitious visits about which I was told 'not to tell Daddy'. Old Mr Evans was not, as one might have supposed, Welsh but a naturalised German. With his bushy grey hair and busy grey eyebrows, one of which was permanently cocked higher than the other from inserting his mysterious black glass under it, and his black leather apron, Mr Evans always made me think of some old man in a fairy tale, one of those poor but kindly cobblers or wood-cutters who rear an abandoned baby as their own child, never guessing that it is some lost prince or princess. His shop was very dark and his jewels almost invisible in dusty glass cases so that when he produced some sparkling ring or brooch he seemed to have produced it from nowhere, like a conjuror. He spoke English with a guttural accent and it was a great pleasure to him that my mother spoke German. Though I could not understand what they said when they relapsed into German I knew that they were conspiring together. The old man would produce some piece of jewellery, usually a ring, over which she would sigh longingly. And usually, some weeks later, the object had found its way into her jewel case, though she did not wear it in my father's presence. When I was very much older I knew that she filched money from the five pounds a week my father gave her for the housekeeping and, sometimes, I suspect, from money that was intended to be spent on me. My shoes were often too tight for me, like Rosamund's, and my pinafore often concealed a dress that I had grown out of or that was shabby with being worn every weekday for months for I seldom possessed more than two frocks, one for best and one for everyday.

Once we had returned home from our shopping round, I did not usually see my mother again, except at lunch, for the rest of the day. Sometimes, in the afternoon, if she was having tea with one of those intimate female friends who were my honorary 'Aunties', she would take me with her. On 'At Home' days or when it was her turn to entertain her woman's bridge four who met weekly in each other's houses, I was sometimes invited, as I have said earlier, to make a brief appearance, in my best frock, in the drawing-room. But normally I spent the rest of the day, apart from my official 'walk' after lunch accompanied by Bessie or Millie, in the nursery.

The nursery was at the far end of the passage on the ground-floor beyond my father's study. Like the study, it looked out on a high brick wall and the backyard and never got any sunlight, even in summer. Nor had any attempt been made to brighten its gloom with cheerful wallpaper or curtains or to pretty it up in any way when it was allotted to me as a nursery. In fact, nothing could have less resembled the modern idea of a nursery than this room with its chocolate paint and dingy wallpaper furnished with some bits of grown-up furniture that had seen better days. The only picture on the wall was of a pale little girl with large upward-turned blue eyes, mauve lips and smooth ringlets, wearing a white, off the shoulder dress, and clasping her hands in prayer. It was enclosed in an elaborate gilded frame and must have been demoted from the drawing-room. For a long time I assumed it was a portrait of some dead relative as a little girl and it was not till I read *Uncle Tom's Cabin* that I identified her as Little Eva. However, it did not worry me that my nursery was not much more than a glorified box-room. Those cast-off pieces of furniture had the great merit of not having to be treated respectfully: I could regard them as mine to do what I liked with. The shabby old table in the window served all sorts of useful purposes. Turned upside down, it made an excellent raft; draped with an old curtain, it made an excellent tent. In any case, when I was in the nursery, I was usually somewhere else in my mind, either in the setting of the book I was reading or in some imaginary place, so that I spent many hours of a normal day alone in my nursery, reading and writing and acting out dramas with my dolls and toy animals. But there was hardly a day when, weary of my own company, I did not escape down the back-stairs, which were just outside the nursery, into the rich underworld of the kitchen. My parents had no idea how much time I spent down in the basement, in the company of the servants and their visitors. Once my father had gone off to afternoon school and my mother too was safely out of the way, especially in winter when my fireless nursery was very chilly, Mr Dash and I would more often than not descend to the cheerful warmth of the kitchen and sometimes spend the whole afternoon there. Officially, Millie was supposed to bring my tea and supper up to the nursery, but as no one checked up on this, I usually had both in the kitchen with her and Bessie, an arrangement that suited us all much better. Bessie and Millie are much vaguer in my memory than Lawrence and Frances, the cook and housemaid who succeeded them when I was five or six, but they were both very agreeable and I learnt a great many interesting things in their company. They were not sisters, like Lawrence and Frances, but 'best friends' who always took posts together. They were so devoted to each other that, out of uniform, they

essed alike. I remember how delighted they were to receive as
Christmas present from my parents a length of silk apiece to
ake themselves blouses. I can see those blouses much more
early than I can see their faces. The silk was pink, with narrow
hite stripes; hot, vivid pink known then as 'crushed straw-
rry' but almost the colour Schiaparelli made famous as 'shock-
g pink'. They had their blouses made up by a dressmaker friend
th quantities of ruching, low necks and elaborate flounced
eves. They were so pleased with the result that they each had
eir photographs taken in them, wearing their identical cat's
e pendants and their brown hair piled up in immense pompa-
urs.

I found their conversation fascinating, especially when they
metimes forgot my presence and discussed topics never re-
rred to upstairs, such as murder, fatal accidents and ghosts.
metimes I used to collect items from their talk to liven up a
wspaper which I wrote from time to time called *The West
ensington News*. I only remember one of them: 'A cabman had
s head bashed in by a lamp-post in Hammersmith.' I suppose
remember it because my mother looked horrified when she
ad it and asked me where I got such morbid ideas, but my
ther was rather amused and said it was a good sensational news
em.

Listening to stories of women discovered with their throats
t from ear to ear – 'an' they never found out who done it' – of
urderers who chopped their victims into little pieces and
ried them in the back garden, of burglars who climbed in at
ght through the windows and strangled people or clubbed
em to death if they tried to raise the alarm was deliciously
ine-chilling when one was sitting by the kitchen fire eating
ipping-toast. But alone in the dark in bed, with only Mr Dash
r company, I sometimes wished I had not listened to them so
idly. Quite often I would wake up from a nightmare and be
rrified at the sound of footsteps on the stairs outside and at the
ght of strange shadows thrown on the frosted pane of the top
lf of the night-nursery door. Then the footsteps would go
eaking up another flight, the frosted pane would go dark as the
s on the stairs was turned out and I would tell myself, not
ways with complete conviction, that it was only my father
ing up to bed. If my parents had ever, as they assured me,
en in the habit of looking in to say goodnight to me, they had
rtainly dropped it by the time I was four. At six, when I was
t to bed, my father was still busy with pupils and my mother

was usually still out, or, if she was in, playing bridge o
entertaining friends.

Without my friends below stairs who included not only
Bessie and Millie, but Mrs Bullock the charwoman who came in
one day a week to scrub floors and various of their male and
female acquaintances whose names I forget, I should have had
much duller time as an only child.

10.

One of the great disappointments of my life befell me at this
eventful age of four. At the time I accepted it fairly philosophi-
cally – what else could I do since my father's word was law
however unjust it seemed? – but I think it affected me for life. At
any rate I have always had a conviction that if something
wanted very badly seemed just within my grasp, it would
inevitably be snatched away from me.

One afternoon, knowing that my father was not yet back
from school, I went into the study without knocking. To my
surprise, it was not empty. A dark young man, evidently a
pupil, was sitting in my father's Windsor Chair. I was about to
scuttle away but the young man called me back.

'Don't run away. Stay and talk to me.'

I was doubtful whether I should, but the young man was very
insistent. He said he had arrived much too early for his lesson
and was bored, sitting there doing nothing. He was obviously
not one of the boys from St Paul's; he was grown up and had an
extremely assured manner. None of my father's Pauline pupils,
if they had arrived early, would have calmly seated themselves at
his desk, in his magisterial chair while waiting for him. He
laughed away my fears that my father might be angry if he found
me in the study, promising he would explain it was all *his* fault
and that he had insisted on my keeping him company. He was so
authoritative, as well as agreeable that he prevailed on me to
stay. I would not, however, sit on his knee, as he wished, but
stood facing him on the opposite side of the double desk. He
asked me a great many questions and seemed interested and
amused by my answers. I was not used to so much attention and
found it flattering. When he asked me if I was learning Greek
yet, I said proudly that I knew the first line of the *Iliad* and
proceeded to recite μηνιν αειδε. Soon I was indulging in the
intoxicating pleasure of showing off as I recited my other bits of
knowledge – the names of the gods and goddesses of Olympus

and some of their history. Finally the young man laughed, said I was such a good pupil that I deserved a reward. Out of his pocket he produced a golden coin and held it up between his thumb and finger.

'Do you know what this is, infant phenomenon?'

I knew very well. It was the coin I coveted most, a half-sovereign. I knew of course that it could not be intended for me, he only wanted to test my knowledge.

'It's a half-sovereign.'

'Do you know how many shillings there are in it?'

'Ten.'

'I bet you don't know how many pennies there are in it!'

'I had to shake my head. 'Not how many pennies. But I know there are sixty twopences.'

I had not worked it out in my head. My mother had told me the astronomical sum half a sovereign represented in weeks of my pocket-money.

The young man laughed. 'Good enough. You've earned your prize.' He reached across the desk holding out the half-sovereign between his finger and thumb.

'Come on, hold out your little paw.'

I did so, and he put the precious coin on my palm.

'Hold it tight, or you'll drop it.'

I still could not take it in. It was too good to be true that he meant me to keep it.

'It's yours,' he said, smiling, closing my fingers over it.

'Mine to *keep*?' I asked, overwhelmed by the magnificence of the gift.

He nodded.

I was too overwhelmed even to thank the young man. I stood staring at him, but hardly seeing him as I envisaged all the wonderful things I might buy with this fortune. I was so engrossed that I did not realise that my father had come into the room till I saw the young man leap up from the chair and heard my father apologising for being late.

'Please don't apologise, sir. It is I who arrived much too early. Your charming daughter has been kind enough to entertain me.'

My father had not yet noticed my presence. He noticed it now, and frowned.

'What are you doing in here, Eirene?'

The young man was true to his promise, assured him that he had detained me against my will and that he was most grateful to me for consenting to stay and amuse him.

'We had a most interesting conversation,' he wound up. 'I really must congratulate you, sir, on having a daughter who's obviously going to follow in her father's footsteps. She's been giving me a Greek tutorial.'

My father's frown partially melted. 'Well, I suppose I can't blame her if you encouraged her to chatter, though I don't approve of her making a nuisance of herself to grown-ups, most of all my pupils. Say goodbye nicely Eirene, and run along now, there's a good child.'

I found my tongue enough to say: 'Goodbye. And thank you *very* much.'

'What's that you've got in your hand?' my father asked with sudden suspicion as I moved hastily towards the door.

I had to show him.

He snatched it from my hand, asking sternly: 'How did you come by this?'

I faltered, speechless, before his renewed and now thunderous frown. Once more the young man came to my rescue.

'I'm sorry,' said my father. 'I'm sure you meant it most kindly, but I can't possibly allow her to accept it. Even if it weren't far too much for a child of her age, I should insist on your taking it back. On principle.'

In vain the young man pleaded that I should be allowed to keep it, or at least that it could 'go into my money-box' and be saved for when I was older. My father was adamant and the half-sovereign went back into the young man's pocket.

As I left the room, just managing to restrain my tears till I was back in the nursery, I heard my father mutter to the young man:

'It was exceedingly generous of you, but I'm sure you'll see my point of view. No, no, she won't be disappointed. I'm sure she knew all along she couldn't possibly be allowed to keep it. Don't worry. By tomorrow she'll have forgotten all about it.'

He was wrong. After seventy-two years I have not forgotten that breathless moment of possession and the bitter sense of injustice when the treasure was snatched away. I wonder if that pupil whose name I never knew and whose face I do not remember, ever realised that, unintentionally, he had sown the seed not only of as pretty a complex about money as any psychologist could be called on to resolve but of a conviction that the more passionately I wanted something, the more un-likely I was to be allowed to have it.

However, that one severe disappointment is the only un-pleasant happening I can remember in that year when I was four.

The rest of it was characterised by the very reverse, a series of interesting, delightful and quite unexpected events which made it an *annus mirabilis* of pleasant surprises, all the pleasanter because they were things that it would never have occurred to me to wish for and, in my limited experience of life, could not even have imagined.

One of the first was that my father planned a treat for me – an expedition all alone with him to the British Museum. Looking back, I wonder whether this may have had some connection with the episode of the half-sovereign. Perhaps I had taken the disappointment 'well' – as I had on the surface – and had earned some kind of reward. Or perhaps, since he was pleased with my progress in my Sunday evening lessons, he thought it was time I saw the Elgin marbles and other classical sculpture of which hitherto I had only seen photographs. He also told me that we were going to see something that, frankly, interested me far more, the Egyptian mummies. I looked forward to these with a delicious trepidation for he told me that they were real dead people and I was very anxious to know what dead people looked like. In the security of his presence I was sure I would not be too frightened, though I was a shade apprehensive when I remembered them alone in the dark.

He was kind enough not to torment me with the suspense of looking forward to an indefinite date. One day he announced that on the following day I was to be ready immediately after lunch to accompany him to the British Museum. Though it must have been either a Saturday or a day in the school holidays, it was rare for him to have an afternoon free of pupils and never before had he devoted one entirely to me. To be taken out all by myself, as if I were my mother, was an honour I have never expected and I felt very important as, washed and combed and dressed in my best, I came downstairs to find him waiting for me in the hall in the black overcoat he wore over morning dress, holding his top hat and his silver-topped ebony cane. My mother spoilt the dignity of our exit by saying to him: 'Now, Cecil, *don't* forget to ask her,' and in a loud whisper to me, 'If you want to . . . you know . . . just say "Daddy, may I wash my hands?"' At that moment I could have killed her, but I forgot the shame and even her very existence as I set off down Perham Road with my chin in the air and my hand in his, almost trotting in the effort to keep up with his quick strides and too proud to ask him to walk a little more slowly.

It was a blissful afternoon. I remember less about the Greek statues than the pleasure of having him to myself. He was in his sweetest, most companionable mood and no grown-up lady could have had a more charming and attentive escort. The way he asked me at intervals, 'Would you care to wash your hands, Eirene?' was so exquisitely tactful that I felt no shame in admitting that I would when this was the case. He would then conduct me to the threshold of the gloomily majestic Ladies Cloakroom, hold the door open for me and await my return a polite distance away. Inside I found a kindly attendant who made the necessary arrangements for someone of my size and felt rather grand and sophisticated as I bestowed on her the two pennies my father had slipped inside my glove. He and I then resumed our tour of the Greek sculptures, identifying various Greek gods and goddesses and, I think, amusing some other visitors by our mutual pleasure when I was able to pipe correctly 'Hermes' or 'Apollo' in response to his, 'Can you tell me who this is?' There was a question I myself should have much liked to ask though it was as well I did not. An object which seemed common to all the photographs of naked gods had always puzzled me and the puzzling object was far more evident now that I could see these marble deities life-size and in three dimensions. I could not make out if it was really part of their bodies or merely an added decoration. This curious boss seemed too elaborately carved to be made of human flesh yet it always appeared in the same place, in that secret spot which, on my own body, I knew was 'not nice' and must never be mentioned, still less exposed. Yet, since the strange object clung there with no visible means of support, it really seemed as if it might be growing out of the flesh. None of the naked goddesses and nymphs had one and where it was possible to see behind the hand with which they modestly covered the same place – proving that they too knew that it was 'rude' to show it – I observed that they were made the same way I was. I had often wondered what really made the difference between boy and girl babies and how parents were so certain which was which. With grown-ups the difference was obvious; women had long hair, full bosoms, smooth faces and soft shrill voices; even if they had been dressed in trousers no one could mistake them for men. I had long ago, of course, discovered that a little girl could not turn herself into a little boy by wearing knickers instead of a frock; it seemed that once one's parents had decided, without consulting one, that one was a little girl, whether one liked it or not, one had to go being one and eventually grow up into a lady.

But what made them decide so early? I had studied several babies in prams and could not guess, without being told, which were male and which female. I noticed that many grown-ups could not either. The only people who were always sure were the babies' parents. Evidently, even for them, it was not a matter of personal choice. I had often heard my mother's friends sympathising about couples who were so disappointed that they had got a little daughter instead of a son or the other way round. Presumably they knew by some sign, invisible to other people, which they had been given, according to my mother, by the fairies, according to Bessie and Millie, by some even more mysterious agency which they refused to disclose. However much I pressed them, I got no more than a teasing giggle and that infuriating retort: 'Ask no questions and you'll be told no lies.' On the subject of the difference between boys and girls, they volunteered the information that little girls were made of sugar and spice and all things nice whereas little boys were made of slugs and snails and puppy-dogs' tails which was flattering but really not much help. However the sight of these curious, foliated bosses which appeared not only on gods and demi-gods but also on beautiful mortal youths who were favoured by the immortals started me off on a new line of speculation. Whatever the unmistakable difference, it could only be detected with no clothes on, and presumably it must be evident even in infancy. The only little boy – indeed the only other child of my own age – whom I knew was my cousin Arnold but, as I had never seen him naked, I could not verify my theory. If this mysterious adjunct was what really differentiated the sexes, then boy babies must have little ones which grew bigger as they grew older. In that case, my father, since he was a man, must possess one too, a large ornate one, like Apollo and Poseidon. No sooner did this thought occur to me than I was stricken with horror at my own irreverence. Whatever would my father think if he had known that I had been on the verge of wondering what he looked like with no clothes on?

It was a relief when he diverted my attention from the statues to some fragments of the capitals of Greek columns and pointed out to me the difference between Doric, Ionic and Corinthian. Anxious to atone for my shameful thoughts, I concentrated on these neutral objects and was soon able to identify which was which. So thoroughly did I master these three types of capital that they have remained ever since as my one sure piece of knowledge concerning Greek architecture.

The mummies were something of a disappointment. Their faces were so shrivelled and brown and leathery and they looked so much of the same texture as the brown cigar-like wrappings of their incredibly small bodies that it was difficult to believe that they really were dead human beings. To me they looked very like very old and dirty rag dolls. I found them rather repellent, but not in the least frightening. My mental picture of human corpses had been very different, life size, with recognisable faces stiffened in a ghastly white rigidity and glazed staring eyes. I was quite sure that when I went to bed that night I should not dream of the faces of dead Pharaohs; they made no more impression on me than a row of coconuts.

When we left the British Museum I was overjoyed when my father hailed a hansom. Not only were my legs very weary, but I had never ridden in a hansom before and to go home in one seemed a magnificent climax to our afternoon's outing. But there was another treat to come, for which I had not been prepared. When the driver opened a little square trapdoor in the roof and called down through it: 'Where to, Sir?' my father did not give our home address.

'I think we both deserve a decent tea after all that intellectual strain,' he beamed at me, when the cabby's whiskery red face had vanished from about our heads and the trapdoor had slammed down again. 'After going to the B.M. I usually treat myself to tea at Appenrodts. In my opinion they have the best cream cakes in London. I hope you'll agree with me.'

I had never had tea in any teashop except the Lyons in Kensington High Street where my mother had occasionally taken me after she had been shopping at Barker's. Even that was a great treat, for I was sometimes allowed a chocolate éclair after my bread-and-butter and a chocolate éclair was the most delicious thing I had ever tasted. But never had I imagined such cakes as appeared on the marble table at Appenrodts or such an orgy of them as he offered me.

'We do not want to waste time on bread and butter, do we?' he smiled. I could not have agreed more heartily. 'And what would you like to drink? Their chocolate's very good and you'd probably prefer it to coffee which is what I'm going to have.'

I could hardly believe my ears. I was actually going to be let off milk as well as bread and butter. Never had I felt so grown-up. The waitress brought us great thick white cups topped with foamy blobs of whipped cream and he showed me how to drink the ambrosial chocolate through a straw so as not to get cream on the tip of my nose. Everything about that meal was gloriously unusual and, as for Appenrodts' Viennese pastries, they surpassed anything I could have imagined. Not only were there chocolate éclairs, lighter and more delicious than any I had ever tasted, but ethereal meringues, delicate cornucopias, airy puffs of buns, all mere shells of exquisitely varied tastes and textures to set off their lavish fillings of fresh whipped cream. My father kept pressing me to 'have one more of these' or 'try one of those' and, when I reluctantly refused, for, with the best will in the world, I could not have managed another, saying politely: 'You don't mind if I do?' Of course I did not mind. It was a great joy to discover that he revelled in cream cakes as much as I did. How human, how approachable, how utterly charming he was, devouring Appenrodts' superb confections, with his blue eyes shining, his cheeks very pink and little flecks of cream dotting his moustache! I felt I had never loved him so much as he sat there, laughingly apologising for his greed and telling me that he had never outgrown the passion for whipped cream he had had as a little boy and that even the experience of making himself sick by eating too much cream trifle had never spoilt his appetite for it. 'I daren't indulge in it in front of your mother,' he confided to me. 'She tells me I'm getting too fat as it is. You won't give me away when we get home, will you, Eirene?'

I shook my head ecstatically. That was my crowning bliss, the thought that he and I were sharing something highly pleasurable from which my mother was excluded.

We drove home in another hansom. I wished the ride could have gone on for ever. By now, I was getting sleepy. At moments I half dozed off to the rhythm of the trotting hooves and the jingle of the harness. Then, as we slowed down or turned a corner, I would open my eyes again and see the horse's hind quarters rising and falling in front of me and find that I was leaning against my father's shoulder and that he did not seem to mind. Now and then he would turn his face to me and smile down at me under the brim of his shining top hat. But all too soon, the heavenly drive was over and we were out on the pavement outside 22 Perham Road and he was fishing in his trouser pocket for his latchkey.

Before we mounted the steps, he paused for a moment and pointed to the two peeling stucco pillars of the porch.

'Let's see if you remember what you learnt this afternoon. What kind of pillars are they?'

Concentrating with all my might, I said, after a moment's hesitation:

'Doric.'

'Quite right,' he said. 'I wish all my pupils were as good as you.' And bending down, he kissed me.

I went to bed, tired and happy, but too excited to go to sleep at once. Lying there, clutching Mr Dash close, I thought about many things, but not about the statues and mummies in the British Museum. How wonderful it would be, I reflected, if life could always be as it had been this afternoon and, since I knew it could not, why was there not some way of storing up all this happiness so that it would be still there to draw on when life was grey and my father severe? I had not had time to take in all the happiness of the afternoon any more than I had had room inside me to take in all the cream cakes I had been offered. How delightful it would be if I could shut away this lovable, approachable Daddy somewhere inside me so that he would be there whenever I wanted him. When he was cross and Olympianly aloof, all I would have to do would be to open this secret cupboard inside me and get him out, as I got my favourite toys out of the toy cupboard. And in another cupboard inside me, I would store all the Appenrodt cream pastries to which I had been legally entitled but had not been able to eat at the time and get them out when I was hungry and there was nothing for tea at home but thick bread and butter and seed cake.

11.

In the early summer of that year 1903, I made my first real appearance in the social world – as a bridesmaid. The subject had been first mooted by the prospective bride at one of my mother's 'At Home' days and I had been banished before I grasped what a bridesmaid was but not before I had overheard the delicious words I was not meant to hear: 'She's so pretty . . . she'd make an adorable one. Do persuade Cecil to let her.'

Perhaps, if anyone but the Mortons had made the request, my father would have refused. The Mortons were very special friends of my parents who led a much more social life than they did and entertained them a great deal. I forget where they lived, but it was in some much more fashionable neighbourhood than West Kensington and my father was rather in awe of old Mrs Norton who had a haughty manner and was given to examining

Antonia aged twenty-five, in the year she married E.E.S., her second husband.

people *de haut en bas* through a lorgnette. My mother was not impressed by old Mrs Morton's *grande dame* manner and refused to kow-tow to her. She pointed out that even if one of her husband's ancestors had come over with William the Conqueror, it did not give his wife any claim to blue blood, still less any right to patronise her children's friends.

The younger Mortons consisted of a son in the Treasury who must at one time, I think, have been one of my father's pupils and was not many years junior to him. At any rate, William, always known as 'Billoy', had gone up to Oxford soon after my father came down from Cambridge and when my parents were engaged he had invited them up for some of the festivities of Commem Week where they had met his two younger sisters, Millicent and 'Toppy', and the five had become great friends. Billoy – I can only guess at the spelling of his nickname, which was pronounced 'Be*loy*' – was tall, slim, distinguished looking and impeccably dressed, the kind of young man whom my father instinctively admired. His youngest sister 'Toppy' – I never knew her real name – unlike her brother, was short, plump and fluffily pretty in a way that my mother declared was very 'common', but which my father found extremely attractive. In falling in love with my mother, he had gone against all his normal inclinations, and even after he married he was never quite proof against the charms of petite blue-eyed blondes with retroussé noses and peachy complexions and quantities of honey-coloured hair. Poppy Morton was a perfect example of his type and long afterwards, when I was grown up, he confided to me that he had been tempted to do more than flirt with her. She was gay, and silly, and the soul of good nature, and I liked her almost as much as my father did. But if Toppy attracted my father, Billoy was equally attracted to my mother, though in a slightly different way. He never missed one of her 'At Home' days and he always seemed to be on hand to escort her to concerts and theatres or to take her to Ranelagh or Queen's Club, to both of which he belonged. I do not think they were in the least in love with each other. Billoy was simply what was almost indispensable in those days to a pretty married woman whose husband was nearly always too busy to take her out, a *cavalière servente*. Billoy never married so my mother was able to rely on him for years as her devoted familiar. They made an elegant couple and they were conscious of it. I do not think my father was jealous of him, he was too much attached to him and had too much confidence in him for that, but I think he

sometimes envied him his tall, slim figure, his pale, distinguished face and his imperturbable poise. He had neither my
father's intelligence nor his wit but he was a very agreeable
person and the nearest thing in our small circle to the 'man about
town' one part of my father secretly longed to be. He did not
aspire to be Lord Henry Wootton but he would clearly have
liked to be Mr Carter of *The Dolly Dialogues*, one of his favourite
characters in fiction along with Colonel de Gray in *The Egoist* –
whom he always said resembled Toby de Courcy – and Saki's
Clovis Sangrail.

It was not Toppy Morton who was getting married – though
next year I was in turn to be one of her bridesmaids – but her
elder sister Millicent, of whom I have not the slightest recollection except that I believe she was tall and pale like her brother. At
the ceremony I was aware of the bride only as the back view of a
veiled figure wonderfully arrayed in cascades of white tulle and
white satin with a wreath of waxy white blossoms on its head. It
was the first time I had ever been in a church but I was too
preoccupied to think of anything but performing my duties with
proper dignity. I felt like a court lady walking in a royal
procession. An older child had the awful responsibility of
holding up the bride's train; all I had to do was to walk slowly up
the aisle beside another fair-haired little girl of the same size,
carrying a silver basket of flowers and, as I had been instructed,
not looking at anybody in the congregation, not even my
parents. I was disappointed that the bridegroom was not splen-
didly arrayed like the bride and her cortège but only wore black
morning dress like my father and all the other men in the
congregation. As to my own clothes, I had never worn anything
so magnificent. My last glimpse of myself in the looking-glass at
home had shown me a reflection I could hardly believe to be my
own. As we stood at the altar, during the boring exchange of
muttered words that went on between the bridegroom, the
bride and an old gentleman, curiously dressed in a black skirt
instead of trousers over which he wore a voluminous white
pleated garment edged with lace, like one of my mother's
peignoirs, I had leisure to gloat on my glorious attire. My
companion was dressed exactly like me so, by glancing sideways at her, I could verify and admire each detail as in a mirror.
Our short, bell-shaped frocks were made of alternate narrow
bands of white glacé silk and écru lace. The lace had a pattern
that looked like shelled walnuts and the combination of stiff,
snowy white and pale coffee colour agreeably reminded me of a

whipped cream and walnut confection I had eaten at Appenrodts. I must have been a very greedy child for I was constantly
associating quite unrelated things with food: for example, when
there was a layer of snow on the top of the dark brown brick wall
of the backyard, I was immediately reminded of iced Christmas
cake. On our heads we wore enormous white felt hats, tied
under our chins with huge chiffon bows and we had white silk
mittens, white silk socks and, of course, white kid shoes. My hat
was uncomfortably heavy, but I gladly bore the discomfort for
the sake of the grandeur of wearing such a magnificently
grown-up hat which vied in size with my mother's plumed one
and must have made me look like a mushroom. Underneath my
frock I wore a white silk petticoat, the first I had ever possessed,
and even my new knickers were of fine lawn instead of nainsook
and edged with lace. As I walked up the aisle, I had made a
delicious *frou-frou*, just like my mother, and as I stood at the altar
I had to clutch my silver basket of forget-me-nots and tuberoses,
in which a lace-edged handkerchief was thoughtfully concealed
in case we needed to blow our noses, very tight to resist the
temptation to pick up the hem of my skirt and admire my silk
petticoat, or feel under the chiffon bow that half-covered my
chest to feel if my brooch was still safely there. For just before
we had left home my mother had produced an exquisite little
brooch composed of three turquoise forget-me-nots set in gold
and seed pearls. It was a present from the bridegroom whose
name I ungratefully forget, and as my mother pinned it to the
bosom of my dress, she said: 'There – now you have a *real* piece
of jewellery! Aren't you a lucky child?' It was so much prettier
than my gold wire 'Eirene' brooch that I wondered if, in future, I
might be allowed to wear it instead. But, rather disappointingly,
my mother said I might lose it and that she had better look after it
for me. So, after the wedding, it officially lived in her jewel case
and she quite often honoured it by borrowing it to pin on her
lace jabots, though I was allowed to wear it on 'At Home' days
or any occasion on which Mortons were likely to be present.

    At the reception, I found myself being made a most flattering
fuss of. I had meant to have some words with my fellow
bridesmaid, for normally it would have been a great treat to talk
to another child of my own age, but she had her own circle of
admirers. Once again I had the intoxicating sense of being a
success that I had had with that pupil in the study. Gorgeously
dressed ladies swooped down and kissed me and told me I was a
little duck and had behaved like a little angel in the church.

Elegant gentlemen plied me with ices and sugar cakes and gave me sips of champagne from their glasses. The champagne was deliciously fizzy and, though I did not care for its taste, it gave me a pleasantly fizzy feeling inside and I became very talkative. At one point I had two or three gentlemen gathered round me laughing and listening to my chatter. On the edge of the group stood a pale dark one whose hair was rather longer than men's hair usually was and who wore a black satin stock instead of a tie. He seemed more interested in my appearance than my chatter and he kept staring at me. Thinking he was admiring my clothes, I picked up the skirt of my silk and lace frock and spread it out so that he could see its full glory.

'I've got a silk petticoat underneath,' I declared proudly, looking up at him. The other gentlemen laughed but the dark one with the stock screwed up his eyes, put his head on one side and muttered: 'Don't move, child. Stay just as you are. Charming, *charming*!'

At that moment, I saw my parents approaching, my mother looking ravishing in a poppy red dress with sweeping skirts, a high-necked bodice trimmed with insets of black lace over white satin and a big black hat trimmed with red poppies. I promptly dropped the pose I had been obediently holding. Though my father was smiling, I knew I was showing off and had better be careful. The man with the stock went up to them, smiling too.

'I was just coming to look for you, Mr and Mrs Botting. I've discovered that this charming little girl is your daughter. My name's Wilson. We've met before at the Mortons. I'm a painter.'

'Of course,' said my mother. 'You painted that beautiful picture of Millicent and Toppy that was in last year's Academy.'

My father nodded appreciatively. 'Ah, of course. I've admired it so much in the Morton's drawing-room.'

'And now I so much want to paint your little daughter. She would make an adorable picture just as she is at this moment.'

My parents looked pleased but embarrassed.

'Of course we should love to have a portrait of Eirene,' said my mother. 'Especially by such a famous artist as you, Mr Wilson. But alas, I fear we couldn't . . . at any rate not just yet.'

'Oh, please don't misunderstand me, Mrs Botting,' broke in Mr Wilson. 'I'm asking you this as a personal favour . . . just to let me use her as a model. I want to do a child subject for next year's Academy but so far I haven't been able to find the right child. Your little girl is exactly what I've been looking for. So fresh and so unselfconsciously natural.'

'In that case, Cecil we can hardly refuse Mr Wilson, can we?'

A few days later, wearing my best ordinary clothes, but accompanied by a cardboard box containing my bridesmaid's finery, my mother took me in a cab to Mr Wilson's studio in Camden Hill. On the way, she said she wished Daddy could have afforded to have *her* painted by Mr Wilson. He had often told her how much he would like to paint her portrait but of course he would have to be paid for it. They would not of course be able to buy the picture of myself, however good a 'likeness', it would be much too expensive, but they would feel proud to have it hung in the Academy. She added, with a sigh, that it was a pity that when Mr Wilson needed a grown-up model, he used his wife. She would quite have enjoyed posing in a picturesque costume as he often painted Mrs Wilson 'in character' as Romola or Portia or some other heroine. 'I think a Spanish dress would suit me best,' she said musingly. 'Spanish *court* dress, like a Velasquez lady. And of course a high comb and a mantilla. I have that lovely mantilla that belonged to Mamma. Yes, I think I'd make a very convincing high-born Spanish Doña or something or other. Or perhaps it would be more fun if he did me as Carmen. But Carmen was rather a naughty lady. I don't think Daddy would like it!'

At the studio I was changed into my bridesmaid's dress and hat and Mr Wilson posed me on a rostrum in various attitudes. When he had finally settled that I was to stand with my skirts raised in both hands and right foot pointed forward at an angle in the 'first position of dancing', a photographer suddenly appeared and took several pictures of me. After that Mr Wilson made some preliminary sketches, drew two chalk marks on the rostrum to fix the place for my feet and I was dismissed, leaving my finery behind for Mr Wilson to 'work on'. For subsequent sittings I was brought in a bus by Millie and collected at a stated time.

I enjoyed my sittings very much. Mr Wilson's studio was full of fascinating objects, tapestries, lengths of rich brocades and velvets, pieces of armour, Venetian mirrors, silver bowls and goblets (he specialised in painting reflections in silver) and various musical instruments including a harp, a spinet and a mandolin. There was also a lay figure whose jointed wood and canvas limbs were usually draped in a Spanish shawl but on one occasion in a mayor's robes with a cocked hat on its faceless head. With so much to look at I did not get bored standing up there on my rostrum while Mr Wilson, wearing a blue smock

and a floppy bow, moved to and fro behind his easel, occasionally peering at me round the canvas with one eye shut and a
paintbrush held perpendicularly at arm's length as if he were
measuring me. I watched him with absorbed interest as he
squeezed out colours onto his loaded palette, mixed them and
dabbed them onto the canvas, sometimes making only a single
dab before he took another brush from his bristling sheaf. He
had a photograph of me pinned to his easel which he consulted
during the frequent rests he gave me from posing so that he
could go on painting through the breaks. Meanwhile I was
allowed to wander about the studio, with its delicious smell of
oil and turpentine – a smell I have loved ever since – and admire
all its furniture which included several framed and unframed
examples of Mr Wilson's work. I was dazzled by his cleverness,
especially by the realistic way he painted materials and objects.
You could see almost every hair in a lady's fur stole and his satin
and silver had the most glorious sheen. As to the famous
reflections, I marvelled at the number of things that could be
reflected in miniature in a bowl or a goblet and be so accurately
reproduced. It was like looking into Mr Wilson's 'magic' mirror
in which all the objects in the studio were visible reduced to the
size of the tiniest doll's house furniture and very slightly dis-
torted so that they seemed more magical still. I got on extremely
well with Mr Wilson who talked to me almost like an equal and
told me I had a very intelligent appreciation of art. I also got on
very well with his dachshund, who was often in the studio
during my sittings – or rather 'standings' – on the rostrum and
showed a marked inclination to sit on my lap during the
intervals. Unfortunately this could not be allowed for fear of
crushing my silk and lace dress. But Mr Wilson consoled me by
promising to paint me again next year, in an ordinary frock,
with Fritz on my lap. I was such a good and biddable model, he
said, that he would like to do *Little Girl with Dachshund* as a
successor to *The Dancing Bridesmaid*.

When I was finally allowed to see the picture I was amazed
how wonderfully Mr Wilson had painted the chiffon bow that
tied on my big white felt hat and the silk and lace of my dress.
You could see every detail of the walnut-like pattern of the lace
and the chiffon looked so like chiffon that you felt you could
have untied the bow. As regards the face, my eyes looked much
bigger and bluer than they ever looked in the glass, my lips
redder and my teeth much more even but I thought it a great
improvement.

'The only thing,' said Mr Wilson, squinting earnestly at the picture, 'is what background to give it. I want something rather striking and original. Out of doors, I think, green grass and daisies, to suggest the springtime of life.'

In the end he found something very striking and original indeed. Behind my white-clad figure, he painted the cricket pitch at Lords, viewed from the nursery end, with the pavilion in the distance.

I do not know whether *The Dancing Bridesmaid* was ever hung in the Academy, or, if it did, if anyone bought it. I often wonder if in some lumber room or junk shop there still exists a very typical example of Edwardian period painting representing a small fair-haired child in a huge white felt hat and silk and lace frock standing all by itself, with its skirts extended and its feet in the first position of dancing, in the middle of the cricket pitch of Lord's which the artist has scandalously scattered with daisies.

The frock remained my best party frock till it was replaced by my next bridesmaid's dress. For, after this initial success, I was a bridesmaid at two more weddings when I was five and six and made my last – and least glamorous appearance when I was nine. As to the great white felt hat which I should dearly have liked to keep for dressing-up, my mother annexed it the moment my portrait was finished. It appeared on her head with various trimmings. Three years later she was still wearing it. She is wearing it in the only photograph of us taken together, when I was seven. By then it had been transformed into a kind of Napoleonic cocked hat, turned up in the front and liberally trimmed with ostrich plumes. My own costume in that photograph is singularly unglamorous for I refused to be photographed in anything but my newly acquired Froebel school uniform, a stark, box-pleated serge tunic with a white collar and belt so stiffly starched that they appear to have been pipeclayed and wearing on my head a hussar cap that I loved so passionately that I sometimes slept in it. But it was to be some time yet before I developed my military phase.

12.

Probably the most important thing that happened to me in that summer of 1903 was my first introduction to Binesfield.

My grandparents went down there every year for their summer holiday and this year it was decided that I should go with them. I was very fond of my grandparents and it was always a treat for me to go to tea with them in their little flat in Owen Mansions, Queen's Club Gardens, within ten minutes walk of Perham Road. My mother resented their living so near and still more that my father paid their rent which she considered absurdly expensive. It was forty pounds a year for an apartment consisting of a bedroom, sitting-room, kitchen and bathroom whereas he paid only sixty pounds for the twelve-roomed house in Perham Road. However, from her point of view, the alterna-tive of their living with us would have been far worse and she much preferred that our spare room should be occupied by a resident pupil. I do not remember whether Mr Henderson, who was tall, dark and a German citizen preceded Mr Hamley, the small, fair-haired English officer, but they both admired my mother greatly and often took her out. Willy Henderson was, I think, more than a little in love with her. They were both very kind to me and often gave me small presents, so that I found them very agreeable additions to our household. My mother certainly liked having them about, especially as she earned a little money by coaching Willy Henderson in German which, after her four years in Hamburg, she knew much better than he did since he had left Germany as a boy and been brought up in England.

She never accompanied me on my visits to 13 Owen Man-sions and I was very glad that she did not. My grandparents and I were much more at our ease without her and even without my father. My grandparents' flat was crammed with heavy Victo-rian furniture and interesting objects, such as glass cases of stuffed birds, a model in different coloured sands of Washington Church where they had been married, and innumerable orna-ments which included painted vases with dangling glass lustres, a severed marble hand emerging from a marble lace cuff and a china boot adorned with forget-me-nots and laced half-way up with gold laces with rose-buds for tags. The atmosphere was almost as pleasantly relaxed as that of the kitchen at home, though of course we ate the delicious home-made cakes and scones my grandmother provided for tea from a table spread with a white cloth edged with her own crochet lace and drank from her best china, a set she had been given as a wedding present, with a different wild flower painted on each gold-rimmed cup and plate. My grandfather had, at that time, a clerk's job in Maple's which had been found for him through his nephew's connection with that firm and which suited him much better than his efforts to run a grocer's shop. His deafness was no handicap and his beautiful copper-plate writing combined with his accuracy at figures made him a model clerk, except on the days when he was 'not well enough' to go to the office owing to having drunk a little more than was good for him.

I could not admire my grandmother's looks as I admired my grandfather's pale, delicately hollowed features and silky white hair and beard but I did not find her plain doughy face, with two onyx-rimmed brown eyes stuck in it like raisins in a scone, anything like as repellent as my mother did. Her hair really seemed to me very handsome; that profusion of rich brown waves ending in a tightly curled Alexandra fringe on her fore-head impressed me much more favourably than my mother's because it was always so tidy. It never occurred to me that it was a wig any more than that her teeth, so much whiter and more even than my mothers, were false. I had often noticed that old ladies had much whiter and more regular teeth than younger ones and wondered why this should be so. Her body was a very queer shape, even for an old lady's, for it was not uniformly stout but shaped like a cottage loaf, with a tiny, shrunken looking bust and a huge protruding stomach which swelled out like a stiff balloon from under a quite small waist encircled by a black velvet belt with a cut steel buckle. She never wore anything but black and told me that she had done so ever since she was thirty – in 1903 she must have been in her late fifties – as she was always having to go into mourning for one of her own or her husband's relatives and it seemed a waste of time and money going into colours. However, her bodices were usually discreetly trimmed with little touches of grey or lilac satin and, unless she was actually in mourning, she always wore a coloured flower or feather in her toque.

At those tea-parties at Owen Mansions, I had of course heard a great deal about Binesfield and Granny's two sisters, my great-aunts Agnes and Clara Jeffery. I had been told stories of the unimaginably long ago – a legendary period like 'Once upon a time' of a fairy tale when they had all been little girls like myself. I loved these stories of their country childhood, but the country for me was still, since I had no recollection of my one holiday in it with Lizzie, a magical place I had only heard about and read about. I longed to see with my own eyes the old house that had once been a farmhouse, the garden with the great tree that had sprung up from the three walnuts the three little girls had planted long before my father was born and was now twice as tall as when he was a little boy, the green with the ducks and geese, the meadows where there were real cows which I had hitherto seen only in pictures and wild flowers which, unlike the flowers in Kensington Gardens, could be picked and taken home. When I heard that I was to see all these marvels this very summer, I could hardly wait for the day the three of us were to set off.

When we reached Partridge Green station, it was already dark and I was half-asleep. I was roused by a voice shouting 'Parr'ge Green' and a lantern flashing in my eyes. As we bundled out on to the platform, the first thing I was aware of was wonderfully fresh cool air and a most delicious smell. My grandfather was sniffing it too appreciatively. I called out loud enough for him to hear: 'What's that lovely smell, Grandpa?'

'Just good Sussex air, my dear,' he told me.

Outside the station, a fly was waiting. 'Good evening, Mr Tidey,' said my grandmother to the man on the box. He had a red face and wore a rough, ridgy straw hat, shaped like my father's panama.

'Evening, Mrs Botting.' His voice too had a burr like the porter's. 'So you've brought little Missy to see her aunties. Reckon the Miss Jefferies will be outway pleased.'

'Say "Good evening, Mr Tidey,"' prompted my grandmother.

'Good evening, Miss. I see you've brought your doggie with you. Does he bite?'

'Mr Dash never bites,' I said haughtily. I was not sure if I liked the red-faced man. I did not care for his loud, condescending laugh as he exclaimed:

'*Muss* Dash indeed. Plain Rover I calls *my* dog. You'd best keep your Lunnon dog out of his way – he'd make two mouthfuls of him, Rover would.'

'Mr Tidey's only teasing,' said my grandmother.

I liked Mr Tidey less than ever, though later we were to become quite good friends. I cuddled Mr Dash protectively as we drove along a road between high hedges. The horse's hooves sounded much louder than they did in London and the wheels made a scrunching sound quite different from the sound of cab wheels in London.

The night was cloudy, though here and there in a rift twinkled a star or two, the first I had ever seen, for I had never been out of doors so late. The excitement of driving at night through the damp, sweet-smelling air almost made up for not being able to see the country I was so longing to see. The light from the fly's lamp, in whose aureole fluttered moths and tiny insects, showed up hedgerows and now and then a white gate or a cottage. I kept asking eagerly 'Is that Binesfield?' every time a dark bulk with a glimmer in some of its windows loomed up ahead of us. But the answer was always, 'Not yet, dear.'

Except for the clip-clop of the horse's hooves and the slither and scrunch of the wheels, it was wonderfully quiet. Nothing passed us on the road but a woman on a bicycle coming in the opposite direction who called out 'Good evening' to us and Mr Tidey and my grandparents called back: 'Good evening, Miss Stepney.'

'I wonder what's she doing, going into Partridge Green so late. You'd think she'd be at home seeing to her brother's supper,' said my grandmother.

'What's that, Ada?'

'Miss Stepney,' my grandmother raised her voice. 'Out so late on her bicycle and coming away from Ashurst. I wonder where she's going.'

Mr Tidey answered from the box.

'Oh she's always gadding here, there and everywhere since she got that cycle. Rode all the way to Steyning last week for a dance after the stool-ball match. Dancing at *her* age!'

'Her brother helps your aunts with their garden,' my grandmother told me. 'Ever since he was fourteen and that's quite a while ago now. Such a quiet man he is too. Such energy she has, always organising things in the village. We can't help laughing a little over Miss Stepney's goings on. But she's a very good-hearted woman.'

I was not interested in Miss Stepney's goings on and I was glad when there was silence again and I could listen to sounds that came from behind the hedges, the lowing of a cow, sudden squeals and rustlings, a melancholy hoot that Granny told me was an owl. Once, right above our heads, there was a very high shrill squeak.

'What's that squeak, Granny?' I asked, looking up, though I could see nothing.

'I can't hear anything. Oh, dear,' she exclaimed with horror, seeing Mr Tidey flourish his whip as if he were trying to hit something in the air, 'I hope it's not a bat. Nasty, horrid things.'

'It was a bat all right. There's a lot of 'em about this summer,' observed Mr Tidey with gruesome relish. 'You ladies don't like 'em, I know. If a bat gets in your hair you can't get it out nohow and all your hair has to come off. You've sharp ears, little Missy, if you can hear a bat squeak. Flittermice we call 'em down here.'

'What are you fidgeting for, Ada?' asked my grandfather.

'A bat!' she screamed at him.

'They'll do no harm if you leave them alone,' said my grandfather. 'Like wasps.'

'Bad summer for wasps too,' said Mr Tidey.

'Oh dear,' said my grandmother. 'That's the worst of the country. All these nasty insects. You must never pick up a plum or an apple off the grass, dear, in case there's wasps in it.'

My grandfather said suddenly:

'I could hear a bat squeak before I lost my hearing. It's not everyone that can. *You* can't Ada.'

'Eirene can,' my grandmother shouted at him.

'That's what I miss most, not hearing the birds. Time was when I knew the call of every bird in Sussex.' He added more cheerfully, 'But I can show you all the birds, Eirene, and I know where to put my hand in and find an old nest.'

The sound of the wheels grew louder for a moment and the horse's hooves echoed as we crossed a little bridge over a narrow river.

'Only a minute or two now,' said my grandmother. 'That's the Adur – well, it's only a canal really but we call it the Adur all the same. When I was a little girl I thought it was called after me. They say the smugglers used to come up it all the way from Shoreham. But nothing does now, not even a barge. It's all overgrown with weeds and water lilies. Look dear, we're going across Bines Green now. That's the house – the last one on the right back from the road.'

I peered ahead eagerly. Beyond two or three other scattered dark shapes of houses was one set higher and further back than the rest, half hidden by the great round bulk of a tree which I guessed must be the walnut.

Mr Tidey stopped the fly in the road, got down from the box and, when my grandmother had got out, he tried, to my great indignation, to pick me up and carry me.

'Please put me down, Mr Tidey,' I said haughtily. 'I'm not a baby.'

It was one of those small incidents that were destined to become a family legend. Year after year I was to be reminded of my first arrival at Binesfield.

'You were only a little mite, but so independent. That was the first we heard of you . . . a high little voice saying very proudly: "Please put me down, Mr Tidey." Poor Tidey, I'm sure he meant so well. It had been raining and he didn't want you to get your feet wet on the damp grass.'

Holding my grandmother's hand, I walked over the damp bumpy grass in the glimmer of light from the open doorway while my grandfather and Mr Tidey followed with the luggage. The sloping stretch of green was too rough for the fly to drive up to the gate in the iron palings. The figures of two old ladies, one taller and thinner than my grandmother, one shorter but not so stout, were standing at the gate. I remember little more of my arrival, for I was very sleepy, but walking up an uneven red brick path, with little yellow flowers growing between the bricks to a porch hidden under a tangle of honeysuckle and amber. Aunt Agnes and Aunt Clara told me that, as soon as I entered the house, I looked all about me, gave a great sigh and said, according to them, 'so quaintly, as if you were quite an old person: "At last!" '

The front door at Binesfield opened straight into the living room. The only illumination was an oil lamp in the centre of the table. That first night, as always, the white cloth must have been spread for supper, cold ham and tongue, salad and cheese and jelly and the two painted hexagonal biscuit tins I was to come to know so well, one with six scenes from naval life on its panels containing plain biscuits and the other with scenes from military life containing sweet ones. That first night I was too tired and excited to do more than drink a mug of milk and eat a few shortbread biscuits. I had never been up so late before and it was maddening the way my eyes kept closing when there was so much I wanted to take in. I had already decided that I liked Aunt Clara better than Aunt Agnes. I found Aunt Agnes, the elder of the two, who looked to me much older than Granny because she had silver hair, rather intimidating. Her pale, bony face, with its steel-rimmed spectacles, had a rather stern expression and she gave me a reprimanding look when I yawned without putting my hand in front of my mouth. But Aunt Clara I loved at first

A map of West Sussex from 1898. Bines Green, the common on which Binesfield still stands, consists of no more than a few farmhouses on the road between the villages of Partridge Green and Ashurst. Horsham, where trains were changed for Partridge Green, and Steyning, at the foot of the Downs, were the nearest small towns.

Inset: Binesfield photographed from the common about 1916. The old walnut tree and the central front door are gone now. In front of the cottage stand Cecil and Christine Botting. Seated are the aunts, Clara and Agnes.

sight. Everything about her was round, her little cottage-loaf figure, shorter but better shaped than my grandmother's, her face which was like a withered, but still glossy yellow apple with here and there a brown stain on it, her eyes which were the colour of faded blue pansies. She did not talk to me very much but every time I looked at her, she gave me a sweet, shy smile. But what had endeared her to me from the first was that when Aunt Agnes had said, 'Put your toy down, dear, and come and sit at the table,' Aunt Clara had stroked Mr Dash and admired his beauty before gently removing him from my arms and installing him in a chair where I could see him.

'I think I'd better put Eirene to bed,' said my grandmother. 'It's long past her bedtime, she's dropping with sleep.'

'No, you finish your supper, Ada,' said Aunt Clara. 'I'll take her up and put her to bed. That is if Eirene doesn't mind.'

I did not mind at all. On the contrary, I much preferred this idea to being put to bed by my grandmother. I knew her too well not to feel rather shy of having to undress in front of her. I had never done so further than my petticoat. For some reason I did not feel in the least self-conscious about undressing in front of Aunt Clara, any more than I minded Millie or Bessie seeing me in my bath. I should have been very nervous indeed if I had had to undress in front of Aunt Agnes and something told me that she would have been equally embarrassed. But there was something so cosy and motherly about Aunt Clara that I knew instinctively that she liked children and understood them.

There were no less than four doors besides the front door opening off the living room. They were not at all like the doors at Perham Road. They were very low and irregularly shaped and made of unpainted dark wood which I afterwards learnt was very old oak. Only the front door and one other had a small brass handle, the others had only wooden latches, worked with a string. Aunt Clara disappeared behind one door and emerged carrying a lighted candle in a saucer-shaped candlestick. When I had collected Mr Dash and said 'goodnight' all round (Aunt Agnes did not kiss me as my grandparents did but just touched my forehead with her lips and murmured, 'God bless you'), Aunt Clara pulled the string of another latch and opened the door on to a winding staircase. Its dark and wedge-shaped steps looked very steep in the glimmer of the candle. There was not room for us to go up side by side so Aunt Clara made me climb ahead of her so that she could catch me if I stumbled. She also carried Mr Dash for me so that I could get a purchase with both hands on the steps above me for there were no banisters. The winding stairs were mercifully short and we soon reached a tiny square landing where Aunt Clara unlatched another door.

'Granny and Grandpa will sleep in here,' she said as we walked through a room containing a huge four-poster with a canopy, 'and your bedroom opens out of theirs. So if you're lonely or want anything in the night, you've only to knock on their door.'

She unlatched a door in the far wall and there we were in the bedroom I was to sleep in every summer holiday for the next twenty or more years and which was to remain unchanged until my father made so many radical alterations to Binesfield on his retirement that it was hardly recognisable as the same house.

Aunt Clara put the candle down on a little dressing table whose legs were concealed with beribboned lace curtains and in its light I surveyed a room full of fascinating objects I would like to have examined more closely if I had not been so absurdly sleepy. The bed was as big as the one in the next bedroom but, instead of being a four-poster, it had a very high wooden footboard and headboard. It also had a patchwork counterpane which, in the candle-light, glowed with a medley of colours. I admired it very much and still more when Aunt Clara told me she had made it herself.

'I save all the scraps from my dressmaking for patchwork,' she told me. 'We find a use for almost everything here. You'll find bits of old cushions and so on from Perham Road in it. And your mother's kind enough to send me scraps of material from some of *her* dresses, such lovely materials too. But I mustn't keep you here chattering. Into bed with you.'

As I undressed and she folded each garment neatly and placed it on a chair, she apologised for my having to go to bed without a bath.

'We haven't a bathroom, as I expect Granny's told you. We've got a hip-bath, but it takes so long to heat the water – we usually don't have more than one a week. I hope you won't miss all the comforts you're used to in London too much.'

I was quite sure I was not going to miss them at all. I washed my face and hands in deliciously cold, refreshing water at a tiny, rickety wash-stand, also skirted with a drapery, whose jug did not match its basin.

'There's a chamber-pot behind the curtain, dear. I put you an enamel one because I thought a china one might be dangerous for a little girl besides being so heavy to handle. If you want to use it, I'll turn my back.'

I did want to use it, but the extraordinary thing was that I would not have minded if she had not turned. I had never felt so uninhibited in any grown-up's presence as I did in Aunt Clara's. She seemed much shyer of me than I was of her and delicately averted her head when I peeled off my vest.

As soon as I was in my nightdress I grabbed Mr Dash and made to scramble up into bed from which she had removed the patchwork counterpane. The top sheet was invitingly turned down. I could not wait to snuggle down on those two vast pillows which smelt deliciously of lavender.

'Just a moment, dear,' said Aunt Clara. 'You haven't said your prayers.'

I stared at her. I had read, of course, about children who said prayers, but prayers formed no part of my bedtime ritual.

'I know you're very sleepy, but don't you think you ought to say just a little one? Just as you do at home.'

'But I don't at home,' I said. 'I never have.'

She looked at me with a sad, puzzled expression. 'You can't surely mean that your mother never taught you to say any prayers?'

I shook my head.

'You poor little thing. But you've been christened. I know you have.'

'Oh yes, I was christened Eirene Adeline.'

'But don't you know anything about God and Jesus? Haven't you ever been to church?'

I could not honestly say I knew anything about God. The word still conveyed to me only the dark man in the long green robe and the white frilled collar in the picture in the dining-room, the one with the young man with the severed foot. But I said proudly:

'Oh yes, I've been to church. I was a bridesmaid. Church is where people get married.'

'Haven't you ever been to church on Sundays?'

I shook my head.

'Oh dear, I don't know what to say,' said poor Aunt Clara. 'I suppose it's none of my business if your parents don't – But I'm surprised that Granny and Grandpa haven't – And I'm sure I don't know what Agnes will say.' She added kindly, 'It's not *your* fault, dear.'

Anxious to console her, I said:

'I'll say prayers if you like. Only I don't know what to say. You kneel down, don't you?'

She looked much happier. 'That's right, dear.'

I knelt down beside the bed, and she knelt down beside me.

'Now put your doggie down for a minute and put your hands together *so*. Now say after me: "God bless me and make me a good girl."'

I repeated the words after her.

'And God bless Mummy and Daddy and Granny and Grandpa. Amen.'

I did so. Then I looked up at her. 'What does "bless" mean?'

'Take care of people and make them happy.'

'Is God the only person who can do that?'

'Yes. But only if they are good.'

'But I had to ask him to *make* me good. Only me, not the other people.'

Aunt Clara cut short our theological discussion by giving me a hearty hug and kiss and lifting me into the bed. At once the mattress rose up in a great billow on either side of me.

'Oh, it's so *soft*,' I exclaimed. 'Not a bit like my bed at home.'

'I don't suppose you've ever slept in a feather bed before,' she smiled. 'We stuff the mattresses ourselves with the goose-feathers from the green. You'd be surprised how many you can pick up in an afternoon.'

'Oh, I so want to see the geese,' I wailed. 'It was too dark to see anything.'

'You'll see everything tomorrow. I'm going to leave you a night-light in case you feel frightened in a strange room in the dark. But you mustn't feel lonely – we're all in the room underneath and you'll be able to hear our voices – the floor is full of chinks. Don't be frightened if you hear funny noises in the walls. It's only the rats scampering about. There are always rats in an old house like this but they mind their own business and don't do anyone any harm. Or it might be birds in the ivy outside. You're not used to country noises but you soon will be. Good-night, my dear.'

I lay awake for a few moments, watching the wavering shadows the night-light threw over the low ceiling that had a sagging bulge in it just over my bed. But before I could sort out my impressions of my first evening at Binesfield, my eyelids came down like shutters and when I opened them again the room was full of sunlight filtering in through a red blind and outside I could hear birds singing, cocks crowing and geese cackling.

13.

I stayed in bed just long enough to take in the fact that I was really and truly at Binesfield, then I got up and went over to the door leading to my grandparents' bedroom. Impatient as I was to see what the country outside looked like by daylight, I thought I had better not try to pull up the red cotton blind trimmed with white crochet so I lifted it up just high enough to enable me to see out. Beyond the palings which fenced off the narrow strip of garden in front of the house was a rough grassy slope which must be 'the green' Aunt Clara had talked of, for there were geese on it. They were the first live ones I had seen; up to now I had only seen dead ones, plucked of all but their neck feathers, hanging up by their yellow feet in Sendall's horrid shop. On the other side of the road along which Mr Tidey had driven us in his fly was another expanse of grass with some more geese on it. At the far end of it was the only house in sight. Except that it did not have a thatched roof it looked like all the pictures of country cottages I had seen on calendars. Its pink front was chequered with dark brown squares like a game of noughts and crosses and there was a creeper growing on the wall and over the porch. A woman came out of it wheeling a bicycle. She jumped on it and after a bumpy ride over the rough grass, pedalled furiously along the road. Before she disappeared out of sight, I recognised her as the woman who had passed us on the road last night and remembered her name was Miss Stepney and that her brother helped the aunts with their garden. I was pleased to have discovered on my own who lived in that cottage and to have identified Miss Stepney so quickly. It gave me an agreeable feeling of already being part of Binesfield and not a mere visitor. Beyond the Stepney cottage I could see a meadow with cows in it and, except where my vision was obstructed by trees, a vista of many-coloured fields intersected by dark green hedges.

At that moment my grandmother came in, saying, 'I thought I'd find you still asleep.' She kissed me and raised the red blind carefully. Together we looked out of the window. She was so happy pointing out the various animals and in being the first to show me all these promised delights, that I was glad that I had not told her that I had already seen one or two of them. There was, however, something new to see. A flock of sheep was coming along the road, followed by a big shaggy grey and white dog and an old man with a red face framed in white whiskers, carrying a crook. The old man was wearing a curious kind of holland overall over his trousers. I asked my grandmother what it was.

'It's the old-fashioned round-frock. Smocks they call them in some parts. But here in Sussex we always call them round-frocks. When I was a girl, all the farm labourers used to wear them. But now you don't often see them except on old men. That's Dumbrell's old shepherd, Harry Nye. He'll be driving the sheep over to Steyning Market. Four miles – it's a long step at his age and it's going to be a hot day. Your grandpa's been out already and says that Chanctonbury looks very far away and has a haze on it. That's a sure sign.'

'What's that mountain over there in the distance?'

She laughed. 'That's not a mountain, dear. It's Nye-timber – the only bit of the downs you can see from the front of the house. It isn't as high as Chanctonbury really.'

The sheep had only just disappeared round a bend, leaving a cloud of dust behind them, when along came a low-sided blue cart with red wheels and shafts, drawn by a huge horse with shaggy legs and the horse was actually wearing a hat – a little straw hat edged with braid for its ears to go through. There was a net fixed over the top of the open cart and under it were a lot of pigs, crowded so close together that they could hardly move. A little later a man came along pushing a handcart with a coop of live chickens on it.

When I descended to the living room the sun was shining through the only window. On a bamboo table in front of it, an old tabby cat was basking among pots of geraniums. The big table where we had had supper last night was laid for breakfast and in the middle of it was a jug of bright coloured flowers, some, like sweet peas that I could recognise, others quite unknown. At the far end of the room, which was so long that it was always in shadow, Aunt Agnes and Aunt Clara, wearing claret-coloured skirts and print blouses like my grandmother's – only theirs were cream-coloured and faded, were dodging in and out of two opposite doors in the wall, Aunt Agnes bringing in plates of bacon and fried eggs and Aunt Clara now a jug of milk, now cut-glass dishes containing butter and plums and gooseberries, all arranged on green leaves. My grandfather, wearing a holland jacket instead of his usual one came forward to greet me, saying: 'Hope you're woken up with a better appetite than you had last night.' I nodded vehemently, I was so hungry I could hardly wait to begin my breakfast. But just as he was about to lift me on to the chair with the extra cushions on it where I had sat last night, my grandmother stopped him.

'Don't sit her up to the table yet, Fred.'

I noticed that she and the aunts were now standing behind their own chairs as if waiting for something. My grandfather went and stood behind his, at the head of the table. There was complete silence. Aunt Agnes nodded towards my grandfather and said loud enough for him to hear:

'Will you ask a blessing, Fred?'

'My grandfather looked a trifle embarrassed, then muttered into his beard, 'For what we are about to receive may the Lord make us truly thankful.'

I gazed at him, astonished. I had never heard him do this. All the grownups, except Aunt Agnes, who said it very distinctly, mumbled 'Amen'. Then we sat down and began talking and eating. I whispered to my grandmother who was sitting next to me: 'What was Grandpa doing?'

'Saying grace, dear' she murmured back. 'We don't say it out loud at home but Aunt Agnes likes us to. Next time, remember to bow your head and fold your hands together.'

As if she had overheard us, Aunt Agnes said to me quite kindly: 'I daresay you'll find our ways different from what you're used to in London. But we keep to the old customs in the country. Though even here many people have given up the habit of saying grace aloud. I think it's such a pity.' She turned to my grandmother, 'I know you think me very old fashioned, Ada. But I'm not ashamed of it.'

'Your Aunt Agnes always set us a good example when she was a little girl. But only after she suddenly became so serious. Up to then she was always the one who made the mischief,' said Aunt Clara. 'Ada, do you remember when she put brown stuff all over her face and dressed up in an old red-hooded cloak and came round to the back door pretending to be a gipsy child selling brooms? Poor Mother was quite taken in and actually gave her a penny.'

Aunt Agnes' pale face flushed a faint pink but she did not look angry though she said reprovingly, 'Really, Clara, I do not think you should tell such tales in front of Eirene. I'm sure she never done anything so naughty.'

I found it quite impossible to imagine that the three old ladies had ever been little girls, and when they began reminiscing about their childhood I listened without much interest. However I was perfectly happy eating my excellent breakfast and looking about me. The whitewashed ceiling was very low; when my grandfather stood up its crooked, whitewashed beams only cleared his head by a few inches and even Aunt Clara, the shortest of the three old ladies, had to stoop when she went through one of the doors in the wall. The paper was the same as upstairs, pale green with white sprigs on it and all round the walls, about a foot below the ceiling ran a dado of the same brown varnished corrugated paper that framed the text and the picture in my bedroom. The walls were bulging and uneven and when I was allowed to 'get down' and walk about, they felt quite soft when I bumped into them as I squeezed behind the grown-ups' chairs. I discovered afterwards that so many layers of wallpaper had been successively pasted over their original oak beams and plaster that they made a kind of padded lining to the room. My great aunts had no admiration at all for bare oak beams and plaster and had laboured hard and with much in-genuity to convert the interior of the old Elizabethan farmhouse as nearly as possible into that of a Victorian suburban villa. But nothing could disguise the ingle-nook, deep enough for two grown-up people to sit side by side, though there was an embroidered screen in front of the bare brick hearth and they had contrived to make a little mantelpiece, covered with a bobbled fringe and loaded with ornaments to mask the low whitewashed beam above it. Two small sunken armchairs in faded chintz covers, draped with crochet antimacassars threaded through with red ribbon stood on either side of the ingle-nook and against the far wall of the room was a horsehair sofa with three patchwork cushions arranged symmetrically against its stiffly curved back. Above it hung a large, spotty steel engraving in a walnut frame showing Lord Strafford on his way to execution being blessed by an Archbishop whose lawn-sleeved arm was thrust out through the grating of a prison cell. There was a paragraph of explanatory writing in fine copperplate but it was too dim at the end of the room for me to read it. Working my way back to the sunny end, I threaded my way between the still-seated grown-ups' chairs and a mahogany sideboard till I came to the only door with a brass handle and the only one which I had never seen opened.

'That's the parlour behind there,' said my grandmother. 'One of us will show it you later on. Don't go in there by yourself in case you have an accident and break something.'

The front door, which was only a little higher than the other four doors, was half-hidden by a screen covered with scraps and varnished over with the yellowish-brown varnish. I admired this very much and asked if the aunts had made it.

'Not the screen itself,' said Aunt Clara. 'Our father made that. But we pasted all those scraps on to it when we were girls. About the time your Granny and Grandpa were married. It was very fashionable in those days, cutting out bunches of flowers and little pictures from old annuals and decorating furniture with them. What was it they called it, Agnes? You're the one for remembering long words.'

'Decalcomania,' said Aunt Agnes.

I approached the old tabby cat lying dozing in the sun on the bamboo table in the window. 'What's your cat's name?'

'He's called Whiff,' Aunt Clara told me.

'May I stroke him?'

'Better wait till he's got to know you, dear. He's an old cat and very shy of strangers. And he's not used to children. He won't scratch you if you touch him; he'll just jump down and run away.'

'He's your Aunt Clara's cat,' said Aunt Agnes. 'I've no objection to animals but I'm not particularly fond of them, as she is. She has a pet robin that follows her about in the garden. She even has a pet toad that comes into the house.

My grandfather suddenly put down the newspaper which he had unfolded as soon as he had finished his breakfast and said, 'Fetch me my pipe. I'm going to take a stroll round the garden. I expect Eirene would like to come with me.'

'She'd better put on goloshes,' said Aunt Clara. 'The grass is very damp after yesterday's rain and it's muddy down by the gooseberry bushes. I put my pattens on when I went out to pick some before breakfast.'

'What are pattens?' I asked, pricking up my ears at the sound of a new word.

'A kind of wooden clog you slip on over your ordinary ones. Come out into the kitchen and I'll show you.'

I followed her through one of the doors into a gloomy, stone-flagged place which could not have been more unlike our cheerful cosy kitchen at Perham Road. There was not even a range in it, only a battered oil stove on which stood a huge black kettle, just beginning to steam. On one wall was a stone sink with pails of water standing beside it.

'Why hasn't your sink any taps?'

'Because we haven't any running water. We have to draw all our water up in buckets from the well. Sometimes the well runs dry when we have a very dry summer and we have to get our water from Mrs Kensett's across the road. Her well is deeper than ours.'

Against the wall of the kitchen which was not even whitewashed but showed all its naked brick and crooked oak beams, were propped all kinds of strange metal and wooden implements, including what looked like a witch's besom.

'Haven't you ever seen a birch broom?' asked Aunt Clara.

I shook my head. 'It looks like the things witches ride on.'

'Don't be frightened, dear, we haven't any witches in Ashurst nowadays. But people hereabouts always make a birch broom with two little pieces of wood nailed together like a cross in the middle of the twigs. Then no witch will ever use it. A witch can't abide to touch anything with a cross on it. When we were little girls, there was a man over in Henfield was said to be a wizard. And our mother used to tell us how one day a boy wanted to find out if the man really was. So he laid a birch broom across a very narrow path and hid behind a hedge to see if the man would step over it. Because if he couldn't, the boy would know he was a wizard. And sure enough, when the man came along, he couldn't step over it and had to go back. But he caught sight of the boy hiding in the hedge and put the evil eye on him. And from that day to the day of his death, that boy walked lame.'

'So the man really was a wizard?'

'So they say. And my mother had seen the boy with her own eyes. But I promise you there aren't any witches or wizards hereabouts nowadays. Ah, there's your granny coming downstairs. You mustn't keep grandpa waiting.'

'You haven't shown me the pattens.' She stooped down and picked up a pair of what looked like solid blocks of wood mounted on four wooden pegs and slipped their straps over her insteps.

'How much taller you look! Oh may I try them on?'

'They're far too big for your little feet. Even if we could get a pair small enough, you'd take a long while to get the knack of wearing them without twisting your ankle.'

My grandmother called from the doorway, 'Come and put your things on, dear. Grandpa's out in front, waiting for you.'

As she knelt down to pull on my goloshes for me, she whispered a question in my ear. I whispered back: 'Yes but where do I go?'

'Aunt Clara will show you. It's down at the bottom of the garden. You can go out the back way, it's quicker.'

Aunt Clara opened a door in the kitchen wall and we emerged into the sunlight. It was my first sight of the real garden for there were no windows at the back of the house and it seemed to me enormous. I wanted to stop and look at everything but Aunt Clara was saying: 'Grandpa will show you it all later.' She took my hand, and stepping along briskly on her pattens, led me down the long grass path between beds that were a jumble of gnarled fruit trees, bright flowers and patches of vegetables to where, long-concealed by tall bushes, stood a little grey wooden hut. Pulling the string of the latch, she showed me what was inside.

'I'm afraid it's not what you're used to at home, dear.'

I found myself gazing at a kind of wooden bench one half of which was lower than the other with two holes, one smaller than the other, placed side by side in it. Looking through them I could see a ditch with long grass and nettles growing in it. Hanging from a hook in the wall was a bundle of neatly-trimmed squares of newspaper. There was no sign of a plug to pull.

'Use the smaller seat, dear, it's meant for children. I'll stay outside the door and keep guard for you.'

It was very dark in there when she shut the door. The only light came in through chinks between the planks and the hole above the latch. Through the bigger hole beside me came up a rather unpleasant smell. At first I was to nervous to 'do' anything, but eventually I succeeded.

It was to take me a little while to get over my distaste for the dark earth closet and the mysterious scrabblings and rustlings I could sometimes hear in the ditch below, but once I had, I came almost to like it. This was one of the many features of life at Binesfield that made it so utterly different from life at Perham Road and gave me a sense of inhabiting another world. Soon that world was to become as familiar to me as the Perham Road one. Summer after summer, I was to find myself happily revisiting every room in the house, every tree in the garden, every person associated with my Binesfield life.

Perhaps the most startling difference between my Perham Road self and my Binesfield self was that the latter had no desire to impersonate imaginary characters or invent imaginary surroundings. My real surroundings were more interesting than any I could invent and with so much to occupy me I felt no need to invent daydreams. Instead of being shut up alone for hours in the nursery as I was at home, I had the garden to play in and the garden provided so many interesting things to do that there was no need to resort to make-believe to keep myself entertained. Moreover the grown-ups took a benevolent interest in my activities and were never, like my parents too busy with their own affairs to be concerned with mine. My grandfather was always ready to play with me, as well as to take me for walks in the fields. In spite of his deafness, he was a wonderful companion. He taught me the names of birds and butterflies and wild flowers, to recognise the different crops and distinguish between barley and bearded wheat, to know mushrooms from toadstools and tell the time by 'dandelion clocks'. I never ceased to be amazed at the wonderful things he could fashion with a penknife out of twigs and odds and ends of wood, whistles that you could really blow on, dog's heads, miniature shepherd's crooks and an endless supply of the little walking sticks I delighted to carry in imitation of his big one when we went off to explore the countryside. He made me a miniature wheelbarrow which was the joy of my life. Sometimes I gave Mr Dash rides in it but more often I used it to 'help' Aunt Clara or Mr Stepney with the gardening. For one of the things that made my life at Binesfield so different from my other one was that the grown-ups did such much more interesting things than my parents, and I often preferred 'helping' them to playing on my own. I enjoyed Aunt Agnes' magnificent fruit tarts all the more because I had helped Aunt Clara pick the gooseberries or raspberries: I felt a personal sense of achievement when the helping appeared on my plate and I could calculate how much I had contributed to it by my own labours. Considering I ate as much as I picked and Aunt Clara always filled up my little basket from her big one before we reached the kitchen door, my actual contribution must have been remarkably small, but I was firmly convinced that everyone's share of the pie was largely composed of it. And everyone, except Aunt Agnes, assured me that my gooseberries or raspberries tasted particularly delicious. Aunt Agnes never made any concessions to my childish vanity. Yet I would not have had her any different.

Such daydreams as I indulged in at Binesfield were of the most blameless kind, such as finding a beautiful pony saddled and bridled tethered to railings, and being told it was a present for me, to ride whenever I liked. Sometimes they were inspired by nobler desires, aroused by such edifying books as *Ministering Children*. I envisaged myself as the Little Lady Bountiful of the entire village, bringing a ray of sunshine into the darkest cottage, distributing chicken broth and jelly to the sick and reading the Bible to bed-ridden old ladies. For my Binesfield self was strongly attracted at times by those model little girls in the pious Victorian children's books which were my Sunday reading.

Every year I renewed my acquaintance with all the familiar figures of Ashurst who always looked the same as when I had first seen then. Miss Stepney with her witch-like brown face and her untidy black hair, always dusty with flour, who seemed to live on her bicycle; the Misses Naylor, who never seemed to appear in public except on their way to church but knew even more about the minutest details of what went on in the neighbourhood than Miss Stepney for Miss Carrie spent the greater part of the day staring out of the front window of South Blows through her binoculars: old Thorne with his bristly face, as wrinkled as a walnut, and his one solitary black tooth.

Yet there were changes. Every year I was alarmed to discover the aunts and their front room had grown smaller. It took me some time to realise that it was I who had grown bigger. Out of doors, however, I quite welcomed changes from summer to summer. In fact, when I went for my first walk in the fields with my grandfather, I got almost as much pleasure from noticing that Mr Dumbrell next door had planted oats instead of wheat in Six Berries this year, that a barn had been re-thatched or a gate mended as from rediscovering the familiar landmarks, the two poplars on either side of Pinfold which made it look different from every other farmhouse in the neighbourhood, the mossy log that bridged the muddy, nettle-filled ditch in front of the Old Man's Stile at the bottom of the lag which I was always relieved to cross safely before the Old Man grabbed my ankle (though my grandfather assured me he would only do so if I ventured there alone), the lightning-struck oak in the hedge of the Long Field and the rich green meadows down by the Adur which were never ploughed up and always filled with grazing shorthorns. Noticing all these changes, especially in 'our own fields' in which I took a proprietary pride, though they were let to Mr Stanford and Harry Dumbrell, gave me a sense of being a real inhabitant of Ashurst, not just a summer visitor.

It was not till I was nine or ten, when it was my parents, not my grandparents, who came down with me every summer to Binesfield that my two worlds became inter-related. Even so, they remained separate. For my parents too underwent a transformation at Binesfield. The life we shared there with the aunts was quite other than our life at Perham Road. Year after year, we would pick it up at a point where it had been left off, resuming our Binesfield selves the moment we arrived at Partridge Green station. By the time we changed at Horsham on the way back to London we had already shed them till the following July.

14.

The streets of West Kensington seemed duller than ever after the fields and the gardens. Never before had the view of that blank brown brick wall from my nursery seemed so depressing. Though I was glad to see my toy animals again, they were a poor substitute for Mr Stepney's rabbits and Aunt Clara's tame robin and Little Maggie's dog Carlo. We no longer had even our cross old cat Sunny. He had mysteriously disappeared in my absence; I suppose he had been destroyed for I got only evasive answers when I asked what had happened to him. Even more than the animals, I missed Little Maggie. It had been so pleasant to have someone near my own age living just across the way. Up to now I had not seriously felt the lack of companionship of other children but now I began to wish badly for another child to talk to and play with. The only other child I knew was my cousin Arnold White who was only three months older than I was but he lived too far away for us to see each other often. Being taken over to spend the day at Uncle Howard's and Aunt Edith's house in St John's Wood was a rare treat. But, though I liked Arnold and enjoyed seeing him, we met too seldom to become real friends. Moreover, being both at that time only children we were so used to playing by ourselves that, after Arnold had shown me his new toys and I had rather enviously admired them for they were much grander than my own, we usually amused ourselves independently at opposite ends of the nursery or the garden.

I fell into a bored and listless state in which it seemed that nothing exciting would ever happen again to me. I clung more than ever to Mr Dash, for he had shared all the delights of Binesfield with me and, unlike my parents, who had at first listened with interest to my accounts of them but by now were heartily sick of the subject, he did not mind how much I talked about them and tried to make us both re-live them. Yes, though I loved him as much as ever, I realised that he had his limitations. I was growing older and beginning to have ideas in my head that even the most faithful and sympathetic of toy dogs could not share. The most important of these was the one that had been implanted into me at Binesfield that God existed and now that I had been told about Him, I was under an obligation to Him.

One morning, several weeks after my return, my mother announced that she was going to take me, that afternoon, for a walk in Kensington Gardens. Now that I had seen the real country, this was not the treat that it had been, but at least it made a change in the daily routine. My depressed spirits rose a little when I was dressed in my best pale blue coat with the white flecks on it that reminded me of snowflakes and my starched muslin bonnet. This could mean that we were going to have tea in a tea-shop after our walk and the possibility of éclairs stimulated me to make myself more agreeable to my mother than I had been for some time. She, naturally enough, supposed that I was showing my appreciation of her company and was proportionately pleased. Our relations, for the past few weeks, had been a little strained, due to my tactless insistence on how much I had enjoyed myself in the country. She was apt to interpret this as a criticism of my own home and to accuse me of alienation of affection. Though she attributed this mainly to my grandmother's fatal influence – she ought to have known that she would take advantage of having me all to herself to turn me against my own mother – she was offended with me. I knew it, and I knew that it would have been easy to restore peace, but until now I had not thought it worthwhile to make the effort. Now that I had, I was pleasantly surprised. I had forgotten what an agreeable companion my mother could be. By the time we reached Kensington Gardens, I had forgotten about those possible éclairs and was enjoying her company for its own sake. So much so that as we were making towards the Round Pond, talking very happily, I was quite annoyed when I saw that our conversation was about to be interrupted. Walking towards us and twirling her parasol in greeting was Miss Louise Edwards, one of my mother's closest friends and one of my unofficial 'Aunties'. Though I liked 'Aunty Louise', I did not welcome her appearance at this moment. I knew that, once she joined us, she and my mother would become involved in one of their animated discussions of topics of no interest to me. The friendship between them was rather surprising for they could hardly have been more alike. 'Aunty Louise' was a slightly austere and very high-minded spinster who cared nothing for clothes, and held opinions that were considered 'advanced'. She was an admirer of

Ibsen and Shaw and a champion of women's rights. Later she was to become an ardent, though not 'militant', suffragette and not only induced my father to support the movement but persuaded my mother to chalk 'Votes for Women' on the pavements of West Kensington. She had a stiff, bony figure and a face which might have been pretty, or at least piquant, had she done her fair hair more becomingly and taken a little care of her complexion. As it was, her dry skin had patches of broken veins on the cheeks and her nose, which she refused to powder to subdue its unfortunate redness, resembled a frost-bitten cherry. Her brother, Osman Edwards, was a master at St Paul's but anything but the conventional type of schoolmaster. He was the nearest thing we had in West Kensington to a literary Bohemian and his background and interests were very different from the rest of my father's colleagues. He had not only spent many years in Paris where he had been intimately acquainted with such poets as Verlaine, but he had also lived in Japan and was

The photographer insisted that she should lie on her back for this picture, claiming that the lines would thus be erased and a more relaxed air conveyed. The picture was taken at the time of her divorce from Tom Hopkinson. Antonia was undergoing a Freudian analysis at the time.

something of an authority on Japanese art and literature. In appearance, as well as in temperament, he was quite unlike his sister. Louise Edwards could not have looked more English, but her brother Osman with his pointed beard, his unconventional clothes and his un-English habit of kissing women's hands and gesticulating with his own suggested an ex-patriate Frenchman. There was a slightly forlorn air about Osman Edwards as of a civilised, cosmopolitan exiled among provincial barbarians. Teaching French at an English Public School was a depressing occupation for a man whose preoccupations were entirely aesthetic and whose spiritual home was in France and Japan. Perhaps to console himself for the loss of both, he had married a French widow who looked not unlike a Japanese and, to the scandal of West Kensington, painted her face like a geisha's.

My father had struck up a friendship with him at St Paul's and I think Osman was thankful to find someone on the staff who appreciated his conversation. My mother, who usually disliked my father's colleagues, found him fascinating. Though he was not a handsome man – indeed he was almost an ugly one, short and fattish, with rather sensual features to which his beard and his moist red lips gave a somewhat satyr-like cast – he was not only witty and intelligent but had a peculiar sweetness of disposition which made him attractive to children as well as to women. 'Bertie', as his mother and sister always called him (perhaps it was his real name and he had discarded it for the more romantic Osman by which he was known to everyone else), had what my mother described as the 'continental attitude' to women, especially to pretty married ones and she often told me in later years that she had to be very severe with him on several occasions though she hinted that some of her friends had been less resolute in their resistance.

When she was first introduced to his sister, my mother did not take to her at all. The antipathy was mutual. My mother thought Miss Edwards stiff and cold and Miss Edwards made it very plain that she considered my mother a frivolous creature, the kind of woman who most impeded the emancipation of her sex by being content to be a 'man's plaything' instead of his intellectual comrade. The friendship between them, which lasted all their lives, developed as a result of an accidental meeting. Miss Edwards and her widowed mother lived in Tennyson Mansions, Queen's Club Gardens, only a few steps away from my grandparents' flat in Owen Mansions. The two old ladies had made friends and one day, on one of my mother's reluctant visits to Owen Mansions, my grandmother told her that she had just learnt from Mrs Edwards that Louise's beloved pug-dog had died and that she was inconsolable. On her way out my mother ran into Miss Edwards in the street, looking red-eyed and sad and said how sorry she was to hear of her loss. Miss Edwards was so touched by her genuine sympathy that she thawed completely and my mother, discovering that under her chill exterior Miss Edwards had a tender heart and sensitive feelings, took a liking to her. Very soon they were 'Louise' and 'Christine' to each other and meeting constantly, not only to play bridge, the only frivolous occupation in which Louise indulged, but to go to lectures at the Pharos Club and to the plays of Shaw and Ibsen and Grenville Barker.

The two friends were soon deep in conversation so I slipped away unobserved to watch the other children sailing their boats on the Round Pond. I had not brought my own little boat. My one experience of trying to sail it on the pond had been a dismal failure. It had promptly keeled over and the contemptuous glances of the owners of those splendid craft which went scudding off from the shore and sometimes reached the far side unaided as I dragged my tiny boat along on the end of a string, lying flat on its side with its immovable sail submerged, had shamed me so much that I had never taken it to Kensington Gardens again. Today the pond was crowded with vessels of all sizes, from ships hardly bigger than my own, but more efficiently rigged and handled, to big model yachts sailed by expert grown-ups. Among all the craft sailed by children one beautiful little three-masted ship with a fine spread of canvas caught my envious fancy. Her lucky owner excited my admiration even more than his craft. He was a fair-headed boy, taller and obviously older than myself but still young enough to be called a child by grown-ups, though to me he seemed almost a man. He was smartly dressed in a fawn overcoat and matching cap and I thought him the handsomest boy I had ever seen. His eyes were large and very blue, his features small and well-cut, and his complexion, instead of being pink and white like that of most English boys of his age was an even, pale golden fawn, a few shades lighter than his overcoat. I stared at him, fascinated even more by his unusual colouring – hair as fair as my own but contrasting oddly with dark eyebrows and eyelashes and that exotic warm pallor – than by his attractive face. Other things about him fascinated me too, the decisive but curiously graceful way he moved so that all the other little boys seemed clumsy beside him, the deft toss with which he launched his boat and drew her in with his boat-hook when she had finished each successful voyage, the intense concentration on his face as he set his sails which made him look almost grown-up and his composed smile of satisfaction as the breeze filled them and sent her scudding on her course. It was with intense annoyance that I heard my mother calling me and realised that I must go back to the grown-ups or there would be trouble. It was all the more infuriating because the last time my hero had launched his boat, he had been close beside me and had actually smiled at me. Now he was far away, bringing her safe to port and gone out of my life for ever.

Reluctantly I rejoined my mother and Aunty Louise. They were beside the Round Pond now and, to my surprise, Aunty Louise was scanning the crowd of boat-sailing children as if looking for someone she knew. Suddenly she cried: 'Ah, there he is. Wait here while I fetch him,' and darted away.

'Who's she gone to fetch?' I asked my mother.

'Her little nephew – or rather step-nephew. Osman Edward's wife's son by her first husband. He's half French and his name is Gérard – Gérard Sinclair-Hill. Such a charming name. I'm sure he's a charming little boy. Louise is devoted to him.'

'How old is he?'

'Quite a lot older than you – seven. He's an only child, like you.'

My interest was aroused and I stared eagerly after Aunty Louise to see which of the little boys she approached. I could hardly believe my eyes when it turned out to be none other than my hero. As I saw him approaching, beside Aunty Louise, he seemed such a lordly masculine figure in his fawn cap and overcoat, carrying his boat-hook and his dripping yacht, that I was overcome with shyness. If my mother had not held my hand and pushed me forward to be introduced, I should have retreated behind her skirts. For a moment we stared at each other gravely. Then suddenly, Gérard did an extraordinary thing. Thrusting his yacht and boat-hook into Aunty Louise's arms, he put his arm round me and kissed me. It was a deliberate, almost solemn kiss, quite unlike the official peck my cousin Arnold unwillingly bestowed on me in response to his mother's 'Come along, dear, give Eirene a kiss.'

Aunty Louise was evidently as surprised as I was. I heard her say to my mother: 'What an extraordinary thing. I've never seen

Gérard do that to any little girl before. I hope Eirene doesn't mind.'

I did not mind at all. I was flattered and overwhelmed. Having kissed me, Gérard took my hand, and gazing at me very seriously with his turquoise-blue, black-lashed eyes, announced, 'I think I'll marry you. You're so pretty. Shall we be sweethearts?'

I had never felt so honoured in all my life. It had been love at first sight on my side but it had never occurred to me that my hero had felt the same. I remember nothing more of that blissful afternoon except that we wandered hand-in-hand, a little apart from the grown-ups and that he told me a great deal about himself and his ambitions and I listened with admiration. Compared to myself, Gérard seemed almost grown-up in his knowledge of the world and his range of speculations. Never had I imagined that so wonderful a thing could happen to me as to be chosen as the future wife of someone so handsome and so brilliant. We were both, I suppose, in some ways, precocious children. At any rate, the love affair which began that afternoon in Kensington Gardens quickly developed into something which both of us took very seriously and which lasted, with most of the characteristics of an adult one, ecstasy, jealousy, mutual (and often justified) accusations of infidelity, until I was thirteen and Gérard sixteen.

Soon after I met Gérard I acquired something which I had longed for but had always supposed to be almost as much beyond my reach as a real pony – a rocking-horse. Like my doll's house, he was second-hand, but, unlike the doll's house, for which I had never had much enthusiasm, I passionately coveted him the moment I set eyes on him. He came from the same source, a family named Royal-Dawson who lived a street or two away from us. Mrs Royal-Dawson was a rather flamboyant lady, with a thickly-powdered face and peroxide hair, who had, I think, once been an actress and gave dramatic recitations at her own and other people's parties. I once heard her recite 'Curfew shall not ring tonight' at one of my mother's 'At Home' days and was so profoundly impressed that for days I could think of nothing else. It seemed to me simply the greatest, most moving poem ever written and when I discovered a copy of it on our bookshelves, I read it over and over again till I knew it by heart. For a long time I could never hear a church bell without thinking of the heroic maiden who clung to the clapper to prevent the tolling of the curfew which was to be her lover's knell. The elder

Royal-Dawson children, the brilliant Oswald, one of my father's many beloved pupils who were to be killed in the First World War and the lovely fair-haired Anka, whom all West Kensington took to be the original of Lily Haden in Compton Mackenzie's *Sinister Street*, were already grown-up when I was four, but there was a younger daughter, Vera, who, though much older than myself, sometimes condescended to play with me when my mother was calling on hers. I suppose Vera was not, in fact, more than nine or ten, but to me she seemed almost grown-up and to her I seemed a mere baby. We would retire to her 'play-room' (she strictly forbade me to call it the nursery) and there she would provide me with toys that she considered suitable for my years though she had long outgrown them, while she herself, an erect, queenly figure, with her long black hair flying, went for long solitary gallops on the rocking-horse. Sometimes, for a treat, she would allow me a short spell in the saddle, and this was such bliss that I could hardly bear it when Vera made me get off again. She was still much attached to Dragon, as his name was then, and, when she was given a bicycle, she assured me that she would never part with him. How she was induced to do so, I shall never know, but one day the incredible happened. I came back from a dull walk with Bessie to be told by my mother: 'There's a surprise for you in the nursery.' And, when I opened the door, occupying nearly half the floor space, was the Royal Dawson's old rocking-horse. I could hardly believe that he was really mine now, mine to keep for ever and to ride whenever I wished. It was the most wonderful present I had ever received, apart from Mr Dash.

He was, indeed, a battered veteran of a rocking-horse. He had already been ridden hard by the elder Royal-Dawsons before he became Vera's sole property. His dapple-grey paint was cracked and peeling, his saddle torn and one ear and most of his mane was missing. Nevertheless, in spite of his scars, he was a fine-looking animal. He had a noble head and flaring crimson nostrils and his real horsehair tail was still magnificent, although it had come unstuck and had to be wedged with paper to keep it in place. Some mischievous boy had once dropped a marble through the hole in which his tail was lodged, so that as you rode you could hear it rattling about inside. He was a real old-fashioned rocking-horse who bumped up and down on his wooden rockers, instead of merely sliding to and fro on iron bars like the new models which were now beginning to appear in fashionable nurseries. He had also a feature, due no doubt to his venerable age, which I have never known in any other rocking-horse. At either end of his rockers was a wooden seat, so that two children could also use him as a see-saw. These seats had another advantage, though when he first came into my possession I was not brave enough to perform the equestrian feat they made possible. By rocking very violently, one could bump the front seat so hard on the floor that the whole horse moved forward. Vera was such a skilled and fearless rider that she could gallop him the whole length of her play-room. It was a splendid sight to see her charging him forward at reckless speed, gaining more ground each time the seat hit the floor, to the accompaniment of the thunderous rattling of the marble in his hollow inside. I used to look on and admire, but never expected to be able to emulate her. It was not a feat to be attempted by 'soppy kids'.

Although I liked the name 'Dragon' and it suited him, I wanted to feel that he was really mine, so I decided to change it. After much thought, I asked our current resident pupil, Mr Hamley, to advise me about this momentous choice. I had a great respect and affection for Mr Hamley. He was in the army, which seemed to me so much the noblest of professions that I was beginning to be sorry I was a girl and could not be a soldier when I grew up. He encouraged my military ardour by giving me my first box of lead soldiers (the Fifth Dragoons), the foundation of a considerable army which I not only still possess but was still manoeuvring in elaborate battles when I had turned eighteen. Mr Hamley suggested Sceptre. I knew that Vera would not be pleased but what was the loss of her occasional patronising companionship compared to the gain of her rocking horse? Sceptre, née Dragon, was now mine to ride whenever I wanted. However much Vera resented his being passed on to me – and she had even said scornfully that she would rather he had been given to the poor had she known I would have the cheek to change his name – she could not get him back.

Moreover, my pride was more than appeased now that someone infinitely superior to Vera favoured me with the most flattering attention. At first it seemed too good to be true that this lordly boy, three years older than myself, should be as eager for my company as I was for his. But with every meeting after our first memorable one in Kensington Gardens I gained confidence. The extraordinary thing was that Gérard actually suspected that he might have rivals and questioned me closely, every time we met, as to what other boys I had seen in his absence. Though the only other boy I even knew was my cousin Arnold he seemed to think I needed constant reminding that I was his exclusive property. Finally one day, he decided to settle our relationship once and for all by marrying me.

We were sitting on the wooden seats at either end of Sceptre, rocking quietly, when he announced his decision.

In any case, what did it matter if Vera despised me? Someone far more impressive than she had singled me out for the highest possible favour. Within a month or two of our first meeting Gérard had promoted me from being his sweetheart to being his wife. Our married name was Mr and Mrs John Barker and we were the rich owners of the grandest shop in Kensington High Street.

15.

Our marriage remained a secret between us. Only when we were alone together did we address each other as Mr and Mrs John Barker and carry on our private domestic life. It was an idyllic life, uninhibited by material cares. We lived in a palatial apartment over the shop and all we had to do, if we wanted anything, was to take a lift down to the necessary department and help ourselves.

Outwardly, of course, we continued to pursue our separate lives in the restricted conditions imposed on us by our families. We were still too young to issue invitations on our own so our official meetings depended on the grown-ups. I dared not ask too often for permission to have Gérard to tea and, as his mother and mine were not intimate friends, I was not, in our early years, invited to his home. However, as he spent a great deal of time with his devoted step-aunt and step-grandmother in Queen's Club Gardens, we managed to meet fairly often. Apart from being invited to have tea with him almost every Sunday at 4 Tennyson Mansions, I seized every chance of an unofficial meeting. I developed a new eagerness to accompany my mother whenever I knew that she was going round to Aunty Louise. There was always a hope that Gérard might be there and, even if he were not, I could gaze fondly at his photograph. Looking at it, I could recapture all the romance of our first meeting. It showed him in a sailor-suit carrying his yacht and boat-hook as regally as an orb and sceptre, just as he had been carrying them that afternoon by the Round Pond before he relinquished both to embrace me.

There were other compensations, in Gérard's absence, for a visit to 4 Tennyson Mansions. Aunty Louise's widowed mother, Mrs Edwards, was not only the kindest of old ladies, but possessed a fascinating collection of Chinese and Japanese knick-knacks which she allowed me to play with. The glass-fronted cabinet in her drawing-room housed all kinds of fascinating objects, miniature junks and rickshaws and bullock-carts, carved jade and ivory animals, bronze dragons and soap-stone pagodas. There was a lacquer box containing exquisite mother-of-pearl counters shaped like four kinds of tropical fish and a wonderful ivory chess set in which the kings were Chinese emperors with long drooping moustaches and the bishops mandarins. Best of all I liked a red lacquer box which contained a whole set of smaller lacquer boxes fitted one inside the other with incredible precision, each one a perfect box on its own, down to the last which was smaller than a lump of sugar. I never tired of exploring this Aladdin's cave of treaures and playing with its contents.

Mrs Edwards herself fascinated me too, now that Gérard had told me a story about her which invested her, in my eyes, with romantic glamour. Having been told it under a strict pledge of secrecy, I had to suppress the questions I was itching to ask her. Nevertheless, every time I saw her now I gazed at her with avid interest, marvelling that anything so extraordinary could have happened to this placid old lady with her smooth grey hair parted in the middle, her black satin dress festooned with gold chains and hair lockets, who seemed as unlikely as my own grandmother to have an unsolved mystery in her life. All the same, there was one, and of a kind familiar to me in fiction but which I had never yet encountered in fact. I know the story was true for when I was older she told it to me herself.

As a young married woman, she and her husband had lived out East and for a time had been stationed in Hong Kong. They had three children, Osman, Louise and a little boy who, when Mr Edwards and his family left Hong Kong, was only a baby. His Chinese nurse was so devoted to this baby boy that they decided to take her with them when they sailed to their next destination. Mr and Mrs Edwards boarded the ship, followed, as they believed, by the Chinese Amah carrying the baby. When they reached the top of the gangplank and turned to look, there was no sign of Amah or baby. Frantic search among the milling crowds on the quayside produced no result. Eventually the Captain refused to delay the ship's departure any longer and Mr and Mrs Edwards had to sail without their youngest child. Every effort was made to trace the Amah who had stolen the baby but neither she nor the little baby were ever found. In books, long-lost children were always restored to their families but I had to agree with Gérard that there was little hope that his lost step-uncle, if he were still alive, would ever find his way from Hong Kong to West Kensington. As Gérard pointed out, even if the Chinese Amah had confessed on her deathbed that he was not really her son, she would not know where his English mother was now so it would be pretty hopeless for him to set out in search of her.

I was constantly impressed by Gérard's powers of reasoning, lordly self-assurance and his superior knowledge of the world. Yet in spite of his greater age and experience, he did not treat me as an inferior. Naturally he exerted his male authority as my husband, but he never bullied me or snubbed me. He discussed all his opinions very freely with me and was even willing to listen to mine on certain problems to which he had not yet found a satisfactory solution any more than I had.

Far from despising my hopeless inefficiency at any kind of outdoor sport, he rather approved of it. It made me an all the more admiring spectator of his own prowess when he sailed his boat on the Round Pond with such expert skill or propelled his iron hoop at reckless speed along the gravel paths of Queen's Club Gardens. I was as proud as he was that he had a real boy's hoop, driven with a dangerous iron hook, as opposed to the stick-propelled wooden ones bowled by girls of all ages and by most of his male contemporaries. The possession of an iron hoop raised him almost to the level of the Olympians in Colet Court caps and blazers, some of whom were actually over ten and entitled to use the junior tennis court, who formed a 'sidey' and exclusive gang in Queen's Club Gardens. Most of us smaller fry were terrified of them: they would charge through us in mass formation, driving their huge iron hoops like war chariots, menacing us with their deadly iron hooks and frequently mowing us down.

Gérard, however, regarded them with reverent admiration for, next year, he himself would be going to Colet Court, the preparatory school for St Paul's, and be entitled to wear their envied uniform; a dark blue blazer and cap emblazoned with a silver Maltese cross. He had already learnt from his step-father enough of their tribal customs to forbid me to call him 'Gérard' in their hearing. At Colet Court, he told me, one's Christian name had to be kept a deadly secret, and his own, being not only unusual, but foreign, must on no account be revealed. I never admired him more than, when accosted by one of the Olympians with: 'What's your name, kid?' he replied with the utmost self-possession: 'Sinclair-Hill. G. A.'

The A stood for Arthur, which he considered almost as inadmissable as Gérard. I did not care for it myself, but I thought Gérard a beautiful name and I knew that he secretly liked it too. He took care to teach me the proper French pronounciation for it irritated him very much to be called 'Gerard' or 'Gerald' as it did me to be called 'Eileen' or 'Ireen'. It was a great comfort to him that his initials spelt GASH, which could command nothing but respect if discovered marked inside his Colet Court cap.

I was as anxious as he was to preserve him from the terrible imputation of 'soppiness' so, if there were any Colet Court boys about in Queen's Club Gardens, I accepted the fact that he adopted a slightly aloof manner towards me and sometimes even appeared to disown me altogether, leaving me to trundle my wooden hoop alone while he dashed far ahead driving his iron one.

In private, however, he could not have been more demonstrative. Though we both preferred to maintain a certain reserve in front of the grown-ups, the moment we were left alone he would hug me and kiss me and I would rather shyly kiss him back. This, he told me, was called 'flirting' and I must never 'flirt' with any boy but himself. For me it was a strange new experience, at once exciting and slightly alarming. The feel of Gérard's arm round me and his warm cheek pressed against mine sent a delicious thrill all through my body, unlike anything I had ever felt before. I enjoyed this peculiar sensation so much that I had some apprehension that 'flirting' might come under the ban of grown-up disapproval, as so many pleasurable things did. In particular, I felt that my father might frown on it. He had given my grandmother a very black look one day when she had referred to Gérard as 'Eirene's sweetheart' and told her not to use that idiotic expression again. He also asked my mother now and again, somewhat impatiently, if there were no little *girls* she could find for me to play with. At any rate, I found it wiser not to mention Gérard too often or too enthusiastically in my father's presence. I learnt to be very careful not to fidget or glance at the clock on Sunday afternoons during my lessons with him, if he knew that it was one of the Sundays on which I was invited to Tennyson Mansions to have tea with my beloved. He was more severe than usual at any sign of inattention and sometimes threatened not to let me go at all if I did not keep my mind on my lesson. I also learnt not to show too much eagerness to be allowed to invite him to tea in my own house. I did not dare ask my father direct for the required permission. It was safer to broach the subject first to my mother and leave her to bring it up with my father. Sometimes the answer was unfavourable: 'She can't *always* be having that boy round here – he was here only the other day. You seem to forget that the nursery is next door to my study and unfortunately not sound-proof.' And even if it was favourable, it was apt to be accompanied by an expression of surprise that Gerard (he always anglicised his name and gave it an emphatically hard G and D) should condescend to play with a girl of four when he might be playing with boys of his own age.

Any meeting with Gérard was a joy to me but having him to tea in my own home was the greatest joy of all. On those occasions, when we had each other all to ourselves, we could talk with an intimacy that was impossible in the presence of even the kindest of grown-ups. When we played together in old Mrs Edwards' drawing-room, she or Aunty Louise or both often joined in our games and conversation so that we could not concentrate wholly on each other. At Perham Road we were entirely on our own and free to pursue our private life without interruption. Even if my mother was at home and not having a bridge-party, she had her tea as usual upstairs in the drawing-room, leaving me and Gérard to have ours in the dining-room. My father, as always, went straight into his study and his waiting pupil as soon as he returned from afternoon school. We never saw him at all unless, when we were playing in the nursery after tea, he burst in on us with a wrathful request to make less noise.

Mercifully, this happened seldom. When it did, it was due to my letting my desire to please Gérard overrule my fear of displeasing my father. His admiration for Sceptre equalled my own and he was a far more daring rider. Without my having told him of Vera's feats he discovered for himself that by violent rocking and bumping the front wooden seat on the floor he could urge him forward. The bumps would grow louder and louder, the rattle of the marble in Sceptre's inside more and more thunderous till I was torn between pride in his prowess and fear that the noise would disturb my father next door and bring him storming out of his study. Luckily Gérard was usually satisfied with one such solo display of his horsemanship and afterwards we would go for long rides together with me mounted behind him as pillion, clasping his waist to preserve my seat on Sceptre's slippery hindquarters and holding very tight when he quickened him to a brisk but not furious pace.

Hitherto I had had to invent all my own dreams and play all the characters myself. Now, for the first time, I had someone to share these imagined adventures; someone, moreover, with much richer powers of dramatic invention than my own. Along together in my nursery, Gérard and I built up a private world which we re-entered the moment the door closed behind us. I cannot now remember the innumerable stories we dramatised from books or improvised as we went along in which we featured as hero and heroine. We were wrecked together on desert islands, we rescued each other from deadly perils, we lay huddled together in dungeons awaiting torture and execution and were rescued in the nick of time by our magic horse who swooped down from the sky and carried us off on his back, high above the clouds, while our enemies gazed up in helpless astonishment. Sometimes we were magnanimous to our enemies but sometimes we inflicted on them the tortures intended for ourselves. Since we both had a taste for horrors, some of the tortures were very horrid indeed. I was very proud when I could think up a better torture than Gérard.

We did not always pretend to be other people. Very often we preferred to be ourselves and have serious conversations. We would sit on the wooden seats at either end of the rocking-horse, Gérard at the head and I at the tail, and discuss life and its problems. Among other things we discussed religion. Now that I had been told about God and Jesus, though since my parents never mentioned them and never went to church, they did not seem quite so real as they had at Binesfield, I was convinced of their existence. I was careful to remember to say my prayers when I went to bed, even though I felt rather shy kneeling down in front of Bessie or Millie, because I knew I would not go to heaven if I didn't. But Gérard had not quite made up his mind whether to believe in God or not.

'How can you know for certain he's a real person? Granny Edwards believes he is, but Papa Osman – I mean my step-father – says he used to but now he doesn't any longer. And he's a lot brainier than Granny Edwards.'

I was sure my father was much brainier than Mr Osman Edwards, but for some reason I had never asked him if he believed in God. Looking back, it seems strange that I never did.

Perhaps the constant praise of my father's goodness I had heard at Binesfield, in particular from Aunt Agnes who said that, apart from poor savages to whom missionaries had not yet brought the Bible, only wicked people did not believe in God, assured me that he must. Perhaps I was afraid to ask him, for if he had said he didn't, I should have been in an agonising quandary. His opinion would have had tremendous weight with me, but would I have dared to take even my father's word against the word of God himself in the Bible?

I did not like to suggest that Gérard's step-father, of whom he was very fond, was wicked. But I was relieved that Gérard was by no means convinced by his step-father's assurance that there was no such person as God.

'I asked him how the world got started and he said no one had found out for certain yet. Well, if they haven't, how can they be sure it wasn't God who started it? Anyway, somebody must have made it. It could turn out to be God after all. And that would be an awful swizz for the people who don't believe in him.'

But what inclined him most to believe in God was the knowledge that it was the right thing to do at Colet Court.

'Everyone has to go to School Prayers, the masters as well as the boys. So anyway it can't be *soppy* to believe in God, even if you're a man.'

Unlike myself, Gérard preferred God to Jesus. 'I think Jesus sounds rather soppy. I like all the heroes who went about slaying their enemies much better than him. God slew his enemies all right, but you say Jesus just let his slay *him*. He didn't even put up a fight when they caught him. I bet God wouldn't have let anyone crucify *him*. He'd have struck them all dead before they'd even started.'

I would argue that Jesus could have, if he'd wanted to, because he could do anything, like his father God only he was so much kinder that he'd rather let people kill him than kill them. But I had to agree with Gérard that if he could really do anything, why had he let people torture him to death when he could so easily have stopped them without killing anybody? Though our arguments about religion usually ended in a deadlock or in our suddenly getting bored with the subject and turning to other problems on which I felt freer to surmise, such as whether fairies still really existed, where we had been before we were born because, whether babies were found under gooseberry bushes or brought by the doctor in a black bag, they must have existed somewhere beforehand, why you couldn't choose your father or mother or whether to be a boy or a girl, I would find myself milling over them when I was alone and sometimes wishing that Gérard and I had been born in ancient Greece where everyone believed the same thing.

The best moments of all for me when Gérard and I were alone together in my nursery were when we stopped talking or playing and were Mr and Mrs John Barker, Gérard would take me in his arms and kiss me and whisper, 'Let's go to bed now and be husband and wife.' We would lie down together on the floor under the table, draping an old shawl we used for dressing-up over it as a curtain to make our bedroom as dark as possible and there we would cuddle close. The warmth of Gérard's body as I lay full length against it with my head on his shoulders, his ardent kisses, the flutter of his long lashes against my cheek melted me into a state of rapture in which I was acutely conscious of that strange thrill deep inside me. I could not wholly give myself up to the rapture for I could never quite forget the presence of my father next door and wonder what he would do or say if he were to come into the nursery and find us lying on the floor, locked in each other's arms. Something told me he would be angry with me in a new way, one more formidable than any I had known before, and that I dared not even imagine.

At night, though I still took Mr Dash to bed with me, I no longer fell asleep clutching him close. After fondling him a little so as not to hurt his feelings and assuring him he was still my favourite animal and that Sceptre had not displaced him in my affections, I would put him gently aside on the pillow and turn over with my back to him. Then I would imagine Gérard lying beside me, so vividly that I could almost feel his arms round me and his body pressed against mine and I would stay awake as long as I could to prolong the delicious sensation. Sometimes, if I imagined hard enough, I could even produce a faint tremor of that curious inside thrill. One night I discovered that by touching the most secret part of my body which I knew it was 'rude' to touch I could produce it all on my own. I began to invent new ways of producing it, sometimes not even thinking of Gérard. I imagined doing extraordinary things which it would have shocked me beyond words to do in real life, such as running out into the street without any clothes on and letting strangers see me naked. They had to be strangers; I should have been horrified if anyone had recognised me. I wanted these strangers to be shocked, but at the same time fascinated by the sight of my nakedness and as I ran past them, the consciousness of all those unknown eyes staring at my bare body made it tingle all over with a mixture of shame and exultation that was feverishly exciting. This fantasy, as I say, had nothing to do with Gérard; the idea of letting Gérard see me naked was too shocking even to entertain. I had a certain guilt about indulging in it because I was afraid that God might disapprove of my even imagining doing something so reprehensible. Sometimes I would fight against the temptation, but the more I did, the more alluring it became and, once my imagination caught fire, I forgot all about God's possible disapproval. Moreover, I vaguely hoped that certain things I thought and did in the dark and which I was never tempted to think or do by daylight were somehow exempt from the ordinary rules and did not count.

However, most of the things I imagined as I dozed off to sleep concerned myself and Gérard. I imagined rescuing him from all sorts of dangers at great risk to myself and dazzling him with my heroism. In real life he was so much braver than I was, as well as always being the invincible hero who rescued *me* in our dramas, that it was very pleasurable to invent stories in which I was the central figure and Gérard the admiring audience. Sometimes I allowed him to undergo a considerable amount of torture at the hands of his enemies before I rescued him and magically healed his wounds. Sometimes I even waited till his stoical courage broke down and he was reduced to tears before I released him from his tormentors. In real life, of course, I had never seen Gérard cry; the most disgraceful thing a boy could do, as he frequently impressed on me, was to 'blub' and I should have felt it an insult to his honour even to imagine him doing so.

But at night I could indulge in all sorts of forbidden fancies and there was a peculiar pleasure in imagining my proud Gérard burying his shamed face on my shoulder and clinging to me for strength and comfort. Of course I healed his physical hurts at once but I often let him sob for quite a long while in my arms before I healed his wounded spirit and turned him back into his indomitable self.

A studio portrait taken at the age of forty, just before the outbreak of the Second World War. Antonia was making a good living as a freelance journalist. Her first novel, *Frost in May*, had appeared six years earlier.

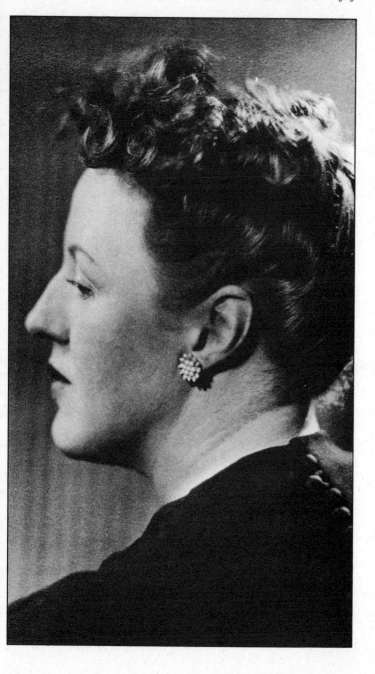

16.

So many new interests had come into my life when I was four that for the next two or three years, though I was often sad and still more often impatient for the next anticipated pleasure to hurry up and come along, I cannot remember any of those intolerable periods of boredom when it seemed impossible that anything exciting would ever happen again. Paradoxically, my passion for Gérard made me more independent of him. Since I could only see him at intervals the only way to appease my longing for his company was to develop my own resources and entertain myself as best I could on my own and with any grown-ups I happened to be with. On the whole, time passed quite pleasantly in the simple business of getting older.

I became conscious of time. Spring, summer, autumn and winter established themselves in an orderly procession which I knew would repeat itself next year. Spring was my least favourite; it seemed to have no particular character in West Kensington and to be a half-hearted compromise between winter and summer without the pleasures of either. It seemed to be always raining or windy when I was taken out for my afternoon walk and the sight of a few sooty hyacinths or daffodils in window boxes was no compensation for the disappearance of the muffin man and the hot chestnut man and the non-appearance for ages of the hokey-pokey man with his gaily-coloured cart from which, if I had a halfpenny left from my pocket money, and was not in the company of a parent, I could buy a cornet, brimming with ice cream, and suck it as I walked along the street.

Spring did however bring my birthday, though I wished it brought it a day earlier than 31 March. I cannot remember a year passing without someone reminding me that I had only just missed being an April Fool. This joke became very wearisome to me, as well as an annual irritant to my pride, because the humourist invariably expressed the conviction that All Fools' Day would have been a most appropriate day for my birth. I was very grateful to my parents for never making this well-worn joke which was trotted out year after year by some grown-up to whom it had just occurred as a flash of inspired wit.

I was also grateful for the privilege of being allowed to choose, on my birthday, what we should have for lunch. This gave me a great sense of importance. It did not require any deliberation beforehand for I always chose the same menu, sausages and mashed potatoes, followed by chocolate blanc-mange, and washed down with fizzy lemonade. At tea-time there was a birthday cake with pink and white icing adorned with my name and my new age which I admired so much that it always gave me a pang to see it cut. As long as its perfection remained I could gloat over it with a regal sense of possession. Every silver ball, every sugar flower was a precious treasure I could hardly bear to have ravished from this splendid tribute to my personal importance. As soon as the knife descended, this glorious confection created in my honour and inscribed with my own name, ceased to be *my* cake and became public property; I was not even entitled to more slices of it than anyone else round the tea-table. I felt almost as resentful when I saw 'Eirene' being mutilated into indecipheral pink squiggles as if I myself were being dismembered and handed round to be eaten. Nevertheless I greatly enjoyed my birthday tea-party even though I could not invite Gérard to it as it was a strictly family affair, attended only by my parents and my grandparents and occasionally by my Aunt Edith and my cousin Arnold. My mother made the dining-room table, spread with the best damask cloth normally only used for grown-up dinner parties, look really festive. There was always a big silver bowl of daffodils in the middle, sur-rounded by crackers, and the food was laid out on lace-edged paper doileys, just as it was on 'At Home' days. It was of 'At Home' day standard too, wafer-thin bread and butter and elegant little sandwiches both shorn of the hated crusts which were always left on the thick slabs provided for my everyday tea and which I had to eat because I was told they made my hair curl, and Bearman's rainbow display best seven-for-sixpence cakes, iced all over with a few currants or a dab of crystallised sugar. I felt very grand sitting in the place of honour at the head of the table, dressed in my best frock and wearing a paper crown from a cracker. Afterwards, I descended to the kitchen to give Bessie and Millie and their successors, Frances and Lawrence, slices of my cake and pull crackers with them. On 31 March I was queen of the house for an entire day; my father even forewent his tea-time pupil to attend my birthday party and cheerfully submitted to the indignity of wearing a paper hat. It was the one day in the year on which I could do no wrong and on which I could be sure of basking in a warm glow of approval.

My mother's birthday on 24 April was not celebrated with any public pomp. There were cards from her sisters in Vienna and my Uncle Howard by her plate at breakfast and sometimes a

326 · AS ONCE IN MAY

package or two besides the one containing the present I had bought, with a conscious sense of virtue, out of my own birthday shilling, but no tea-party and not even a birthday cake to announce her age. I once asked her 'How old are you today?', a question I was always delighted to be asked on my own birthday and was told sharply that one must never ask a grown-up person's age, most of all a lady's. It puzzled me very much that grown-up people's aged should be forbidden subjects of enquiry whereas the first thing grown-ups asked children when they were introduced to them was, 'How old are you?' More-over children had to reply promptly and truthfully. I once answered an 'At Home' day visitor with the formula I had learnt in the kitchen, 'As old as my tongue and a little older than my teeth', and was sent out of the room for impertinence.

If my mother's birthday was only a minor feast, it was preceded only a few days earlier by the major one in both my parents' calendar; their wedding anniversary. April 18, referred to by them as simply 'the eighteenth', was celebrated every year by a glorious evening out together. Naturally, I had no share in this celebration but I caught the infection of their excitement, as for weeks beforehand, 'What shall we do on the eighteenth?' was a recurring topic of discussion at mealtimes. I was also allowed to stay up late to see them depart in all their glory, both in full evening dress, my father looking very grand, wearing an opera cloak with silk facings over his tails and white waistcoat and his gibus hat – the fascinating top hat which crushed flat when you sat on it and sprang up to its full height again at the flick of a finger – and my mother dazzling in the new frock he always bought for her on 'the eighteenth'. The prettiest one I remember was a foam of yellow chiffon, shading from pale primrose to orange and glittering with sequins and she wore a butterfly of golden sequins in her dark brown hair. She always had her hair done by a hairdresser on the eighteenth so that it was piled up in the luxuriant wavy puffs that she could never successfully achieve by her own efforts and made her look positively queenly. My father always gave her orchids to wear on the great night and wore a white carnation in his own buttonhole. It was the one night in the year on which he loved to be really extravagant and enjoy the illusion of being rich. He would take her to dine at the Hotel Cecil or the Carlton, then to a box at the theatre and finally to supper. Before he left I was sometimes allowed to see him fill his sovereign purse – a fascinating object like a fat little silver watch which opened with a secret spring. Inside was a disc just the size of a sovereign which worked on another spring and on which you pressed the golden coins one by one to fit snugly under a clip. Only the top one was visible but when you slid it out another sprang up to replace it. I called it his purse of Fortunatus. Even if it was not bottomless, there were times when my father enjoyed spending as recklessly as if it were, and his wedding anniversary was one of them.

My mother was fond of reminiscing about her wedding day. It was always a slight grievance to her that she had not been married in white satin with a train and a veil and orange blossoms. 'I don't know what dear Mamma would have said if she'd been alive. But your Grandfather White was so selfish he grudged spending anything on his daughters, even on me though he was fonder of me than any of the others. "You've got the pick of the bunch," he said to Daddy when we got engaged. Well, I suppose I *was* the beauty of the family, though it was rather naughty of him to keep saying so in front of my elder sisters. But the very fact that I was pretty was an excuse for his never buying me anything pretty to wear. "Beauty unadorned adorns the most" was his favourite motto – and how sick I used to get of hearing him say it! So I had to save up every penny for my trousseau out of the wretched little salary I got at the Garrards and of course I couldn't afford a proper wedding dress. It was so sad, because I could have worn the lovely Honiton lace veil that poor Mamma wore at her wedding. So I was married in my going-away costume, peacock blue, with white satin facings and a white satin and lace blouse – it looked quite bridal – and a hat I had trimmed myself. Still, though it wasn't what I longed for, I think I looked rather nice. At least everyone said so. One thing I did have – a really magnificent bouquet. It came from the hot-houses at the Crystal Palace. One of the old gardeners there who had known me as a child and was very fond of me insisted on making it up as a wedding present. It was quite exquisite – tuberoses and white orchids and gardenias – fit for a princess! I expect it was all against the rules, but wasn't it touching of him? It was so lovely, I could hardly bear having to leave it behind when we went off on our honeymoon. I kept the withered remains of it for years put away in tissue paper.'

Sometimes my mother dwelt more on how she had felt than how she had looked on her wedding day. 'I trembled so much as I walked up the aisle that your Grandfather White thought I was going to faint and kept muttering, "For heaven's sake, bear up,

Christine, you're not going to the scaffold." But it really was an ordeal for such a shy, sensitive creature as I was. I felt that pledging oneself for life to the man one loved should be something secret and sacred. It seemed to me almost a profanation to have to make one's marriage vows in front of other people. I was so romantic and idealistic. And some of the things in the marriage service – though some of them are very beautiful – are really rather embarrassing. And of course such an *oriental* attitude to women. I don't wonder that Louise says she shudders every time she hears a bride say "obey".'

I did not need to be told how my mother looked on her wedding day for there was a photograph of her on the study mantelpiece, an unfamiliarly slight, almost flat-chested figure in a curious compromise between a dress and a coat and skirt. The top half simulated a close-fitting jacket with tucked leg o'mutton sleeves and broad white revers, opening over a white blouse with a frothy lace jabot, and the skirt belled out from the tiny waist in ample folds, half-hidden by the famous bouquet. And, tilted a little forward, on her head was the famous hat she had trimmed herself, a round white straw toque decked with bridal tulle and white flowers looking like nothing so much as a wedding cake. From under it, her great dark eyes gazed out seriously and a trifle sadly, and her unsmiling face had a wistful, faintly apprehensive expression. As a child, what struck me most about the photograph was that my mother could ever have been so thin. I had never known her as anything but lusciously curved above and below a waist that required rigid control to achieve fashionable slenderness. Though she always brought her corsets in waist size twenty-two, in my role of 'little maid Marie' I had to tug very hard at the middle laces of the stiff cuirass of steel-boned coutil to try and make its edges meet in the small of her back. But however hard I tugged, there was always a little gap where her wool vest showed through the criss-cross laces and the squeezed flesh bulged through their lattice. Nevertheless, she would never admit to more than a twenty-two inch waist, for only a woman who had given up any attempt to be smart would have let another woman overhear her ordering a corset even one size larger. But the waist concealed behind the enormous bouquet had been, as even my grandmother conceded, hardly more than the coveted eighteen-inch one. 'Oh, she was skinny enough in those days not to need tight lacing. Much too thin, in my opinion. There was even talk of her being consumptive – anyway she was delicate – or supposed to be, and always suffering from some complaint or other, though half the time it was just nerves, in my opinion. I didn't think your father ought to marry such a sickly-looking girl. I was so afraid she would turn into one of those nervous invalids who make a man's life such a burden. Besides, she was so unlike the girls he had always admired, pretty fair ones with lovely pink and white complexions and happy, contented natures, like his cousin Eva. He was engaged to her at one time, you know. Such beautiful golden hair she had and such a blooming complexion – such a sweet disposition too. I was quite upset when he broke it off. Well, he certainly went from one extreme to the other. Still he obviously knew his own mind for he had plenty of time to change it, considering they were engaged four whole years.'

Even as a small child, I could hardly help knowing how much she wished he had changed it. I suppose because she dared not disparage my mother to my father or even to my grandfather who by no means shared her dislike of their daughter-in-law, she found me a more sympathetic listener. At times I was a little ashamed of being such a sympathetic one for when my mother was not being irritable or irritating I quite liked her. But when I was annoyed with her, and even when I wasn't, I disloyally urged my grandmother to finish every sentence which began: 'Well, dear, I suppose this is something I oughtn't really to say to you about your own mother . . .'

Soon after my parents' wedding anniversary it would suddenly be summer. The coal carts were replaced by the watering carts trailing their great sprinklers which left dark wet tracks in the dusty roads and gave them the peculiar sweetish, earthy smell that heralds a thunderstorm. The hokey-pokey man replaced the muffin man and the Punch and Judy man reappeared now that his audience of children and nursemaids could be relied on to stand through the show instead of hurrying off to warm their cold feet before dog Toby took the hat round. I never much enjoyed Punch and Judy shows. I found the story incomprehensible and the guttural squeaks and squeals and the endless belabouring of poor Judy and the baby by the cruel, hideous Mr Punch distasteful and rather frightening. Though I knew from Gérard, who had now acquired a toy theatre, that they were only puppets and that the man behind the scenes manipulated them and used his own voice to interpret all the characters, I could never quite believe, even when Gérard was with me, criticising the show with professional interest, that those grotesque gibbering creatures had not some kind of life of their own.

The only thing I liked was dog Toby but always felt rather sorry for him. He had such a resigned expression as if he did not at all enjoy being dressed up in that shabby ruff and feathered hat and when he came round with the hat I felt guilty if I did not drop at least a half-penny of my precious twopence pocket-money into it, for I had once read of a cruel Punch and Judy man who beat his dog if it did not collect enough coppers.

In the summers of 1904 and 1905, I made two more appearances as a bridesmaid. I have no idea who the brides were; all I remember is what I wore and what present I was given. The dress had become very important to me now that I had begun to go to children's parties for it would be my party one next winter. My first bridesmaid's dress, the white silk and lace one in which Mr Wilson had painted me when I was four, had been of the kind all the other little girls were wearing and I had felt perfectly happy in it. Not so with my second. The bride I attended when I was five decided that her bridesmaids were to be dressed in yellow ruched chiffon, trimmed with black velvet ribbon. The bridegroom's gift of a gold chain curb bracelet was no consolation for the misery I knew I was going to endure at parties all next winter wearing something so conspicuously unlike everyone else's party-frock. My apprehensions were justified. Mine was the only yellow frock at every party and the other little girls, all in white or palest blue or pink, stared and giggled till I was in agonies of self-consciousness. Worst of all, Gérard did not approve of it. He had just gone to Colet Court and was terrified of the unfavourable impression my unconventional dress might make on his school friends. At his own party at Tennyson Mansions, he said, 'Look here, do you mind awfully if I don't sit next to you at tea? I'm as keen on you as ever but I don't want everyone to know it. A chap in my form has just asked me who was the silly kid who'd turned up in fancy dress by mistake and what was she supposed to be – a scrambled egg?'

Mercifully, the bride of the summer when I was six had less eccentric tastes and my next dress was one I could wear to parties without suffering any humiliation. It was white silk with lace flounces and a pink satin sash, just the kind all the other little girls were wearing and once again I could hold up my head. This third time I acquired a gold brooch adorned with a clover leaf in seed pearls to add to my collection of bridegroom's presents. I rather regretted boasting to one of the grown-up bridesmaids at the reception that it *was* my third time for she said: 'Don't you know the old saying, "Three times a bridesmaid, never a bride"?' This made me somewhat anxious since I had long ago known that Gérard and I were not really married. Now that Gérard was a nine-year-old schoolboy and I myself was six, we could look back on the early days with tolerant amusement. 'Gosh, what a rum pair of kids we were then,' Gérard would say, 'Pretending we were Mr and Mrs John Barker and all that bosh.' Nevertheless he still considered me his exclusive property and glowered if any other boy called me out at parties at 'Postman's Knock' to pay a forfeit of kisses. After all, as he pointed out, he was quite likely to want to marry me in earnest when we were grown-up so I must consider myself 'bagged' as long as I remained his official sweetheart.

So far I had retained that proud position, though that hated yellow frock had jeopardised it. But I was not sure that I would retain it through the endless years that stretched ahead before we were grown-up. Even my small experience of parties had shown me what a number of girls there were, other than myself, who were eager to attract Gérard's attention and who could attract it not only by being pretty but by performing dazzling feats of which I was incapable, such as doing skirt dances and giving recitations. I myself, of course, was quite sure that I should never want to marry anyone but Gérard, so if he decided to marry someone else, the fatal saying would come true. I fervently hoped it would not, but I could not help fearing that it might.

Summer brought more exciting things that being a bridesmaid, such as being taken to the zoo. Oddly enough I remember nothing about the animals I saw on my first visit; perhaps the lions and tigers and elephants were so much like the ones I was familiar with in picture books that they produced no effect of surprise. What impressed me far more was a pretty little spotted red creature that alighted on my frock as I sat on my father's knee on the way home in the hansom and which I was told was a ladybird. I had never seen a ladybird before or even a picture of one so it was a thrilling new discovery. I gazed at it entranced, sitting very still so as not to disturb it and hoping it would stay there till I got home so that I could keep it as a pet. I was deeply disappointed when it flew away, though I accepted my mother's explanation that it had only done so because a fairy had told it its house was on fire and it must fly back at once to rescue its children. However, going to the zoo soon became one of my greatest treats. We went quite often on Sundays in the summer, for my father had two great friends among the Fellows, the eminent Belgian zoologist, Monsieur Boulenger and his son Edouard who was to become equally eminent. We used to lunch with them in the Fellows' special preserve and afterwards they would take us round the various houses. Going round the zoo with the Boulengers was very exciting for we were able to go into places forbidden to the ordinary public and see behind the scenes. Old Monsieur Boulenger was Curator of the anthropoid apes and his son Edouard Curator of reptiles so that we were allowed to accompany them into the precincts behind the cages. Old Monsieur Boulenger was passionately attached to his chimpanzees and they to him so that when he appeared at the bars of their cages quite a crowd would gather to watch the spectacle. The dignified old bearded gentleman in his frock-coat and top hat would gesticulate wildly in front of his chimpanzee friends and chatter to them in a language they seemed to understand and they would chatter and gesticulate back with obvious pleasure. Sometimes one would reach out its hairy arm through the cage and snatch the end of a cigar from his mouth and finish smoking it itself, closing its eyes in ecstacy. Old Monsieur Boulenger would laugh delightedly and say: 'You see how *intelligently* he smokes, like a real connoisseur!' My mother was less amused when a chimpanzee grabbed her lace handkerchief and refused to surrender it. Monsieur Boulenger, however, was intensely interested to see what the ape would do with it. After examining it thoughtfully for some moments, it put its on its head and, running over to a square of looking-glass on the wall of the cage, gazed at its reflection with a positive smirk of satisfaction. This greatly pleased the old zoologist, for it was a female chimpanzee and – 'You see, she has learnt by observation that a pretty hat so enhances a lady's charm. Putting it on her head and studying the effect with all the satisfaction of a woman in a new bonnet is a truly reasoned action, not a merely instinctive one. How fine an example of the remarkable capacity of the chimpanzee brain. Who knows, given the correct education, of what further developments it may be capable?'

He had innumerable stories to tell of the remarkable intelligence of what he called 'our biological cousins'. Personally, though I was amused by their antics, I did not greatly like the big anthropoid apes. They bore too much resemblance to ugly, misshapen human beings for me to think of them as real animals and I found something rather frightening in their gibberings and gesticulations just as I did about those of Punch and Judy.

Monsieur Boulenger, however, doted on them like children and they seemed to return his affection. When he went behind the cages, they would leap into his arms when the keeper released them and cuddle up to him, pressing their faces against his and stroking his beard with their long leathery fingers. Sometimes one would remove his top hat and rummage in his grey hair. But even this produced no more than an indulgent smile. 'You see, my dear, he thinks I too am a chimp. It is most friendly on his part to try and rid me of my fleas and it would be most rude of me to rebuke him. Chimps have most sensitive feelings and one must be careful not to wound them even if it means suffering a little discomfort.' He not only visited the sick chimpanzees in the animal hospital, but often sat up with them all night. Sometimes he would take a patient home and nurse it himself, 'in my bosom' as he said. I never had any ambition to have a chimpanzee, even a baby one, as a pet but I longed passionately to adopt two baby lion cubs whose mother had died. I knew, of course, that I should never be allowed to, so I had to be content to be allowed to stroke the two enchanting creatures where they lay curled up together on a nest of straw like two big woolly yellow kittens. Their eyes were not yet open and they were being fed by the keeper from a baby's milk bottle, which they clutched between their paws which seemed a size too large for them and made them look as if they were wearing furry bootees. When I heard that Edouard Boulenger was really going to be allowed to take them home and rear them, I nearly wept with envy.

My mother, who had a horror or snakes, refused to accompany us when Edouard took us into the long stone passage behind their cages. He would lift the iron shutters and let me peer through at the great coiled-up boa-constrictors and the brown-hodded cobras with their flickering double tongues which I thought were their poison fangs until Edouard corrected me. He was almost as fond of his snakes as his father was of his chimpanzees and he was pleased with me for not being afraid of them. I was rather pleased with myself for even my father could not bring himself to touch the ones that he took out for our inspection though Edouard assured him they were perfectly harmless. I was a little nervous when first invited to stroke a snake for I expected it to be cold and slimy but on the contrary it was dry and quite warm and had a delightfully smooth, firm texture like polished leather. After that I became bold enough to let a black and ivory King snake coil itself round my bare arm. I quite enjoyed the sensation of feeling it winding its way up my arm, gripping it so firmly with its incredibly supple body that I could feel the muscles working under its scales in one long continuous ripple as it coiled itself at surprising speed into a living spiral bracelet. But I enjoyed even more the admiration of my audience. Not only the keepers but the curator applauded my courage and my father looked on with a flattering expression of almost awed surprise. Never before had I had such an intoxicating moment as when he said in front of them all: 'You're considerably braver than I am, Eirene. With the best will in the world I don't think I could bring myself to handle a snake.'

Even Gérard was impressed when I told him I had had a great live snake climbing up my arm. 'Bet you it wasn't a cobra, though. Or any sort of poison snake.'

'It *was* a poison snake. It was a King snake. They're so poisonous that they can kill every other kind of snake.'

'Gosh. Weren't you afraid it would bite you?'

'Not a bit,' I boasted.

'Anyway, I bet its fangs had been drawn.'

'No they hadn't. None of the snakes in the zoo have their fangs drawn. The keeper has to put on goggles when he goes in to feed the cobras in case they spit poison in his eyes and blind him.'

'You know what would have happened if that old snake *had* bitten you? They'd have had to gouge the flesh where it bit you out with a penknife. And if they didn't do it at once or cut out a big enough chunk you'd have swelled up and died in awful agony. Of course *I* wouldn't be frightened of having deadly snakes crawling all over me. But I must say that for a girl you were jolly plucky.'

I did not think it necessary to tell Gérard that King snakes were only deadly to other snakes and quite harmless to human beings.

The only thing I did not like about snakes were their eating habits. I was horrified to discover the reason why they kept cages of mice and rabbits in the back precincts of the reptile house, where they also kept other creatures not on view to the public, including enchanting baby crocodiles only nine or ten inches long with delicate buff coloured scales and teeth tinier than a kitten's. In my innocence I had supposed the mice and rabbits, though they looked quite ordinary ones, must be rare specimens which needed special care. But one day I saw a keeper take a white rat from its cage, and holding it by its tail, dash it to death against a stone wall. Then, raising the iron shutter at the back of a snake's den, he thrust the still twitching body into the gaping mouth of its occupant. 'They likes their meat fresh, you see, miss. Very particular about that, snakes are.' I was too sorry for the white rat to marvel at the way the snake swallowed it whole, its slender body expanding to accommodate the bulk of its victim as if it were made of elastic. After that, though I continued to handle snakes without repugnance and to enjoy showing off my prowess, I was relieved that my father had politely but firmly refused Edouard Boulenger's kind offer to procure me one as a pet.

One summer when I was still very young, perhaps five, I was given a really grown-up treat. I was taken by my grandparents to the Earls Court Exhibition – *at night*. I cannot remember what the exhibition was, but I rather think it must have been Venice since I have a recollection of real gondolas floating on real water against a painted background of marble palaces. What I do remember is the excitement of being up so late, long after my bedtime, and of being transported into a world of so many marvels that I could not possibly take them all in. We were swept along with the crowd through scenes of magical splendour, past pavilions outlined with rows of glittering lights, through gardens with trees festooned with garlands of coloured lamps, and fountains spurting plumes of rainbow spray, under arcades where all sorts of rich merchandise was displayed in tiny shops presided over by people dressed in strange, foreign clothes.

High above this magical city towered an enormous illuminated wheel which revolved very slowly against the dark sky. When I looked hard at it, I could make out dim box-like shapes hanging from it and being carried round with it. As they mounted to the top of the dizzy height they grew smaller and smaller till I could not see them at all, then they slowly reappeared again coming down the other side and growing gradually bigger as they descended. I was awed when my grandfather told me there were people in those boxes. Even though he assured me that they could not fall out, I thought what an alarming experience it must be, hoisted so high above the earth and, if the Big Wheel stopped turning, left suspended there. It seemed that this had been known to happen, so once when I glanced up at the great circle of brilliant lights and saw it was no longer turning I had a gruesome thrill. I was half relieved, half disappointed to be told that it had only stopped to take on a new load of passengers. I had no ambition at all to be one of them but I was sorely tempted to ride one of those splendid horses, obviously relations of Sceptre's, who pranced up and down on a roundabout. Moving slowly at first, then galloping faster and faster till they seemed to be flying through the air like the horse in the Arabian Nights whose rider had only to turn a peg in its ear to make it soar like a bird. My grandfather offered to mount one himself and hold me on in front of him but my grandmother shouted at him that I should get giddy and very likely be sick. The mere possibility of being sick in front of all those people was so fearful that I was not brave enough to risk it. However, in spite of my grandmother's nervousness for my safety, he took me for a ride on the water-chute. I admit I felt rather frightened myself, when, wedged tight between his knees, I felt the boat begin to slide down from what seemed a dizzy height towards the dark lake whose shimmering reflections only emphasised the blackness of the water. The next moment we were plunging downwards faster and faster, so fast that I could not breathe and my insides seemed to have been left behind at the top of the slope. I shut my eyes tight and just when I thought this terrifying sensation would never come to an end, there was a bump and a tremendous splash and I was no longer whizzing downwards through space but being rocked to and fro with a violence that gradually subsided. When I opened my eyes and recovered my breath, the boat was floating on the water, sending ripples over its dark surface that made the reflections in it dance and quiver in tongues of yellow flame. Back on dry land, I was so proud of having gone through such a tremendous ordeal that I felt almost brave enough to go through it all over again. However I was decidedly relieved that this was not suggested. I preferred to rest on my laurels and feel immensely superior to my grandmother who had been too timid to accompany us.

Of all the experiences of my first visit to the Earls Court Exhibition, two thrilled me more than all the rest. One was the scarlet-coated military band on its illuminated bandstand. What fascinated me most was the conductor who could produce whatever tune he liked from the shining brass instruments and make them play loud or soft, fast or slow, merely by waving his little stick. I stood behind him, entranced, trying to imitate the movements of his arm with my own and pretending that the

Antonia around 1965 at 42 Courtfield Gardens, South Kensington. The cat is Minka, her Siamese, about whom she wrote two children's books.

band was obeying *me* as well as the magnificent officer in command of them. From the amount of gold braid on his uniform and his proud, erect bearing I was sure he might even be Lord Kitchener himself. The crowd realised his importance too. Every time he laid down his wand and the band stopped playing, he turned round and bowed and everybody clapped him. The other soldiers remained seated, gazing modestly down at their instruments, so that it was obvious that all the glory belonged to him. I decided then and there what I would be when I was grown-up. I had long wanted to be a soldier but to be a soldier commanding a band, with hundreds of people admiring me, seemed to me the most splendid thing imaginable. For several days afterwards, I conducted an invisible military band with my hoop-stick, turning at intervals to bow to the storm of applause from my invisible audience.

   The second experience occurred not at the exhibition but on the way home. It was the first time I had been out in the streets after dark. As I walked between my grandparents, I was amazed how mysterious and beautiful dull old West Kensington looked at night. It had been transformed into a city almost more magical than the one I had left – a city of dusky palaces, glimmering here and there with oblongs of golden light, of pavements whose flagstones suddenly sparkled like diamonds when we walked under a street lamp and turned so dark as we entered the shadows again that I could not see them under my feet. All at once I looked up and for the first time noticed the sky. It had gone the colour of blue-black ink and scattered all over it were tiny glittering lights.

   I tugged at my grandparents' hands, crying, 'Oh, do look up there! All those little lights up in the sky! Whatever *are* they?'

   'Why, stars, dear,' said my grandmother. 'You've never been out late enough to see stars, have you? Isn't it lucky it's such a fine night and you can see lots of them?'

   'You mean they're *real* stars?'

   'Why of course. What makes you think they're not? Can't you see them twinkling?'

   I stared hard up at the blue-black sky. The bigger and brighter lights were indeed twinkling but even the biggest ones were very small and the tiniest no larger than pin-heads and did not twinkle.

   'But they're so weeny,' I objected. 'And they haven't got any points round them. Why don't they *look* like stars?'

   'Come along, dear,' said my grandmother hastily. 'We

mustn't stand here dawdling any longer. It's high time little girls were in bed.'

I tried to question my grandfather but I could not make him hear me. He merely nodded benevolently and we walked on in silence. All the rest of the way home, I gazed thoughtfully at the sky. So that was what real stars were like. Even brighter than I had imagined, but so much, much smaller; just thousands of glittering dots spangling the darkness overhead. I had always supposed they would be even bigger than the silver-paper star on top of Aunt Edith's Christmas tree and, of course, the same shape. All the same they seemed to me the most wonderful of all the wonderful things I had seen that night. Nothing excited me more than seeing for the first time with my own eyes something I had only imagined or read about. When my father asked me next morning at breakfast what I had enjoyed most of all of the splendid treat Granny and Grandpa had given me, I replied without hesitation: 'Oh, seeing *real stars*!'

It had indeed been a splendid treat but, like other treats, it was not something I could count on happening again. Summer in London might produce pleasant surprises such as visits to the zoo, but there was only one thing I could safely look forward to, my annual holiday at Binesfield.

EPITAPH

(Published in Delta*, April 1938)*

The metaphysical tone of this poem, where love and death weave a macabre dance, must owe something to John Donne, whose work Antonia so much admired. It was written at the time of the affairs with N.H. and I.H.

The poem appeared in the first, and almost the last, issue of *Delta* in April 1938. *Delta* was the successor to the *Booster*. It was a French and English poetry monthly whose editors were Alfred Perlès, Lawrence Durrell and Henry Miller. Among Antonia's fellow contributors were her friends Dylan Thomas and David Gascoyne. It ceased publication with the outbreak of war.

'Epitaph' was later included in *The Distaff Muse*, an anthology of poetry written by women, edited by Clifford Bax and Meum Stewart and published in 1949.

By man came death;
Not by my love, my single sun,
Did this seed ripen to its monstrous bloom
But by the moon's unquickening breath
I was undone.

Bury me deep
Lest my love look on me asleep
And see the time-stained face with which I died.
This hasty, swollen mask of yellow wax
Which fear, the clumsy workman botched me up
Blasphemes death's patient marble.
Calmer my living brow,
Purer my cheek that flushes now
With dark decay like rouge.
I wear the face of one who could not stay
For heaven's slow marriage day
That stamps me as death's whore and not his bride.

And from that greedy coupling, hour by hour,
My bastard death grew like an iron flower
Transmuting blood to metal, bone to ice
Between the abhorring thighs.

But my eternal travail is not yet.
Not till this waxen mommet turn to flesh once more
Shall I my true-born death beget.
Not yet, not yet may I put on
Majesty and corruption.